It's All About

JESUS

Daily Considerations of Christ in Us

Jim Fowler

C.I.Y. Publishing
17102 Blanco Trail
San Antonio, TX 78248

IT'S ALL ABOUT JESUS

Daily Considerations of Christ in Us

Volume four in the "Jesus series"
of daily Christ-centered readings

© 2022 by Jim Fowler

Published by
C.I.Y. Publishing
17102 Blanco Trail
San Antonio, TX 78248

ISBN 10 digit – 1-929541-67-8
ISBN 13 digit – 978-1-929541-67-6

Printed in the United States of America

FOREWORD

The "Jesus series of daily readings on the Christ-life" keeps expanding. This is the fourth volume in the series. Despite my declaring that each present volume will be the last volume, thoughts keep coming to my mind that beg to become another reading, first appearing as a daily post on Facebook, and then as a daily reading within a year of readings in another volume.

I keep awakening early every morning with a thought on my mind that I jot down in my "ideas" folder, and then it expands into a three-paragraph article, followed by another, and another, and another. They accumulate until there are 366 readings, enough for one year of daily readings.

If a reader were to read and digest all of the readings in the various volumes of this "Jesus series of Daily Readings on the Christ-life," that individual would have a fairly good grasp of the Christocentric theology that I espouse and teach. It is a theological perspective that has developed over 50 years (since 1973) of progressive growth in understanding how Christ lives in me and desires to be every facet of life within me and through me and as me. "Christ who is our life" (Col. 3:4) desires to re-present His life and character within our behavior to the glory of God – the very purpose for which we were created (Isa. 43:7), and the very objective of the risen and living Christ living in us (Col. 1:26,27).

What a privilege it has been to enjoy the inner Christ-life drawing me to ever-greater-intimacy with the

Triune God – allowing me to participate in the inner sanctum of God's holy fellowship. Yes, I have faltered. Yes, my faith has been tested. In fact, in this volume, the readers will see several readings written in the anguish of having both of my lower legs amputated due to the disease of diabetes. I wanted to be honest enough to reveal that my humanity was fragile, requiring me to exercise trusting faith in the sufficiency of God's grace in Jesus Christ despite much pain and uncertainty.

I trust that the readers of this volume will find in these readings a biblically revealed and spirit-tested explanation of the Christ-life that I have had the privilege to experience for some fifty years, and I would hope that readers will be encouraged to exercise the faith (our receptivity of His activity) that allows the living Lord Jesus to live out His life by His grace in their lives.

Jim Fowler
2022

Table of Contents

WORDS OF APPRECIATION

There are several persons who deserve a note of appreciation for their involvement in my life as these various readings were written. I begin with a few that I am in contact quite often. These friends: Don Burzynski, Ken Grief, Matthew Morizio, and Don Frantz share the understanding of the organizing premise of my theological thought, the concept of "derivative man," allowing us to explore where that premise leads in all facets of Christian theology.

Others whom I have appreciated during the development of these readings are those who have interacted with the daily posts on the Facebook platform. I will mention those I can remember presently, knowing that there are many more that are deserving of mention. Thank you, Diana Busby, Muriel Ruppert, Larry Eis, Glenn Webb, Bernard Gemeroth, Phil and Kathy Gemeroth, Chris Moore, Sheila Barr, Nicole Waters, Jodie Wilcox Armstrong, Mary Wilkinson, Dan White, Michael Elliot, Dennis Clark, Steve and Nancy Talbot, Katherine Rutledge, Deb Switzer, Darwin East, Jean Rittenberg, Brooke Haakinson, Beba Mayer, Frank Cole, Joyce Hamm, John C. Seekins, etc. Your comments and participation have been most helpful.

I should also thank the Facebook website which has allowed me to post my thoughts on its social media platform almost every day for approximately seven years – and that without charge! What an opportunity for ministry.

Most of all, I appreciate my wife, Gracie, who must put up with the time I spend "thinking" and writing on my computer. Since the amputation of my feet, she has assumed double duty as both helpmate and caregiver. Thank you, sweetheart!

Jim Fowler
November 2022

JANUARY 1

A NEW YEAR

The word "new" has numerous nuances of meaning. A person may declare that he acquired a new car. Is the car the latest model just off the assembly line – a recently manufactured vehicle with the "new car smell"? This would be the "new" of recent origination or construction. Or is the automobile this person has acquired a used older model vehicle that is "new" to the individual in terms of ownership and possession? This would be the "new" of recent acquisition; new to me, as contrasted with my previous car. Is the new car "new new" – newly built or manufactured – or is it "new to me" – recently acquired? Or both?

Interestingly, the new covenant literature, the New Testament, uses two Greek words for "new" – *neos* and *kainos*. These two words are occasionally used as synonyms, but there are important differences in meaning and implication in these two words. Generally, the word *neos* refers to something that did not previously exist, i.e., the most recent vintage or model, "brand new," unprecedented. In contrast, the word *kainos* generally refers to that which is new in contrast with an older model; that which is new and improved and superior. As intimated above, something can be "new" in both senses.

The new covenant, for example, is a *neos* covenant (Heb. 12:24), unprecedented and spectacular. It is also referred to as a *kainos* covenant (Heb. 8:8,13; 9:15), because it is contrasted with, and superior to, the prior old covenant. The "new (*neos*) wine," the most recent vintage, needed to be put in "new (*neos*) wineskins, else the expansion of fermentation would explode the old wineskins. In Christ, we become a "new (*kainos*) man" (Eph. 4:24), contrasted with the "old man" who has been crucified with Jesus (Gal. 2:20). As we commence a "new year," it can be a *neos* year like nothing before it, but it is also a *kainos* year contrasted with the years that have gone before it.

1

JANUARY 2

A RESTLESS SOUL BECOMES A RESTFUL SOUL

Most of us can probably think of someone we have known who could be described as a "restless soul." Most of these persons could probably have been diagnosed when children as having had ADHD (Attention Deficit/Hyperactivity Disorder). They were/are often full of energy, and always on the move like the "Energizer Bunny." Not knowing how to channel their energy in constructive ways, they are often impulsive and "at loose ends." They are often driven to do something, even if it's wrong. Throughout their lives they have been told to "settle down" and "be quiet," for they tend to be over-talkative and interruptive.

These personality characteristics are not something these persons can simply determine to change. Developed early in life in the midst of the circumstances they experienced, these action and reaction patterns are an integral part of their personality. Many such persons are introduced to Jesus and are receptive by faith to His saving life. Spiritually they become "new creatures" (II Cor. 5:17), but their fellow Christ-ones are often advising them to "be still and know that He is God" (Ps. 46:10). The means by which to do so often eludes them, as their "flesh" patterns of restless personality remain firmly entrenched in their soul.

How can a restless soul become a restful soul? The Christ-one must go beyond merely understanding that Jesus saved them and "got them off the hook." As they understand that the living Jesus is their life (cf. Col 3:4), the indwelling Spirit as their teacher will lead them to understand the means of entering "the rest of God" (Heb. 4:1-11). This occurs as they begin to understand that the dynamic of God's grace in Jesus Christ by the empowering of the Holy Spirit is sufficient to do all that needs doing in their lives. The Christian life is not a new context for hyperactivity (despite what the church might teach) but is an opportunity for restful involvement in what Jesus wants to do in us.

TRAPPED IN THE BOOK

For many Christians, the Person of the Holy Spirit is an ethereal abstraction. They may assent to the orthodox Christian teaching of a Triune God comprised of Father, Son, and Holy Spirit, but on a practical, personal level the Holy Spirit remains an untapped mystery. In the process of my early theological training, the topic of the Holy Spirit was relegated to a plaything of the Pentecostals and the neo-Pentecostal Charismatics. The only teaching about the Holy Spirit seemed to indicate that it was "trapped in the Bible-book," and could serve as an "influence" to facilitate interpretation and understanding of the Biblical text.

Such teaching exhibits a severe misunderstanding of the Christian Trinitarian God, and diminishes the relational heart of the Christian gospel. To view the Holy Spirit as merely an interpretive influence for understanding the Bible elevates the Bible above God. It is important that we understand the ontological reality of the Holy Spirit as a divine Person to Whom we can relate, and Who can enter into the human spirit of an individual (Rom. 8:16), thereby restoring the presence of God in humanity. To recognize that the Holy Spirit is a divine Person means that he is more than a vague influence or power.

It is also important to consider the Christological reality of the Holy Spirit as the "Spirit of Christ" (Rom. 1:4; 8:9; Phil.1:19; I Pet. 1:13). Though Jesus and the Holy Spirit are distinct Persons of the Trinity, they are also indivisibly "one" in the divine Trinity. When Jesus was explaining to His disciples what was to transpire after His crucifixion and resurrection, He said, "I will send Another (not Greek *heteros* – another of a different kind, but *allos* -another of the same kind) who will be with you forever" (Jn. 14:6). He promised that He would be with them in Spirit-form. Paul explained that "the last Adam (Jesus) became the life-giving Spirit" (I Cor. 15:45) in His resurrection-life form.

3

JANUARY 4

WATER-WITCHING THROUGH THE BIBLE

My first introduction to Christianity was in the context of a group that believed that water-baptism was essential for salvation. They used Acts 2:38 ("repent and be baptized for the remission of your sins") as their primary proof-text, and this was the watermark of their entire theology – their formulation of baptismal regeneration using the explanation that an individual comes contacts the blood of Jesus in the baptismal water. Like using a forked stick to dowse for water, their interpretive grid was that all references to "water" or "baptism" necessarily pointed to water-baptism and its necessity. As they read through scripture and come to the word "water," their metaphorical forked-stick dove toward the thought of water-baptism and its being essential for salvation.

Of course, Paul's reference to "the washing of regeneration" (Titus 3:5) was thought to refer to baptismal regeneration. Peter's reference to "eight souls being saved by water in the time of Noah" was also considered a reference to baptism. Such direct, literalistic, linear logic leads to eisegetical interpretation (reading into the text and using the text as a pretext for one's preconceived ideas). Physical water-witching is generally associated with divination, sorcery and the occult, and baptismal regeneration is likewise a questionable means of understanding God's re-creation of mankind in Jesus Christ
The purpose of the rite of water-baptism is to illustrate the over-whelming of our human spirit by the Spirit of Father, Son, and Holy Spirit. The orthodox teaching of the Church has always indicated that water-baptism is an external representation of an interior spiritual reality. The rite does not effect the reality of this spiritual overwhelming, but provides a pictorial representation of such, identifying the baptismal candidate with what God has effected in his or her spirit.

THE ORIGIN OF EVIL

Human beings are often inquisitive about the origins of things around them. Many are asking about the origin of evil. The origin of evil, like the origin of all things, is *ek Theos* ("out of God"). Rom. 11:36 – "For from (*ek*) Him, and through (*dia*) Him, and to (*eis* - "unto") Him, are all things." This has long been the traditional Jewish and Christian explanation from the biblical narrative. God is the originating source, the Creator, of all things, but never the direct and culpable source of evil, contrary to His nature. Lucifer, the angelic light-bearer chose to defy and usurp God in a selfish quest to "be like God." He became the antithesis of the character of God, the ontological Evil One.

Since the time of the Enlightenment (17th and 18th centuries) when human intelligence was elevated above God's revelation, there has been increasing skepticism about God, the scriptures, and the origination and existence of the Evil One. Spiritual realities are regarded as superstitious medieval beliefs that cannot be verified by empirical evidence via the scientific method, and thus to be rejected. Even so, it is difficult to avoid the recognition that there is much evil in the world in which we live, and it is destructive and devastating to many people's lives. The pain we experience due to evil is adequate evidence.

The Evil One is alive and well in the world today. He is the Tempter who counters the loving and just character of God, soliciting humanity to derive from his character of selfishness and sinfulness. His ego-centric character was revealed in his stated desire, "I (*ego*) will be like the Most-High God" (Isa. 14:14). John explains, "The one doing (committing) sin is of (*ek* – derives the character of what he is doing out of) the devil" (I Jn. 3:8). Humanity's derivative function allows us to derive character either from God or from the Evil One, resulting in either sinfulness or godliness.

5

JANUARY 6

WHAT LOVE IS THIS

God is for us, not against us. Think about it! God seeks our highest good at every moment in time. That is what it means to say, "God is Love!" (I Jn. 4:8,16). God is undergirding us with His sovereign Love amid anything we might be doing, whenever and wherever we might be doing it. Not just when we are doing good things, or religious things, but even when we are engaged in selfish or sinful things, God continues to love us without measure. "What wondrous love is this...", declares the Christian folk hymn from the American South, first published in 1811. "When I was sinkin' down, sinkin' down," the words of the song declare, God's' wondrous love is there to sustain me.

"Who shall separate us from the love of Christ? Shall tribulation, or distress, or persecution, or famine, or nakedness, or peril, or sword? Nay, in all these things we are more than conquerors through him that loved us. For I am persuaded, that neither death, nor life, nor angels, nor principalities, nor powers, nor things present, nor things to come, nor height, nor depth, nor any other creature, shall be able to separate us from the love of God, which is in Christ Jesus our Lord" (Rom. 8:36-39). "Behold, what manner of love the Father hath bestowed upon us" (I Jn. 3:1), that we should be called the "children of God."

To know unreservedly that we are loved by God in Christ, and nothing we might do can cause us to be unloved is such a comforting thought. To wake up every morning with the thought on our mind that "I am God's beloved child, for whom He sent His only begotten Son to live and to die to bring me in to participation in His triune family of love, the love of the Godhead – that should wrap us in a sense of security that prepares us for whatever trials the day might bring. What love is this – it has and does go to the ultimate extreme to allow us to be the recipients of His loving embrace – the extreme Love of God in Christ.

CONTEMPORARY EXODUS

A few years ago (2017), a friend of mine, Don Burzynski, and I made a trip to Egypt, and followed the path of the Israelites in their exodus out of Egypt. The Greek word *exodus* is derived from *ek* = out, and *hodos* = way, thus "the way out." (Every exit sign in Greece today is marked "exodus," the way out). On our trip, we went to the southern tip of what is called "the Sinai Peninsula," and went to Mt. Moses. Don spent many hours climbing and descending what many call "Mt. Sinai," but I chose not to make that climb, reasoning that I had spent most of my life figuratively climbing "Law mountain," and it simply wore me out.

We continued our trip travelling up the east side of the Dead Sea in the nation of Jordan, visited Petra, and came to Mt. Nebo where the Israelites looked over at the Promised Land of Canaan. From there we crossed the Jordan River into the present-day nation of Israel, and visited many Biblical sites, including Caesarea Maritima, Mt. Carmel, Megiddo, Nazareth, the Sea of Galilee, Magdala, Capernaum, Caesarea Philippi, and other sites. We also visited Qumran on the Dead Sea, Masada, Bethlehem, and the many sites in Jerusalem such as the Temple Mount, the Pool of Bethesda, the Garden Tomb, the Mount of Olives, etc.

Of late, I have noticed a contemporary exodus that has many similarities to the Exodus of the Israelites from their slavery in Egypt. I am referring of the exodus of God's new covenant people out of the slavish performance within the institutional Church. Christ-ones have realized that they are just spinning their wheels on the religious treadmill of religion, and are leaving their religious and denominational churches, seeking a place of promised rest (cf. Heb. 4:1-6) wherein the living Lord Jesus is experienced as the total sufficiency for the Christian life. Performance-oriented religion has shown itself to be irrelevant to the genuine spiritual needs of people in the 21st century.

JANUARY 8

THE DISTRACTIONS OF LIFE

Life is full of distractions that draw us away from what is really important to our lives. It is the living Lord Jesus Christ who is the supreme reality of Life to the Christ-one. The "ruler of this world" (Jn. 14:30; 16:11), the enemy (Matt. 13:39; Acts 13:10), the adversary (I Pet. 5:8), the Evil One (Eph. 5:16; II Thess. 3:3), the devil (Jn. 8:44; Eph. 6:11), Satan (Acts 5:3; 26:18) is persistently active in his attempts to distract Christ-ones from their focus on (Heb. 12:2) and intimacy with Jesus, and from "growing in the grace and knowledge of our Lord and Savior Jesus Christ" (II Pet. 3:18) becoming mature (Eph. 4:13) sons of God.

This may come as a shock to some readers, but I am inclined to think that the greatest distraction to the Christ-life is religion and its performance practices. Religion is the devil's playground and serves as a great distraction to personal participation in the life of Jesus. Religion wants all its "members" to be involved in churchy-busyness, committed and loyal to the performances that they regard to be the essence of faith and faithfulness. Religion always wants you to "join their club," so you can "serve" on leadership committees and be coerced into believing and doing what they want you to believe and do.

Religious activity distracts us from discerning what and how Jesus within desires to function in, through, and as us. Religion always has a slot to plug interested inquirers into their machine, but their involvement therein will always be a distraction to genuine spiritual growth which is the process of allowing Jesus to function as one's Life. Distractions are innumerable in the world in which we live, but to add the distraction of religion with its many counterfeit activities and performance routines makes it all the more necessary that Christ-ones understand God's grace is the dynamic empowering of everything that is to be done in the Christian life.

SPIRITUAL GIFTEDNESS

The entire subject of spiritual giftedness has been distorted by religion and its attempts to package this wonderful reality into specified job descriptions and skills. Misunderstanding the indwelling presence of the living Christ in every Christ-one, religion develops a mechanical business model that encourages all members to "find their spiritual gift" and employ it by getting involved in the function of the church. Notice, we refer to spiritual giftedness rather than to an entity or commodity of a "spiritual gift" that is to be sought or identified. Spiritual giftedness is the ministry of the living Christ through you. The Greek word is *charismata*, meaning expressions of God's grace.

Every Christ-one who has received the life of Jesus into their spirit in regeneration has all the expression of spiritual giftedness – every spiritual gift, if you will. When we received Jesus, He came complete with His ability to minister to others through us. He did not put separated spiritual gift entities somewhere on the top shelf of the religious shop, asking Christ-Ones to find the particular gift they would like to possess and employ, and then get busy in accord with their spiritual job description. We simply need to be aware of and available to all that the living Christ wants to be and do through us.

Every Christ-one has the full cluster of the fruit of the Spirit (Gal. 5:22,23) by which to manifest the character of Christ. Christ came to dwell in us complete with the full complement of the fruit of His character. Will we be receptive in faith to allow Him to manifest such? Every Christ-one has received the entirety of the spiritual giftedness of the Spirit of Christ by which to manifest the ministry of Christ. Christ came complete with the fullness of His ability to minister to others. Will we be receptive in faith to allow Him to minister in whatever manner He chooses, in the portion of the *ecclesia* we are involved?

JANUARY 10

THE MESSAGE IS THE MEANS

The message of the gospel, of the Christ-life, is not an informational-content message incentivizing those who hear it and accept it to respond by providing the personal means of its fulfillment and performance. Yet, that is the message proclaimed in the majority of pulpits of thousands and thousands of churches week after week, advising the religious adherents of what they need to do and perform in order become Christians or be better Christians. "This is it; now do it!" Such a humanistic incentivization to self-betterment by means of independent self-generating activation is not the gospel message.

Our gospel message, our "good news," is **JESUS**, and inherent within Him is the grace-means by which His life is lived out and manifested in our bodily behavior (cf. II Cor. 4:10,11), allowing Jesus to re-present Himself in the context of our individual lives. The "good news" of Jesus is the message, and He is the means to facilitate and implement the outliving of His Christ-life – the Person of Jesus constitutes the Christian message which carries with it the intrinsic means by which He lives out His life in, through, and as us. All that God has to give and extends to us is His Son, Jesus Christ

The living Lord Jesus is in Himself the empowering of the Spirit (cf. I Cor. 15:45; II Cor. 3:17). The dynamic means of Spirit-manifestation in the life of the Christ-one is not some external and additional booster shot that is acquired subsequently to His coming to dwell within us. Jesus comes to indwell us with everything necessary to live out His life through us in the sanctification of holiness (cf. I Thess. 4:3), exhibiting the character of godliness in all that He does (cf. II Pet. 1:3,4). The gospel message is the "good news" of the Person of Jesus – all He is, and all He does because He is who He is, as He lives out and re-presents His life in us.

JANUARY 11

A SEPARATED AND DETACHED DEITY

Many who call themselves "Christians" today seem to have more of a deistic concept of God than a "one spirit" (cf. I Cor. 6:17) Christian concept of God. Deism conceptualizes a deity who is "out there," outside and beyond the one who is pondering God. Deism speculates that God is separated and detached from the created world, and from involvement and interaction in the daily personal lives of those who might believe in such a deity. The concept of God among many Christians is often couched in such ideas. Ex. How often have you heard Christians refer to "the god out there" or "the Man upstairs"?

Deism seems to conceptualize god as an irrelevant abstraction of logical thought. "He must be; therefore, He is!" is a common logical formulation of a deistic and/or theistic god. Such a deistic conception of god fails to consider the personal and relational reality of the God who is love (I Jn. 4:8,16). God is much more than an ideological power-source out there in the universe, far-removed from where we live our lives. He is an ontological reality, a triad of Persons, Father, Son, and Holy Spirit, who mutually desire that we, His human creatures, might participate in the loving community of the interactions of the Godhead.

Jesus, the second Person of the Godhead, the "only begotten Son of God," is not merely a transcendent Being who joined the Father in the heavenlies after His resurrection and ascension. Many Christ-ones fail to realize the implications of the resurrection of Jesus, that Jesus is indeed alive today and immanent within every person who has become a "new creature in Christ" (II Cor. 5:17), His Spirit indwelling our spirit (Rom. 8:9). This "one spirit" union (I Cor. 6:17), facilitates the experience of "union-life" with God in Christ, allowing for the incarnational expression of Jesus (cf. II Cor. 4:10,11) in human behavior. A deistic conception of God precludes such incarnation.

11

JANUARY 12

THE BEING AND THE DOING OF JESUS

The most basic dialectic in human thought is the juxtapositioning of "being" and "doing," considering both the essence and function of all things, including living things. This contradistinction was posed and discussed by the early Greek philosophers, centuries prior to the incarnation of Jesus as the God-man. Plato emphasized essential being, whereas his pupil, Aristotle, emphasized the visible functionality of things. In subsequent theological considerations, Augustine followed Plato's emphasis on essential being, whereas Thomas Aquinas tended to follow Aristotle in attempting to explain God by His functionality.

These philosophers were prior to and could not have fathomed the Christian explanation of the Being and Doing of Jesus Christ, the God-man. Since the being and doing of God and His created humanity are so contrary, how do we explain that Jesus could be God and be man at the same time, but could not behave (do) as God (Self-generating) and behave (do) as man (derivative and dependent) at the same time. His derivative doing as a man necessitated His emptying (Phil. 2:7) Himself of the prerogative of acting as God, even while maintaining His oneness of Being in equality with God the Father and Holy Spirit (Phil. 2:6).

Jesus' being and doing as the God-man is unique. He cannot do what He does apart from Being who He is. He cannot BE who He is apart from doing what He does. His doing in inherent in His Being. He does what He does because He is who He is! His Being implicitly implies and includes His doing. Jesus is never just a passive object of adoration. We participate in the ontodynamic of Jesus – the Being of Christ in action through us. The Eastern Orthodox churches refer to *Theosis*, the manifestation of God's activities in Christ-ones via the divine "energies" of Christ. This is not deification; we do not become Christ, but it is the expression of the living Lord Jesus in the Christ-one.

12

GRACE IS GOD IN ACTION

Grace is not merely the benevolence of God, nor the initiative of God, nor the "undeserved favor of God." Grace is not a commodity that God gives to us. It is not a static gift. Grace is not God's benefits (benes), not an additional empowering, not an extra booster-shot to implement what He requires of us. Grace is not acquired by means of engaging in ecclesiastical activities, such as the Eucharist, even though the institutional church has long referred to such as a "means of grace." God exercises His grace because He is who He is, in accord with His character and will, not because we do something to obtain such.

In the most general sense, Grace is God in action, the expressive agency of the active God. Grace is God being God, acting in accord with who He is. God does what He does (grace) consistent with and in expression of His character – Who He is. God never acts out of character. Grace is the ontodynamic of God's being in action. In the more specific sense, Grace is God's action in Jesus Christ, inaugurated in the incarnation of Jesus (Jn. 1:17). Grace is God acting in a distinctively Christian sense, God doing what God does, and He does what He does through the agency of the Son who was sent to reveal the Father.

Although we can use the word "grace" as a noun to refer to a phenomenon, or a thing, it is better to conceive of grace as an active verb, as the activity of God – God in action through Jesus Christ! Grace is dynamic; it cannot be passive because God is always an active God. The religious institution of the church has attempted to formulate grace as a static commodity that can be dispensed in the process of ecclesiastical performances. In that manner religion tries to use grace as a leverage to coerce its religious adherents to engage in the human activities that best serve the institution's benefit. That, however, is not grace; it is a disgrace that camouflages God's action.

JANUARY 14

ABERRANT GRACE CONCEPTS

Grace is God in action, energizing and empowering all that is of God, all that is in accord with God's character of righteousness, holiness, perfection, etc. as revealed and summed up in Jesus. Everything that God does, He does *ek autos* (out of Himself). Everything that God does is *ek Theos* (derived out of God.) Grace must always be sourced in God, and expressive of God, enacting God's character. God always acts "in character." Such grace-activity of God's action can only be received by human faith, as derivative, dependent, contingent creatures are drawing from God, available and receptive to God in faith.

Some religionists view grace as a commodity, a packaged principle, that God grants to "those in the know," granting them freedom from legalistic religious restrictions, rather than freedom to be the derivative humans that God intended by deriving character from God. Grace is God's action to make available His character through His Son, Jesus Christ. Whenever grace is thought of as contra-something else: contra-sin, contra-law, one will end up with a humanistic-skewed concept of grace. Grace is always pro-Jesus – God's action in making Jesus available to manifest His life and character in the lives of Christ-ones.

As absurd as it may be, those who fail to understand that God created humanity as derivative creatures often distort God's divine grace into a form of aberrant humanistic grace. Grace is then thought of as an autonomous self-action tool of religion – activity that can be controlled by man. If grace is simply contra-sin or contra-law, and we have been set free from such by the work of Jesus, then grace can be conceived as a personal freedom to live independently, as one sees fit, in ways that often violate God's character of purity, holiness, righteousness, etc. In such a context, grace is reduced to license and liberty to engage in whatever man deems right in his own mind.

FLAUNTING GRACE

It will be important to begin with a definition of grace. Grace is the dynamic divine activity of the Triune God by which He manifests Himself by means of the Son, Jesus (cf. Jn. 1:17), by the power of the Spirit (Rom. 15:13; Eph. 3:16) to exhibit His character in a tangible behavioral expression among His creation unto His own glory. Misunderstanding such a definition, some think that grace is a personal freedom to behave in contra-distinction of the religious regulations by which they have been constrained, and to do so without regard for their "weaker brethren" (I Cor. 8:11), regardless of what anyone else thinks.

Those who then act with the misunderstanding of grace as contra-law or contra-sin, i.e., with a concept of grace as personal freedom to express one's natural desires of the "flesh" in a libertarian and libertine manner, end up misrepresenting the character of God in sinful behavioral expressions. They are usually attempting to "push the limits of grace," as if grace had behavioral parameters. Those who engage in such sinful behavior are not really flaunting grace; they are disdainfully spurning the religious rules, challenging the restrictions thereof, and choosing to manifest character that is not derived from God, but from the diabolic source of all sinful behavior (I Jn. 3:8).

When one understands the proper definition of grace, it is difficult to see how it can be flouted or flaunted. I recall a young man, who after a lesson on God's grace, went out to "cut donuts" in the parking lot. Returning with a smirk, he declared, "Now, that's grace!" No, that is license to sin, and "in your face" taunting of regulations and flaunting of sin. Others who misconceived grace to be personal freedom, have touted and flaunted their freedom to smoke cigars, to drink alcoholic beverages to excess, to flirt with people other than their spouse, and even to engage in intimate relations with such persons. Grace is not freedom to sin!

JANUARY 16

OPERATIVE GRACE

I have observed that there are many who share the message of "Christ in you," often quoting Gal. 2:20, and referring to "God's Grace," but they seem to have a skewed perspective of what is entailed in such realities. What is lacking is the foundational understanding of how grace operates, and the means by which humanity can allow for the operative enactment of God's grace. Operative grace demands that we accept its corollary –that man is essentially a derivative creature. Grace without human derivation is but an ethereal abstraction.

When grace is not understood with the corollary of man's derivative receptivity of such by faith, we often observe the oxymoronic conceptions of "autonomous grace" or "humanistic grace," whereby humans think that by becoming a Christ-one, they can now operate and manipulate grace to their own ends. Grace is not a benefit (a "bene") of becoming a Christ-one, of having "Christ in us." Grace must not be viewed as detached or separated from the dynamic of the very Person and work of Jesus Christ. "Grace is a Person," but such divine grace is only realized in the human derivation of such grace by the receptivity of faith.

Grace is always the derived activity of God in Christ operative in a Christ-one with the operative objective to manifest the character of Christ in the behavior of the Christ-one. Any definition or explanation of grace that suggests that the intent of grace is freedom from law or sin or ecclesiastical restrictions usually fails to appreciate the positive operational intent of God's grace to provide everything necessary for humans to function derivatively from the divine activity of God's grace. Derivative human beings must derive everything from God in Christ to function as God intends, i.e., to allow the Person of the living Lord Jesus to actively express Himself in our behavior, as us. God's grace will always be expressive of His character.

THE MISUSE AND ABUSE OF GRACE

The word "grace" has become a widely used theme in religious circles. Hundreds of ministries, podcasts and Facebook pages claim to be based on grace and to proclaim grace. The majority of them are advocating a false grace, a pseudo-grace, a misused grace rather than the activity of God to express His divine character in man through Jesus Christ. Grace is so much more than God's initiative to redeem man, to forgive man, and to "get man off the hook" for the consequences of sin. Grace is so much more than the lubricant of the Christian life, or the octane booster by which man is enabled to perform what God requires.

When grace is conceived of as a grace-freedom to avoid the performance responsibilities and restrictions of religion, it soon becomes "grace in a vacuum," grace without a divine source. Such an idea becomes exactly opposite of God's divine character-grace provision for His Christ-ones. It becomes Satanically inspired autonomous humanistic "grace" wherein man thinks he is able to be and do whatever he desires to be and do, often flaunting his alleged grace-freedom in license and libertarianism before other believers who are regarded as less enlightened and less free to enjoy the pleasures of unrestrained sin.

It is a tragic abomination how some religionists are misusing and abusing the theme of God's grace in Jesus Christ. Grace is being gutted of its divine dynamic and provision of God's action. True grace is always *ek Theos* (out of God), directed toward a positive expression of God's character. It becomes a disgrace when the behavioral expression of character is misrepresentative of the character of God, i.e., in manifestation of sin. The grace of God never leads to sin! Sin is always derived from Satan, not God (cf. I Jn. 3:8). Grace is God's positive action – God doing what He does because He IS Who He IS, and has revealed Himself to be in the Son, Jesus Christ, and is desirous of re-presenting in Christ-ones.

JANUARY 18

GRACE AND FREEDOM

There are some who have a confused understanding of God's grace, having equated grace with freedom from the legalistic restrictions of religion. There is a connection between grace and freedom, but it most certainly is not that grace facilitates an unrestricted and unloving freedom to trample on and make a mockery of the religious sentiments and sensitivities of those who have not yet understood God's grace. It is most unkind, and certainly not the character of Christ, to kick the religious crutches out from beneath those who are unknowingly relying on those supports to prop up what they consider to be their religious relationship with God.

Divine grace in Jesus Christ does facilitate freedom, but such freedom must be consistent with the essence and objective of God's grace. God's grace in Jesus Christ provides the divine dynamic to manifest His character, the "fruit of the Spirit" (Gal. 5:22,23) in the attitudes and action of those who have received His grace by the receptivity of faith. The freedom that is facilitated by grace is a freedom to be all that the living Lord Jesus wants to be in us. It is not a freedom to attempt to impose and force grace on those who have not yet grasped what grace means. We must allow the Spirit of God to do His work gracefully.

Jesus, who is the Truth (Jn. 14:6), told His listeners, "You will know the Truth, and the Truth will make you free" (Jn. 8:32), and clarified such by saying, "When the Son makes you free, you will be free indeed" (Jn. 8:36). Such freedom is the freedom to allow God's grace to manifest the very character of Christ in what we do, our human behavior. Paul advised the Galatians, "It was for freedom that Christ set us free" (Gal. 5:1). Yes, that freedom was from the tyranny of religious performance regulations, but the freedom of grace is always the freedom to be a Christ-one who allows the character of Christ to be exhibited through them.

BACKDOOR GRACE OR FRONTDOOR GRACE?

When grace and freedom are boxed together too tightly, one risks the possibility that the concept of grace is morphed into a form of freedom that eschews this or that, grace-freedom *from* law, sin, flesh, devil, etc., rather than grace-expression of God at work via His Son, Jesus Christ, and the power of the Holy Spirit; grace-freedom *to* re-present the life and character of Jesus in love, joy, peace, goodness, etc. I am differentiating the two by calling grace-*from* a "backdoor" understanding of grace, and grace-*to* a "frontdoor" perspective of grace and suggesting that God's grace is better understood as a leading-edge vanguard of God's work than as a tail-gunner defending from the rear.

The Bible seldom refers to "grace-*from*" tyranny or restriction, or "grace-*from*" as avoidance of what is onerous. "Grace-*from*" is instead "grace actuated *out of* the Triune God," and as such is "grace *to*" with a forward-looking direction whereby we observe God actively manifesting His character of love, joy, peace, and reconciliation. I have observed much grace-teaching that seems to be back-loaded rather than front-loaded; it approaches grace by looking back at what has been vanquished (law, sin, flesh, devil), rather than looking forward to what God is doing (loving, giving, serving), manifesting the life of the living Jesus.

Ours must be a positive expression of God's work of grace in Jesus Christ, rather than a negative survey of conquered foes. Instead of focusing on grace-suppression, we want to proclaim grace-expression. Grace is not a mole whacker, but an ice-breaker that expands the parameters of the possibilities of all that God wants to do in Jesus Christ. We do not want to present ourselves as "aginners" (against this, against that), but as positive "good news" bearers of God's grace expressing the character of Jesus. When the world sees the love and joy and peace of Jesus re-presented in us, it will sit up and take notice of His grace.

JANUARY 20

DOES FAITH WORK?

The final statement of the love chapter reads, "Now abides faith, hope and love, but the greatest of these is love" (I Cor. 13:13). I recall preacher, Bernard Briscoe, saying, "Love gives, hope expects, and faith works." If there are no works resulting from faith, then there is no faith. That seems to be what James wrote, "Faith without works is useless, dead, of no value, impossible" (James 2:14-26). If there is no out-working resulting from our faith, then it simply evidences that there is no faith. There may perhaps be assent, belief, trust, desire, expectancy, loyalty, but without the evidentiary works of God, there is no faith.

Faith is aptly defined as "our receptivity of God's activity," or "our availability to God's ability." Faith responds to and receives from the willing action of God's grace (God in action). Faith without the consequential out-working of God at work evaporates into a vacuum of nothingness. Of course, if there is nothing to respond to or be receptive of, then faith is impossible. If there is no grace activity of God to receive, then there can be no faith-receptivity to God's working. Faith is responsive in allowing God to work on our behalf. In and of itself, faith does nothing, but faith allows God to do His divine work.

Paul explained to the Ephesians, "For by grace are you saved through faith; that (salvation) is not of yourselves, it is the gift of God; not as a result of works, so that no one may boast" (Eph. 2:8,9). There are no meritorious works of man that can effect our salvation; it must be received by faith. However, faith without the outworking of God's grace-activity evidences that whatever we are calling "faith" is not biblical faith. We are defining faith here in a dynamic sense (as a verb), rather than in a static sense (as a noun). The stated question was, "Does faith work?" Not in and of itself, but it allows God to work, and if there is no divine outworking, there is no faith.

GODS GRACE-DYNAMIC

It is a sad indictment of the "Church," to observe that so many Christians have such a vague and nebulous understanding of God's grace. When I graduated from Bible college, my understanding of grace was simply that God took the initiative to send His Son as our Savior. While it is true that God's grace was inaugurated in the incarnation of the Son of God as the God-man (Jn. 1:17), any understanding of grace that fails to go beyond the objective historical data of the birth, death, and resurrection of Jesus remains static and ineffectual. Understanding grace must move on to a subjectively experienced receptivity of the dynamic activity of God whereby He reveals and expresses Himself and energizes His character and activity in His people.

I remember the day when a retired pastor, over 80 years old, came to me and said, "I am just now beginning to understand God's grace. How did I miss it for all those years? Everywhere I look in scripture, I now see it." We rejoiced together in the sole sufficiency of God's dynamic grace whereby everything "Christian" is enacted. He continued to acquire and read every book he could find on the subject of "grace," but divine grace is like the wind (Jn. 3:8,9), and human beings cannot get a handle on it, even to describe or define it, much less to use it as a tool to attempt to make believers more "spiritual."

It is NOT God's grace dynamic employed that we should know more, store more, and regurgitate more data and facts. It is God's grace-dynamic to allow Jesus to live-out His Christ-life in our behavior. It is God's grace-dynamic to manifest His divine character in His human creatures, those who have received the life of Jesus Christ into their spirits (Rom. 8:9,16). It is God's grace-dynamic to energize the "fruit of the Spirit" (Gal. 5:22,23), as the trademark or Christ-mark of the behavior of Christ-ones. "See how they love one another," the world remarked.

JANUARY 22

GRACE-MINISTRY

Grace has often simplistically been defined in the acrostic, God's Redemption at Christ's Expense. Some, who recognized that God's grace went farther than just redemption, used another acrostic, God's Restoration at Christ's Energizing. Proceeding beyond these trite acrostic tools, we want to explain that all genuine ministry must be grace-ministry or the message becomes damaging condemnation. Grace is God's dynamic empowerment to serve, to minister, to love others. Grace should never be misused or as a club to "beat the hell" out of others' misunderstandings of law, sin, flesh, death, etc. Grace is best utilized to introduce heaven to a sin-weary world. Jesus said, "I came not to judge the world" (Jn. 12:47), rather "I came that you might have life, and have it more abundantly" (Jn. 10:10).

Any grace-ministry that shares His life will of necessity be energized by the grace-giftedness of Jesus Himself. Grace (Greek *charis*) is expressed in ministry by means of the *charismatoi*, the grace-gifts of Jesus' desire to minister and serve through us (Rom. 12; I Cor. 12). It's not what we roll up our sleeves to do for Jesus, but how Jesus wants to serve others in love through us by means of His own grace-ministry intentions and empowering. Grace is the dynamic, the dynamo, of the Christ-life that always ministers to others. It is always Christ in us, for others.

The result of grace-ministry will always be the grace-expression of *eucharist* (eu = good; *charis* = grace). Both the one ministering God's grace and the one who receives such will be compelled to respond with thanksgiving for the "good grace" of God in Jesus Christ. *Eucharist* is far more than partaking of the bread and the fruit of the vine in a sacramental rite. Eucharist is a divinely inspired attitude of "giving thanks" (I Cor. 11:24. *Charis* (grace) employed by means of the *charismatoi* (grace-gifts) will produce *eucharist* (giving thanks for God's "good grace").

GRACE-DATA *AND/OR* GRACE-LIFE

Those who teach God's grace in Jesus Christ must determine whether they are repetitively teaching grace-data or whether they are sharing the grace-life of the living Lord Jesus with their listeners. By "grace-data" I am referring to the necessary preliminary understanding of the objective and historical details of the work of Jesus Christ on the cross and in the subsequent resurrection. This will include the explanation of the "finished work" of Jesus Christ on the cross, including the elimination of the Law, the overcoming of sin, the defeat of the devil, and the power of the Holy Spirit to override our "flesh" patterns.

Grace-data, standing alone, can be sterile informational tidbits, the knowledge of which may puff a person up (I Cor. 8:1) with the pride of being "in the know." But the data may be of no more practical value than knowing that $E=mc^2$. The need of mankind is that we build upon the foundational grace-data and explain to receptive people the dynamic provision of the indwelling life of Jesus Christ, and how grace energizes the vibrancy of that life of Jesus as He lives out His divine spiritual life in our behavior. People want to know the practicalities of the means and manifestations of the grace-life, i.e., the Christ-life.

Though I might know all the data about discerning the "flesh," facing the trials of life, and avoiding the solicitation of temptation, if I do not experience the love-life of grace-life in the Christ-life, I am but a befuddled buffoon filled with spiritual pride – yet still yearning for all that Jesus wants to be in me. Yes, I must personally plead "guilty" to the very misemphasis I am exposing, for I have taught the preliminary grace-data to many audiences, while failing to proceed from the informational data to the relational sharing of the vitality of the grace-life. It is my personal desire to simply live by His Life, and to allow the ministry overflow of the Jesus-life to be realized by others in the *ecclesia*.

JANUARY 24

"GOOD GRIEF!"

If I may quote the perennial philosopher-counsellor, Nancy, I might exclaim, "Good Grief!" Many Christians are like the character of Pigpen in the Charles Schultz "Peanuts" cartoon series. They seem to be most comfortable functioning in the dust-cloud and playing in the muck and mud of everyday life. If one suggests or directs them toward a world of clean air and cleanliness, they will quickly reply, "Yes, BUT..." They have lived so long in the dust and dirt, that they find it unfathomable to focus on anything other than what they are familiar, and they will remain in that mind-set repetitively. It has become so common-place to them, that they cannot see themselves differently.

When you speak of God's grace in Jesus Christ to some people (yes, Christ-ones), they will look backwards and say, "Yes, BUT..., we have to watch out for legalism; we must beware of sinning;, we must recognize that all people have "freedom of choice" (they usually say "free-will"), and they will usually veer toward that which they are most familiar. And that's where most of us go, you know, right back to our selfishness and sinning." For many, it seems that God's grace is to no avail; they would rather sputter and cough in the dust-cloud, than to even consider breathing freely in the rarified air of God's grace.

Charlie Brown seems to accept Pigpen's condition and mind-set as inevitable – "That's just the way he is!" Nancy keeps decrying in despair, "Good Grief!" What will our response be to the abundance of Pigpen characters in the religious mud-puddle and the polluted air of religious thought? I am not willing to take the *laissez-faire* attitude of Charlie Brown, nor am I content to cry "Good Grief!" like Nancy. I want to pray that God will reveal (as only God can) the wonderful provision of His grace, and cause that to be so desirable in the hearts of His people they will put-aside their dust-cloud dysfunctionality to live in God's grace.

THE GRACE–FAITH CONNECTION

The grace-faith connection is really the God-man connection, and the very essence of the gospel, the "good news," is encapsulated in that reconciling spiritual union between God and man. The Creator God created the creature man is such a way that humanity was designed to function by the grace-faith connection. Apart from such connection, humanity is dysfunctional. Grace is God in action consistent with His eternal character (God is the Doer and Giver); Faith is the prime function of human beings, as they have the freedom of choice to receive what God is doing in His grace (Man is the receiver). Faith is man's receptivity of God's activity. Faith receives God's action of grace.

The utmost historical action of God's grace was evidenced by the giving of His Son, Jesus Christ. "Grace and truth were realized through Jesus Christ" (Jn. 1:17). Jesus is God's Word (Jn. 1:1,14) for mankind, incarnated as a human being (Phil. 2:5-11), enduring our experiences, even to the point of death (Phil. 2:8). Rising in the resurrection, the life-dynamic of the living Jesus was available to all mankind from Pentecost onwards in the form of the Spirit of Christ (Rom. 8:9). God, the Three in One, continues to act and give by providing the dynamic of grace for the implementation of His character in receptive man.

The human receiver can partake of the Person and work of Jesus Christ by faith. "For by grace you are saved though faith" (Eph. 2:8,9). Yes, Jesus said, "I will draw all men to Myself" (Jn. 12:32), and His grace-action does so without violating man's choice of receptivity. "Without faith it is impossible (Greek *adunaton;* (*a* = no; *dunamis* = dynamic) to please God" (Heb. 11:6). Without faith-receptivity there is no connection with grace-dynamic. James explains, "Faith (man's receptivity of God's activity) without the dynamic outworking of God's grace-activity is the denial of the grace-faith connection (cf. James 2:17,20,26).

JANUARY 26

LEGALISTIC GRACE?

The title combines two words, "legalistic" and "grace," that together form an oxymoron, an incongruous connection of words. Legalism and grace should not be put together for they are in opposition to one another, to the extent that each cancels out the other. So, the topic under consideration is not really "legalistic grace," but we seek to address a legalistic form of teaching grace whereby some grace-teachers and grace-ministries think they "have a corner" on the correct words, phrases, concepts and diagrams with which to properly explain God's grace operative in Jesus Christ. If you do not present the subject of grace in the manner they do, then you are doing it wrong – not in accord with the regulations (i.e. laws – hence legalism) they have determined acceptable explanation.

Since grace is the activity of God in accord with His character, it is nigh unto impossible to define God's grace, or to encapsulate grace into acceptable words, phrases, concepts, or illustrations. To explain the grace of God is like trying to explain the wind. Jesus used that analogy with Nicodemus, "The wind (*pneuma*) blows where it wishes and you hear the sound of it, but do not know where it comes from and where it is going; so is everyone who is born of the Spirit (*pneumatos*)" (Jn. 3:8). Matters of the Spirit (*pneumatikoi*), whereby God enacts and puts in motion His grace by means of the empowering of the Holy Spirit are quite inexplicable; beyond human paradigms of thought.

Thus, when we attempt to teach about grace, or minister grace, or share the subject of God's grace, we are dealing with a subject that is beyond full or finite explanation – even more than trying to explain the wind. God's grace is always enacted in accord with His wise foreordination, and always consistent with His own character, for God does what He does, because He IS who He IS. Human explanations may vary greatly. That is to be expected.

WHY IS ECCLESIASTICA AFRAID OF GRACE?

In the organized and institutional Church (*instituta ecclesiastica*), in the denominational structures with their prescribed leadership flow-charts, it's all about control of those deemed to need to be controlled, i.e., the erratic flock of sheep that tend to go their own way. The Institutional Church is all about control of the *hoi polloi* (the commoners), and that is why they demand that you be a "member" under their control, and why when you become a member they often present you with written expectations of your performance – attendance, committees, giving – and sometimes demand that you "sign on the dotted line" to legally agree to such control, i.e. the "church contract."

In *Ecclesiastica* they have "a handle on what's going on," but there is no way to "get a handle on what God is doing by His grace. God's grace cannot be controlled or determined by the presbyters, the episcopators, the bishopry, the superintendents, the pastors, the pope, or any leadership structure. God's grace is as erratic as the wind (Jn. 3:8). Grace might be described as the pneumatological activity of God, and no human leaders can get a handle on where the wind will blow, or how God will act by His grace. God can't be figured out. He can't be organized or orchestrated. There's just no telling what God will do, except that He will always act according to His character! Church leaders are afraid that God is capricious and dynamic and will act outside of their control-box.

Ecclesiastical leaders have constant fears that the intangibility of grace may lead to chaos, to anarchy, to a grace-movement outside of their control. They are afraid that God has a lot more power than they do, and that He is going to do things His way, despite any plans they may have developed for "church growth." It all boils down to whether Church leaders and all Christians will be receptive in faith to God's grace action.

JANUARY 28

GRACE AS DIVINE ONTODYNAMIC

Many have attempted to define God's grace as His nature, His character, His Being, or His essence. In the Greek language, this would be to define God's grace by His *ousia* or His *ontos*. It is certainly true and accurate to indicate that since God is the personally active divine Being, He is always acting in accord with, and expressive of, His Being; He is consistent Being in action. God does what He does because He IS who He IS. His absolute Being and character and essence of goodness, love, holiness, righteousness, perfection, etc. will of necessity be activated and manifested in expression of who He is. Such actuation of His divine nature and Being is grace! God in action!

Philosophical considerations have always noted the most basic dialectic of all human thought pertains to persons and things: the conceptual differentiation between "being" and "doing; between essence and function; between nature and manifestation; between character and behavior. To speak with philosophical technicality, grace is not God's nature, essence or Being, but the outworking, the doing, the expression and manifestation of His nature, character and Being. Grace is the operational process by which God expresses His character of goodness, loving kindness, holy righteousness, etc.

Every action of God is not only expressive of His Being but invested with His Being. God is at work in His every action. There is no divine action without such being His Being in action. This is the important connection: no action of God can be separated from His Being. There is no divine action of grace, but what God's very Being and presence is integrally and personally involved in the action. That is why we can speak of grace as divine ontodynamic (*ontos* = Being; *dunamis* = doing, empowering, action). Grace is the divine Being of God in action, always expressing His divine character in His every action of grace.

WHAT IS HYPER-GRACE?

Numerous teachers and authors have referred to "hyper-grace," or been charged with teaching "hyper-grace." What is "hyper-grace"? Can God's grace rightfully be described as "hyper-grace"? Let us begin by noting that God's grace is always hyper-grace, above and beyond anything that we could ask or think (Eph. 3:20). In the well-known passage of Ephesians 2:6-10 where Paul speaks of our "having been saved by grace through faith" (2:8), Paul leads-in to his discussion of grace by explaining that God's intent was to "show us the surpassing riches of His grace in kindness toward us in Christ Jesus (2:7).

The Greek word that Paul used to describe "the *surpassing* riches of God's grace in Jesus Christ" is *hyperballon*, which obviously employs the preposition "hyper" to explain God's grace as exceeding, immeasurable, unlimited, boundless, exaggerated, extravagant, incomparable, beyond imagination, incapable of overstatement, inexplicable, even hyperbolic. So, yes, it is biblically proper to speak of hyper-grace. What, then, is the phenomenon of "hyper-grace" that some are concerned about?

Some grace-teachers have sought to "accentuate the positive and eliminate the negative" so often emphasized in religion, that they seem to "be soft on sin," and fail to recognize that the Satanic originator of sin (I Jn. 3:8) is still active in his world-realm. Also, among those of Reformed persuasion, some so emphasize the sovereign grace of God and the sin-corrupted inability of human beings to even respond to the grace of God; they discard "limited atonement" and push the idea of "unconditional grace" into a form of hyper-grace," to the extent that it becomes the universal reconciliation of all humanity in the vicarious humanity of Jesus, and the hypostatic union of deity and humanity applies not only to Jesus, but to all mankind, a form of universalism. That may be an aberrant hyper-grace requiring no human response of faith.

JANUARY 30

VIRTUAL-REALITY CONFLICT

I have observed my grandchildren wearing their virtual-reality face-screens, fighting off virtual-reality foes that only they can see. Oblivious to the tangible world around them (even the furniture in the room), they assume different stances and flail their arms to counter the virtual-reality images that appear right before their eyes as they wear their projected-image goggles. The entire scenario reminds me of some of the so-called "grace-ministries" operating today. Instead of projecting an image of God's victorious, all-sufficient, joyous grace, they are flailing around and "beating the air" in a virtual reality conflict, fighting images of sin, the Law, the flesh, and the devil.

They are involved in a virtual-reality conflict because they are fighting a battle already won by Jesus on the cross. Their repetitious focus on the repelling of sin, dying with Christ, the enemy of legalism, the overcoming of the "flesh," and the defeat of the devil are but a "beating of the air" attempting to finish the "finished work" (Jn. 19:30) of Jesus on the cross. Jesus accomplished both the redemption and restoration of mankind once and for all (Heb. 7:27) in His death on the cross of Calvary. In the grace-dynamic of His resurrection-life, we must proceed to allow the living Lord Jesus to live out His Life re-presented as us.

We must cease playing around, lurking in the past, and fighting the already defeated virtual-reality foes of the past alleged to be coming at us from every direction to overcome us. Instead, we want to focus on the present reality of the grace-life of Jesus, and how by the receptivity of His activity by faith, we allow Him to live out His resurrection-life in our behavior. The purpose of Christian teaching is to encourage Christ-ones in the daily out-living of the Christ-life. Whenever teaching, from the pulpit or the podium, fails to provide practical encouragement of the Reality (cf. Jn. 14:6) that is ours in Christ Jesus, we should "press mute."

FAITH IS AN ACTION, BUT NOT A "WORK"

God created humans as choosing creatures with freedom of choice (not free-will). Such choices are an essential function of humanity – the choice to receive (not to self-generate our own activity). Faith is an action of choice to receive from a spirit-source (either God or Satan). God's intention in creating humans was that they might choose to receive from the provision of His Self-enactment and allow for the expression of His character in His creatures to His glory! That divine action - human reception exchange (God's grace received by human faith) was the operative intent of God for the human race He created.

Some (usually those inclined to a closed-system theology wherein God sovereignly controls every action, and man is thought to be so corrupted as to be unable to respond) have argued that the very act of faith is a "work," because it is something that a human being does. No, it is a choice that a human being makes, but not a "work," for a "work" is an action deemed to have meritorious benefit before God (cf. Eph. 2:8,9). To receive a gift is a choice to act via receptivity, not a "work" designed to accomplish a goal. Neither is faith "a gift of God," a forced imposition of divine action on our behalf.

This grace-faith connection between God and man (God's activity and man's receptivity) is evident in the life of Jesus. The Son of God emptied Himself (cf. Phil. 2:7) of the divine prerogative to function as God (though never less than God) and was incarn-ated as the God-man (fully God and fully man). How, then, did Jesus live the life that He lived? As all men do – by faith-reception of God's grace. Jesus explained (Jn. 14:10), "I do not speak on My own initiative (*God always acts at His own initiative*), but the Father abiding in Me does His works (*as I am receptive to such by faith*)". Jesus lived by faith-receptivity of the Father's activity for every moment in time for 33 years – the Perfect Man!

FEBRUARY 1

WHAT GOD DOES; NOT WHAT MAN DOES

The entire Christian gospel is the narrative of "what God does, and not what man does." When man rejected God's operational intent of man's deriving all from God's grace, and in disobedience (Rom. 5:19; Eph. 2:2; 5:6) sought to be his own center of reference (the lie of humanism), man couldn't do anything to remedy such. Man could not save himself. He was helpless and hopeless, unable to function as God intended and designed in the grace-faith connection. God's redemption and restoration of mankind could only be accomplished by God's grace-activity. God took the initiative (Rom. 5:6-8) to remedy man's death for sin.

We do not mean to imply that man's response to what God has done and is doing is just a "do-nothing" passivity. What man does is not to engage in any activity to contribute to or to supplement what God is doing. Man's action of doing never adds to what God has done for our redemptive salvation. So, what can man do? The only thing man can do is to receive by faith what God has done and is doing by His grace. In such reception, man is not doing anything to provide a reciprocal benefit to his own salvation. Just because you receive a gift offered to you does not mean that you have "worked" for it, or earned it in any way.

Some have a clear message of redemption emphasizing what God does, not what man does (often among the Reformed brethren, and a few Baptists), but they often fail to carry it over the same understanding to the restoration of sanctification. They revert back to human works for living the Christian life; they drift into legalism (what man can do in attempting to keep the Law, the performance requirements); they implement liturgical necessities. Jesus advised His disciples, "Apart from Me, you can do nothing' (Jn. 15:5). The dynamic source of everything that glorifies God must be empowered by the Spirit of Christ. All we can do is receive by faith what He gives by His grace.

THE FINISHED WORK OF THE CROSS

It was from the cross, Jesus exclaimed, *"Tetelestai"* (derived from the Greek *telos* = the end). He was declaring (Jn. 19:30), "It is finished, accomplished, completed done, *fini, fait accompli."* The question is: "What was finished, completed, and accomplished? Not the physical life of Jesus, for He arose in the resurrection. What, then, was "dead and done," as effected in the death of Jesus on the cross, whereby it might be declared, "The End –Mission accomplished?" Let us consider the Law, sin, death, and the devil, and how they (or the effects thereof) were terminated (or exterminated) when Jesus was executed on the cross.

The Law was henceforth, from the occasion of the cross onward, a dead dodo bird. It never was intended for Gentiles in the first place, The Law was not even applicable and viable for the Jews after the cross. Even among those Jews who became Christ-ones., there were those wanting to dabble in the Law, ex. the Judaizers who were trying to fabricate a house of cards, or construct an air-castle, as they took certain/select performance regulations of the Law and tried to impose them on persons they were never intended for in the first place (Gentiles and Christians), yoking them in unnecessary bondage and slavery (Gal. 5:1-9).

Sin, and its consequences, were totally forgiven on the cross. Sin was dealt a deathblow in the death of Jesus Christ. Sin, being the character of the Evil One (I Jn. 3:8), was overcome by love. Death was conquered on the cross. The death-dealing devil (Heb. 2:14) was vanquished (I Jn. 3:8). We see the death of death in the death of Jesus. The devil was defeated (Col. 2:15; Rev. 12:9) in Jesus' death on Calvary, and from that time on he was but an impotent imp, a hollow hobgoblin, just a defeated dog on a chain waiting for his final execution (contrary to the concerns of the ASPCA). The death of Jesus, the God-man, on the cross was the divine victory over all that occurred in the Fall (Gen. 3).

FEBRUARY 3

PAIN IN PROGRESS

Pain in the human life is inevitable. There is no such thing as a utopian pain-free life. How we react and respond to the painful incidents of life, either by acceptance, or in the fight, fright, or flight of personal disturbance, will determine whether the pain paralyzes and defines us, or whether it is merely another hurdle to be vaulted. None of us would want a stagnant, go-nowhere life without progress, change, and growth. Such progress and growth often expand the parameters of our status-quo normality, and this is the reason personal pain is often experienced in the midst of progress. Progress can be painful.

Progress implies growth and change. For progress to be realized there will be things that are displaced, dispensed of, and discarded in order to be replaced by what is new and different. The progress of the fulfillment of God's covenant promises required the dispensing and discarding of the old covenant with the Israelite peoples to inaugurate and implement the new covenant of Christ's life. Jesus explained that the old wineskins were dried and brittle and would burst with the vital and dynamic action of His life by the Spirit, therefore new wineskins were required (cf. Lk. 5:37,38).

All of life involves pain during progress. This is true in physical growth as well as spiritual growth (cf. II Pet. 3:18). Writing to the Philippians, Paul explained some of his pain in "counting all things as loss in view of the surpassing value of knowing Christ Jesus my Lord" (Phil 3:8), "desirous of knowing Jesus and the power of His resurrection and the fellowship of His sufferings, being conformed to His death" (Phil. 3:10). Writing to Timothy, Paul encourages him to "take pains with these things (personal discipline, manifestation of Christ's character, ministry to others via your personal giftedness); be absorbed in them, so that your progress will be evident to all." (I Tim. 4:15).

FEBRUARY 4

DO YOU SEE WHAT I SEE?

This title question is from a Christmas song, the lyrics of which were written by Noel Regney in 1962, and the music composed by Gloria Shayne, who later became his wife. The song was made famous by Bing Crosby in his Christmas album of 1963. Carrie Underwood and other artists have more recently recorded the song, making it popular again.

What we see with our physical eyes is most often not the really real. That is why scientific observation is not reliable for knowing reality that is beyond the visible physical world. What we hear, see, and know is not entirely empirically based on our physical senses; there is another plane of spiritual understanding. Paul prayed "that the eyes of our heart might be enlightened" (Eph. 1:18) and advised that we "fix our eyes on Jesus, the author and perfecter of faith" (Heb. 12:3). He explained his mission to King Agrippa, "to go to the Gentiles, to open their eyes so that they may turn from darkness to light, and from the dominion of Satan to God" (Acts 26:18).

The Greek philosopher, Plato, wrote, "Those who are able to see beyond the shadows and lies of their culture, will never be understood, let alone believed, by the masses." Christ-ones are to be "in the world, but not of the world" (Jn. 17:11,14). We are expected to understand what is going on in the world, as the "ruler of this world" (Jn. 12:31; 14:30; 16:11), Satan, operates in his antichrist manner. When we see with spiritual insight what is happening behind the scenes, beyond the out-front visible world, and "see-through" the operational machinations of evil in the world-system, we become an enigma to the world of mankind around us. We can see answers to world-problems and people's problems that those who are "of the world" cannot grasp, much less incorporate into their humanistic solutions. Such spiritual discernment recognizes that the world's solutions are ineffective.

FEBRUARY 5

OUR RESPONSIBILITY AS CHRIST-ONES

There was a time in the early instruction of the Spirit-teacher (Jn. 14:26) in my life, as He was teaching me the content and the actuation of the Christ-life, when I used to say to myself and to God, "I am only responsible to be and to do what God wants me to be and to do today." Gradually, over time, I came to realize that my understanding of my responsibility as a Christ-one was misguided. My responsibility-statement focused on what I could and should allegedly do to be pleasing to God. So, I changed my responsibility-statement to: "I am only responsible to be and to do what the Lord Jesus wants to be and to do in me today."

What is the difference between those two assertions of responsibility? The difference is not in the intent to be involved in what Jesus desires to be and do in me, but the difference is in understanding who is doing the doing. It is not what I do, but what Jesus is wanting to do in me. Jesus told His disciples, "Apart from Me, you can do nothing" (Jn. 15:5). Apart from our drawing from, depending on, deriving, and receiving from the living Lord Jesus by faith, we cannot do or achieve anything that pleases God or accomplishes His purposes. Since we were created to glorify God (Isa. 43:7), we can only do so by allowing Jesus to manifest God's character and action in us to the glory of God.

In the minds of some English speakers, the word "responsibility" carries with it the connotation that "I must do this." For that reason, I have chosen to think and speak of personal "responsibility" as personal response-ability – the ability to freely respond with freedom of choice to what God has made available (and does make available) by His grace-dynamic in Jesus Christ. God is the dynamic for all that He demands and desires in our lives. We do not, and are not, to attempt to "crank out" the actuation of God's intents by our own self-effort. Instead, we respond with faith-receptivity to God's grace-activity.

FEBRUARY 6

JESUS AND THE HOLY SPIRIT

The Christian faith is unique in its understanding of a monotheistic Trinitarian God, comprised of Father, Son and Holy Spirit – three Persons (not three gods) in one Divine Being (cosubstantial and indivisible). The first council of the Church, convened at Nicea in A.D. 325, addressed the co-equalilty of the Father and the Son (questioned by Arius, but asserted by Athanasius), determining by consensus that Jesus was "the only begotten of the Father, begotten not made, being of the same substance with the Father." The co-equality and co-deity of the Holy Spirit was agreed on by consensus at the Council of Constantinople in A.D. 381. God is three Persons in one Being.

These statements of church leaders in the fourth century have been, and still are foundational to orthodox Christian doctrinal understanding. The three Persons of the Triune God are distinct, but not separate; capable of being distinguished but not disjoined. The main issue of practical Trinitarian misunderstanding in the Western Church in the twenty-first century is the correlation of the risen Jesus and the functional operation of the Holy Spirit – how are they to be distinguished, yet not identified in equivalence of Personage? Is there a difference between the living Lord Jesus and the Holy Spirit in the Christ-one?

The co-equal, yet indivisible correlation of the Son of God (Jesus) and the Holy Spirit of God is a mystery beyond the full understanding of the finite minds of mankind. Paul explained, "the last-Adam (Jesus) became the Life-giving Spirit" (I Cor. 15:45), and later "the Lord (Jesus) is the Spirit" (II Cor. 3:17). In one sense there is no difference between the living Lord Jesus and the Holy Spirit, and yet in another sense they are to be differentiated as distinct persons of the Divine Trinity. On a practical level, every Christ-centered Christian will of necessity be a Spirit-empowered Christian, and *vice-versa*.

FEBRUARY 7

JESUS: GOD AND MAN

The Christian doctrine that Jesus is divine and human simultaneously and equally from the time of His incarnation was formulated at the Council of Chalcedon, convened in Asia Minor (now Turkey) in A.D. 451. There were numerous ideas of how Jesus could be God and man at the same time, but the conclusion of the assembly of 520 delegates to the council was that Jesus was fully God and fully man, one Being (*homoousion*) with God and one being (*homoousion*) with mankind. This union of God and man was defined as the hypostatic union of God and man in one Person having two natures (*duophusis* or dyophysite).

This was a council where consensus did not ensue in the Church at large after the creedal formulation; disagreements that remain today, almost sixteen centuries later. The divergent opinions that remain in the Church are for the most part unified in understanding that Jesus is the *Theanthropos*, the God-man, but their differences arise in how to explain such, and the word-semantics to be used in such explanation. The Greek word *phusis* that is translated as "nature" lacks clear definition. Can a person or object have more than one nature or "essential reality"? There are differing interpretations of the Greek term, *hupostasis* used for "hypostatic union."

When travelling in Egypt a few years ago, our travel guide was a member of the Coptic Orthodox Church of Alexandria which does not accept the Chalcedonian Creed formulation of Jesus having two natures. Their teaching is that Jesus has one nature (*miaphusis*), His deity and humanity combining into a singular divine-human nature. This is not the same as one nature (*monophusis*), either God or man, while denying the other. It should be obvious that Christian theology and its attempted explanation of Christology is not an easy task, but we are obliged to formulate our Christian teaching as precisely as possible.

PERFORMANCE RELIGION

Religion is comprised of a myriad of "to-dos" and "bullet point lists" of productivity and performance. The impoverished people who participate in religion always seem to think that "they have not done enough" to please God and failed to live up to the expectations of the leaders of the organizations who claim to represent God. These poor abused people need to have their blinders removed to understand that performance religion is entirely antithetical to the reality of the Christ-life and is counter to the grace-dynamic of empowerment that is intrinsic to the activity of God in the living Lord Jesus.

Performance religion knows no mercy. It swallows up the hard-working people who mistakenly commit themselves to its task, and then condemns them for not doing enough, or being good enough. Performance religion is a taskmaster who cannot be satisfied, always demanding additional and more specific performance. And just when one thinks they have the techniques mastered to perform as religion requires, then they "raise the bar," requiring a higher level of performance. How fair is that? It soon becomes a no-win situation, wherein all incentive to keep performing is gone. "I give up!"

That is the only real benefit of performance religion. If a person works hard enough and long enough until they have expended all their energy and they "hit the wall" of exhaustion and arrive at the recognition of their inability to perform, then such person will be receptive to the provision of God's grace in Jesus Christ. God never intended that his created human beings work themselves to death. His intent from the beginning was to provide everything for man that he could not accomplish for himself. To be man as God intended man to be, God would by the dynamic (grace) of fulfilling all His own desires in man, that as man was receptive to such in faith.

FEBRUARY 9

TRUTH

In the world of spiritual reality, Truth is a Person. Jesus said to
His disciples, "I am the Way, the Truth, and the Life" (Jn. 14:6).
"Truth was realized in Jesus Christ" (Jn. 1:17). "Truth is in Jesus"
(Eph. 4:21). "You will know the Truth (the Son), and the Truth
will set you free" (Jn. 8:32,26). Jesus is the "Spirit of truth" (Jn.
14:17; 15:26; 16:13; I Jn. 4:6).

The world thinks in terms of propositional or ideological truth;
truth statements that agree or are in accord with the facts that
are provided. Such an evaluation of truth allows for a wide range
of conclusions allowing for constant argumentation. Many people
want to find a single absolute truth that has no variance and is
without question. Our legal court system, for example, asks each
witness if they will promise "to tell the truth, the whole truth,
and nothing but the truth." Any omission or altered personal
opinion is regarded as fallacious and untrue. From that
perspective of truth statements, "a half-truth is a whole lie."

A Christian teacher or preacher intends to share the truth of the
gospel. Even if they understand that Truth is a Person, they must
still formulate verbal expressions of such in propositional truth-
statements. When they do so, they will find it impossible to
formulate and express every truth-factor in every message. That
is why Dr. Fred Craddock, professor of preaching, explained that
"every sermon is heresy," in and of itself incomplete and omitting
some aspect of truth. What about the pastors who knowingly or
unknowingly, teach a partial gospel, inclusive of redemption,
regeneration and reconciliation (cf. Rom. 5:10), but fail to teach
the indwelling Christ and spiritual union with Christ, thereby
omitting what Dan Stone called "the rest of the gospel," the
remainder you seldom heard from the pulpit. If it be true that "a
half-truth is a whole lie," can we then conclude that "every
sermon is a lie?" Propositional truth can be hard to ascertain.

THE WAYS OF A LEGALIST

A legalist does not understand the provision and dynamic of the grace of God in Jesus and thinks that he must "keep the rules" of the Law to be right with God. His dilemma becomes greater and greater with time, for the legalist knows that he is unable to keep all the rules that he is attempting his hardest to keep. The frustration of defeat is constantly nagging at his fractured resolve to do things right for God. His performance resolve is always at the tipping point of collapse, so the legalist is always fleeing from the inevitable – the public exposure of his inability to keep the rules in order to be right with God.

Have you ever wondered why legalists are always seeking others to join them in their misery of inadequate performance? Is it like the mythological behavior of lemmings; they love company as they barrel toward the precipice of the abyss in a mass suicide? The old maxim is true, "misery loves company." The misery of failing to "measure up" is only bearable when there are others to commiserate with in the camaraderie of languishing losers hanging on to the last vestiges of false hope that in keeping the religious rules there will be some benefit in the persistent striving of trying harder and being committed.

Those who might consider joining with the legalists should understand that they will involve themselves in perpetual provisional standing in the company of legalists. You will be held at arm's-length, and only be invited into the innermost circle of rule-keepers when you have become an entrenched hypocrite willing to perpetuate the pretense that inadequate performance is the best that anyone can do. If they were anything other than religious legalists, they would meet at the bar and cry in their beer, but as it is, they can only gather in small groups of masochists who seem to love the pain of their failure and the continued manipulation of their collective guilt.

FEBRUARY 11

ADDICTION AND ANGER

When one gives in to their habituated weaknesses, succumbs to their addictive tendencies, and acts out in ways they have vowed and tried to avoid, they often become angry with themselves. They are dismayed and discontented with themselves and with everyone else around them. It's their way of trying to alleviate the self-imposed condemnation and guilt over their own failure, by beating up on themselves in masochistic behavior and lashing out at others in sadistic behaviors that cause physical and emotional pain, as well as the ruination of relationships that are so important to addressing the problem of addiction.

Those of us who have addictive tendencies (and by the way, that is every one of us) have usually attempted to overcome such by trying to muster up the self-effort to be what we think we should be, and do what we think we should do. It is extremely difficult to get it through our minds that self-effort and will-power will never be how we will overcome our propensities. Such discontent with ourselves and others will eventually cause us to act out again in our area of addiction and obsession. "If I cannot solve my own problems, then I will just bury my woes and worries once again in the dead-end problem.

It's a vicious circle – succumbing to the addiction; developing a disposition of discontent and anger; then succumbing to the addiction again. Some seek an addiction transference, thinking they do better in another addiction category such as an anonymity group or religion. Religion is full of angry addicts of one form or another. Contentment will only result when we come to the Lord Jesus and admit, "I can't; only You can; and I am willing to let you do it Your way in Your time. In the meantime, Lord, You know and I know that I will likely act out in continued compulsive behaviors that are self-destructive and damaging to those around me. You Lord are the divine change-agent."

OUGHT TOS & SHOULD DOS

Christians who have not developed an adequate perspective of God's grace as the total provision and dynamic of Christian living are often unduly concerned about the "ought tos" and "should dos" of how they think they should be performing as Christians. This performance-oriented perspective is indicative of all religion, as they require regular and ardent activity to keep people busy and involved, to measure their success in attempting to live the life that no one can live under their own self-effort. It's an exercise in futility but the religious leaders are never going to tell you that. That's what keeps people coming back week after week to "give it another shot."

This performance-oriented perspective of the religious life is so subtle. Many times, Christians have been led to believe that they are responsible to preserve and maintain a "Christian image;" and be concerned about what other people, both Christians and non-Christians, think of what and how they are doing. One fellow was hyper-concerned about getting his lawn mown in a timely manner, because he was convinced that the failure to keep it meticulously manicured would present "a bad testimony" to his neighbors. "It was for freedom that Christ set us free" (Gal. 5:1).

I have often grieved at the performance inculcations that religion has heaped on sincere Christian people. I have personally known pastors who were unduly burdened with the personal obligation to perform in accord with what they thought God and the congregation expected of them. One self-driven pastor was constantly concerned that "I haven't done enough for the Lord. There are many more ministry opportunities I should be assuming." Another pastor had such a sensitive heart for the needs of his flock, that he would mull over their problems night and day. He suffered an emotional breakdown and was only restored to health when he realized the dynamic of God's grace.

FEBRUARY 13

PARANOID UNCERTAINTY

Several brothers and sisters in Christ have expressed to me their uncertainty, verging on anxiety, about what is happening in the world around them. Some have asked, "Do you think the world is getting worse and worse? Are present events a prelude to the last days for the world? Are we nearing the end?" I must confess that these are not questions I have concerned myself with, for I have preferred to focus on all we now have in Christ Jesus, despite what is going on in the world. The world is going to do what the world is going to do, for the "ruler of this world" (Jn. 16:11), is the antithetical, adversarial antichrist.

We must avoid the anxiety that leads to paranoia, the suspicious mistrust of what people or agencies might be engaged in behind the scenes. The word "paranoia" is derived from two Greek words: *para* = alongside; *nous* = mind. When thoughts of current events and people's actions cause us to feel worried and threatened, such can leave a person in a state of hopeless insecurity and powerlessness. The suspicious mistrust of what is happening tends to cause people to distrust that God is in control of all that is happening. This is often due to a disproportional self-referential perspective of possible personal harm or loss.

How can people overcome the doomsday scenarios that are concocted by the devil in their minds? These often occur after a crisis in one's life, when things take a turn for the worse. It may be a pandemic. It may be after an election when the party of our preference did not emerge victorious. The tempter can play with our minds in ways that can become delusional, projecting a multitude of "what ifs" and conspiracy theories. Instead of paranoia, we should seek pronoia, a state of mind that sees the positive perspective that "God is love" (I Jn. 4:8,16), always seeks our highest good, and we can trust Him to continue to do so, for He has conquered evil once and for all at the cross.

THE EXISTENTIAL LIFE

Most Christians are unclear about the meaning and implications of the word "existential." It must be admitted that the various man-made systems of philosophical existentialism are obfuscated and confusing. The adjective "existential" is based on the noun "existence," and pertains to the considerations of how individuals ask and answer the most meaningful questions of human existence, such as "who am I? and "why am I?". These existential questions can lead an individual to an existential crisis as they search for meaning in their lives in the midst of the sorrow, misery and despair that are indicative of the world.

The Greek philosopher Socrates is quoted as saying, "The unexamined life is not worth living." The existentialist is unwilling to accept that examination of our human existence must lead to meaningless or nothingness (nihilism). Humanistic, existential thinkers like Camus, Sartre, and Nietzsche did conclude that life in this world was miserable, absurd and without teleological hope. Soren Kierkegaard, on the other hand, known as the "father of existentialism," was a Christ-one, who despite his melancholy and sorrow found meaning, joy and hope in his faithful receptivity of the life of Jesus Christ.

In alignment with Kierkegaard, my entire existence and identity is caught up in the individual moment-by-moment faith-choices by which I continue to derive spiritual life from the living Lord Jesus during the circumstances of misery, sorrow and despair that present themselves in the world. That is the "existential life" of the indwelling presence of the life of Jesus Christ who serves as my *raison d'etre*, my reason for being. With Paul, I declare that "for me to live is Christ" (Phil. 1:21), and I focus not on the externals of circumstances, but on the interiority and subjectivity of "Christ in me, the hope of glory" (Col. 1:26,27) who "is my life" (Col. 3:4).

FEBRUARY 15

RESTING, RESTING

These words are from a hymn written by a rather obscure Irish poet, Jean Sophia Pigott (1845-1882). Pigott's brother, Thomas, was a missionary to China, martyred in 1901 in the Boxer Rebellion. The first two stanzas of the hymn are as follows:

> Jesus, I am resting, resting, in the joy of what Thou art;
> I am finding out the greatness of Thy loving heart.
> Thou hast bid me gaze upon Thee as Thy beauty fills my soul,
> For by Thy transforming power, Thou hast made me whole.
>
> O how great Thy lovingkindness, vaster, broader than the sea!
> O how marvelous Thy goodness lavished all on me!
> Yes, I rest in Thee, Beloved, know what wealth of grace is Thine,
> Know Thy certainty of promise, and have made it mine.

This hymn became a favorite of J. Hudson Taylor, founder (1865) of the China Inland Mission (CIM). Burdened with administrative responsibilities of the new mission, Hudson received a letter in 1869 from his trusted colleague, John McCarthy, explaining his new awareness of "trusting Christ to supply the Holy Spirit, and ceasing to work so hard to become holy." Taylor was greatly affected by the content of McCarthy's letter, and wrote to his sister, "A sentence in a letter from dear McCarthy was used to remove the scales from my eyes, and the Spirit of God revealed the truth of our oneness with Jesus as I had never known it before. McCarthy, who had been much exercised by the same sense of failure, saw the light before I did, and wrote: 'Not by striving after faith, or to increase our faith, but by resting on the Faithful One, resting in the Loved One.'" The terms they used to refer to this new awareness were "the exchanged life," and "union with Christ." Those phrases are still used to this day to refer to the life of "rest" wherein Christ-ones allow the Christ-life to be the full sufficiency of God's grace, desirous of seeing Christ lived out and working in all that Christ-ones do.

POSITIVE PSYCHOLOGY

In the past couple of decades, there has been a movement within the psychological community that seeks a more positive approach to human behavior. This is a reactive correction to the popular psychological approaches that dwell on the negatives of human problems and mental illnesses (cf. *Diagnostic and Statistical Manual of Mental Disorders*, DSM5, 2013). Called "Positive Psychology," some trace the commencement of this movement to a book by Christopher Peterson and Martin Seligman, *Character Strengths and Virtues* (2004). Certain basic premises and principles, however, can likely be traced back to Aristotle in his *Nicomachean Ethics*.

In the 19th century, Soren Kierkegaard (1813-1855) laid philosophical foundations for existentialist thought and the critical moments of an individual's life as they search for meaning in life. In the 20th century, Victor Frankl (1905-1997), Austrian neurologist and psychiatrist, wrote *Man's Search for Meaning* (1946), recounting some of his thoughts while surviving the holocaust in Nazi concentration camps. Frankl built upon, yet reacted to, his predecessors Freud and Adler, insisting that to help people, one must address subjective well-being, moral virtue, personal happiness, and *eudaimonia* (the good life).

This recent movement of "Positive Psychology" is certainly based on humanist and existentialist premises. As such, this means that they regard humans as "independent selves" who are simply "the products of their own choices (self-made individuals), with no consideration of a Being beyond themselves, i.e., a God who is at work in His creation, and has set His creation aright in His Son, Jesus Christ. But it appears that their emphasis on positive development, looking to a person's future and not just their past problems, might provide a structure to help people if they would only accept the spiritual source of character in God or Satan.

FEBRUARY 17

SIN MANAGEMENT

Many who call themselves "Christians" are overly concerned about their past or on-going sin. They view the Christian life as a constant process of sin-management, attempting to avoid sins of commission and omission, and attempting to evaluate whether certain actions are to be considered as sin (or not). This becomes a miserable and vicious cycle of sin-avoidance, sin cover-up, sin confession, and an over-all consciousness of sin. Eating constantly from the "tree of the knowledge of good and evil," they fall into the WYSIWYG syndrome – i.e., "what you see is what you get," so if one's focus is on sin, one will veer toward sin, and spend most of their time trying to manage their sin.

Those who view the Christian life as sin-management are still operating in the religious paradigm of concern about external misrepresentation. The quicksand of the sin struggle is a futile effort of trying to overcome what has already been overcome. The victory has already been won! The sin of mankind was taken care of at the cross, when Jesus defeated the Satanic originator and source of sin (I Jn. 3:8) once and for all (I Pet. 3:18), and "broke the power of sin" (Heb. 2:14). Satan and his character of sin and evil was conquered (Col. 2:15) on the cross in the death of Jesus Christ, wiping out the consequences of sin.

Those who receive the Spirit of the living Christ into their human spirit by faithful receptivity of His presence and activity are safe "in Christ" (in union with Christ), having been "freed from sin" (Rom. 6:18,22; 8:2), and are now "dead to sin" (Rom. 6:11). Satan and his defeated power of sin and death cannot overcome the dynamic of God's grace in the Christ-one. He has no authority or power to steal the one who now belongs to Christ. That does not mean that the believer cannot exercise the freedom of choice to behaviorally plug-in to the devil's misrepresentative character expressions of sinfulness and selfishness.

COUNT ME OUT – COUNT ME IN

People have such a propensity to attempt to classify one another. We want to identify and label other people with the thought and action of a particular subgroup. There are many such identifiable groups that I do not wish to be lumped together with in identification. Of course, I have always been an "odd man out," seeking to avoid any boxes of thought or action. I think the spontaneity of God's grace in each Christ-indwelt individual will cause that person to be unique and for the most part unclassifiable. As that unique Christ-one that I am, there are categorized boxes that I want to avoid ("count me out") and categories that I am willing to identified with ("count me in").

For example, I do not want to be lumped together in the over-all box of American cultural Christians. Count me out; I don't want to be included! In the United States today, those identified as "evangelicals" have morphed into a cultural and political religious voting bloc of attempted social action and persuasion. This subgroup of cultural Christians is identified by their shared beliefs and ideology. They are identified as conservatives and are predominantly Republican in their political persuasion. General public opinion views them as self-absorbed and in-grown hypocrites who are narrow-minded and unstable.

Now if you want to talk about Christ-ones within whom the living Lord Jesus Christ indwells and lives out His character, then "count me in." I am desirous of being fully invested in the Body of Christ, in the company of those who have received the living Lord Jesus by faith and are longing for the contemporary re-presentation of Jesus's life and character. Many of these Christ-ones are not church-going folks, because they do not want to be identified as mere cultural Christians. They desire to experience the freedom of God's grace as they operate "in the world, but not of the world" (Jn. 17:11,14). Count me in!

FEBRUARY 19

TIE ME UP; TIE ME DOWN

WARNING: The following reading may be offensive to the sensitive-minded reader. "Tie me up; Tie me down" was a 1989 Spanish dark-comedic love story adjudged by some critics to be pornographic. I have not viewed the movie; I simply want to key off the words in the title, which referred to the practices of BDSM (bondage, domination, sadism, masochism) within sexual relationships. I am not making any judgment on these sexual practices, but I am seeking to make an analogy from such practices to religious practices, which have been referred to as a psychological or spiritual form of BDSM.

The word "religion" is derived from the Latin words *religio* and its cognate *religare*. These words refer to the action of "binding up" or "tying down." The words "ligament" and "ligature" both find their origin in this Latin word group. Popular usage of the word "religion" is rapidly developing a negative connotation of binding or tying people to various rules and regulations, and/or rituals of devotion. This is consistent with how the word "religion" is used in the New Testament, where it usually has a negative connotation of human self-effort (cf. Col. 2:23) but can refer to a positive binding devotion to Christ (cf. James 1:27).

There is a great need in our contemporary English-speaking world to differentiate between the binding performance regulations of religion as contrasted with the vital dynamic of God's grace that imbues Christ-ones with the reality of the Christ-life to manifest His character in human behavior. We must recognize that Christianity is not religion, though on the popular level of understanding that will take a long period of time to change, because Christ-ones have long presented the faith in the terms of a religion, i.e., Christian religion. Christians are tired of being tied to performance, and long to experience the freedom of living spontaneously by means of God's grace in Jesus Christ.

LONGING IS PART OF THE PROCESS

Some Christ-ones seem to think that there should be no more longing or yearning in their lives. They may rightly understand that God has provided everything they need in Jesus Christ, and they are "lacking nothing" (James 1:4). Whereas the Psalmist cried, "My eyes fail with longing for Your salvation, and for Your righteous word" (Ps. 119:123), Christ-ones realize that God's salvation has been given in Jesus, the Righteous Word (cf. Jn. 1:1,14). That does not mean, however, that that there is not an ongoing experiential longing for an ever-deeper intimacy in our relationship with Jesus, and for an increase in our "growing in the grace and knowledge of our Lord Jesus Christ" (II Pet. 3:18).

Longing is part of the process in our desire to participate in all that God wants to be and do in our lives. Sometimes, we do not even understand the object of our longing. We are longing for what we do not know; for the unknowable, for the mystery that is only in God Himself. Prolonged longing allows us to clarify our focus of what we really desire, our deepest desires. God uses that sense of longing, so we will appreciate what He only can provide; our longing is really for Him, for only He can satisfy our deepest, earnest, passionate longing to be everything we were intended to be; man as God intended.

We may be longing for deeper intimacy with God, for pure love, for genuine fellowship with others in Christ. God means for us to go through the process of longing. We must not disparage such or despair and give up on our longing. Jesus said, "Seek and you shall find; knock and the door shall be opened" (Matt. 7:8). Those who seek Him will be drawn into deeper intimacy of relationship with Him. Longing can be a part of faith; the willingness to receive all that God has for us. Our longing may even include "the groaning and longing to be clothed with our dwelling in heaven" (II Cor. 5:2); an eschatological sense of longing.

FEBRUARY 21

THE SUBTLETY OF IDEOLOGICAL IDOLATRY

Christianity has to do with personal relationship with Jesus. We do not want our Christianity, our Christian faith, to be faith in a "concept," an ideological construct, instead of the living Lord Jesus; for as accurate as the idea may be, such often becomes concept-idolatry. Even if our conceptualization has to do with the "finished work" of Jesus Christ, or "Christ in you," or our being "complete in Christ," or that we have received all that God has to give, or "new covenant" ideology, these can become a form of ideological idolatry if they are not experientially known and behaviorally manifesting the character of Jesus.

Yes, even the idea of "Christ in you" (Col. 1:26,27) can become Christ-in-you-ism (an idolatrous ideological construct). Then there are those who so adamantly emphasize the "finished work" of Christ (Jn. 19:30) that they conceive of themselves as a "finished Christian." If we think we have arrived at the summit of understanding an idea, it is likely we are engaging in idea-idolatry (ideolatry). Mere ideological information without the continuous experiential and relational intimacy with Jesus is arid, and leads only to pride and arrogance, rather than to the humility of recognizing all that we do not yet know.

We must not settle for a plateau of settled sufficiency in any corpus of ideas or concepts. The fifth century mystic known as Pseudo-Dionysius wrote, "God hates ideas." Every ideology is based on taking a part out of creation's totality, raising it above the creation, and making the latter revolve around and serve that conceptualized idea. Augustine wrote, "idolatry is worshipping anything that ought to be used or using anything that ought to be worshipped." Paul stated, "Not that I have already obtained *it* or have already become perfect, but I press on [h]so that I may lay hold of that [i]for which also I was laid hold of by Christ Jesus (Phil. 3:12). May we continue to press on.

THE NEEDINESS PANDEMIC

The recent Covid-19 pandemic has made us more aware of what is involved in a comprehensive pandemic that affects and infects most people in the world. What I am suggesting in this article is that there seems to be a pervasive "neediness pandemic" that is affecting many people and infecting the social interactions of our society as a whole. Christ-ones are well-aware that the world of mankind in their natural condition are a needy people, needing to discover the spiritual solution to their spiritual need, found only in the living Lord Jesus.

The sense of neediness that needs to be addressed in general society today goes beyond the regenerative spiritual need of mankind, for we are seeing so many people debilitated by psychological, emotional, and social neediness. This condition is prevalent, not only in those who are unregenerate but also in those who identify themselves as "Christians" – those who have not chosen to allow the living Lord Jesus to be their total Life-sufficiency. Retaining their natural self-oriented patterns of the "flesh" (Gal. 5:19), many people are paralyzed by their fear of inadequacy and insecurity, their fear of not being in control of their situations and their fear of not being able to solve those perceived problems.

Many of these people suffer from bouts of anxiety and panic over their perceived inadequacy. Paul explained, "Not that we are adequate to consider anything as coming from ourselves, but our adequacy is of God" ((II Cor. 3:5). Christ-ones need not be "needy"! They are "complete in Christ" (Col. 1:28) and "lacking/*needing* nothing" (James 1:4). "God will supply all our needs according to His riches in glory in Christ Jesus" (Phil. 4:19). The solution for the neediness pandemic is that Christ-ones might understand their spiritual identity and strength in Jesus Christ and trust in His competent sufficiency in their lives.

53

FEBRUARY 23

RELIGION'S TEACHING FETISH

It seems that the preoccupation of contemporary Christian religion has to do with correct teaching, with orthodox ideological formulations. This is not a new phenomenon. The history of Christian thought records that the Christian religion has long been preoccupied with correct doctrinal teaching, teaching a correct corpus of information, to the extent that it often becomes ideolatry (the idolatry of ideas). Now don't get me wrong: there is a necessary foundation of correct historical and theological thought that underlies the reality of Christ-thought, but it should not become our foremost objective to teach such.

The prime objective of Christian faith is not correct teaching – not the teaching of Jesus as found in the gospels – not the teaching of the apostles, Paul, John, James, Jude, etc. – not the teaching and creeds of the church – not the teaching of anything! Christianity is not a didactic process, but the process of life, of the living out of JESUS' life (cf. II Cor. 10:11). Christianity is a PERSON, not a teaching – not ideas and information about that Person, but the indwelling life and character of the living Lord Jesus lived out. Paul wrote, "As you received Christ Jesus the Lord, so walk in Him" (Col. 2:6); Jesus lived out!

The story is told of Gautama Buddha: As he was dying, some devotees asked how they could share his legacy. Buddha replied, "It is not about me; just share my teachings with all you meet." Many seem to think that Jesus might have said something similar. Not so, absolutely not! In contrast to Buddhist thought, the Christ-life is all about Him, the resurrected and living Lord Jesus living in Christ-ones by His Spirit indwelling their human spirit. The Christian faith is a PERSON, not a teaching about that Person, or a repeating of the teachings of that Person, but the ontological dynamic of the Person of the living Lord Jesus.

"LIFE BY JESUS"

Many readers, especially those with a few years under their belt, will remember the prestigious-looking badges attached to General Motors cars until the mid-1990's, marked "Body by Fisher" or "Fisher Body." The Fisher Body Company began as an independent coachbuilder building high-quality horse-drawn carriages in the first decade of the 20th century. They soon converted to building enclosed automobile bodies, and were acquired by General Motors in 1919, which continued to use the distinctive and iconic logo, "Body by Fisher" on their door sill plates until the final decade of the 20th century, the 1990's.

Playing off that memorable 20th century image of "Body by Fisher," I am proposing an even more distinctive and iconic label inscribed "Life by Jesus." When people open the doors into the lives of Christian people, they should recognize a distinctive intangible marking of "Life by Jesus." Yes, they will know us by our given name, but they should recognize a quality of excellent character in us that is a result of a derived identity as a Christ-one – Life by Jesus. This is much more than a logo plate or badge attached to our body. This derived spiritual identity should be evident to all whom we come into contact, identifying us by our distinctive character of Christ-life.

Christ-ones do not need an exquisite badge or placard to identify that they live by the Life of Jesus. In His sermon on the mount, Jesus explained "by their fruit you will know them" (Matt. 7:16,20), and later stated, "everyone will know that you are my disciples, if you love one another" (Jn. 13:35). The familiar chorus, "One in the Spirit," with the words, "They will know we are Christians by our love" was written in the 1960's by Catholic priest, Fr. Peter Scholtes. The love we exhibit is Christ's love, "given to us by the Holy Spirit" (Rom. 5:5), and we "bear fruit in every good work" (Col. 1:10) only by means of the life of Jesus."

FEBRUARY 25

CHRISTUS INTERRUPTUS

Surely you have noticed that life seems to be a series of interruptions. Some blame these on fate, or on the devil, or on God. We want to consider how it is that Christ repetitively interrupts the daily routine of Christ-ones to reveal what He wants to do in our lives today. As busy humans, on the fast-track of life, we set out daily agendas comprised of the things that we think we need to do today. As Christ-ones, we experience the living Lord within orchestrating situations and circumstances in our outer lives that we might think are nuisances and inconveniences, but Christ is revealing the next opportunity for Him to exercise His grace sufficiency in the midst of the situation.

Solomon wrote, "The mind of man plans his way, but the Lord directs his steps" (Prov. 16:9). Jesus Christ, as Lord of our lives, is directing the steps of Christ-ones today. We make our plans, our agendas of the things we want to get done (man's ways), but we are often interrupted, stopped short in our tracks, and our "flesh" reactions consider these as irritations and annoyances. What we need to do is to realize that God has another idea (God's ways), and say in deference, Okay, Lord, obviously you have something else in mind, so let's proceed to address what YOU have in mind, and YOU will accomplish by YOUR grace.

The living Jesus in us has a way of interrupting our objectives and plans, causing us to evaluate our ways and consider the ways of God, and in the process allowing us to make the faith-choice to see what God wants to do in our situation, and to rely on His grace-dynamic to implement and orchestrate. This re-direct process of *Christus interruptus* changes our plans and direction and presents opportunities to see Jesus working in the situation. These may be car troubles, a flat tire, a broken appliance, a cancelled meeting, family needs and interruptions, and we have the choice to say, "Okay, Lord, let's do it YOUR way!"

DO DOGS HAVE A SOUL?

First, we must ask "What is a soul"? The functionality of a soul is comprised of thought processes, emotive passions, and the willed determination of making choices. The Greek word for soul is *psuche*, from which we get psyche and psychology. Most of us have taken a course in psychology and learned that the function of the psyche involves the mentality of thought, the affectations of passions, and the volitional determination of choices that usually follow the thoughts or passions. But the question at hand is whether such a behavioral process of function is operative not only in human beings, but also in the animal kingdom, particularly in canines and domesticated dogs.

We have two small white poodles named Peaches and Sofie. As I sit and watch the interactions of these two dogs, I notice a certain degree of psychological function that affects their behavior toward one another. Sofie is playing with a favorite stuffed toy they are both fond of. Peaches desires that toy with emotive passion, but she sits down about a yard away from Sofie, thinking about whether she should snatch the toy away (knowing that she could do so, for she is larger), but she knows that Sofie might get angry and snap at her, so she determines to make a willed choice to refrain from snatching the desired toy from Sofie.

All the functionality of the psyche, the soul, are operative in the dogs. But didn't the preacher say that "What separates humans from the animal kingdom is that humans have a soul."? The misinformed pastor is confounding the functionality of the human soul and the capacity of the human spirit (which Christian teachers have done for centuries). Yes, only humans have the spiritual capacity to be indwelt by one of the two spiritual sources, God or Satan, and to allow the character of one or the other to influence their psychological functionality, and thus activate the behavioral manifestations within the body.

FEBRUARY 27

THE LOVE OF GOD

All Christ-ones are aware that "God is love" (I Jn. 4:8,16), but I wonder whether this statement has become so common-place that it is an over-familiar flippant phrase, not invested with the depth of meaning that it contains. First, we must note "the love of God" can refer both to our love for God or God's love for us. It is the latter that we are addressing in this article. I don't think any human being with finite understanding can fully comprehend the infinite love of God for His human creatures, but to the extent that we are capable, we must attempt to understand and experience the love of God as He has revealed Himself to be, particularly by means of His Son (cf. Jn. 3:16).

Every Christ-one should be involved in a process of realizing the depth and intensity of God's love for them. not merely as an objective fact, but as a deep subjective reality that affects our emotions and spiritual sensitivities. Do we comprehend what it means to be loved by God so much that He would have sent His only-begotten Son to die in our place if we were the sole sinner among mankind. We are God's beloved son or daughter. Can you feel the weight of that love? Can you say to yourself, "I am God's beloved child!", and feel the privilege of that familial and spiritual union (I Cor. 6:17) deep within your soul?

We love because He first loved us (I John 4:19). As we personally experience and appreciate God's love for us, we can thereby be used as the conduits through which Christ expresses His love for others. We can never muster up and self-manufacture manifestations of love for others; it must the love of God shed abroad in our hearts by the Holy Spirit who has been given to us (Rom. 5:5) at regeneration, who expresses His divine love in and through us – the "fruit of the Spirit" (Gal. 5:22,23). The love of God grips us with an inescapable bonding that will necessarily desire to share that love with others.

SYSTEMATIC IDOLATRs

My early desire was to be a student of systematic theology. I enjoyed studying Christian doctrine when I was in Bible school. I went on to study dogmatics, the study of the dogma of the Church, at the seminary in Edinburgh, Scotland. I acquired hundreds of volumes (maybe over one thousand) of systematic and dogmatic theology from as many theological perspectives as I could find. I am here to tell you – the reading of such theological categorizations can leave a person thoroughly befuddled, tied up in mental knots that take much untangling, and does not lead to any definitive conclusions of understanding.

Then, I began to read some books by the late French sociologist, philosopher, and social analyst, Jacques Ellul (1912-1994). Ellul pointed out that the systematization of thought, as well as the systematization of procedural actuation (what he called "technique") – such systematization can be a form of idolatry whereby the process becomes the end-all, the deified objective. The teleological objective of such does not lead to complete comprehension, and certainly does not end in the worship of the Creator God who controls all that transpires in the world. The technique of systematization can lead to idolatry.

You see, if something is systematized, it can be mentally boxed up for distribution with alleged guaranteed outcomes, and presented to the world as "this is the way" to understanding; the cure-all to all functional proceduralism – it smacks of a form of idolatry. In that Jesus declared, "I AM the way, the truth, and the life" (Jn. 14:6), to pronounce any human procedure or thought process as "the way" is a defiant contradiction that can be termed "systematic idolatry." Is it not ironic that I set out to study systematic theology and realized that such a process can and often does lead to systematic idolatry? Our human search for systematics defies the loving relationality of the gospel.

FEBRUARY 29

THE ROGUE'S GALLERY

The eleventh chapter of the book of Hebrews is revered as "The Faith Chapter," with a recitation of numerous personages recorded as persons who exercised faith in God. There are those, however, who have referred to the list of personages in Hebrews 11 as "The Rogue's Gallery." Those extolled as people of faith in God also have a history of less than admirable behavior. The value of this is the recognition that people who have roguish behavior in their past, people who do not have clean records, people who have less than perfect and righteous behavioral manifestations, can still be identified as people of faith, and can still be included in the Faith Hall of Fame.

Hebrews chapter 11 is not a list of the most righteous people in Hebrew History, yet they are known as the "Heroes of Faith." This just goes to show that religious self-righteousness does not exclude or eliminate a person from the possibility of exercising the faith-choice of receptivity to God's activity or availability to God's ability. Misrepresentative behavior does not disqualify an individual from faithfulness when God wants to use them and work through their lives. God takes great pleasure in working with failures, because it reveals that it is not something that we have done, but what we have receptively allowed Him to do.

Yes, Noah was available to build the ark and take his family aboard to survive the flood, but then, he was discovered nude and drunk. Abraham lied in passing his wife as his sister and chose the logical alternative to faith by copulating with his wife's servant girl, Hagar, to produce a progeny, Ishmael – but he was receptive to God's action in leaving Ur of the Chaldees and in his willingness to sacrifice his son, Isaac. Moses murdered an Egyptian slave and fled for his life but was available to lead his people out of Egypt in the Exodus. These less than perfect individuals chose to exercise faith that allowed God to function.

JUSTICE

Political progressives and religious theological progressives constantly rant about the need for justice. Their concern is social justice to be orchestrated and implemented in accord with humanistic premises that elevate a false freedom founded on personal rights and social equity in race, gender, religion, etc. Those considered victims *de jour* may receive temporary benefit and betterment, but ultimately such a quest for human-centered social justice results in injustice, enslavement, inequality, and dehumanization. Justice derived from humanistic aspirations does not have the authority nor the endurance of longevity to meet man's deepest needs for justice and a just society.

Justice must be rooted in God and His character, rather than in the humanistic aspirations of man. Jacques Ellul wrote, "The only justice resides in God and comes from Him." The just and righteous God (cf. Rom. 8:33) acts in the highest benefit of the humanity He has created, and human creatures who realize such will derive justice and righteousness from God (*ek Theos*), thus availing themselves of genuine human personalization and socialization. The Greek word *dikaiosune* in the New Testament can be translated both "justice" and "righteousness." Just righteousness commences within the character of God

Justice is only realized among men when divine justice is allowed to become operative in humanity. Jesus did not come to establish social justice in the humanistic paradigm that liberals promote. The full essence of justice was implemented when Jesus Christ, the Just One or Righteous One (Acts 3:14; 7:52; 22:14) brought justice within Himself (Rom. 3:26). The objective is that "we might be made the righteousness of God in Him" (II Cor. 5:21), functioning as "servants to righteousness unto holiness (Rom. 6:13,19), "filled with the fruits of righteousness, which come through Jesus Christ" (Phil. 1:11).

MARCH 2

FREEDOM

Human beings around the world, individually and collectively, are clamoring for freedom – freedom from genuine and perceived oppression – freedom from an imperceptible enslavement of misused and abused humanity. There is an oppression of humanity in the world-system that offers a false freedom leading to the dehumanization of mankind, to the failure of social structures – to a disguised dead-end that ends in death rather than living freedom. The freedom that fallen humanity craves will never be found by means of humanistic pursuits and self-constructed remedies.

Freedom based on humanistic premises of self-potential is contrary to God's purpose and character, i.e., sin. It amounts to attempting to put ourselves in God's place, which is precisely what Adam and Eve sought to do in the Garden when tempted by the serpent's declaration, "You will be like God" (Gen. 3:5). It was a pseudo-freedom wherein they became enslaved to their own desires, and that because they were enslaved to the Evil One (II Tim. 2:26). Humanity is enslaved to the vain glory and pride of declaring, "I can do it myself, I am my own center of reference, my own resource" – self-potential.

Freedom is inherent in the character of God as he desires His human creatures to be and to freely function as He intended. It is not true freedom if it is detached from God's purpose, which is to affirm man in his intended purpose to glorify God (Isa. 43:7). The freedom that allows for the full dignity of humanity is only in the receptivity to God's activity, allowing the God of liberty to do as He wills in our lives. Real freedom is the freedom to be man as God intended man to be. It was for such freedom that Christ set us free (Jn. 8:32,36; Gal. 5:1,13). Christ-ones are free to express God's righteousness (Rom. 6:20), and to be the instruments of God's love one another, and the instruments of righteousness.

FAITH-REST IS NOT PASSIVISM

Though we emphasize that the Christ-life is what God does and not what we do, we do not want to give the impression the Christian individual is totally passive in the actuation of the Christ-life. We certainly do not want to imply that the human individual should just sit on his duff and wait for God to hit him over the head with a wooden 2x4 to advise him that He wants to energize divine action in and through Him. The Christian life is not a do-nothing attitude of acquiescence or passivism, just "waiting on God" to act in me. That is not what we mean when we state that "Christ is the doer of the Christ-life in the Christ-one."

Do you remember your school grammar lessons? A passive verb is when an object or person is acting upon the subject. If "you," the Christ-one, are the subject, then Christ is the one who is acting upon and in you. That does not imply that Christ's action is an inevitable imposition that you cannot resist, or that there is no act of willingness or receptivity that "you," the subject, are not reponse-able to make. The Christ-one must make an active choice of faith, a volitional determination to be receptive to the activity of Christ in our life. It is a definite act of purposed determination in the human will to allow for Christ's divine action in us.

The very definition of faith we employ is a denial of passivism. Faith is "our receptivity of His activity." The receptivity is our active availability; the activity is Christ at work in us. There is no passivism in that arrangement – not in the Christ-one or in Christ as He is allowed to do what He wants to do in us. But this reveals the necessity of obedience, i.e., "listening under" Christ to ascertain the next action He wants to enact in us. Yes, "God is at work in you to will and to work for His good pleasure" (Phil. 2:13), and Jesus said, "Apart from Me you can do nothing" (Jn. 15:5), but we are response-able to respond in faith and "present our bodies a living and holy sacrifice" (Rom. 12:1).

MARCH 4

CHANNELS ONLY

This is the title and theme of a 19th century hymn, the authorship of which has been attributed to both Mary E. Maxwell and Ada Gibbs, with little known about either of these authors. This hymn is not contained in many hymnals today, and it is rare to hear it used among Christian groups.

> How I praise Thee, precious Savior,
> That Thy love laid hold of me;
> Thou hast saved and cleansed and filled me
> That I might Thy channel be.
>
> Just a channel full of blessing,
> To the thirsty hearts around;
> To tell out Thy full salvation,
> All Thy loving message sound.
>
> (Refrain) Channels only, blessed Master,
> But with all Thy wondrous pow'r
> Flowing through us, Thou canst use us
> Every day and every hour.

The truth contained in these stanzas and refrain is biblically and spiritually accurate. Christ-ones are but the channels through which the Christ-life is expressed and manifested. We do not manufacture or produce the life of Christ by our self-determined behavior, but we are the channels or conduits through which the character of Christ is lived out to the glory of God.

The scarcity of modern use of this hymn may be due to the 20th century use of the notion of "channeling" within occult societies, where they believe a person can "channel" a spirit guide to achieve expanded consciousness. We must not allow such usage to hijack the legitimate use of the word "channel" as a course or conduit of conveyance and manifestation of Jesus Christ.

CHRONIC COMPLAINERS

Without doubt you have noticed that there are some people who are unhappy and discontent about almost everything they encounter. They will complain that it is too cold, and as the temperature changes that it is too hot. They will complain that the room is too still and stuffy and then when the fan is turned on that there is too much draft in the room. They will complain that they have nothing to do, and when events change that they are too busy and have too much to do. They will complain they are poor and lacking, but then when they have plenty, that their domicile is cluttered with unneeded things. Whatever the circumstance, a chronic complainer will be dissatisfied.

Job, who had much to complain about, declared "my complaint is rebellion" (Job. 23:2). His declaration reveals that complaining is active resistance against what God has provided or allowed. It is a self-centered desire that all circumstances should be favorable to my wishes. It's all about me, and whether I consider what is happening suitable to my whims of self-pleasure. Chronic complainers have an attitude of defiant discontent with what God has provided and are contentious with people in God's *ecclesia*. "Do not complain against one another, brethren" (James 5:9); "Be hospitable, without complaint" (I Pet. 4:9).

The Israelite people in the old covenant were chronic complainers, constantly dissatisfied with their plight during the forty years they were being led to the promised land. Neither Moses nor God Himself was pleased with their grumblings of discontent (Numb. 11:1; 14:27), and there were consequences. God has provided everything He promised to the Abrahamic people in His Son, Jesus Christ (II Cor. 1:20), and Christ-ones should find joy and contentment with everything that God has provided and continues to provide in our daily circumstances. Chronic complainers are in jeopardy of God's displeasure.

MARCH 6

FOUL!

When the rules are violated in many games of sport, the referee or the one overseeing proper play of the game may call "FOUL!" In baseball, for example, if the batter hits the ball outside of the field of play between the first baseline and the third baseline, the hit is called "FOUL!" In basketball, when a player makes illegal contact with another player on the opposing team, he is called for a "FOUL! In American football, a "FOUL" against the rules may be committed by a player and is assessed against the team, resulting in moving the football back 5, 10, or 15 yards toward their own goal. Some flagrant fouls may result in disqualification from continued involvement in the game. In track and field, a "FOUL!" may be called when the runner jumps the gun at the start of a race, or a player goes outside of the acceptable field of play (ex. shot put, javelin). In soccer (football) a "FOUL!" is called when one player makes illegal contact with an opposing player. A gymnast commits a "FOUL" when he/she goes outside the lines on the floor routine. In horse racing, a "FOUL!" may be called when one horse comes into contact with another horse, or otherwise impedes his run. Most sports have rules – the violation of which constitutes a "FOUL!".

In correlation to what occurs in the world of sports, I am suggesting that a "FOUL!" might be called when a Christ-one attempts to do what only the living Lord Jesus can do, i.e., live the Christian life. The self-effort of human performance to "live like Jesus" is a "FOUL!" against the grace dynamic by which the Christian life is designed to be lived. But if a "FOUL!" were rightfully called on all Christians who are trying to live the Christian life by their own self-effort and trying to perform in a way that they falsely think will please God, the on-going game that the church plays would come to a stand-still. The game would have to be "called" and discontinued for lack of legitimate participants, because the vast majority had "FOULED OUT!"

JESUS IS ENOUGH

The story is told of John D. Rockefeller that he was once asked, "You have so much wealth; how much is enough?" His reply was, "A little bit more than I presently have." For the Christ-one, there is not a little bit more than we presently have in the full sufficiency of the living Christ Jesus dwelling in our human spirit. Jesus is enough! Jesus is all that God has to give. He gave His only begotten Son, who continues to live after His resurrection by the presence of the Spirit of Christ living in those who become Christ-ones by receiving Him into their human spirit by faith (cf. Jn. 1:12,13; Jn. 14:16; Rom. 8:9).

Jesus is God's provision to be and do all that God wants to be and do in us. Jesus is God's gracious gift that allows human beings to be man as God intended man to be. To say or indicate in any manner that we need more than what we have in Jesus is to say that Jesus is inadequate or insufficient. May it never be! The proper equation is Jesus plus nothing; Jesus + _____ (nothing that can rightfully be added here). No additive is needed for the Christ-life – no spiritual STP, Lucas, STA-BIL, or Seafoam. We need nothing more than the dynamic of God's grace via the empowering of the Holy Spirit to be and do all that God desires.

The Christ-one is "complete in Christ" (Col. 1:28). "God has blessed us with every spiritual blessing in heavenly places in Christ Jesus" (Eph. 1:3). "His divine power has granted to us everything pertaining to life and godliness" (II Pet. 1:3). "All spiritual things belong to us" as Christians (I Cor. 3:21,22). There isn't anything more than ALL! What we have been given in Jesus is ALL that God has to give and ALL that we need. Jesus is enough! We do not need to seek additional blessings, additional experiences, or additional teachings to build us up and "make us more spiritual." Jesus is enough, and He wants to be All that He is in us by manifesting His life and character in ALL we do.

MARCH 8

SELFLESS SERVICE

Colin Luther Powell was a four-star general in the United States
Army and went on to become Chairman of the Joint Chiefs of Staff
in the U.S. Department of Defense and became the United States
Secretary of State under George W. Bush. He died on October 18,
2021, of complications from the Covid-19 virus. In the many
words of commendation and admiration after he died, it was
noted that a dominant emphasis of Powell was his value of and
constant call for "selfless service" to the nation of the United
States of America. Does such a call for "selfless service" to our
nation seem to be an admirable objective?

In the world-system that advocates a worldview calling people to
"do your own thing," and "be the best self you can be," it might be
that a call for "selfless service" to one's country might be the
highest calling one can achieve. It seems that many Christians
might concur with such a call for "selfless service," both to the
nation of the United States and to the church where they have
identified. The question must be asked: "Is it possible to muster
up 'selfless service' for God or country if one has not broken free
of the humanistic premises that promote self-concern, self-
gratification and selfish aspiration?

Paul advised Timothy that until the last days, "men will be lovers
of self... and haters of good" (II Tim. 3:2). Jesus explained, "If any
man will come after Me, let him deny himself, and take up his
cross, and follow Me" (Matt. 16:24; Mk. 8:24; Lk. 9:23). The only
way to overcome our natural self-interest and self-concern is to
experience a spiritual exchange "from the dominion of Satan to
God" (Acts 26:18), "to be rescued from the domain of darkness,
and transferred to the kingdom of the Son" (Col. 1:13). When the
living Lord Jesus is our Lord and our life, then "selfless service"
on behalf of others in need (not the institution of government or
religion) is possible (cf. Phil. 2:4).

FOR OTHERS

It is important that we emphasize that the Spirit of Christ comes to live in us, and that as Christ-ones, we are to allow Him to be our Life. But we do not want to become self-absorbed in our awareness of the indwelling Jesus. When we keep referring to Christ in us, we need to realize that it is always Christ in us for others. Jesus Christ does not live and exist for Himself, but the character of love that is inherent within Him is necessarily desirous of seeking the highest good of others. If we do not have a heart for people, for their spiritual, psychological, and physical well-being, then it is to be questioned whether we know Jesus and His heart for needy people.

The contrast with, or the opposite of Love is selfishness. We are either occupied with our own self-concerns with a centripetal gravitational pull to fulfill our own desires, or we are occupied with the needs of others with a centrifugal motion that allows the Persons of the Trinity to push out to others with the divine character of Love. There has to be motion – either inward or outward, for without motion there is but static stillness, i.e., death. "God is love" (I Jn. 4:8,16), and He always reaches out to the needs of others. In the process of the manifestation of His other-directed Love, He overcomes our natural self-orientation.

Even after we have received Jesus Christ and have become a Christ-one in whom the Spirit of Christ lives, we still have the residual patterns of selfishness in the desires of our soul. These patterns of selfishness and sinfulness are what the apostle Paul refers to as "the flesh" (cf. Gal. 5:16-21). These patterns of selfishness need not be the driving force of our behavior. The Spirit of Christ living within our spirit (Rom. 8:9) is the empowering to overcome our selfish flesh-patterns, and the means by which we allow our selfishness to be overcome by the Spirit of Love in the day-by-day process of sanctification.

MARCH 10

JESUS' EFFECT ON OUR HEART

When you ponder the reality of Jesus living within you, or simply hear or say the name of "Jesus," what are the inner emotional feelings that arise in your heart? Is there an overwhelming sense of being loved? Is there a sense of security that you are kept in His love? Is there a sense of awe and wonder that the Lord of the universe has descended to inhabit your spirit ...your heart ...your very being? Is there an awareness that the presence of Jesus in you has changed everything about you? Some Christ-ones get goosebumps or warm-fuzzies when they ponder the intimacy of being "one with Jesus" (cf. I Cor. 6:17).

Despite my tendency to be a cerebral believer, that does not mean that my emotive sensitivities are not part of my Christian faith as well. I am willing to share that I get a warm and secure feeling in my heart as I ponder the presence of Jesus. My heart, my inner being, is warmed by the awareness that He is my life – He is my everything! I am nothing apart from Him. In fact, I find it inconceivable that I should or could be without Him. He is the basis of who I am, the essential constituency of my being. In the words of a contemporary song by Dennis Jernigan, "Nobody fills my heart like Jesus."

These considerations about our spiritual and emotional sensitivities are not all that dissimilar to Asaph's sharing of his heart in the 73rd Psalm. With utmost honesty, he admits that he questions how God works, that he has been envious and bitter about the prosperity of the wicked. "Nevertheless," he goes on to conclude, "God is the strength of my heart and my portion forever" (26). "The nearness of God is my good" (28). "Whom have I in heaven but You? And there is nothing on earth that I desire besides You?" (25). Christ-ones will feel likewise about Jesus who dwells within our spirit. We want nothing more than Jesus, and to allow Jesus to be our everything.

WHAT'S GOING ON IN THE WORLD?

Considering what is going on in the broader world around me, I tend to take a "stand-back" approach and observe what happens. "The world is going to do what the world is going to do!" The character of the "ruler of this world" (Jn. 14:30; Eph. 6:12) is always that of discord, disputes, dissension, strife, selfishness, greed, etc. (cf. Gal. 5:19-21). The prevailing axis on which we can explain what goes on in the world-system of evil is "conflict" – this goes back as far as the discord between Cain and Abel (Gen. 4:1-9). Jesus told His disciples, "When you hear of wars and rumors of wars, do not be frightened; those things must take place; but that is not yet the end. (Mk. 13:7).

As Christ-ones, we are "in the world, but not of the world" (Jn. 17:13-19). The Son of God "became flesh" (Jn. 1:14) in the form of the man (Phil. 2:7,8), Jesus Christ. He was not of "the world of evil" and His divine character was diametrically opposite to the character of the "ruler of the world." By His incarnation, He came into the world of God's creation, and into the world of humanity. Jesus, by the Spirit, living in every Christ-one (cf. Gal. 2:20; Col. 1:27), is not trying to escape the world-context into which He was sent, but desires to exhibit the contrast of His character from the character of the Evil One in the world.

Christ-ones are called both individually and collectively to engage with and disengage from the world-system of evil – a dialectic few have understood. Is our nation appointed to police the conflicts of other nations of the world? Sometimes our elected leaders will choose to engage and challenge the rulers of the world to alleviate suffering and death. Sometimes our leaders will choose to disengage and let the conflict play out as they have throughout the history of mankind. Likewise, individually, we may engage by functioning as salt and light in the world or disengage by remaining pilgrims in an alien world.

MARCH 12

ALL THINGS NEW; YET PROCESS CONTINUES

"If anyone is in Christ, he is a new creature; the old things passed away; behold, all things have become new" (II Cor. 5:17). This verse refers to the new spiritual condition that a Christ-one has when he has been spiritually regenerated and received the Spirit of Christ into their human spirit. He has new life – the very life of the risen Lord Jesus (Rom. 6:4). He has become "a new man" (Eph. 4:24; Col. 3:10). He is constituted a "new creature" spiritually. The "old spiritual things have passed away," i.e., he is no longer an "old man" (Eph. 4:22; Col. 3:9), inhabited by "the spirit that works in the sons of disobedience" (Eph. 2:2), enslaved to do the will of the devil (II Tim. 2:26). A spiritual exchange has occurred (cf. Acts 26:18; Col. 1:13) – "behold, all things" pertaining to his spiritual condition "have become new" (the Greek perfect tense verb indicates that this action transpired in the past and remains to the present). This individual has become totally new spiritually, a "new creation" (Gal. 6:15).

"Yet...", on the other hand, as many new Christ-ones have noted, there is a process of ongoing conflict taking place in the soul. Though there is a settled reality in the spirit of the Christ-one, the soul remains unsettled. Why? Paul explains, "the flesh sets its desire against the Spirit, and the Spirit against the flesh; they are in opposition to one another" (Gal. 5:17). There remains in the soul of the Christ-one the patterns of selfishness and sinfulness in the desires of the soul. Though Satan has been expelled from the spirit, he continues to work from without (cf. I Jn. 4:4) to tempt the Christ-one to act and react with the old patterns of behavior. The Spirit of Christ within the spirit of the Christ-one works to counter this solicitation to return to the old ways, but His action is not imposed upon the Christian. We must make the behavioral choice of faith, as to whether we will allow the Spirit of Christ to manifest "the fruit of the Spirit" (Gal. 5:22,23), overcoming Satan's "deeds of the flesh" (Gal. 5:19-21).

GOD IS NOT A GOD OF "HOW TOS"

Almost every week we receive a package or two from Amazon with objects that need to be assembled. We are thankful for the "assembly manual" that explains "how to" put the object together, despite the fact that it has usually been written by someone whose native language is not English. We are even more appreciative that when God sent His Son Jesus to us in the incarnation, He did not (as many seem to think) send Him with an assembly manual (the Bible?) to explain how to make the Christ-life work (by the self-effort of performance), including a warranty card to explain the limited parameters of the expected duration of usability and dependability.

Have you noticed how extensive the section of "How to" books is in any retail bookstore? That seems to be what the public is craving today – a "how-to" book to inform them of the means and manner by which they might do and perform any task they desire. That is in accord with what humanistic philosophy advocates – you can "do it" if you just know "how to" do it. If a person cannot find or does not wish to purchase a "how to" book, they can simply go to YouTube and find a video that explains "how to" accomplish whatever task they want to do. We live in a world of activistic individuals who desire "how tos."

God is not a God of "how tos." God has not provided mankind with a performance manual to explain the "how to" of performance that will please Him. Yes, there are people who think that is the purpose of the Bible, a performance manual of behavioral rules and regulations by which we can do what God allegedly wants us to do. Not so! What we learn from the Bible is "grace and truth were inaugurated and realized through Jesus Christ" (Jn. 1:17). Grace is the dynamic of the life of the risen Lord Jesus by which Christ-ones can do everything that God wants to do in our lives. God is the God who operates by grace.

MARCH 14

TRYING TO BE WHAT WE CAN NEVER BE

The first one who tried to be like God was Lucifer; "I will be like the Most High God" (Isa. 14:14). He became the antithesis of God, the Evil One, still deriving from God but turning God's character into its opposite (Acts 13:10) – into evil. This was all part of God's design so mankind could have a legitimate either/or choice. Satan, as the serpent, tried to foist his selfish desire upon mankind, saying, "You too can be like God" (Gen. 3:5). What a lie! When we try to be our own center of reference and our own resource of action, we are deceived by the Deceiver and will fail in all of our humanistic attempts of trying to be and do what we can never be or do – what only God can do.

But the temptation of the Evil One is constantly with us, even as Christ-ones. He urges us to try to be good, try to be strong, try to be in control, try to be righteous, try to be the "top dog," try to know everything, try to be like God. Because we were all conditioned by "the spirit that works in the sons of disobedience" (Eph. 2:2), we have all developed patterns of selfish action and reaction in our soul, called the "flesh" (Gal. 5:16-21), So, when we are tempted. we are susceptible to the tempting solicitations to try to be what we can never be. But the Christ-one who knows their identity "in Christ", knows their inability to be and do what Satan tempts them to be and do.

We have all fallen into that temptation trap. We have all attempted to cover-up our inabilities in trying to be what we can never be – trying to fake it in our falsification of our ability. Oh, how exhausting it is to keep trying to be totally sufficient, like God. When we come to end of ourselves, we can say with Paul, "Not that we are sufficient in ourselves to consider anything as coming from ourselves, but our sufficiency is from God" (II Cor. 3:5). When we know the living Lord Jesus lives in us (II Cor. 13:5), then He can be what He wants to be in us and as us.

JESUS: ALL IN ALL

This has been a much-misused phrase. Some have declared that Jesus is "all things to all people," in which case He is not anything to anyone. Clarity will only be achieved when we identify what the two "alls" refer to, if it is possible to clarify such. In Ephesians 1:23 Paul refers to "the church which is His body, the fulness of Him who fills all in all." Through the centuries, commentators have disagreed with one another as to the meaning of the "all in all" phrase. The abundance of English translations likewise show a multiplicity of variant translation alternatives. We will proceed to consider some of the interpretations.

When Paul wrote of Christ "filling all in all," did He mean: ...ALL Christ-ones in ALL portions of His Body? ...ALL Christ-ones in ALL situations? ...ALL that is needed in ALL Christ-ones? ...ALL spiritual realities in ALL Christ-ones? ...ALL functionalities of our being with ALL sufficiency? ...ALL sufficiency in ALL Christ-ones? Or the less likely possibilities of ...ALL things in ALL ways? ...ALL things in ALL people? ...ALL the universe with ALL of Himself? These latter suggestions seem to suggest a more monistic or pantheistic concept that fails to take into consideration the context of the *ecclesia*, the Body of Christ.

Taking the context of the passage into account, we observe that the *ecclesia* is the fulness of Christ, the collective Body of Christ, the re-presented manifestation of Jesus on earth in every age. In that context the divine fulness (*pleroma,* the divine essence and divine sufficiency of power) of Jesus fills/is constantly filling ALL of His Christ-ones (those who are "in Christ" and Christ is in them) with ALL that He is and does (His divine being and His divine doing, His divine essence and function, *ontos* and operation), with ALL of His character fruit of the Spirit (Gal. 5:22,23) and with ALL of His ministry giftedness of the Spirit (I Cor. 12-14; Eph. 4:11,12; I Pet. 4:10,11). All of Him in all of us!

MARCH 16

FREE TO BE HUMAN AS GOD INTENDED

Jesus proclaimed to the Jewish crowd that was following Him, "Disciples of Mine shall know the truth, and the truth shall make you free (Jn. 8:32). He followed that with, "When the Son makes you free, you shall be free indeed" (Jn. 8:36), thus identifying Himself as the truth that would set mankind free. "I am the way, the truth, and the life" (Jn. 14:6), He told His disciples as He prepared to go to the cross and die. Jesus is the reality/truth (Greek word *alethia*) that can make mankind free to be human as God intended when He created human beings. Otherwise, we are held captive by the devil and relegated to dysfunctionality.

Paul explained, "It was for freedom that Christ set us free" (Gal. 5:1,13). It is important to note that the freedom Christ-ones have "in Christ," is both freedom *from* that which enslaves us, as well as freedom *to* be what God intends us to be. Christian freedom is freedom *from* sin (Rom. 6:7,18,20,22), freedom *from* the law (Acts 13:39: Rom. 7:3; 8:2), and freedom *from* the world (I Cor. 2:12), freedom *from* love of money (I Tim. 3:3; Heb. 13:5. Christian freedom is freedom *to* enjoy our liberty, freedom *to* live in righteousness (Rom. 6:18,20), freedom to be human as God intended human to be, free to love the unlovely, free to pay back insults with loving kindness (II Cor. 12:10).

Notice that the title refers to being "free *to BE*...". This is not a freedom to DO what you could not do when you were not a Christ-one, but the freedom *to Be* the Christ-one that you have become with all the godly manifestations of the character of Jesus evidenced in our behavior as Christ-ones. The freedom of truly functional humanity is realized in allowing the living Lord Jesus to live out through us, loving one another. The freedom *from* is for the most part objective realities gains by Christ's death on the cross, whereas the ***freedom to BE*** involves the subjective ramifications of the free expression of Jesus' life and character.

THE DEATH OF JESUS ON THE CROSS

The death of Jesus on the cross of Calvary for the sins of mankind is so easily and quickly warped by the human mind into concepts of legal pardon based on the penal substitution of punishment inflicted on Jesus, or it is turned into an economic transaction of pay-off wherein Jesus paid the ransom-debt to an unidentified extortive debtholder. The conceptual theories of atonement that men have applied to the death of Jesus through the centuries need to be rethought and reframed. Christian thinkers have identified some of these logical conjectures for almost two millennia: If Jesus paid a ransom price or debt payment in His death, who did He pay the ransom and debt payment to? To God? How can Jesus, the Son of God, be paying a penalty to an apparently punitive God, His Father? That divides the oneness of the Trinity. How could He be paying the ransom price or debt payment to the devil, for there is nothing owed to that adversarial supplanter of God. The cost of the cross needs a different explanation.

Might we explain that Jesus paid a great price, the cost of His own death, and in so doing absorbed the consequence of sin by submitting to the death that the devil has power over (Heb. 2:14), thus showing that the "sting of death" (I Cor. 15:56) is a pointless metaphor? This would be the substitutional absorption of the consequences of sin in the death of Jesus. The ransom price and the debt payment are dissolved by the absorption of all sin consequences of death in the death of Jesus. God's forgiveness and pardon do not require the penal penalty of punishment or an extortive debt payment. In His death, Jesus rescued, redeemed, and freed mankind from the clutches of Satan's power of death, the consequence of his character of sin. Jesus died to extend to mankind, to all individuals who might receive Him by faith, the divine life that is in Him alone (Jn. 14:6).

Such absorption of sin and death allows for a reversal and exchange of the spiritual condition of mankind (cf. Acts 26:18; Col. 1:13). It pulls together the redemption and restoration of mankind, bringing together salvation and sanctification. In this explanation, all the symbols, models, and theories of the atonement are decoded and put aside in a simpler explanation of Christ's dying on the cross for mankind's sin.

MARCH 18

STUDYING A TEXT IN CONTEXT

A text out of context can soon become a pretext – a disguise to say anything one wants to say. Here are some interpretive considerations:

1. The **overall context** of the Bible as a whole – the BIG PICTURE. One must understand the metanarrative of God's covenant with His people. The Old Testament is the Jewish Bible, and the New Testament is the Christian new covenant literature.
2. The **literary context** considers the type of literature. Is it history? Is it poetry? Is it prophecy? Is it epistolary? Is it apocalyptic?
3. The **personal context** must be reconstructed to the extent possible. Who is the author? To whom was it written? What is the purpose of it being written? Is there a problem being addressed?
4. The **cultural context** should be considered. Every writer is a product of his time, even though he may be writing under the inspiration influence of the Holy Spirit. Inspiration is not dictation of words, but allows the author to employ his own vocabulary and style of writing in the culture in which he lives.
5. The **paragraph context** recognizes that a verse is part of a larger flow of thought. The paragraph is the immediate context, and the preceding and following paragraphs give context to the paragraph and verse being studied.
6. The **verse context** within the paragraph allows us to understand the flow of the author's thinking. We are trying to "get into the head" of the author and understand his heart.
7. The **intended meaning context**. A portion of scripture cannot mean now what it did not mean then – else it can mean anything to anyone at any time. The intended meaning is the only correct meaning.
8. The **language context** allows us to go back to the original language in which the words were written. The New Testament was originally written in *koine* (common) Greek, which is different than classical or modern Greek. The verbs provide the action. The nouns must be considered both etymologically and linguistically. The prepositions explain where the action of the verb is directed.

These contextual considerations can be utilized to assist all readers to read their Bibles in context.

MY CAREER AS A SYNOPSIZER

As I look back over my physical lifetime approaching almost four decades, I recognize that much of my life I have served as a synopsizer ... not a synthesizer, ...not a stimulator, ...not a syncopator, ...but a synopsizer. What in the world is a synopsizer? Perhaps you will recognize the word "synopsis," which refers to a condensed or abbreviated summary of the topic at hand. Many will be familiar with the *Reader's Digest Magazine*, which provides condensed and synopsized articles from other sources, along with original articles. With a readership of over 100 million, it is one of the most popular periodicals in the world.

Along the lines of *The Reader's Digest*, I often take concepts and ideas, mostly biblical, philosophical, theological, and particularly new covenant concepts boiling them down into condensed synopsis articles of approximately three paragraphs in length that state the subject in a way that is concise and understandable by the average reader. These short articles then become daily readings on social media and are eventually put into a book of readings for every day of a calendar year. I am presently developing volume four in the series of readings, identified as "The Jesus Series of Daily Readings" on Amazon.com.

Like a general systems analyst, my tendency is to consider the whole system and then to boil it down into its constituent parts and functions. By thus analyzing the dynamics of the interactions within a functional system, whether it be a personal, mechanical, or social system, one can consider the options for each functional part. A synopsizer considers how the various parts or ideas should function together and provides a synopsis of explanation for proper function of the system. My perspective as a synopsizer differs from many of the mechanical and instructional systems by recognizing that the Christian faith is not a system that can be broken down into constituent performance parts.

MARCH 20

KINGDOM CONDUCT VS. WORLD'S WAYS

Many are attempting to participate in kingdom-living by employing the ways of the world. In fact, since religion is constantly engaged in trying to produce the things of God and create a semblance of the kingdom by human works of self-effort, there are few who call themselves "Christians" who can even differentiate between religion with its operative "ways of the world" and the function of the Kingdom that Jesus came to set in motion in Himself. Jesus is the Kingdom in Himself (*autobasileion*) – where the King, the Lord Jesus Christ, is reigning and ruling, there is the kingdom. Kingdom living is when Jesus is in control of our lives; when our single focus is Jesus, rather than the peripherals of the world's concerns. When we are deriving from the sufficiency of God's grace in Jesus, it becomes obvious that the religious and worldly ways of performing and producing are but a temporal and superficial production requiring the publicity of self-promotion to perpetuate itself and will never produce kingdom righteousness.

Jesus explained to Pilate, "My kingdom is not of this world ... not of this realm" (Jn. 18:36). The kingdom of Jesus is on another plane of operation. It does not employ the ways and tactics of the world. The kingdom perspective "sets its mind on things above" (Eph. 3:2), instead of setting its mind on things of the earth (Matt. 16:23; Mk. 8:33) and the things of the flesh (Rom. 8:5-7). Christ-ones are advised not to love the world and its things (I Jn. 2:15). "We have received, not the spirit of the world, but the Spirit who is from God" (I Cor. 2:12). The kingdom of the Lord and King, Jesus Christ, involves union with (I Cor. 6:17) Christ and submission to God (James 4:7), allowing Christ-ones to see and function in the eternal unseen presence of God (II Cor. 4:18). Kingdom function is totally opposite of the ways of the world. The ways of the world will never bring about or accomplish the kingdom-living Jesus came to bring by His own presence.

THE IDOLATRY OF METHODOLOGY

It is a natural tendency of mankind to develop methods that will lead to the desired human performance and production results. Our entire educational system seems to be the instruction of the latest methods in every discipline. There inevitably develops a competition of methods in every field of study concerning which method works better – "This is how to do it right or most effectively." The social sciences and humanities studies, in general, seem to engender a broader spectrum of methodological variation, having less definitive operational criteria. Methods, procedures and techniques are necessary, but they must not be allowed to become the ultimate objective or end-all. When that occurs, we have the "idolatry of methodology" wherein people have faith in the method to achieve their ends.

We observe this proliferation of methods in almost every category of thought and action these days. Business methods. Production methods. Educational methods. Writing methods. Exercise methods. Diet methods. Health methods. Spirituality methods. Religious methods. This methodological diversity contributes to the abundance of books and popularity of the "how-to" section of the remaining general bookstores.

The idolatry of methodology is particularly apparent in the field of religion and the church. Denominational methods. Preaching methods. Worship methods. Sunday School teaching methods. Discipleship methods. Counselling methods. Faith, commitment and adherence to human methods, procedures and techniques often runs contrary to the personal direction and spontaneity of the work of the Holy Spirit. It can be, and often is, emphasis on what man does, rather than what God does, thus failing to be receptivity to the dynamic grace of God in the function of the living Lord, Jesus Christ. "There is a way that seems right to man, but the end thereof is death" (Prov. 14:12; 16:25).

MARCH 22

GRACE COUNSELING

There are many ministries offering what they call "Christian counseling," "Biblical counseling," "Spiritual counseling," Faith-based counseling," Exchanged Life counseling," "Grace-life counseling," etc. I have no doubt that many of them are helping some people with some of their behavioral and psychological problems, but I still question whether Christian people are receiving the highest quality of counsel that is available. Apart from all these methods and models of attempting to counsel, teach and instruct people, we must remember that Jesus told His disciples that the Holy Spirit would be their counselor (Jn. 14:16).

The friends of Job attempted to give him counsel concerning his life problems. They were of very little help. In fact, God was angry with the three so-called "counselors" because of their humanistic counsel. Many of the counseling methods used in both secular or Christian counseling today are of no more benefit than was the counsel of Job's friends – just humanistic blather about increased human performance. Writing to the Roman Christians, Paul explained that any Christ-one who has received the Spirit of Christ and understands how He operates by grace should be "competent to counsel" (Rom. 15:14), for such person is simply instructing a fellow Christ-one in faith-receptivity to Jesus.

Genuine Christian counseling must involve a receptive Christ-one who recognizes that the man-made methodologies are not the means of achieving God's intent. One who would be a counselor to hurting Christian people will constantly be aware that the Spirit of Christ within is the divine Counselor functioning through his/her actions. Such is best explained as "grace counseling," because by the divine dynamic of grace, the counselor will listen in obedience to ascertain what the living Christ would say to the person seeking counsel, and simply be the vessel of God's communication of Spirit-directed advice.

IT'S ALL ABOUT JESUS

The gospel, the good news, the message of the Christian faith is all about Jesus. Yes, there are the historical events of His incarnation, His life, His death, His resurrection, His ascension, and the Pentecostal outpouring His Spirit. But it doesn't stop there! The Spirit of the living Jesus poured out at Pentecost has come to dwell within every Christ-one (Rom. 8:9). The Christ-life in every Christ-one is meant to set the world on fire with a zeal for His dynamic life. Jesus said, "I have come to set the earth on fire, and how I wish it were already blazing!" (Lk. 12:49). This is no docile namby-pamby life that we have received in Jesus.

The Christian life is not what it has been made out to be in the contemporary context of religion, where they have suffocated the life out of the Christ-life. They emphasize all the peripherals of joining the church, asking every attendee to be a "member" and to serve by donating one's time and talent, to attend all of the services, and to contribute a tithe to fund the ongoing projects. To this they add all the expected conformity rules to "live like Jesus." Get this: Religion has as its objective – performance compliance; the grace-life has as its objective – obedience to Jesus, i.e., listening under the Spirit of Jesus within to ascertain what He wants to be and do in us today.

Satan does not want the Christ-life to be lived out with the dynamic phosphorus/potassium ignition of the fire of the Spirit. The tempter seeks to pull us away from the realization that the Christ-life is all about Jesus – what He wants to be and do in one's life moment by moment. It is all about Jesus! The reformers were trying to say that in their formulation of *Solus Christus* i.e., Christ alone or Christ only. The living Lord Jesus wants to live out His life in us, through us, and as us, and our only responsibility is to get out of the way and allow the nuclear fission of His character to produce the chain reaction that affects the world.

MARCH 24

MAY I DIE WITH GRACE

Living, as I am, in the eighth decade of my physical life, my thoughts sometimes go to the realization that I am living in the twilight years of my life expectancy. This is no macabre longing to meet the grim reaper (more correctly the death-dealing devil – Heb. 2:14), but a realistic appraisal that the trajectory of my life on earth has a termination point. When I think of my inevitable physical death, and ponder what might lead up to that expiration, I pray that I might die with grace, in the continuation of the manner in which I have lived in the dynamic of God's grace in Jesus Christ. I want to die in like manner as I have lived.

I have ministered to many dying persons through the years of my ministry opportunities, and I have observed many of them grasping at the false promises of the elongation of physical life, for the latest medical or religious elixir to postpone the great opportunity to experience the heavenly realm in the presence of the eternal Jesus. Many have been fearful and filled with anxiety, fighting tooth and nail to stay alive here on earth. I have no fear of death (cf. Heb. 2:15). I have been on the brink of death on more than one occasion, and I am ready to go home to meet Jesus face to face whenever He decides to call me home.

Please note: when I say, I want to "die with grace," I am not asking to die alongside or at the same time as my dear wife, Grace, who has put up with me and my "big ideas" for so many years. What I am saying is that I want to approach the big transfer of residence (cf. II Cor. 5:1-9) with the grace of divine character that exhibits "love, joy, peace, patience, kindness, goodness, faithfulness, gentleness, and Godly control of oneself" (Gal. 5:22,23). I want others to see Jesus living in me up to that very moment that we take leave in union with one another (cf. I Cor. 6:17) to participate in the heavenly continuation, extension, and perpetuity of His life for eternity.

PLEADING WITH GOD

In the days after my double amputation surgery (Apr. 25,22), I was pleading with God during my prayers. I pled that He might allow me to escape this life, and slide into the place prepared for me in heaven. Then, God seemed to pull me up abruptly, and said "Stop the pleading! I will not listen to or respond to your pleading. I determine the end from the beginning of all things, and your pleading will not change such." I came to realize that I was every so subtly attempting to dictate to God what He should so. It was just me expressing my discontent with the present circumstances and seeking a self-directed way out.

I came to realize that only when I was content with what God was doing, and aware that God always acted "in character," expressing His "love, joy, peace, patience, kindness, goodness, faithfulness, gentleness, and Godly control over myself" (cf. Gal. 5:22,23), could I ever settle in to trust Him in what He was doing, and thereby enjoy His love and His peace. Instead of pleading for a change, I needed to simply trust that God knew what He was doing and was acting in my best good – in the very midst of what sometimes seems to be unpleasant and uncomfortable on the physical, mental, and emotional level.

It was as if God was saying, "Do you want to continue to attempt to do is your way, or are you willing to accept My way as your best way?" My only answer could be, "Yes, Lord, I want what You want for Me. I want to take my eyes off of myself and focus on You and the others who You Love." So, that is the daily relational process that God and I are engaged in time and again. It's a never-ending process – our natural tendencies keep drawing our attention back to ourselves, and God has His ways of drawing our attention to Himself and what He is doing in our lives. That either-or process of self-focus or seeing what God is up to in drawing us into His love for others will last through our lifetime.

MARCH 26

WHAT ARE YOU AFRAID OF?

We had just begun to talk about what God was doing in our lives, and my friend rather abruptly asked, "What are you afraid of Jim?" I thought for a minute and could not think of anything that I was afraid of at that time. The question, however, stuck with me throughout the day, and I eventually began to formulate what I was afraid of. I was not afraid of dying. I was not afraid of having to live with physical limitations, but I was afraid of not functioning as "god" of my own life. I was afraid of losing control of determining what was going on in my life and the life of my family, and the situations of my home-life. These are matters which I am sure that most men are concerned about.

My fears in the days immediately following the double amputation of my lower limbs, have exposed my tendencies to want to be in control, and the fear of losing such alleged control in my life. I have never actually been in control of my life, it is just that I thought I was in control, and probably exerted control over my family, my wife, and my friends in ways that were overbearing. I have no doubt had an attitude of self-sufficiency (II Cor. 3:5) and self-reliance which revealed my lack of complete trust in God. Trials such as I am experiencing have a way of revealing our self-determinations and our fears based on such.

"Perfect love casts out fear" (I Jn. 4:18). We know who "Perfect Love" is – He is the Triune God who is love (I Jn. 4:8,16). God has no reason to be self-concerned about what is going to happen. He knows all things from beginning to end. His love is always concerned about others and how they are functioning in their faithful trust in Him amid every circumstance of life. When we are doing so, we can rest and relax in what He is doing. The fears of what might happen to us are swallowed up in His love. I can assure you that I am "preaching to the choir" at this point, for these are the thoughts I need to incorporate in my life.

WHAT WILL IT BE?

Love and selfishness are another of those either-or dichotomies. It is one, or the other. Where there is selfishness, it precludes love. Where there is love, it drives away selfishness.
Now, our natural human character tendency is that of selfishness. When we were born with "the spirit that works in the sons of disobedience" (Eph. 2:2,3), Satan's indwelling character of selfishness predominated in everything we did. Our entire perspective was obscured with self-consideration. Many people go through life without any consideration of how this situation might be changed (or whether they want it to be changed).

God's character, on the other hand is Love. "God is love" (I Jn. 4:8,16), and His Love always takes into consideration the needs of others (beyond ourselves). God's love is antithetical to self-considerations. No person can manifest the character of God's love apart from the presence of God. God does not allow a stand-apart expression of His character. He requires that we receive Him and His inherent character if we are ever to experience a radical reversal of our selfishness to love others. "God so loved the world of fallen mankind that He gave His only begotten Son" (Jn. 3:16), whose death on our behalf allows His life of love to be made available to all men.

In my recent experience of physical handicap (double amputation of my legs), my self- concern was brought to the forefront of my experience. Yes, there were some "poor me, pity-party" occasions – some of them quite severe, to the point of my wanting to give up if I couldn't have it my way. Gradually, God's love began to overcome and override my selfishness, and bring to my attention how God wanted to love and minister to others through me. I can't say that the process is completed, for the choice of selfishness or divine love is always an ongoing process – the natural versus the supernatural. What will it be?

MARCH 28

IF IT ISN'T A MYSTERY, IT ISN'T GOSPEL

I used to think that I had life and the gospel of Jesus Christ fairly well figured out – figured out with my cerebral reasonings and logical connections. Well, after this most recent major medical situation with the amputation of both legs (6 in. below the knee on both legs), I have had to rethink all my easy answers. Christianity is not primarily about informational data of history or theology. Christianity is the relational faith-mystery of how we keep our eyes on Jesus in full reliance that it is He who is our life, and that only by drawing from Him moment by moment do we experience His sufficiency.

Oh, what a mystery is our Lord Jesus. Yes, a mystery in the biblical sense that though once concealed, He is now revealed and available to all mankind. But I am thinking more of the experiential mystery of how the living Lord Jesus functions and operates in individual Christians. The Spirit of the living Lord Jesus works uniquely in every Christ-one. No one can tell you "how to" make the Christ-life work in you. There is no standardized pattern by which we are conformed to Christ. In a most personal manner, Jesus is functioning in every scenario of our lives, making Himself evident in the smallest and even obscure situations, right where we need what only Jesus can be.

During my recent medical situation, I struggled with seeing Jesus for a few days. During discouragement and depression, my only mental image of the Lord was a light shining through a crack by the door. I kept looking at that light, knowing that it represented the "light of the world" (Jn. 8:12), and knowing that He was the only way (Jn. 14:6) out of the darkness that encompassed me in my grief. This is not a pattern for others but was the mystery of God working to refocus my mind and spirit on the One who was to be my Life. The good news of the gospel is constantly revealed in God's mysterious ways.

SAFE IN HIS ARMS

"You've got me, Lord Jesus. I am safe in Your arms. No matter what happens; despite any of the 'what ifs' that I might conjecture as possibilities that might occur, I can rest assured that You have everything covered and I need not concern myself or worry about such." What a safe and restful place to be – safe in His arms. My mind conjures and conjectures all kinds of "what if" scenarios, and then I have to change my focus and assure myself that "I am safe in His arms." Safe in His arms, it does not matter what might transpire. I need only focus on Him who holds me in safety and will see me through the situation to the best outcome.

"Safe in His arms" is certainly indicative of the child-like faith that Jesus spoke of. "Jesus called to Him a child, and put him in the midst of the disciples, and said, 'Truly, I say to you, unless you turn and become like children, you will never enter the kingdom of heaven. Whoever humbles himself like this child is the greatest in the kingdom of heaven'" (Matt. 18:2-4). A child feels safe and secure in the arms of the father or mother, not attempting to orchestrate the circumstances of every situation. The child knows that in the safety of the parental arms, his best interest will be served whatever might occur.

It seems somewhat strange that in my time of crisis and inability to change the circumstances, I am brought back to the simplicity of being "safe in His arms." I would have thought that I had passed the child-like faith stage of the Christian life. No, not at all. The child-like faith is for every stage of the Christian life and is really brought to light amid disability and inability. I have laid in bed, both day and the night, and found myself recognizing that I am safe in the arms of the Triune God, and I need nothing more than to trust Him. "Okay, Lord, You have the situation covered. I need not fret or concern myself with how I might handle it. I need only rest, safe in the arms of Jesus.

MARCH 30

"IT IS WELL WITH MY SOUL"

In the midst of my physical disturbances and inconveniences of late, I keep coming back to the words of the song, "It is well with my soul!" Paul explained, "The outer man is decaying, but the inner man is being renewed day by day" (II Cor. 4:16). God is so faithful to keep reminding me that the loss of body parts need not affect the settled state of my spirit and soul. My spirit is joined to the Lord, and I am "one spirit" with Him (I Cor. 6:17). I am spiritually complete in Christ (Col. 1:28). To the extent that the character of Christ within my spirit permeates into my mind, emotions, and the decision- making of my soul, "it is well with my soul" for it is functioning as God intended.

The well-known song, "It is well with my soul," was penned by Horatio Spafford in 1873. After suffering many losses from the Chicago Fire, he put his wife and four daughters on a passenger liner to England. While crossing the Atlantic the liner struck another ship and sank to the bottom of the sea. The four daughters perished, but his wife was spared. His wife sent a telegram which read, "Spared alone!" Spafford rushed to join his wife in England, and as his ship passed over the approximate position where his daughters' lives were lost, he was inspired to write the words of this meaningful hymn:

> "When peace like a river, attendeth my way,
> When sorrows like sea billows roll;
> Whatever my lot, Thou hast taught me to know
> It is well, it is well, with my soul."

The song has particular meaning for me because my friend, Tony Napier, director of the Youth for Christ in Wichita, KS was killed in a tragic accident. At his memorial service, Ernest Alexander sang this song. Everyone present was moved. Amid the present circumstances of my life, the song has come to have more meaning than ever before.

GOD'S IN CHARGE!

The infinite, eternal, all-knowing God is in charge of every detail of our lives. We like to think that we are in charge of some of the details, or that we at least contribute to the causation of what is transpiring. We like to think that in some way we can "play god" in our situations, but the ways of man never serve to the glory of God. All we tend to do is mess things up and get in God's way as He continues to do what He had divinely determined to do. Yes, we do have freedom of choice to accept and receive what God is doing, but God is in charge, and our part is only to be "in on" what God is "up to," willing to participate in what is in our best interest, because God's love always seeks our highest good.

The fact that "God is in charge" has been repetitively reinforced upon my thinking and realization within my recent hospitalization and physical rehabilitation. During Satan's natural suggestions of hopelessness, I am often comfited by the awareness that God is in charge of everything that is happening, that nothing is going to happen that would derail what God wants to do in my life and body. I had to keep readjusting my mind to the awareness of God's providential, moment-by-moment control over every detail of what was happening. Over and over again, I had to "let go, and let God" do what He wanted.

I am a slow learner when it comes to these on-going lessons that God is working into my life. I didn't realize what a "control freak" I had become. I had developed an elaborate pattern of thinking that I was in charge (and that is Satan's humanistic premise that prevails in the world's thinking today – that's why the "self-help" section of every bookstore is so large!). So, time and again, as I prayed and besought God amid the healing process, I was "pulled up short" when God seemed to say "Whoa – Who's in charge here anyway?" And I was forced to say, "You, God, are in charge, and I must agree to keep my hands off the situation."

APRIL 1

A NEW AWAKENING

After six difficult days of stomach cramps and uncontrolled diarrhea during the second week of rehab following the amputation of both of my legs, I awakened on the morning of the seventh day at 2:00 am. I was lying in a pool of sweat, but I sensed that something new had happened physically in my body – that all would be well. It was as if I had been released into a new freedom of life, kind of like I had broken free from a restrictive cocoon and was now free to fly like a butterfly. It was as if I was a new man, ready to face what might remain in the remaining process of my rehabilitation and physical recovery.

I could do nothing other than pray eucharistic prayers to the Triune God, expressing my gratitude and thanksgiving for His "good grace" (*eu* = good; *charis* = grace). I was rejoicing over whatever it was that had happened in my body. As I have no medical training, I do not know what happened that morning, but I awoke invigorated and ready to proceed with whatever might be ahead of me, to proceed with enjoying life despite my restrictions and physical disabilities. Who needs feet to do what God has called me to do? It is not my feet that allow me to think and type out my thoughts in digital form. Thank you, Lord!

What a coincidence (really God's providence) that this occurred on the very weekend of the resurrection celebration of God's people around the world. It was already Easter Sunday somewhere on the far side of the world. It is the resurrection of Jesus from the dead that really brings the freedom of new life spiritually. That is why one of the major symbols of Christ's resurrection is the butterfly, symbolizing the breaking free from the restrictive cocoon into the newness of life! Christ-ones from every people-group around the world who have received the resurrection-life of Jesus into their spirit, have "passed from spiritual death into spiritual life" (Romans 6:4).

APRIL 2

ON A PERSONAL NOTE

Since the double amputation of my feet due to diabetes, numerous people have noted that these daily readings have taken on a more personal tone where I have been sharing what God has been teaching me during "the dark night of the soul." Since my primary thought-processes for over fifty years have had to do with philosophical and biblical theology, this internal glance into how I have responded to deep pain, suffering, and grief has involved a subjective element that has not been the norm in my writing. I have even been able to share my failings. "Help Thou, mine unbelief" (Mk. 9:24).

Though quite willing to share what is going on within me, I do not want these readings to be about me – I want them to reveal and revere the living Lord Jesus. I believe the personal sharing has done just that, because the deep internal refocusing was constantly the nudging of the Spirit to "keep my eyes on the living Lord Jesus" (Heb. 12:2). I certainly needed that during the confusing stimuli that were bombarding my senses, unsettling my faith, and disturbing my thoughts and emotions. My heart-felt desire is that those who have read these readings will have in like manner seen Jesus at work in the personal conflicts that I have encountered in my medical situations.

As I proceed on my personal journey as a double amputee, I intend to intersperse these readings with both objective biblical and theological teaching as well as the personal sharing of the ups and downs (physical as well as psychological), difficulties and triumphs of my walk of faith (II Cor. 5:7). I do want to say "thank you" to those of you who regularly read the readings on my Facebook page, and I want to say "thank you" to all of you who have expressed your concern and have prayed for me during this most recent incident. How humbling, yet how uplifting it is to know that so many people have cared enough to pray for me.

APRIL 3

HOMECOMING

It has been approximately a month since I left the family home and was admitted to the hospital. The first surgery was just an attempt to create a bypass using the veins of the left leg to provide a way to allow for blood flow to provide oxygenated circulation for the right leg. That proved to be not possible, so with the feet dying and turning black without circulation, the necessary decision was quickly made that to avoid gangrene, both legs would need to be amputated six inches below each knee. I certainly did not have much time to process the severity of what was happening, and that was probably all the better.

Just over a week after the bilateral amputation surgery, I was moved to the rehab hospital a short distance away. It was during the early days of facing rehab that my mind was racing with the unknown factors of what was happening. I was fearful and had to settle down to trust God in the midst of the whole ordeal. Now, in the middle of the third week of dealing with the excruciating muscle building in rehab, they have advised that I have a dismissal date from this hospital on Thursday. Oh, the joyous anticipation of homecoming, of being able to return home after many weeks, to be with my wife and our poodle pups.

I was considering the correlation that might exist between this anticipated homecoming back to the family home after several weeks in the hospital and the eternal homecoming that Christ-ones anticipate, when they will move from this life here on earth and enter into the heavenly presence of Jesus. What many Christians need to realize is that the heavenly homecoming does not offer or provide anything other than what they already have received in Jesus. There isn't anything more to receive than what we have in Jesus. "We are complete in Christ" (Col. 1:28), lacking nothing. The heavenly homecoming simply allows us to experience a perfect unhindered presence of Jesus.

THINKING OF DYING

In the process of pain and a prolonged recovery process, my mind has pondered the idea of suicide (self-effecting of one's own death). I am not ashamed to admit my thoughts on this almost socially taboo subject because I do not consider such thoughts to be a sign of an unstable mindset that might act upon those thoughts. I consider such occasions as being the tempter trying to interject his thoughts into my mind. "The one having the power of death, that is the devil" (Heb. 2:14) is always focused on death and destruction in contrast to the life more abundant (Jn. 10:10) that is in Jesus Christ alone. The death-dealing devil is always conniving to undermine the life that is in Jesus, and even to suggest terminating the physical life of one in whom Jesus lives.

We need not go into the various grotesque and macabre suggestions of Satan concerning how his objective might be accomplished. They are as myriad and unmeasured as are the persons that the tempter might tempt with such thoughts of self-death. What we want to keep our focus on is the Satanic source of such thoughts. Satan may introduce such thoughts to one's mind, but he cannot impose such thoughts upon one's action. He cannot even cause the death that terminates our physical life, for God is the One who controls the beginning and the end of all things. We do, however, remain choosing creatures who can succumb to Satan's tempting suggestions

Those in the medical fields and the fields of social science are not wrong to warn people about the signs of possible suicidal people. We do not want to see people take Satan's alternative and take their own lives. Even people with strong faith in Jesus Christ can reach the point of desperation and respond in their painful and desperate moment to the temptation of suicide. We must continue to encourage Christ-ones to strong receptivity of faith to what God in Christ wants to be and do in their lives.

APRIL 5

DISAPPOINTMENT

We are often disappointed when what we are planning does not transpire in the manner and in accord with the timing that we have planned. Does that mean we should cease to have expectations and plans? Of course not! But it may mean that we should allow our expectations to be adjusted and modified by what God wants to be and do in our lives. It is our self-projected plans and expectations that seem to lead to many of our disappointments with how our lives are progressing. Our disappointments may reveal that we have been making our own plans, often expecting that God will abide with and bless those plans and allow us to have our own way. God does not exist to "rubber-stamp" what we determine to do.

The circumstances of life can throw monkey-wrenches into the trajectory that we had anticipated and longed for. It was Robbie Burns, the famous Scottish poet, who wrote in his poem *To a Mouse*, "The best-laid plans of mice and men oft go awry and leave us nothing but grief and pain for promised joy." Both mice and men often suffer disappointments. Not always because of improper expectations, but simply because the grander scheme of life circumstances creates interruptions and disruptions – unforeseen events.

The recent double amputation of my legs due to diabetes was definitely an unexpected disappointment. The ambulatory mobility that I had enjoyed for more than seven decades has been taken away, and I am left to relearn how to move around in the world in which I live. Not easy, I must admit! But overcoming disappointment will never come by "crying over spilt milk;" only by aligning our expectations with God's sovereign plans and continuing to move forward by His empowering grace in Jesus Christ.

WHERE IS JESUS WHEN WE SUFFER?

Some have questioned whether Jesus is hiding His eyes or has departed from them during intense suffering. Every Christ-one has the presence of the living Lord Jesus in his/her spirit. Rom. 8:9 – "If anyone does not have the Spirit of Christ, he does not belong to Him," i.e. that person is not a Christ-one. Jesus does not come and go through a revolving door but is a constant resident within everyone who has taken His name as a Christ-one. When we have received Jesus as our Life and Being, then we can be sure that when the going gets tough in this earthly life, He is right there living as us amid the pain and suffering. He has been through it before!

Jesus "learned obedience through the things that He suffered" (Heb. 5:8), and in the process of our suffering episodes, we too learn obedience. In the new covenant, obedience is not keeping the rules (that was the law-based old covenant), but the Greek word used for "obedience" in the New Testament (covenant) is *hupakouo* (*hupo* = under; *akouo* = to listen – the word from which we get "acoustics"). So, new covenant obedience is "listening under" the direction of the Lord Jesus Christ (both immanent and transcendent) to ascertain what it is that He wants to do in the midst of the present circumstances. Jesus does not leave us or forsake us (Heb. 13:5); rather He is living "as us" through any circumstance that might come our way.

So, where is Jesus when we suffer? He is right there within us, enduring the suffering "as us," while we are "filling up what is lacking in His sufferings" (Col. 1:24). Though Jesus died and rose again as a physical personage, His continuing spiritual life in us remains a sacrificial and suffering life. Jesus was not one who eschewed suffering, but knew the benefits of suffering, and He continues to endure suffering amid our suffering.

APRIL 7

"YOU'LL NEVER WALK ALONE"

When we hurt and are in the midst of suffering, we often feel as though we are trudging through uncharted territory without clear directions of how to proceed. We often feel so alone and unprepared to trudge through the rigorous and unknown paths of pain. One fellow's comment was, "There is no manual to prescribe how to act in the midst of suffering. What we have, instead, is the living Emmanuel, who serves as the personal and living manual that provides everything we need in terms of direction and the strength of His grace to move forward in the difficult (and otherwise impossible) situations of life."

The 1945 musical, *Carousel*, contained a song written by Rogers and Hammerstein, entitled "You'll Never Walk Alone." The words were, "When you walk through a storm hold your head up high, and don't be afraid of the dark. At the end of a storm there's a golden sky, and the sweet silver song of a lark. Walk on through the wind; Walk on through the rain; Though your dreams be tossed and blown; Walk on, walk on with hope in your heart, and you'll never walk alone." The words do not explain why we'll never walk alone but seem to be a humanistic encouragement for people to pursue their dreams.

When the living Lord Jesus dwells in the heart/spirit of a Christ-one, we then have the explanation of why we will never walk alone through the trials and struggles of life. In the famous "Footprints in the Sand" poem by an unknown author, the questioner asks the Lord why there were only one set of footprints in the sand during the lowest, saddest trials and testings of life. "Why would you leave me to walk alone during those times?" she asked. The Lord responded, "When you saw only one set of footprints, it was then that I carried you!" Even better than that, we can say that the Lord and you were walking as one, having been made "one spirit with Him" (I Cor. 6:17).

"DO YOU WISH TO GET WELL?"

That was the question Jesus asked the man who had been ill for 38 years and was brought to the Pool of Bethesda hoping to be the first to get in the water when the water stirred (John 5:6). It was not a foolish question, for there are many who would rather sop sympathy from their present situation than to really get well. My present situation elicits the question, "Do you really want to walk again? Do you really want restored mobility?" I can transfer to my wheelchair and have limited mobility, but do I want to go through the painful process of preparing for and adjusting to the prostheses that need be fitted to each leg?

Preparation for and the fitting of prostheses involves shrinking the stubs right where the wounds are located, shaping them into a round-shape that will fit into the prostheses. This will be followed by a lengthy process of fitting and refitting until an acceptable comfort level is reached. Then begins the process of learning to stand, to balance, and to walk with the prostheses, often requiring additional rehab. Do I have the drive, the desire, the resolve, the motivation to endure this process? The question Jesus asked is the question addressed to me as well, "Do you wish to get well?"

Believing that the living Lord Jesus still wants to use me to share what He has taught me through the years, concerning the gospel of the indwelling Christ-life, I think that my choice will have to be to face the additional pain in order to achieve increased mobility of walking with prosthetics. Yes, this will require enhanced effort on my part in accord with the grace-dynamic that works within me – not an easy process! But, like Paul in his letter to the Colossians (Col. 1:26-28), I seek to share the gospel of "Christ in you, the hope of glory" in order to present every person complete in Christ, i.e. the full restoration of humanity to God's created intent.

APRIL 9

FEARFUL PRAYERS

The story is told of a farmer who was working with his son out in the field in Kansas as a tornado bore down upon their farm. The farmer heard his son behind him praying frantically. He yelled back at his son, "Run son – a scared prayer ain't worth spit!" Well, I beg to differ with the farmer. In my recent prayers, since the amputation of both of my legs, I have engaged in many scared prayers. My mind and emotions were overwhelmed in the aftermath of my surgery as I faced the unknown of what the future might hold. I admit that I was scared and fearful. But during those times, God spoke to my heart with the assurance of His presence and providential care.

As I read the gospel accounts, I notice that Jesus' disciples prayed when they were afraid, especially when the storms came up on the Sea of Galilee. Jesus appeared to them and said, "Fear not; I am with you!" When the disciples met the living Lord Jesus in Galilee after the resurrection, Jesus assured them again saying, "I am with you always, even to the end of the age" (Matt. 28:20). In the midst of our fears and concerns, Jesus often assures of His presence and His loving concern for us in the midst of our scary situation. Divine comfort is often made known to us in the midst of our most discomfiting circumstances.

What better time to come to God in prayer than when we are fearful and disconcerted with what is happening in our lives? It is in that context that we recognize we do not have the resources in ourselves to deal with the situation at hand and need to turn to the One (actually the Three in One) Divine Being who is always adequate in every situation, for He is the sovereign God in control of all things within His creation. In the midst of our fear, we seek what we know to be unwavering stability of the Triune God, who by His expression in the living Lord Jesus and by the power of the Holy Spirit is the all-sufficient One.

"HOW BEAUTIFUL ARE THE FEET..."

Having recently had both of my feet amputated because of diabetes, I decided to do a word study on the significance of "feet" in the new covenant scriptures. I was thinking particularly of Paul's statement in Rom. 10:15, "How beautiful are the feet of those who bring good news of good things," i.e., the gospel (Rom. 10:15). Paul was quoting from Isa. 52:7: "How lovely on the mountains are the feet of him who brings good news, who announces peace and brings good news of happiness, who announces salvation, and says to Zion, "Your God reigns!" I had to ask myself, "Am I now disqualified because I have no feet?"

In biblical times, there were no means of mass transit, nor the personal means of transport that most of us enjoy today. They travelled from place to place, even great distances, by walking. Human feet were the primary method of conveyance by which those who were sent by God to preach the gospel went about doing what they were called and sent to do. After a mission trip to India, we collected funds to buy bicycles for a number of village evangelists who travelled from village to village to share the gospel. What a sight of beauty were those bicycles to those who received a new means of conveyance to share the gospel.

Those who walked the dusty roads in biblical times were often afforded the respect and hospitality of the washing of their dusty feet. On one occasion, when Jesus visited the home of a Pharisee, a woman came and anointed and washed His feet. The Pharisee objected that a sinful woman would be allowed to do this. Jesus responded, "You did not anoint My head with oil, but she anointed My feet with perfume. (Luke 7:46). She was the one who demonstrated humble reverence and subservience. In like manner, when Jesus washed the disciples' feet at the Last Supper, He was demonstrating His willingness to be the servant of mankind, even thought He was the Lord of the universe.

APRIL 11

"PRAY WITHOUT CEASING"

How can one "pray without ceasing," as Paul exhorts in I Thess. 5:17, if we must consciously verbalize our prayers in conversation with God? It is imperative that we stay focused on the task at hand in order to accomplish what we are called to do in life. Perhaps, we have developed an idea about prayer that is restricted to the formulation of the right words. What if prayer involves a spiritual communion with God that does not require words? It took me many years to relax and expand my concept of prayer to the point that I realized that much of what I was doing in my walk with the Lord was indeed prayer.

For example, I would be reading a book and come across a passage that emphasized the reality of the indwelling Lord Jesus and how the Spirit of Christ was functioning within us. I would do a fist-pump and declare, "Yes, Lord," indicating that the truth of the passage resonated with my inner being and my own experience. After reading a book by Jean LaFrance on the life of prayer, I realized that these "A-Ha" moments were indeed a form of prayer communion with God that could be included in an expanded awareness of prayer that genuinely included a sense of "praying without ceasing" in a comprehensive life-long awareness of our "one spirit" union with Christ.

On other occasions, I would pull up to a stoplight, knowing that it was going to take a minute or two to change so I could proceed. I would begin singing (my wife would question whether it could really be called singing), "Thank you, Lord for saving my soul. Thank you, Lord for making me whole. Thank you, Lord for giving to me, Thy great salvation so rich and free." That is a form of praying and expressing one's gratitude for all that God has provided for us in His Son, Jesus Christ. The Christ-life lived out in a Christ-one is itself a form of communion and prayer that is constant and "without ceasing."

ONLY BY THE GRACE OF GOD

So many people are trying to perform what can only be done by the grace of God in Jesus Christ. Foremost among them are those who are trying to "be like Jesus" and "live the Christian life." It is impossible to "be like Jesus." And it is impossible to "live the Christian life" by one's best religious efforts. No one can "pull off" the Christian life, despite the preachers' incessant inculcations to engage in this or that discipline, to "do this" or "don't do that" to be a better Christian. The only One who can live the Christian life, the Christ-life, is the living Lord Jesus, the Christ-one, who is simply willing to be Himself in us, re-presenting the Perfect Life He has previously lived.

Many married couples are trying their best to implement the guidelines they learned at the latest marriage conference or retreat to keep their marriage healthy and vibrant. With the best of personal resolve, they are trying to "love one another" in accord with what the Bible advocates, and in a manner that will appear like they have "the perfect marriage." The problem is that no husband can "love like Jesus" (Eph. 5:26), and no wife can "be subject to her husband" as the church, the bride of Christ, is to the bridegroom, Christ. Both husband and wife can only love one another by the Holy Spirit given to them (Rom. 5:5).

Many a father and mother are attempting to parent their children by the myriads of directives in the parenting books, in the parenting seminars, and by the advice of the child psychologists – constantly wondering whether they are doing it right. Teachers teach; preachers preach; parents parent; but none affects our children the way culture enculturates. Parenting children who turn out to be constructive citizens of society is only accomplished by the grace of God. Try as they might, every parent will look back and recognize that it was only by the grace of God that their children turned out as they did.

APRIL 13

"LEAVE THE DOING TO US"

Greyhound Bus Lines began over 100 years ago (c. 1914), and gradually developed into the largest inter-city bus line in the United States (with some routes crossing into Canada and Mexico). In 1956 they began using the advertising slogan, "Go Greyhound and Leave the Driving to Us." Might we suggest that a similar slogan could be employed among Christian people who understand that the Christ-life is lived only by the living Christ in those who have received Him into their spirits and become Christ-ones (cf. Rom. 8:9,16). Just BE who you are "in Christ" and leave the DOING to Us (the three Persons of the Triune Godhead).

Religion, and perhaps foremost the Christian religion, has always emphasized what faithful believers should DO to become and be the Christians that God wants them to be. This is characteristic of all religion – the need to perform in accord with behavioral requirements. "Do this; don't do that," "Thou shalt; Thou shalt not," "This is permissible; That is not permissible." The concept of grace that is distinctive to the Christ-infused new covenant was subjugated to but the historical initiative of God to send His Son, as expressed in John 3:16, "God so loved the world that He gave His only begotten Son, that whoever believed in Him would not perish, but have eternal life."

Christians who understand the grace-distinctive of the new covenant, have come to realize that the religious performance of "DOING things for God" is alien to the good news that is proffered and made available in the living Lord Jesus. All the moralistic DOING is jettisoned; our salvation is "not of works, lest any man should boast" (Eph. 2:9). It is the privilege of every Christ-one to enter God's "rest" (cf. Heb. 4:1-11), and thereby to "leave the DOING" to the divine action and expression of God's grace. What a refreshing freedom is to be found in allowing the living Lord Jesus to manifest His life as we remain receptive to His activity.

GRACE-STRENGTH

In the tough times of life, particularly, I often repeat to myself Paul's words, "I can do all things through Christ Who strengthens me" (Phil. 4:13). Christ's strengthening work in our lives is God's grace. We are strengthened by the grace of God in Jesus Christ by the power of the Holy Spirit – God at work by His grace! Grace is God doing what God does, providing strength where there in none in frail human creatures. "Not that we are adequate to consider anything as coming from ourselves; our adequacy is of God" (II Cor. 3:5). All of God's provision for us is grace, as He provides, enables, and strengthens us with His adequacy, competency and sufficiency for all that He wants to be in us.

Unless we are "strengthened by grace" (Heb. 13:9), we are but weak creatures attempting to be strong in our own strength, and the result is that we are abject failures in all our attempts to be better. "But the God of all grace, who hath called us unto his eternal glory by Christ Jesus, after you have suffered a while, will make you perfect, establish, strengthen, and settle you" (I Pet. 5:10). There you have it – God's grace is the strengthening agency for all that He seeks to do in our lives. It may require some suffering, which certainly exposes our inadequacy, but we can rest assured that the grace of God will strengthen and settle us into the established trajectory of God in our lives

Paul advised the younger Timothy, "my son, be strong in the grace that is in Christ Jesus" (II Tim. 2:1). The strength to remain steadfast in Christ must come from God's grace. It is not a self-strength gained by personal resolve to be all we can be, to be as good as we can be, to do as much as we can do, or to be the ultimate exhibit of a self-wrought Christian life (there is no such thing!). The grace-dynamic of God at work in us is the basis of our strength. God working His strength in us. "Be strong in the Lord and in the strength of His might" (Eph. 6:10).

APRIL 15

THE SELF-INVESTED GOD

God does not operate by "remote control." We cannot operate God by "remote control," nor does God ever function in His world or His people by "remote control." The very word "remote" means far off in terms of place or time. This would imply a detached deity, a separated Savior, removed from what He is doing. He never stands back to tell others "what to" or "how to" do what is expected. God never acts, but what He is fully invested in His entire action. When God is at work, we can be sure that the very Person of God is right there at work. When God acts in grace, we can be sure that it is the very Triune God, the Creator God, the God of Abraham, Isaac, Jacob, the God who revealed Himself in His Son, Jesus Christ, who is present in His every work.

God does what He does because He IS who He IS. Never can it be said that He IS who He is because He does what He does. The Being of God is always active. His every action is fully invested with His very Being. God never stands back to observe what "divine action" is doing. He is in that action! Personally invested. God in action – that is what God's grace is.

The Christian God is not a God who is "way out there," uninvested in our lives (Deism). "Invested" here does not have to do with economic or financial investment. We are referring more to a sense of being enrobed, enclothed, enwrapped (think of clerical investments.) God's Being is always wrapped up in His every action. God is not removed from us; not a God who is separated from us, who we allow to serve as a handyman to fix our daily needs. Neither do we want to think of God in an immanent, pantheistic manner that fails to distinguish between what God is doing, and our willingness to allow Him to do so.

AN INDEPENDENT-DEPENDENT CHRISTIAN

If someone were to inquire about what sets my Christian life apart from others who call themselves Christian, I would have to explain to them that I have been an independent-dependent Christian. That oxymoron would of course confuse them, so I would have to go on to explain that I have, for the most part, been independent from any denominational structure of the church. My thinking has been rather "outside of the box," as I felt rather constricted and restricted by having to agree to a particular theological party-line. I aspire to be thoroughly biblical in all that I believe and teach, but I do appreciate the personal freedom to share with others how the Spirit of God has worked the things of the Spirit into my life.

Though independent of the paradigm of any theological belief-system, I want always to remain dependent on the living Lord Jesus for every facet of my Christian life. Faithful dependence of deriving all from the grace of God in Jesus is fundamental (not fundamentalism) to allowing the Christ-life to be re-presented in and as one's life. No one can live the Christian life under their own power (that is the fallacy of all religion). In dependence, we must rely on the Lord Jesus to be our life, our righteousness, our holiness, our everything. The Christian life is the Christ-life uniquely formulated and manifested through our personalities to express the character of the living Lord Jesus today.

Independent of the religious folderol of a rigid, carefully crafted belief-system and codified moral and behavioral conformity pattern, I seek to remain entirely dependent on the One who has become my Life. I want to be denominated only as a Christ-one, a Christian who by the presence and empowering of the living Jesus within chooses to allow Him to live-out in my thought and behavior – an independent-dependent Christian.

APRIL 17

SATANIC SELFISHNESS

Despite how God continues to reveal the Satanic selfishness that counters what He is doing in my life, the Evil One is persistent and will not back off. Like the caricature of the little devil on one's shoulder constantly suggesting selfish ways to sin, Satan is so quick to prompt and tempt us to exercise his character of selfishness. His character patterns of selfishness in the desires of my soul (what Paul seems to identify as "the flesh" – Gal. 5:16-18) are quick to rise and oppose what the Spirit seeks to do. I must keep remembering that the Spirit is superior to the flesh patterns. "Greater is He who is in you than he who is in the world" (I Jn. 4:4).

Some Christ-ones have not thought that selfishness is the character of Satan. They have tended to attribute selfishness to the fallen and corrupt nature of humanity after the fall of Adam into sin. It appears to me, however, that neither good nor evil are to be attributed intrinsically to human beings, but that mankind derives such character (good or evil) from a spirit-source outside of himself, either God or Satan. Thanks to Adam and Eve, we all begin by deriving from "the (Satanic) spirit that works in the sons of disobedience" (Eph. 2:2), during which time we develop our unique patterns of selfishness in our soul.

Our selfishness patterns are unique to us. Every individual has their particular patterns of selfishness (and this often helps to shape their personality). When we receive Jesus Christ in regeneration, and God's character of good is available to us, that does not mean that the patterns of selfishness do not remain within us (not within our spirit, but within our soul, creating the internal conflict that Paul refers to – Gal. 5:16-23). Our physical circumstances provide opportunity to choose to operate in accord with our selfish patterns or to make the choice of faith whereby we are receptive to God's Spirit action in our lives.

RESENTMENT AND CONTENTMENT

When a person is discontent with their circumstances and the people around them in those circumstances, their discontentment soon turns to resentment of the presence and activity of those they are dealing with. It is a resentment of having to tolerate what others are doing, even when those persons are engaged in loving gestures to facilitate our highest interests. Isn't it strange, that in the very times when we should be appreciating those who are helping us, we blame them to the point of resentment, for intruding in our time of pain, for inserting themselves into our time of pondering the plight of our circumstances, for encroaching into our time of self-pity wherein we selfishly want to wrap ourselves in our own security blanket?

Whereas resentment is dissatisfaction with the circumstances that life has presented us with, and with the people involved in those circumstances who do not seem to be able or willing to resolve the pain and disability – contentment, on the other hand, is satisfaction with our God-ordained circumstances, and with the people who are associated with those circumstances. Contentment is a willingness to accept and abide in what God has ordained for our lives, despite whether we consider such to be the most pleasant path. Paul could say, "I have learned to be content in whatever circumstances I am" (Phil. 4:11).

Does that mean that we can be content even when being assaulted and insulted? Paul wrote, "I am well content with weaknesses, with insults, with distresses, with persecutions, with difficulties, for Christ's sake; for when I am weak, then I am strong (in His strength)" (II Cor. 12:10). What evidence of genuine godliness (which is always the result of God at work In us). To Timothy, Paul explained, "godliness is a means of great gain when accompanied by contentment (I Tim. 6:6) – i.e., when we are content with what God is doing.

APRIL 19

JESUS IS NOT WITHIN US TO HELP US

Big rig truckers often use a tool called "the trucker's helper" or "the trucker's friend." It is a heavy-duty, multi-purpose, combination tool that helps to provide leverage when needed, while also serving as an ax, a hammer, and a cutting edge. It can be used for many purposes and serves as a great "helper" to a trucker in many different circumstances. Another tool is called a "come-along" winch or puller that ratchets to lift or pull objects together. Jesus does not want to serve as a "helper" or a "come-along" who is going to provide leverage to help us to live the Christian life or a winch to bring things together in our lives.

Jesus told His disciples that He would send another "helper" (Jn. 14:16,26; 15:26; 16:7). The Greek word *paraclete* (*para* = alongside; *kaleo* = to call) means "to call alongside" to comfort, help, aid, intercede, or advocate on behalf of. The word "another" is not *heteros*, another of a different kind (cf. heterosexual), but *allos*, another of the same kind, i.e., the Spirit would be another of the same kind, it would be the risen Lord Jesus in Spirit form (cf. I Cor. 15:45) who would serve as the provision for the Christian from the inside out. Our help is not an external, separated, or detached agency of helping assistance, but Jesus living and abiding in us is our more than adequate sufficiency.

We have all heard Christians testify that Jesus helped them to become successful in their business, or Jesus helped them to lose weight, or Jesus helped them to overcome an addiction. The dynamic grace of the Christ-life may well have empowered them to accomplish such things, but we must be careful not to think of Jesus in a detached sense, constantly realizing that He is our Life, our everything, our total sufficiency as He dwells within us. We have "union life" with Him (I Cor. 6:17). "Apart from Him, we can do nothing" (Jn. 15:5). We must not think that we are to do our best, and Jesus will help us do the rest."

LIVING BY THE LIFE OF ANOTHER

Everyone lives by the life of another, but few are aware that they are deriving their being and character from someone beyond themselves. The pervasive philosophy of humanism has convinced people that they can "go it alone," "run their own show," "do their own thing," and "be their own boss." It's a lie, my friends! God did not design us that way. He created us as derivative creatures who will, of necessity, derive from one spirit-source of the other, from God or Satan. God's intent was that we should derive from Him, from His nature, His Being, His character to be "man as God intended man to be."

When the devil seduced the original couple, Adam and Eve, the "father of lies" (Jn. 8:44) lied to them about their self-potential and self-sufficiency. What he failed to tell them was that when they rejected derivation from God, they would be deriving from him, Satan. "The prince of the power of the air is the spirit now working in the sons of disobedience" (Eph. 2:2). Though humanists rail about "the tyranny of derivation," they derive from "their father, the devil" (Jn. 8:44). It is time for the fallen human race to "come to their senses and escape the snare of the devil, having been held captive to do his will" (II Tim. 2:26).

Paul explained spiritual conversion as "turning from darkness to light and from the dominion (deriving from the being) of Satan to God, that one may receive forgiveness of sins and an inheritance among those who have been sanctified by faith in Him" (Acts 26:18). Such an exchange of spiritual presence and derivation allows an individual to be restored to proper God-ordained function. Paul wrote, "It is no longer I who lives, but Christ lives in me, and the life I now live in the flesh, I live by faith in the Son of God" (Gal. 2:20). Paul was aware that he was living by the life of Another, a manifesting the living Lord Jesus (II Cor. 4:10,11).

APRIL 21

GALATIANS 2:20

"I have been crucified with Christ" – Jesus took every person in the
human race with Him to the cross. He died for, on behalf of, and
in the place of every human being who has, is, and will exist.
"He died for all, so that they who live might no longer live for
themselves, but for Him who died and rose again on their behalf."
(II Cor. 5:15). This objective reality is true whether a person
believes and accepts it or not.

"It is no longer I who lives" – Those who observe me will see the
same exterior person they have always known, but the real me of
my spiritual identity has radically changed. When I became a
Christ-one in spiritual regeneration, the "old man" (Rom. 6:6; Eph
4:22) died and was laid aside, and now I am a "new man" (Eph.
4:24; Col. 2:10), a "new creature" (II Cor. 5:17) in Christ.

THIS DOES REQUIRE ONE TO BELIEVE & ACCEPT

"Christ lives in me" – my new spiritual identity is formed by the
presence of the risen and living Lord Jesus living in my spirit. "If
any person does not have the Spirit of Christ, that person is none
of His" (Rom. 8:9). I now participate in the mystery of the ages,
"which is Christ in me, the hope of glory" (Col. 1:27). Jesus
promised, "because I live, you will live also" (Jn. 14:19); "you in
me and I in you" (Jn. 14:20). "If Christ is in you, though the body
is dead because of sin, the spirit is life because of righteousness"
(Rom. 8:10). I recognize that Christ lives in me; my faith in Him is
not in vain (II Cor. 13:5).

*"The life which I now live in the flesh I live by faith in the Son of
God"* – I still live as a human being in the flesh; I am "in the world,
but not of the world" (Jn. 17:11,14). The life by which I live is
Christ's life, and I allow that life to be lived out through me and as
me, by faith, the receptivity of His activity providing the
character expression in my behavior. Christ-life in the Christ-one.

COLOSSSIANS 1:26,27

"The mystery which has been hidden from the past ages and generations, but has now been manifested to His saints, to whom God willed to make known what is the riches of the glory of this mystery among the Gentiles, which is Christ in you, the hope of glory."

Mystery here is not as in a "who done it" novel; biblical mystery (Greek *musterion*) is something that was in the past concealed, but is now revealed, or as Paul says, "has now been manifested to His saints (i.e., Christ-ones). That mystery of Christ the Messiah was concealed in the old covenant era, with only promises, allusions, and types of what God had planned to do from eternity past (Gen. 3:15; Gen. 12:1-3; Isa. 53:1-8), but in the incarnation of the Son of God (Jn. 1:14; Phil. 2:6-8) when the Word was made flesh, the mystery of the God-man Savior (cf. I Tim. 2:5) unfolded until He was "obedient unto death, even death on a cross" (Phil. 2:8), and then raised up again (Acts 2:24,32) in resurrection.

"God willed to make known the riches of the glory of this mystery among the Gentiles." The Jews thought they had exclusive rights to God. Imagine their surprise (cf. Acts 10:9-48), when the glorious new covenant realities were made available to Gentiles, the *goyim*. But that was the promise to Abraham, that what God would do was "for all the nations" (Gen. 17:4,5).

The mystery is "Christ in you, the hope of glory." Religion deals with externals; the mystery of the gospel is that Christ comes to dwell within us (cf. Jere. 31:33; Heb. 10:16), to function as God within the human spirit (cf. Rom. 8:9,16). Why is it that so many Christ-ones have failed to understand that the risen and living Lord Jesus lives within them? Paul asked the Corinthians, "Do you not recognize that Jesus Christ is in you, unless you fail the test (of faith in Jesus)?" (II Cor. 13:5).

APRIL 23

JESUS WILL NOT BE YOUR SPIRITUAL CRUTCH

We have all heard the cliché, "Do your best, and God will do the rest." Some even believe that it can be found within the bible. Not so! It is not a biblical dictum, and is, in fact, a non-scriptural and unscriptural phrase. God doesn't want "the best you have to offer." Isaiah, speaking as God's prophet, explained that "all our righteous deeds are as filthy rags (literal Hebrew = "dirty, bloody menstrual cloths")." God is not impressed with our best efforts at righteousness – anymore than He is impressed with a dirty Kotex. He is only desirous of and glorified by Jesus manifesting the divine life and character in us.

Crutches are devices to assist one in getting along by supporting part of the weight as an individual seeks to ambulate. Jesus wants to bear all the weight as we walk by faith – so much so that there will only be one set of footprints in the sand – HIS! Jesus doesn't want to be our helper, assisting us in doing what we think you can do for Him. Jesus wants to be our ALL in ALL. He wants to be everything in us that pleases what the Father, Son, and Holy Spirit desire to be and do in us. The entirety of what we call "the Christian life" – better termed as "the Christ-life" – is to be the risen and living Lord Jesus living out through us.

Dispose of all your crutches, all of your religious assistance devices with which you have attempted to hobble through your Christian walk. Even Jesus does not want to serve as a crutch by which we seek to lean on Him and do our best to ambulate through life. The Christian life is the Christ-life – His life being lived out through us and as us. "As we received Christ Jesus (by receptivity to His activity on our behalf), so we are to walk in Him (by receptivity of His activity to live out His life in our behavior)" (cf. Col. 2:6). The Christian life is not our best effort to perform up to some religious behavioral expectations, but rather the life of Jesus within us lived out through us.

ARE YOU ENJOYING JESUS?

I have visited church after church, met together with groups of Christians denominated by all sorts of pedigrees, and I must report that the vast majority of those who self-identify as Christians do not seem to be enjoying Jesus. Who am I to question whether they believe in Jesus, but the majority of these people do not seem to exhibit any "joy of the Lord." Instead, they seem to be "down in the mouth," with a puckered resolve to be the best Christian they can possibly be, and to do everything that the preacher keeps advocating they should do to "be like Jesus," They are fully aware by personal experience that religion produces discontent and burn-out – not enjoyment!

A familiar chorus uses the words, "The joy of the Lord is my strength" (Neh. 8:10). In the new covenant, it might be said that "the joy of the Lord" is JESUS. It is by "the working of the strength of His might" (Eph. 1:19), that we are "strengthened with all power, according to His glorious might, for the attaining of all steadfastness and patience; with joyfulness" (Col. 1:11). Christ-ones operate "by the strength which God supplies; so that in all things God may be glorified through Jesus Christ" (I Pet. 4:11). There is great joy in allowing Christ to live in us to the glory of God (Col. 1:27).

We enjoy Jesus when we realize that the Christ-life is what He does, not something we are required to conjure up or perform. The joy of the Lord is experienced when we are functioning by the GRACE of God in Jesus Christ by the Holy Spirit. There is not much joy in the "go, go, go," and "do, do, do" that is encouraged by the religion in the churches today. Rather, we can enjoy Jesus when we recognize that He wants to manifest (II Cor. 4:10,11) and re-present His life in us today, and we can enjoy the "Sabbath rest" (Heb. 4:9) of resting from our laborious works, just as God rested from His work on the seventh day (Heb. 4:10).

APRIL 25

WHAT IS JOY?

Having encountered so many joyless Christians along the way, I have asked the question, "What is joy?" Those who attempted to respond gave such answers as: "Well, it is like contentment." Or "It is the willingness to accept the circumstances." Is joy merely acceptance or contentment? If so, then joy is a self-evaluation of whether things are going my way in life. That is the definition of "happiness," based on the fact that the Old English word *"hap"* meant chance, and if perchance I can accept and be content with how things are going my way, then I can be happy or have joy (in accord with the foregoing popular perceptions).

I cannot accept that the biblical concept of joy is synonymous with happiness – the chance that one might enjoy how the circumstances are randomly turning out in accord with their selfish desires. There is a far greater depth to the joy that Jesus promised to give to His disciples (Jn. 15:11), i.e., to all Christ-ones. The Greek word for "joy" is *chara*, derived from the Greek word for "grace," *charis*. By God's grace-action, He manifests His character of "joy" in our lives. "The fruit (divine character) of the Spirit is love, JOY..." (Gal. 5:22). The Christ-one has the distinct privilege of experiencing and expressing God's character of joy.

Biblical joy is knowing Jesus and rejoicing in the oneness we have with Him – our spiritual union with Christ (I Cor. 6:17). We are overwhelmed with joy that the grace of God in Jesus is sufficient for our every need. "Let us fix our eyes on Jesus, the author and perfecter of our faith, who for the JOY set before him endured the cross, scorning its shame, and sat down at the right hand of the throne of God" (Heb. 12:2). Paul could write, "I am overflowing with JOY in all our affliction" (II Cor. 7:4). James likewise wrote, "Consider it all JOY, my brethren, when you encounter various trials" (James 1:2). We can experience the JOY of Jesus while in the midst of unpleasant external circumstances.

un broken Communion & union with God

116

RELAXING IN JESUS

Many Christians have fallen into the rigorous ruts of the world-system. It's a rat race in the fast lane of trying to keep up with others regarded as more successful than we are. The incentive mottoes are constantly brought to our attention: "Give it your all," "Try to make a name for yourself," If you can conceive it, you can achieve it," "Sweat and hard work will make you successful," "Just do it!" When we try to keep up in that way, where does that leave us? Exhausted, ready to give up, ready to say, "To hell with it all!" Psychologically, we find ourselves uptight, high strung, stressed, and tired of trying to do all that is expected of us, knowing that it is leading to another nervous breakdown.

We do not have to go down that highway. "There is a way that seems right unto man, but the end thereof is death" (Prov. 14:12; 16:25). Instead, we can say, "I want to choose God's way of Life. I am who I am in Christ. That's all I want to be." That is not the same thing as saying, "I yam who I yam; I'm Popeye the sailor man," and popping another stimulant or drinking another energy drink in order to continue the pursuit of a false goal. It is simply knowing our identity "in Christ" as "a child of God" (Rom. 8:16,17,21), a Christ-one, a Christian; knowing that we are but "a vessel for the Master's use" (II Tim. 2:21).

Oh, the peace in knowing that "it is not what we do for Him, but what He does in us." I am not concerned with whether others adjudge me to be successful. I just want to sit back and enjoy the life that God has given me in His Son, Jesus – to "rest" in Christ (cf. Heb. 4:3-11) – knowing that Jesus cannot be other than actively expressing Himself. My objective is to be "relaxing in Jesus," finding everyday life as relaxing as laying in a hammock on the beach in Fiji; all the while cognizant that faith is "our receptivity of His activity." I have no reputation to protect, for when Jesus is my life (Col. 3:4), Jesus is my reputation.

APRIL 27

ONE REJECT TO ANOTHER

The fallen world, of which Satan is the ruler (Jn. 12:31; 16:11), is a rejective environment. Lucifer rejected God and has been fomenting personal rejection among men (cf. Gal. 5:19-21) since he first convinced Adam and Eve to reject their idyllic arrangement in the Garden. Living in that rejective world-system, we have all been rejected at one time or another in our interpersonal relationships. Parents reject children. Children reject parents. Friends reject friends. Christians of one denomination reject Christians of different denominations. People of one political persuasion reject others of another political persuasion. We have all been rejected. That is why I say, "I am just one reject writing to other rejects."

Rejection can be divided into two general forms. There is overt rejection when it is obvious that the rejecter does not want to be friends or to be associated with us any longer. This rejection may involve hurtful and hateful words. It may involve violent and abusive expulsion. It may involve verbal repudiation or being taken advantage of sexually. The covert forms of rejection may include criticism, ridicule and attack on character, as well as distrust, lack of communication, unkept promises and inadequate provision. Even overprotection, permissiveness and indulgence can be forms of covert rejection.

Contrary to Satan's rejective character that causes "enmities, strife, jealousy, outbursts of anger, disputes, dissensions, factions" (Gal. 5:20), God's character is always love and acceptance. "God is love" (I Jn. 4:8,16). God wants to build us up, not tear us down. When Jesus is our life, He will manifest divine character in our behavior, the "fruit of the Spirit" – "love, joy, peace, patience, kindness, goodness, faithfulness, gentleness, and Godly control of oneself" (Gal. 5:22,23). This will be particularly evident in our interpersonal relationships.

NO HOPE FOR THE CHURCH

I have heard pastor after paster decry and bemoan the plight and the condition of the church in our day. They offer no solutions for correcting the problems, but they are chagrined that the church is not what they think it should be. The churches certainly do not need any more programs, as they slavishly try to duplicate the techniques utilized by what they regard as the "successful" churches, i.e., those local churches who report increasing attendance, larger numbers of baptisms, and larger income via contributions. They are particularly enamored by those congregations building larger church buildings.

Most pastors will be quite shocked when I explain that "There is no hope for the church." I need to explain what I mean by that statement. When Wm. Tyndale first translated the New Testament into English (1525-1526), he correctly translated the Greek word *ecclesia* as "assembly" or "congregation," not as "church." The institutional "church" authorities who authorized subsequent translations demanded that the word be translated as "church." The English word "church" is derived from the German word *kirche*, meaning a religious building. So much for the oft-repeated statement that "the church is not a building."

Tyndale was correct in translating the Greek *ecclesia* as "assembly, congregation, or gathering." Every Christ-one (Christian) is part of the assembly of God's saints and should relish the privilege of gathering or congregating with other Christ-ones. "Where two or three are gathered together in My name, I am there in their midst" (Matt. 18:20). While I hold no hope for the "church," its institution and its buildings, I have the greatest of expectant hope for the new covenant *ecclesia*, the greater assembly of Christ-ones and saints. Jesus said, "Upon this rock (the faith exhibited by Peter), I will build my *ecclesia*, and the gates of hell (*hades*) will not prevail against it" (Matt. 16:18).

APRIL 29

AUGUSTINE OF HIPPO

Augustine of Hippo is one of the most pivotal personages in the history of the Church. The question is: was he a saint or a heretic? Some theologians in the Eastern (Greek speaking) Orthodox Church consider Augustine to be a heretic based on his novel ideas of original sin, predestination, and particularly the *filoque* doctrine of the origin of the Holy Spirit. The Western (Latin speaking) Catholic Church, on the other hand, often refers to Augustine as a saint, and he is often quoted as such in both Roman Catholic churches and Protestant churches.

Augustine (A.D. 354-430) was born in Hippo (now Annaba, Algeria). He excelled as a student of rhetoric, the study of oratory persuasion. His early religious influences included a decade in the Persian religion of Manichaeism, and later fondness for the philosophy of Neoplatonism, which also had a dualistic base. His language competency was primary in Latin, and he admitted his incompetence in the Greek language. He moved to Carthage in Tunisia, and then to Rome and Milan in Italy, having abandoned his mistress and son in Algeria. After meeting the Christian rhetorician, Ambrose, in Milan, he converted to Christianity in A.D. 386 at the age of 31. In 391 Augustine was ordained a Catholic priest in Hippo, and in 395 he became the bishop.

Augustine wrote voluminously (cf. *The City of God, On Christian Doctrine, On the Trinity*, and his *Confessions, et al*), and these became the predominant resources for church leaders in the centuries following the 4th century (the Medieval period, which some call the "Dark Ages"). The overarching influence of Augustine is evident in that Martin Luther was an Augustinian monk in the Roman Catholic Church. The other great reformer, John Calvin, was a lawyer who quoted Augustine many times in his *Institutes of the Christian Religion*. Calvin's thought is often referred to as Augustinian-Calvinism, which many still ascribe to.

SPIRITUAL IDENTITY

There is so much instruction and talk about "knowing one's identity" in some Christian circles. Much of such teaching is confusing, if not downright false. Yes, the Christ-one has a new spiritual identity "in Christ." But we must never forget that the new spiritual identity is always "in Christ." It is not an identity that we can claim to be our own inherently. "God is Holy," but no one can claim to be holy in the same sense that God is Holy – essentially and intrinsically in Himself. Holiness is who God IS essentially, absolutely, inherently, *a se* in Himself. What God IS, nothing and no one else IS. God alone is Holy and Righteous.

We are only "righteous" (Rom. 5:19; II Cor. 5:21) because the "Righteous One" (Acts 3:14; 7:52; 22:14), Jesus Christ, has come to dwell and live in our human spirit. Our new spiritual identity is formed by His presence. We are only "holy ones" (saints – Rom. 1:7; 8:27; I Cor. 1:2; Eph. 1:18; Jude 1:14) because the "Holy One" (Mk. 1:24; Jn. 6:69; Acts 2:27; 3:14; 13:35; I Jn. 2:20), Jesus Christ, has entered in to occupy our human spirit. We can only claim that identity because of Him. We are only "perfect" (Phil. 3:15; Heb. 10:14; 12:23) because the "Perfect One" (II Cor. 5:21; Heb. 7:28) came into our spirit with His perfect character.

If anyone comes saying, "You are perfect" – beware. It' not about YOU. Spiritual identity is always derived identity – it is not intrinsic or inherent to the Christ-one but is derived from the presence of a spirit within us. Paul explained that we were all "made sinners" in our unregenerate spiritual condition because of Adam's sin (Rom. 5:19). That was a derived spiritual identity based on "the spirit that works in the sons of disobedience" (Eph. 2:2). When we become "new creatures" (II Cor. 5:17), and the risen and living Lord Jesus dwells within us (cf. Rom. 8:9), then our spiritual identity is derived from Christ. We are "made righteous" (Rom. 5:19) and perfect by His presence in our spirit.

MAY 1

THE SIN OF RELIGION

A few readers might think that I have lost my mind by indicating that religion is a sin. They will be those who have not differentiated between Christianity and religion. In Colossians 2:23, Paul refers to the inadequacy and impotency of "self-made religion." Is all religion man-made? God seems to have given the Mosaic Law to the obstinate Israelites, but the nation of Israel then made it into a religion of performance, thinking that by such they could work their way to the fulfillment of the Abrahamic promises. We might define "religion" as the mind-set that demands performance-conformity to a code of conduct or to authoritative religious advisors telling one how to live.

Religion, by definition, is the attempt to keep the rules and regulations, as well as the rituals of devotion as defined by the religious authorities. Such process serves the interest of man by promulgating self-effort, self-achievement and self-betterment. It does not, however, serve the interest of God in manifesting His character in His people to His glory. In fact, God hates such religion: "Bring your worthless offerings no longer; Incense is an abomination to Me. New moon and sabbath, the calling of assemblies – I cannot endure iniquity and the solemn assembly. I hate your new moon festivals and your appointed feasts, they have become a burden to Me; I am weary of bearing them" (Isa. 1:13,14).

Christianity, on the other hand, is the risen and living Lord Jesus living out His life in His Christ-ones. Those around such person see only the external and physical individual, who goes by her given name and family surname, but other Christ-ones know she is living by the life of Another. In opposition to all self-glory, Christ-ones seek to allow the Christ-life within them to be lived through them to the glory of God as His divine character is manifested in the behavior of His creatures.

"ALL THAT IS IN THE WORLD..."

The apostle John explains, "All that is in the world, the lust of the flesh and the lust of the eyes and the boastful pride of life, is not from the Father, but is from the world (I Jn. 2:16). All that is in the world has to do with self-concern, self-centeredness, and selfishness of one form or another. Satan is the initiator and perpetrator of all self-concern and egocentricity. It was he who said, "I (*ego*) will be like God" (Isa. 14:14). Satan is "the ruler of this world" (Jn. 12:31; 14:30; 16:11), and his self-centered character is constantly offered to human beings by every means of temptation within the world-system in which we reside.

The summation of all Satan's solicitations to self-concern, John identifies as "the lust of the flesh, the lust of the eyes, and the boastful pride of life." The word "lust" here is simply the word for "desire." Paul gives us a short listing of the desires and deeds of the flesh in Galatians 5:19-21. They are all self-pleasing and self-justifying actions. Everything around us in the world-system is oriented to self-gratification, self-aspiration, and self-reputation. They are summed up in the desire to please myself, the desire to possess for myself, and the desire to promote myself – the desires of the flesh, the desire of the eyes, and the pride of life.

Selfishness is so subtle and pervasive as we navigate through Satan's world-system. Words that utilize the prefix "self-" are almost innumerable: self-potential, self-satisfied, self-righteous, self-love, self-possessive, self-image, self-worth, self-control, self-absorbed, self-magnifying, self-justifying, self-starter, self-initiative, self-generative, self-actuating, self-help, self-directed; the list goes on and on. The self-absorption and self-concern of the world is all about ME. In contrast, the gospel of Jesus Christ offers the character of love which is always directed toward others. "The love of God has been poured within our hearts by the Holy Spirit who has been given to us" (Rom. 5:5).

MAY 3

WHAT IS THIS WORLD COMING TO?

People are often bemoaning how evil the world is becoming, and have often asked if it is worse now than in the past. I recall a poem by Jeanette H. Walworth, first published in 1910. "My grandpa notes the world's worn cogs and fears the world's going to the dogs. His grandpa in his house of logs, swore things were going to the dogs. His dad among the Flemish bogs, vowed things were going to the dogs. The cave man in his worn skin togs, said things were going to the dogs. But this is what I wish to state: The dogs have had a long, long wait."

Since the fall of man into sin and Satan's presence in fallen man as the "ruler of this world" (cf. Jn. 12:31; 14:30; 16:11), his character has always been that of the Evil One (cf. II Thess. 3:3; I Jn. 5:19). His mission is always that of the anti-Christ (cf. I Jn. 2:22; 4:3), desiring to counter the character of Christ and overcome everything Christian. It may appear that the evil in the world is getting worse, but it is likely that the technological advances have simply made evil more obvious via increasingly deadly weaponry, ever more clever schemes and scams, legal systems that favor the evildoers, and media that more blatantly portrays evil deeds.

Christians are "in the world, but not of the world" (Jn. 17:11,16), and should not be deceived into expecting the world to get better via its touted progressive agenda. The world ruled by Satan cannot be saved or made better. The devil will continue to inject his character and anti-Christian agenda into the affairs of the world, and it will certainly appear that the world is getting worse as Christians are increasingly targeted. The Christian mission of the future will be Christians willing to "stand in the gap," bucking the political correctness that regards Christian proclamation as a hate crime, and unafraid to suffer loss and death as they stand in Jesus, the only solution for the world's ills.

THE INCONGRUITY OF HUMILITY

The world-system with its humanistic premises of "be all you can be," "just do it!" has little understanding of humility. Humility is an anomaly that "just doesn't fit" with the age of narcissism and entitlement, with the modern aspirations of self-realization and enhancing self-worth. Humility is regarded as shameful self-abnegation and self-abasement that is contrary to the world's focus on self-aggrandizement. Self-effacing humility is regarded as the attitude of the bottom-feeders in the world's hierarchy of value – those persons who want to pull into their own shell and hide from the exciting possibilities of self-exaltation.

The perspective of the kingdom of heaven is so opposite to that of the world-system. Humility is the spiritual modesty that "does not think more highly of oneself than we ought to think" (Rom. 12:3). Humility is the attitude that is not preoccupied with elevating our self-importance – not comparing and competing for the highest place. Humility is a realization of our proper place before God – a premise that the world has rejected as "out of hand;" a carry-over from a time when humanity believed in myth. Humility allows God's grace to function in our lives. "God opposes the proud but gives grace to the humble" (James 4:6).

Despite the incongruity of humility in the perspective of the self-oriented world, humility is not incongruous with the character of the Lord Jesus Christ (Eph. 4:2; Phil. 2:3; Col. 3:12). In fact, humility is the consistent expression of Christ's character. The self-focus of the world's self-orientation and self-preoccupation will only be overcome by God's love that seeks the highest good of others – when by the grace of God in Christ, we focus on the needs of others rather than on ourselves. Christ-manifested humility does not imply any sense of self-deprecation or "dying to self," as encouraged by some religious teaching, but a healthy awareness of the "new self" that we have become "in Christ."

MAY 5

GOD THE GIVER OF ALL GOOD THINGS

Through the years I have made the acquaintance of many firmly entrenched people who have trusted in their own self-sufficiency. These were, for the most part, very good persons – hard-working, law-abiding, civil, willing to assist others if there was a legitimate need. Church going just wasn't their thing. They had observed those who were involved in the church, and there were many of them who didn't live out the "good life." So, these individuals decided they would "go it alone," continue to be as good as they could be in every circumstance, and if there was a God, He would have to be satisfied with that.

Most of these acquaintances were known in their community as "good persons," friendly, helpful, someone you could trust, and usually willing to be involved in community service. It wasn't as if they didn't believe there was a God. Most of them could be categorized as theists who would have said, "I believe in God," but they were reticent, verging on adamant, that they didn't want to get too close to a relationship with this God-figure they tentatively believed in. They preferred to think of God as "out there" somewhere (deism), as a deity they could hold at arm's length, and perhaps call on if they had a catastrophic need.

Most of these God-cautious friends would have even gone so far as to agree that "God was the giver of all good things." "Every good thing given and every perfect gift is from above" (James 1:17). When one believes that God is the giver, they believe in God's natural grace. The hump of hesitancy comes in whether they will give in and accept what God has made available to them, whether they will exercise the faith-receptivity to say, "Yes, Lord, I will receive what you have to give to me," and then go on to accept that God has given His own Son, Jesus, to be the Savior and Lord of our lives. Some of these acquaintances were willing to surrender their self-sufficiency and receive Jesus. Some were not.

WHAT ABOUT "GOOD WORKS?"

When some people hear that the Christian life is all by the grace of God – what He does and not what we do – they respond with the rejoinder, "What about good works? Aren't we responsible to do "good works" in order to show our appreciation to God?" The simple answer to the latter question is "NO!" Paul explained, "We are His workmanship, created in Christ Jesus for good works, which God prepared beforehand so that we would walk in them" (Eph. 2:10). God prepared beforehand the "good works" that He providentially intended that we should walk out as He energized such by His grace in our lives.

In the words of Maj. W. Ian Thomas, "Good works are those works that have their origin in Jesus Christ – whose activity is released through your body, presented to Him (God the Father) as a living sacrifice by a faith that expresses total dependence, as opposed to the Adamic independence." I would have said, "the alleged Adamic independence," because the fall of man into sin did not make mankind independent creatures – simply dependent on the wrong spiritual source (cf. Eph. 2:2; I Jn. 3:8). Human beings are always dependent and derivative creatures, deriving from one spiritual source or the other – God or Satan.

Thomas is correct, though, in noting that "good works are those works that have their origin in Jesus Christ." In the benediction to the letter to the Hebrews we read the explicit statement, "Now the God of peace, who brought up from the dead the great Shepherd of the sheep through the blood of the eternal covenant, even Jesus our Lord, equip you in every good thing (or good work - KJV) to do His will, working in us that which is pleasing in His sight, through Jesus Christ, to whom be the glory forever and ever" (Heb. 13:20,21). "Good works" are derived out of the "good" character of God, manifesting His goodness in our behavior by the empowering of His Holy Spirit.

MAY 7

PERSONAL REVELATION

There are those who maintain that scripture is the revelation of God, and beyond the apostolic revelation recorded in the text of the scripture there is no additional revelation. According to such an understanding of revelation, the personal impact of reading the scriptures is limited to the insights that one gains from proper interpretation of the text. Such an understanding reinforces the biblicism that elevates the physical Bible to a deified place of reverence, and muzzles God from any ability to speak to His people (Christ-ones) in the midst of a personal relationship of intimacy and the leading direction of their lives.

There seems to be three basic meanings of "revelation" within the new covenant scriptures. The first and primary reference is to the historical revelation of God in Jesus Christ. By the incarnation of the Son of God becoming flesh (Jn. 1;14; Phil. 2:7,8; I Tim. 3:16; II Tim. 1:10) as the God-man, the Triune God enacted the divine Self-revelation of Himself and His saving objectives to humanity. The new covenant literature does not refer to itself as a revelation of God, but it is certainly the record of the incarnational revelation of Jesus Christ, and thus serves in a secondary sense as the "word of God" concerning the Word of God. But the biblical record is not to be diminished or deified.

There are definite references to the personal revelation of God to individuals within the new covenant record. We do not want to put God into a straitjacket that disallows His personal revelation to His people in a personal relationship. Paul received personal revelations (II Cor. 12:7; Gal. 1:12; 2:2; Phil. 3:3), and so can every Christ-one (Matt. 16:17; Phil. 3:15;). The expectation of a future second coming revelation of Jesus Christ is well attested (Rom. 8:18; I Cor. 1:7; I Pet. 1:5,7,13; 5:1). Christ will be revealed in praise and honor and glory in His consummation of His entire mission as Savior and Lord.

CONDUITS

When running the electrical wiring for a home or business, the building codes often require that the electrical wires be run through metal or PVC conduits to avoid the wires getting cut, wearing through the plastic coating, or getting eaten through by varmints such as rats or squirrels. The conduits do not provide any energy to the home or business; they are just the channels through which the electrical wires are run in the best interest of preserving the wiring from damage, and thus avoiding a possible fire. Christ-ones are conduits of the life of the risen and living Lord Jesus. We do not provide the energy to live – He does! We are simply the channels through which the life-energy of Jesus flows out to others.

The apostle Paul refers to human beings as "vessels," indicating that we are meant to be containers that contain the contents that might be put in the cup, vase, jar, glass, etc. The container never becomes the contents, just as we never become the Christ who is in our spirit-container. The "vessel" analogy does not always convey the dynamic of the contents. Water in a jar is often quite static, even to the point of becoming stagnant. But Christ-ones have the content of the "Living water" (Jn. 4:10,11; 7:38) of the living Lord Jesus that always flows out to others. Then the vessel metaphor illustrates the dynamic of Christ in like manner as the conduit picture.

"We (Christ-ones) have this treasure (the living Lord Jesus) in earthen vessels (physical bodies), so that the surpassing greatness of the power (dynamic) will be (derived out of) God and not (out of) ourselves" (II Cor. 4:7). We are response-able, however, to make the continuing choices of faith (receptivity to His grace activity) so that we "will be a vessel for honor, sanctified, useful to the Master, prepared for every good work" (II Tim. 2:21).

MAY 9

BEWARE THE HUCKSTERS

Why is it that Christ-ones are so gullible and susceptible to being conned and taken advantage of by hucksters offering pseudo-medical panaceas and promoting misinformation about legitimate medical treatments? Is it because spiritual belief in general has scientifically unprovable tenets, and therefore Christ-ones and religionists are generally more willing to accept scientifically unsupportable claims of health benefits and physical remedies to health problems? That is just my conjecture, for I do not really know why Christians, or the general public are so willing to take the bait and buy into pseudo-explanations.

The world of fallen mankind, energized as they are by "the ruler of this world" (Jn. 12:31; 14:30; 16:11), are so prone to be deceived by the satanic Deceiver who deceives so many in the promulgation of false remedies, false religions, and false reasonings. "There are many rebellious men, empty talkers and deceivers...teaching things they should not teach for the sake of sordid gain (Titus1:10,11). The hucksters, the snake-oil salesmen, want to get in your pocket and take your money by means of deceptive marketing and scams that claim to offer an elixir for all your physical, psychological, and spiritual needs.

Christ-ones are encouraged to be discerning (Phil. 1:9; Heb. 5:14) and to "test the spirits" (I Jn. 4:1) that are behind every phenomenon. Those who belong to the living Lord Jesus are to recognize that Christ is their wisdom (I Cor. 1:24,30), and will provide by His Spirit the necessary insight and empowerment to avoid their being taken advantage of as they "listen under" Jesus in obedience. Christians who fail to listen to the Spirit of Christ will indeed be susceptible to the false information, the quackery, the nostrum, the fraudulent cures, the conspiracy theories, the deceitful false promises that always have been and will continue to be offered by the hucksters and charlatans of this world.

SINCERITY

The etymological origins of the word "sincere" have been debated and remain in question. A popular and understandable attribution is that the English word "sincere" is derived from the Latin *sine cera*, (*sine* = without; *cera* = wax). Proprietors in the ancient world, ex. Greece and Rome, were known to attempt to sell a less than perfect piece of pottery or statuary by filling in any imperfections or cracks with wax. If the object being sold was fully intact, had complete integrity, and was not falsified or adulterated, it was said to be *sine cera*, i.e., without wax, unadulterated, and could be sold *bona fide* (in good faith).

Other linguists and etymologists have explained that our English word "sincere" is derived from the Latin *sincerus*, meaning clean, pure or sound, singularly whole. This latter derivation may be the best linguistic explanation, but the etymology still goes back to the Latin words *sine cera*, without wax. In the Greek New Testament, Paul refers to "*sincere* faith" (I Tim. 1:5; II Tim. 1:5), using *ana* = without; *hypocritos* = hypocrisy. Peter uses the same Greek word in reference to "having in obedience to the truth purified your souls for a *sincere* love of the brethren." Whether from Greek or Latin, sincerity has to do with what is honest, truthful, unfalsified and without hypocrisy.

To say that a person is sincere doesn't say anything about the spiritual condition of that person. It is possible to be sincerely devoted to religious practice and churchy busyness. It is possible to be sincerely committed to the denominational tasks of your church institution. It is possible to be sincerely confident that your belief-system is accurate. It is possible to be sincerely wrong, sincerely deceived, sincerely stupid, and sincerely exhausted. Sincerity does not imply the accuracy or propriety of anything one says or anything does – it simply indicates that you are not attempting to be hypocritical.

MAY 11

JOYFULLY EXUBERANT

Many people attending the churches today are fully aware that Jesus died on the cross for their sins. They appreciate the historical events of Jesus' crucifixion and resurrection, but after a period of time (for some, years and years) engaged in mere historical remembrance, the question arises, "Is that all there is?" Feeling obliged to gather with like-minded Christ-ones week after week, they perpetuate the routines and listen to the monotonous teaching of "how to get saved." They appear to be blissfully ignorant of anything beyond the entry level redemptive teaching that Jesus will keep people from going to hell.

There are always a few who begin to question whether the "eternal life" they have received in Jesus when they "got saved" has any elements of vitality for the present, prior to the expected eternal extension in the heavenly future. What did Jesus mean when He said, "I came that you might have life, and have it more abundantly?" (Jn.10:10). Is it possible that the living Lord Jesus raised from the dead in the resurrection might function as our life in the here and now? Paul explained affirmatively, "He who raised Christ from the dead will also give life to your mortal bodies by means of His Spirit who lives in you" (Rom. 8:11).

The resurrected Christ-life is available to function in every Christ-one every moment of every day. Rather than being "blissfully ignorant" about anything other than being rescued from the death consequences of sin on the cross, it is possible to be "joyfully exuberant" about the life of Jesus experienced abundantly in the present. His life has become our life. "Christ is our life" (Col. 3:4) "It is no longer I who live, but Christ lives in me" (Gal. 2:20). "For me to live is Christ" (Phil. 1:21). The grace of God dynamically expresses the life of Christ through us by the empowering of the Spirit of Christ (Rom. 8:9). Which will you choose? Blissfully ignorant or joyfully exuberant?

THE DIVINE FLOW OF FREEDOM

God does what He does because He is who He is. His freedom to manifest Himself as God is contextualized by His character – who He IS. For example, "It is not possible for God to lie" (Numb. 23:19; Titus 1:2; Heb. 6:18). His character is that of truth/reality. Freedom is inherent in Who He is, and He exercises that freedom in the consistent manifestation of His Being and character. The incarnated Son of God, although fully God, "emptied Himself" (Phil. 2:7) of the prerogative and privilege of functioning as God to become a derivative human being, who would derive the character of God in every moment for thirty-three years.

The humanity of Jesus is evidenced in His human obedience (*hupakouo* = to listen under), to exercise His freedom of choice to choose faithful derivation from the Father (Jn. 14:10), despite being "tempted in all ways as we are (every other human), yet without sin" (Heb. 4:15). God does not obey anyone or anything, but humans are granted the freedom of choice to do so, and Jesus did so. Jesus was "obedient unto death" (Phil. 2:8), despite the temptation to avoid such (Matt. 16:22,23; Mk. 8:32,33). Operating in the freedom of human derivation, Jesus chose obedience to allow the divine freedom of God's consistent manifestation of His character in His (Jesus') human behavior.

Christ-ones who are "in Christ" (in spiritual union with Christ – I Cor. 6:17) have human freedom of choice (as did Jesus). We also have the freedom of obedience, to listen under the living Lord Jesus and to choose by faith to be receptive to His divine activity. The emphasis should not be on freedom *from* sin, law, flesh, (though true), but to recognize the human freedom *to* derive from God's freedom to consistently manifest His character in His creation and in our behavior. This is the divine flow of freedom when humans exercise the freedom of choice and of obedience to participate in God's freedom to express Who He IS.

MAY 13

A MATTER OF EMPHASIS

Just as it is possible to place the em-PHA-sis on the wrong syl-LAB-le in our English pronunciation, it is likewise possible to place emphasis on an accurate and biblical truth while failing to place that truth within the greater context of divine presence and activity. An example of this might be the emphasis on a Christian's identity in Christ, emphasizing that a Christ-one is perfect or has an identity of being perfect, that a Christ-one is righteous or has an identity of being righteous, that a Christ-one is holy, a holy one, a saint, without pointing out the source of such. Having such a spiritual identity can be misrepresented if it is not clearly stated that such identity is derived from the presence of the perfect, Righteous and Holy One, the living Lord Jesus, dwelling within us with the intention of manifesting His perfect, righteous and holy character in our human behavior.

Those emphasizing the spiritual identity of Christ-ones, often proceed to advise Christians that they need only to BE who they are "in Christ," and not concern themselves with any doing. They fail to realize that the being of our identity is in the divine BEING of God in Christ. We can only BE who we are in Christ, when we are derivatively allowing by faithful receptivity the BEING of the divine-human One, Jesus Christ in and through us. The focus and emphasis must be on the BEING of Jesus Christ, rather than on the identity of the Christian that is only derived from the presence and activity of Jesus. We can only BE in the sense of a derived identity that is in reality the very BEING of Jesus in us.

Our emphasis as Christ-ones must be JESUS, rather than focusing on ourselves. Who we are "in Christ" is not an intrinsic, independent, individual identity that we can claim and declare as our own. We must always remember and explain that our identity is "in Christ," and His presence and activity in us. It is His BEING that we want to declare and proclaim and live.

CONFLICT IN THE CHRISTIAN LIFE

Some who have become Christians seem to have been misinformed that the Christian life would be a panacea, elixir, or magic formula whereby there would be no problems, and everything would move along swimmingly as they enjoyed smooth sailing on the seas of life. They may be shocked and disappointed when they recognize that there is struggle and conflict in the Christian life. Christianity is not membership in God's "red carpet club," whereby we are transported into the peaceful perfection of heavenly existence while still living in this world. The powers of evil are still experienced by Christ-ones.

Some Christians are perplexed when they realize they still have residual sinful and selfish desires in their soul that contradict and wage war again the new impulses of the Spirit in their life. "I thought that 'old things were to have passed away' (II Cor. 5:17)," they may exclaim. Yes, "old things have passed away," and there has been a radical exchange in our spirit (cf. Acts 26:18), but within the desires of our soul we still have patterns of selfishness and sinfulness that remain. This is an example of the necessity of distinguishing between one's spirit and one's soul, which Christian religion tends to regard as the same and synonymous.

The apostle Paul explains this conflict, struggle, and behavioral war in his letter to the Galatians. "But I say, walk by the Spirit, and you will not carry out the desire of the flesh. For the flesh sets its desire against the Spirit, and the Spirit against the flesh; for these are in opposition to one another, so that you may not do the things that you please" (Gal. 5:16,17). It is important to note that it is not the Christian's responsibility to wage war against the "flesh" – "the Spirit sets its desire against the flesh." Once again, we allow the Spirit of Christ to overcome our soulical tendencies of selfishness and sinfulness. The positive swallows up the negative and Christ prevails.

MAY 15

"ALL THINGS ARE LAWFUL"

In the restrictive context of the Jewish religion into which Jesus was born and lived, the ever-present question was, "Is it lawful to do this or that?" "Is it lawful to heal on the Sabbath?" (Matt. 12:10) asked the Pharisees, to which Jesus replied, as He often did with a counter-question, "Is it lawful to do good on the Sabbath?" (Matt. 12:12). Religious legalism is always occupied with juridical concerns. Then came the radical paradigm shift of the new covenant, allowing for the freedom of the Christ-one to function in the grace of "the perfect law of liberty" (James 1:25; 2:12) and in accord with the "law of love" (Rom. 13:10) wherein Christ in the Christ-one always seeks the highest good of others.

In the new covenant context of freedom, Paul twice states the open-ended dictum, "All things are lawful, but..." (I Cor. 6:12; 10:23). Paul isn't using "lawful" in the sense of the Mosaic Law, but in the sense of being right before God in the context of the grace that is in Jesus Christ. The conjunctive "but" is not that of restriction or negation. The question is, does "all" mean "all"? Yes, "all" means "all" without restriction, contextualized by divine love empowered by divine grace. Everything is legal (if we want to use juridical terms); everything is permissible; "anything goes" (*Message*); "love God and do what you please" (Augustine).

Do not let religion impose any restrictions on the freedom of the "all." The only contextual qualification of the broad permission is that we live in God's loving grace. In this paradigm of grace-love, God's love does no wrong to one's neighbor (Rom. 13:19). The compulsion of Christ's love (II Cor. 5:14) means we are lovingly responsible to be socially constructive, to edify, build up, and assist others to grow "in the grace and knowledge of our Lord and Savior, Jesus Christ" (II Pet. 3:18). Our response-ability is to be receptive to Christ's character expression for others. Christian freedom does not trample, trump, or override Christ's love.

HOW FAR DOES CHRISTIAN FREEDOM GO?

How free is Christian freedom? Are we really free to do as we please? Are we so free that any action in itself is not right or wrong? Paul seems to have articulated an open-ended freedom when he wrote, "all things are lawful (or permitted)" (I Cor. 6:12; 10:23) but points out this must be contextualized by God's grace in Jesus Christ to love others and to do all to the glory of God. Our Christian freedom is prescribed by the character of Christ. We are free to go as far as the character of Christ might take us, which means what we do will not be self-serving, nor will Christ's character do harm to others but serve to lovingly build them up.

We are free to push against the boundaries that religion prescribes, to eschew "the tree of the knowledge of good and evil," to go beyond static "right and wrong" categories by living in the dynamic of God's grace. Christian freedom gives us great latitude to conform to religious convention and tradition or to defy such as did Luther. We are free to give or not to give. Free to marry or not to marry (I Cor. 7:37-39). Free to be rich or to take a vow of poverty. Free to be a Democrat or a Republican. Free to engage in structured liturgical worship or to choose spontaneous expressions of worship. Free to make a choice, and then turn around and make the opposite choice.

Dare to be free and resist all temptations to revert to religious prohibitions. "If you have died with Christ to the elementary principles of the world, why, as if you were living in the world, do you submit yourself to decrees, such as, 'Do not handle, do not taste, do not touch!'" (Col. 2:20,21). Limits to our freedom always seem to be negative – dare to be positively radical. How far does Christian freedom go? As far as "Christ in you" takes it and you! The love-limit of our freedom will do no harm to others but seek their highest good in building them up. "It is no longer the (selfish) I who lives, but Christ lives in me" (Gal. 2:20).

MAY 17

YOU CAN'T DO IT!

The world around us constantly bombards our senses with the message that "You can do it!" "Just give it your best effort, and you can do it". "You can be everything you were meant to be and want to be." "Just do it!" The humanistic message of self-ability, self-potential, self-effort, and self-enactment constantly bombards us with the fallacious premise that we are "like God" (Gen. 3:5) and capable of creating a world of our own making that will suit our every fancy. To counter this tsunami of misinformation is like trying to hold back or divert the waters of the Niagara River to keep them from going over the famous Falls.

Despite its being so contrary to all that is being proclaimed in the world, there are a few who are willing to stand as lone heralds on the river's edge crying, "You can't do it!" "All your labors are in vain." "You will never produce the end-results you have been promised." Christians, meanwhile, are encouraged by the propagandizing preachers to "do it right." "Live the Christian life." Live "like Jesus." Our cry *au contraire* is "You can't do it!" "You cannot produce righteousness!" If any human being could produce righteousness, then Jesus would have died on the cruel cross to no avail – needlessly (Gal. 2:21) – or as one fellow explained, "Jesus would have died on the cross for the fun of it!"

Tune out both the secular and evangelical humanists with their inculcations to "Do it!" There is only One who can "DO IT!" The living Lord Jesus, who died on the cross and rose from the dead, He can do it, and wants to do it. He stands ready to do all that is required for humanity to function as He intended when He created us. He stands available as the grace dynamic living within every Christ-one to enact all that God wants to do in us, through us, and as us. Only Jesus can live the Christ-life. Only the "Righteous One" (Acts 3:14; 7:52; 22:14) can manifest the righteous character of God in our human behavior.

GRACE: THE DYNAMIC OF CHRIST'S LIFE IN US

Many Christians seem to have a limited view of divine grace. First, they limit God's grace action to simply the motivational incentive of God the Father to send the Son in the power of the Spirit to be incarnated as the God-man. The veracity of this understanding is explained by John when he wrote that "the Word became flesh, full of grace and truth" (Jn. 1:14) and in this incarnation "grace was realized through Jesus Christ" (Jn. 1:17). The divine action of redemptive grace continued as Jesus submitted Himself to the Father (Jn. 14:10), was "obedient unto death, even death on a cross" (Phil. 2:8; Heb. 2:9) and was resurrected by the Father (Acts 2:32; 5:30; 13:34; I Cor. 6:14).

By such divine grace-action the Triune God effected the redemption of mankind (Rom. 3:24) and "the forgiveness of our trespasses, according to the riches of His grace" (Eph. 1:7). Our salvation (past, present, and future) is enacted and energized by God's grace (Rom. 3:24; Eph. 1:7; 2:8,9; Titus 2:11). The grace given to Paul (I Cor. 3:10; 15:10; Gal. 1:15; 2:9; Eph. 3:7) was the impetus for the founding of the early *ecclesia* communities.

We must understand that God's grace is not a relic of God's action in the historical past but is dynamically active in the lives of Christians and in the *ecclesia* of Christ today. The Christ-life is made viable and visible by the present-day operation of divine grace. No Christian can live the Christian life by his/her own effort to "be like Jesus." It is only by the free-flowing abundance of God's constant grace-dynamic that we "reign in life through Jesus Christ" (Rom. 5:17) – it's not what we do, but what He does. Divine grace is never static as events in history, or personal experiences of the past, or doctrinal explanations of "sovereign grace. By God's grace we continue to "grow in the grace and knowledge of our Lord and Savior, Jesus Christ" (II Pet. 3:18).

MAY 19

WHO'S IN CONTROL?

The psychological world often refers of persons having "control issues" or colloquially as being "control freaks." A person who always wants to be in control of every situation or to be in control of the actions of others is often diagnosed and classified as having controlling traits brought on by narcissism, paranoia, anxiety, perfectionism, or obsessive-compulsive personality disorders. Such psychological factors of controlling behavior can always be traced to the deeper activity of the spiritual control exerted by Satan or God as they attempt to influence human beings with their contrasted natures and characters.

Ultimately, God is in control of all that He has created. His allowing (or determining) that an opposing spirit with disparate character should have developed through Lucifer's self-chosen determination to become Satan appears to have been for the purpose of providing mankind a genuine spiritual freedom of choice. Both the spirit of the Evil One with his character of sin and selfishness and the Spirit of God in Christ with His character of love and righteousness vie for influencing control over the minds, emotions, and behavioral expressions of human beings who inevitably derive character from one or the other.

Human beings are derivative creatures who derive their nature and character from the spirit of Satan or the Spirit of God, and thus are under the domain and authoritative control of one or the other. Adam and Eve's choice of sin put them under the control of "the spirit that works in the sons of disobedience" (Eph. 2:2) as "slaves of sin" (Rom. 6:20). Paul explained that he was sent to "turn (convert) Gentiles from the dominion (control) of Satan to the dominion (control) of God" (Acts 26:18). Paul later explained to the Colossians that "He (God) rescued us from the domain (control) of darkness (Satan) and transferred us to the kingdom (control) of His beloved Son" (Col. 1:13).

THE GRACE-CIRCLE OF GOD'S ACTIVITY

There seems to be a circle of grace as God works in the lives of His people. We do not spontaneously dream up something we can do for God. God inspires impulses of action in Christ-ones by the prompting of the Holy Spirit. We sense the prompting to pray and communicate with God. We choose by faith to be receptive to His activity. But "we do not know how to pray as we should, so the Spirit intercedes with inexpressible utterances too deep for human words" (Rom. 8:26). The Father delights in our personal communication with Him by the Spirit and is glorified by such.

We sense the prompting and desire to worship God, whether in collective worship, private worship, or the worship of lifestyle. Responding to such by faith, we engage in Spirit prompted and directed worship (Jn. 4:23,24; Rom. 12:1). Doing so to the glory of God, God is glorified by the worship and communion with His creatures. We sense the Spirit-prompted opportunity to share the glorious gospel of life in Jesus with another person. We sense the opportunity to engage in the "good works" which God prepared beforehand that we should walk in them (Eph. 2:10). Receptive to such by faith, God "equips us in every good thing to do His will, working that which is pleasing in His sight through Jesus Christ, to whom be the glory forever" (Heb. 13:21).

This cyclical process of grace received by faith thereby allows the Spirit-energized actions to bring glory to God. When we act at the impulse of the Spirit of God, all glory for such goes back around to God. Whenever the all-glorious character of God is expressed in our human behavior, the glory for such activity goes to God, for the impetus and dynamic of the action was His activity expressed in our actions. God is glorified when His own all-glorious character and activity is expressed in His created derivative beings. "For out of Him, and by means of Him, and unto Him are all things; To Him be the glory" (Rom.11:36).

MAY 21

WHAT HAPPENED AT THE CROSS?

Human attempts to explain the spiritual realities that transpired at the historical death of Jesus on the cross have been quite diverse. Theologians have long debated what they have called the "Theories of the Atonement" – the Moral Influence theory, the Ransom theory, the Satisfaction theory, the Penal Substitution theory, the Governmental theory, the Scapegoat theory, etc. They are all unsatisfactory in one way or another, and for the most part fail to account for the spiritual powers of the universe that collided at the cross and resulted in the life-giving restoration of humanity effected by Jesus' death and resurrection.

In Jesus' death He absorbed all the blows that the death-dealing devil (Heb. 2:14) could throw at Him, all the throes of death itself. He absorbed death itself (Satan's last salvo) by dying on the cross on our behalf, in our place. He rose victorious over death (*Christus Victor*), making His resurrection life available to all mankind who would receive His life into themselves, His Spirit in their spirit, the "saving life of Christ" (Rom. 5:10) operative within each Christ-one. "It is no longer I who lives, but Christ lives in me" (Gal. 2:20). "Do you not recognize that Jesus Christ is in you, unless you believed in vain?" (II Cor. 13;5).

The death-dealer was defeated by the Life-giver. The Evil One was defeated by the Righteous One. For those who grasp this and accept this, the fear of death is overcome because the power of death has been defeated (Heb. 2:14,15). Jesus absorbed all death into Himself by His willingness to die on the cross in our stead. "Death could not hold Him. It was impossible for the Sinless One to be held in the power of the devil's hold (Acts 2:24). He was raised from the power of death to be the reality of Life within receptive Christ-ones. Death was now defeated (in an objective sense), and the LIFE (Jn. 14:6) was now available for all who would receive Him (subjectively).

RESTING IN THE ADEQUACY OF JESUS

We live in "a world of want." Looking over the mass of humanity around the globe, there seems to be an existential dissatisfaction among mankind. Many people, regardless of their external circumstances, whether they live in a third-world country or in America, seem to be haunted by a sense of insufficiency, by the discontent of an uncertain well-being, by the fear of loss and dying. This sense of inadequacy both for the present and the future can be observed in non-Christians as well as Christians. Discontent and dissatisfaction seem to be the darkened mind-set that pervades the perspective of people around the world.

Is it possible to find the rest and relaxation of a settled mind, heart, or spirit in the turmoil of a troubled world? Jesus said, "Come unto Me, and I will give you rest" (Matt. 11:28). There is the possibility of an inner "rest" that can be found in the presence of the living Lord Jesus, despite the external turmoil and uncertainty that surrounds us. "The one who has entered His rest has himself also rested from his works, as God did from His; therefore, let us be diligent to enter that rest" (Heb. 4:10,11). Though we can rest in Jesus' sufficiency due to His "finished work" (Jn. 19:30) on the cross, our subjective mind-set must correspond with the objective reality of Christ's work.

"The Lord is my Shepherd, I shall not want" (Ps. 23:1). Christ-ones who are receptive to Jesus as Lord, will recognize the adequacy and sufficiency of His life for all their needs. By faith we recognize that we are not adequate/sufficient to consider anything as coming from ourselves, but our adequacy/sufficiency is from God (II Cor. 13:5). Having received the divine sufficiency, it is totally incongruous to continue to be seeking, desiring, wanting, trying to make something else happen, grumbling with discontent, dissatisfaction, and ingratitude as if God had not loved us and graced us with His only begotten Son, Jesus Christ.

MAY 23

SELFISHNESS OR LOVE

It all boils down to two diverse types of character expressed in human behavior. These opposite character-orientations – selfishness or love – are derived from the two contrasted spirit-sources of Satan or God. Antithetical to each other, these are expressions of evil or good, derived either from the Evil One (II Thess. 3:3; I Jn. 2:13,15; 5:19) or from the Righteous One (Acts 3:14; 7:52; 22:14) who is love (I Jn. 4:8,16). These are not generated *ek anthropos* ("out of man"), but are generated from the antithetical spirit-sources; selfishness out of the devil (*ek diabolos* – cf. I Jn. 3:8), and love out of God (*ek Theos* – cf. I Jn.4:7).

All human beings are born "by nature children of wrath" (Eph. 2:3), deriving the character of selfishness from "the spirit that works in the sons of disobedience" (Eph. 2:2). From his formation when Lucifer became Satan, after declaring "I will be like the Most High God" (Isa. 14:14), Satan has been the ego-centric initiator and perpetrator of selfishness. Human beings are not essentially or inherently selfish or sinful (*ek autos*), despite Augustine's doctrine of "original sin" blaming Adam for the corruption of humanity, but Adam's fall into sin did set in motion Satan's indwelling presence and character in mankind.

The character of love, on the other hand, is always derived from the character of the God who is love (I Jn. 4:8,16), *ek Theos* (I Jn. 4:7). Love is never generated or energized by man (*ek anthropos*). "The love of God is shed abroad in our hearts by the Holy Spirit who has been given to us" (Rom. 5:5), and "the fruit of the Spirit is love..." (Gal. 5:22). Divine love, *agape* love, overcomes and overrides the selfish ego-love (*eros*) that has been patterned into the desires of our soul (called the "flesh" Gal. 5:16-21). The character of selfishness is always concerned about me. The character of divine love is always concerned about others – seeking the highest good of others.

RELIGIOUS TRAPPINGS

Trappings are just the fancy wrapping, ribbon and bows on the package. They are the external things associated with something, designed to make it look pretty and presentable, i.e., the decorations. In the religious context, the trappings may include the architecture of the building, the elaborate choreography of the worship services, the pastoral vestments, the organ, the choir, the variety of Sunday school classes, and the necessity of membership in the church – all the pomp and circumstance of gathering together with the particular group of religious adherents one has chosen to associate and assemble with.

The problem arises when people are trapped into thinking that the trappings are the reality, the reason for their gathering together. The object in the package is the same whether it has fancy wrappings and trappings or not. The substance and reality of the gospel is JESUS, the vital life of the risen Lord JESUS who lives in receptive individuals who have received Him by faith. Different churches wrap Him up in different trappings of theological nuances, ecclesiastical polity, liturgical or non-liturgical worship styles, preaching styles, and musical preferences ranging from classical to praise to rock and roll.

When people cannot distinguish between the religious trappings and the reality of the living Lord Jesus, they have inadvertently fallen into a subtle form of idolatry, reverencing and worshipping the fancy packaging rather than the Person of Jesus Christ. In the earliest years of the Christian faith there were no decorative trappings. Christians gathered in the homes of fellow believers in Jesus (cf. Acts 2:46; 20:20; Rom. 16:5; I Cor. 16:19). In the simplicity of the home fellowship, they shared transparently with one another their personal struggles and victories. They sang some simple songs, shared a psalm that was meaningful, and prayed for each other and encouraged each other.

MAY 25

THE CHASM BETWEEN RELIGION AND GRACE

Just as there was a great chasm between the rich man and Lazarus in Hades (Lk. 16:26), there is a great chasm between those involved in religion and those who have accepted the dynamic of God's grace in Jesus Christ. The religious folk on one side of the chasm busily engage in performance exercises to prove themselves worthy and outstanding members of their religious organization. Those participating in grace on the other side of the chasm are just as active, but they are "resting" in God's grace activity, aware that "it is not what they do but what God does in and through them" that is of any consequence.

The religious workers on the one side occasionally get a glance at the grace-folk on the opposite side. They have been told that the grace motif disincentivizes people from giving their best efforts to build God's kingdom – that these are people who have put their hand to the plow but having looked back are not fit for the kingdom (cf. Lk. 9:62). They shake their heads in disbelief. Those living in grace periodically glance over the chasm to see the sweaty religious workers, and they feel a sense of compassion for those enslaved to the religious work-ethic unaware that their best efforts are to no avail in God's economy.

Is there a bridge across the chasm whereby the religious workers might cross over into Graceland? Yes, it is a bridge that was constructed almost two millennia ago in the Person of Jesus Christ when He voluntarily submitted to be crucified on the cross of Calvary. It is a "narrow way" however, and few there are that pass over. The fear of grace instilled in the religious folks makes them think that grace is akin to social welfare, wherein lazy people are riding on the backs of the hard workers. Very few of the grace participants give any thought to crossing back over the bridge to religion, but occasionally there is one who succumbs to the temptation of religious fellowship with prior comrades.

HANDICAPPED?

Yes, I am quite aware that both of my legs were amputated earlier this year due to diabetes, and I am no longer ambulatory or mobile. Yes, I do have a "handicap placard" that I hang from the rearview mirror of our automobile when we park in "handicap parking spaces." Yes, I must use a "slider board" to transition from my wheelchair into the passenger seat of my wife's car, and then she must fold-up the wheelchair and lift it into the back of her car, before taking me wherever we must go – usually to one doctor's office after another. But I don't feel handicapped despite my limitations and disabilities.

The loss of my feet was the best thing that could have happened to me. When they cut off my feet, they cut off the pain of the neuropathy I had endured for several years forcing me to shuffle and use a cane and sometimes a walker. When the dead feet were removed, the pain was removed. Thank you, Lord!

Via Paul's "thorn in the flesh" (II Cor. 12:7-10), he learned to be content, and even to boast in his weakness that the grace of Jesus Christ might dwell and be operative in him. Paul indicated that he would choose the weaknesses that God's strength might be evidenced, rather than his own self-sufficiency. I have come to understand what Paul was saying. I would choose my physical limitations and disabilities in order that God's all-sufficient grace in Jesus Christ might be exhibited in the character of my life. I would choose the bilateral amputation of my lower legs again if thereby I could continue to be the vessel through whom the living Lord Jesus might manifest His life and character, and God could use such to His glory. The really handicapped person is the proud self-confident and self-sufficient person who thinks he can do everything by his own strength and "be all he can be." That person is handicapped by the humanistic lie that he can function as an "independent self."

MAY 27

GOOD AND EVIL

Satan's temptation of Adam and Eve in the Garden of Eve was that if they would eat from the forbidden tree of the knowledge of good and evil "you will be like God, knowing good and evil" (Gen. 3:5). Doesn't sound like an unreasonable conjecture, does it? They ate the fruit from the tree of the knowledge of good and evil and "God said, "Behold, the man has become like one of Us, knowing good and evil" (Gen. 3:22). It appears that Satan's suggestion had some degree of veracity, but on the other hand, we know that a half-truth is a whole lie. The question now is, "what does it mean to be like God, knowing good and evil?"

How does God know good and evil? "God is good" (Mk. 10:18), and anything consistent with and expressive of His good character is "good" (Gen.1:10,12,18,21). Anything not consistent with the inherent good character of God is necessarily "evil," and derived from the Evil One (I Jn. 3:8). Good is determined by the intrinisc character of God. So, how can man be like God, knowing good and evil? After the original couple rebelled against deriving from God and were necessarily deriving from "the spirit that is working in the sons of disobedience" (Eph. 2:2), they fallaciously thought that everything that they determined to be good was good, and everything they did not agree with was evil – self-determined "good and evil."

Such self-determined "good and evil" (really Satan-determined good and evil) was not actually like God's Self-determined "good and evil," for human creatures have no intrinsic character. Human beings are derivative creatures who derive character, direction, and energizing from a spirit-source. Humans are incapable of self-determining and self-generating either the character of good or evil out of themself (*ek autos*). The character of goodness is derived from God (*ek Theos*). The character of sin and evil is derived out of the devil (*ek diabolos*).

ARE WE ALL BORN "SINNERS"?

Short answer to the question – it all depends on what freight is carried by the word "sinners." We need to consider two scripture verses, one in the Old Testament and one in the New Testament that have been used to address the question before us:

The first is the comment of David in Psalm 51:5 which is variously translated: "I was brought forth in iniquity, and in sin my mother conceived me" (NASB). "I was born guilty, a sinner when my mother conceived me" (NRSVA). "I was born a sinner—yes, from the moment my mother conceived me" (NLT). Various theological premises underlie these translations. The Augustinian-Calvinist doctrine of "original sin" is often read into this verse to support the idea that Adam's sin tainted and corrupted all humanity leaving all men depraved and incapable of functioning as God designed humanity to function, incapable of responding to what God does for mankind in Jesus Christ. Their thesis – sinfulness is intrinsic to humanness from Adam onward – in other words Adam's sin undid God's creation of humanity, and reversed His declaration, "It is very good!" (Gen. 1:31).

The second verse we need to consider is Paul's assertion in Romans 5:19 that ""through the one man's disobedience the many were made sinners" (NASB). "All persons were made sinners as the result of the disobedience of one man" (GNT). "through the disobedience of one person many received the status of 'sinner'" (NTE). "through the disobedience of the one man many were constituted sinners" (NET). Neither this verse nor the previous verse document that any human being has an inherent character of sinfulness. Satan is inherently sinful – God is inherently righteous. Because of Adam's sin the entire human race was alienated from God, and every child is born with a spiritual identity of being a "sinner," based on the indwelling presence of "the spirit that works in the sons of disobedience" (Eph. 2:2) – i.e., Satan, the devil, the Evil One.

149

MAY 29

THE FATAL CHOICE AND THE CHOICE OF LIFE

God ushered Adam and Eve to the middle of the Garden and pointed out all the trees they were free to eat of, but also pointed out the one forbidden tree, the "tree of the knowledge of good and evil." "In the day that you eat of that tree," God explained, "dying you will die" (Gen. 2:17), i.e., the ominous death process will ensue. Enticed by the serpent's false statement, "You will not die," Adam and Eve made the fatal choice to partake of the fruit of the forbidden tree. Death set in that very moment. Death was not merely the absence of life but was the activity of "the one having the power of death, that is the devil" (Heb. 2:14).

Adam and Eve died spiritually that day with extended consequence for humanity. There was a spiritual exchange from the indwelling Spirit of life (Gen. 2:7; Jn. 6:63; Rom. 8:2) to "the spirit that works in the sons of disobedience" (Eph. 2:2), the spirit of death. Spiritually dead by the indwelling presence of Satan, sinful character began to permeate the desires of their soul issuing forth in behavioral "dead works" (Heb. 6:1; 9:14) which could not glorify God, the purpose for their existence (Isa. 43:7). The death process of the Evil One was operative in man and all would become "dead in trespasses and sins" (Eph. 2:1,5).

Spiritual death led to death permeation in soul and body, to the mortality of physical death. The life and death options for humanity were set up when Jesus, the Son of God having life in Himself (Jn. 5:26; 11:25; 14:6) chose to become a human being, avoiding spiritual death by His virgin birth but choosing to submit to physical death on the cross to destroy (I Jn. 3:8) and render powerless (Heb. 2:14) the death-dealing devil. Diabolic death could not hold the sinless Jesus (Acts 2:24), and by His resurrection to life out of death Jesus made divine life available to mankind in regeneration, the spiritual exchange from spiritual death to spiritual life. The choice is ours – life or death?

CULTURELESS CHRISTIANITY

Christianity, i.e., Christ-in-you-ity, can function in whatever cultural setting Christ-ones might find themselves. Christianity is, foundationally, the internal reality of the Spirit of the living Lord Jesus dwelling in the human spirit of a faith-receptive individual. That reality of the indwelling Jesus must then be lived out in practical behavior that exhibits the "fruit of the Spirit" (Gal. 5:22,23), the character of Christ, and such can be exhibited within whatever culture the Christ-one lives. It must be admitted that some cultural settings are easier than others to live out Christian thought and behavior, but it is possible within all.

Christianity is cultureless. It functions beyond (or should I say, spiritually "within"), the bounds of any culture. Christianity transcends culture, and is not to be equated with culture, nor should it have as its objective the conformity with or advocacy of any culture. The reality of Christianity cannot legitimately be assimilated with any distinct cultural phenomena and must always resist becoming enculturated with any cultural criteria. Perhaps the most insidious temptation is presented when a Christ-one is called upon to function within the religious culture of so-called Christian religion.

Religion can be, and inevitably is, enculturated. It often becomes syncretized with the culture and thereby synonymous with the culture wherein it operates. For example, it is nigh unto impossible to separate religion and culture in many societies around the world, whether the religion be Muslim, Hindu, Buddhism, Taoism, Shintoism, animism, or Christianism. Religion easily adapts to cultural behavioral regulations of the society where it finds itself, because that is the definition of religion ("bound to" expected regulations). The religion of American Christianism has adapted to the culture of conservative nationalism as well as to the culture of traditional liturgism.

MAY 31

COUNTERCULTURAL CHRISTIANITY

In the humanistic culture of our society, the gospel of Jesus Christ is like a square peg that some keep trying to pound into a round hole. The gospel is an anomaly that defies truth as society has determined it to be, i.e., the consensus of the majority.

Popular social culture keeps preaching the mantra, "you can be whatever you want to be." Since God Himself cannot do that, they must be elevating themselves higher than God, having a self-generating self-potential to be anything they can conceive – and anything they can conceive, they can allegedly achieve. Countercultural Christianity simply says, "Be available to all that God can be and do in you, and His perfect character of *agape* love will mold you into His highest good for you – for eternity.

A second tenet of the popular self-help gospel of humanistic self-betterment is the encouragement to individual striving to be successful in the false evaluative bubble of the world's standards of success. It's somewhat like climbing a ladder with no rungs. We were taught this philosophy on our mother's knee as she read to us *The Little Train That Could* with its repetitive self-talk, "I think I can; I think I can; I did it!" And those who are successful in such pseudo-success can sing with Sinatra, "I did it my way!" Counterculturally, Paul wrote, "To this end (to proclaim the gospel of "Christ in you, the hope of glory'), I strive with all the energy whereby Christ works (by His grace) in me." (Col. 1:29).

Human freedom, specifically individual freedoms, are the highest goal of all people in society, the popular culture maintains. Freedom, as they define such, is the right of independence to be and do all that you want to be and do. Counterculturally, we retort, "Man can never be an 'independent self', i.e., a god unto himself." God created us as derivative creatures, intended to depend on God in Jesus Christ and the Holy Spirit.

SPIRITUAL PARADIGM SHIFT

A paradigm is the cluster or collection of thoughts, opinions, and convictions one has about a particular subject. The word is taken from Greek, (*para* = beside or alongside; *deigma* = to show or demonstrate). However, what we want to address is more than just a paradigm shift in our collection or cluster of ideas, but a life-altering spiritual exchange from spiritual death to spiritual life within our human spirit that will necessarily provide a paradigm shift in our thinking and orientation.

There is "a spirit (the spirit of Satan) working in the sons of disobedience" (Eph. 2:2; I Jn. 5:19), and he is the source of death (Heb. 2:14), sin (I Jn. 3:8), and selfishness (Phil. 2:3). The spiritual exchange is clearly stated by God Himself to Saul who was being sent to share the gospel with the Gentiles, "that they might turn from darkness to light and from the dominion of Satan to God" (Acts 26:18). That commission encapsulates the spiritual exchange from the indwelling presence of and identification with Satan to the indwelling presence of and identification with God in Christ. If anyone has not experienced that spiritual exchange and "does not have the Spirit of Christ, that person does not belong to Him" (Rom. 8:9), i.e., is not a Christian. The bottom-line reality of being a Christian is the living Lord Jesus dwelling in one's spirit, and "the Spirit bears witness with our spirit that we are a child of God" Rom. 8:16).

Such a spiritual exchange from spiritual death, regenerated with the spiritual life of Jesus Christ dwelling in us, having "Christ in us, the hope of glory" (Col. 1:27), will necessarily provide a paradigm shift in the orientation or our thinking. Formerly "alienated and hostile in mind toward God" (Col. 1:21), the Christian has been given "the mind of Christ" (I Cor. 2:16) in spirit and is to be engaged in the transformation (paradigm shift) of the "renewing of one's mind" (Rom. 12:2) in the soul.

JUNE 2

"OUTSIDE OF THE BOX"

"Thinking outside of the box" is a figure of speech that means to think differently, unconventionally, or from a new perspective. The "box" being referred to is the mental parameters that constrain our consciousness, or the rules and traditions that limit our thinking of perceived possibilities. According to a *Psychology Today* article "Thinking Outside the Box: A Misguided Idea," was a concept originated with the work of psychologist J. P. Guilford, who, in the early 1970s, was one of the first academic researchers to conduct studies of human creativity, ingenuity, inventiveness, originality, and divergent thinking.

I am quite willing to own up to the fact that I have been one who thinks "outside of the box" with divergent thinking. I have never been satisfied with the status-quo thinking without considering other possibilities. Uncomfortable with "herd-mentality," I have always sought to think for myself. But "outside of the box" thought can be risky, and one must be willing to pay the price of personal criticism for not conforming to the acceptable "party line," the charges of arrogance for thinking that you need a bigger box than others, and the social ostracism of being "out of bounds" in other's thought, maybe even a "little bit crazy."

Divergent, "outside of the box" thinking, can also be applied to those who choose not to conform to the traditional religious "big-box" denominations. Interestingly, the independent and non-denominational groups are the fastest growing Christian categories in the U.S. today. Of even greater suspicion for being "outside of the box" are those who espouse a dynamic reality of Christ-in-you-ity that functions outside of the church-building boxes; those who conceive of an *ecclesia* without walls, a living organism that is Christ-centered and Spirit-led. The home-church movement is a burgeoning manifestation of vital Christianity that is "outside of the organized ecclesial boxes."

DARK MATTER AND DARK ENERGY

These matters of contemporary scientific conjecture are subject to the changing lenses of scientific observation and explanation. Current calculations speculate that ordinary visible matter (seen through our microscopes and telescopes) accounts for only 0.5 percent of the constitution of our universe. "Dark matter," an unseen component of our universe whose presence is discerned from its gravitation attraction rather than its luminosity, is thought to make up 30.1 percent of the matter-energy composition of the universe. "Dark energy," an unobservable counteractive force to gravity that causes the universe to expand is thought to comprise 69.4 percent of the universe.

Many scientists have admitted that these calculations are a matter of faith-speculation. These matters go far beyond the static-universe parameters of directly observable phenomena in the scientific exercises of the past, taking us to the theoretical considerations of a dynamic-universe wherein everything is in motion. Does this new science have any relation to the considerations of spiritual thought? One must use caution given the ever-changing perspectives of modern science, but we will draw some analogies nonetheless, aware of the dictum that states, "fools rush in where angels fear to tread."

Just as there was a necessary paradigm shift in the science of astrophysics, there is a needed shift in Christian theology from a static observation of known religious phenomena to a dynamic perspective of the expansive unseen grace-faith spiritual realities. The dynamic grace-attraction of divine activity in Christian experience has the counterforce of the repulsive dark energy of the Evil One. We praise the Triune God of the universe who "has rescued us from the domain of darkness and transferred us to the kingdom of His beloved Son" (Col. 1:13). He "called us out of darkness into His marvelous light" (I Pet. 2:9).

JUNE 4

GETTING THINGS ALL FIGURED OUT

It is a natural tendency of fallen mankind to want to get everything figured out. We think our human minds have unlimited potential capable of figuring out the most complex intricacies of any subject. There is an egoistic pride in the acquisition of such knowledge for when we think we have something figured out we think we "have a handle on that topic" and can control its usage. There is no doubt that mankind has figured out many intricate details of our created world, microscopic and macroscopic, by employing scientific methods and utilizing instruments for observing physical phenomena.

As much as we might seek to understand everything, our finite human understanding will never get everything figured out. The infinite knowledge and ways of God are past finding out. Job declared, "God does great things past finding out, Yes, marvelous things without number" (Job 9:10). Paul may have been considering Job's comments when he wrote, "O the depth of the riches both of the wisdom and knowledge of God! how unsearchable are his judgments, and his ways past finding out!" (Rom. 11:33). Man will never figure out the totality of God's created order, and certainly not the mysterious ways of God.

Many a human has been driven to madness trying to figure out every detail in a particular subject area. Philosophers and theologians have attempted to reason out the wisdom of men and the logic of God. Musician and artists have attempted to figure out every variation in their respective areas of expertise. Religionists have attempted to solve all the possible scenarios through eschatological speculations. We must cease our human quests to figure it all out. To know Jesus in personal relationship is the most important point any person needs to know. Beyond that, we trust God by being receptive to His ever unique and spontaneous manifestations in our lives.

NON-DENOMINATIONALISM

Traditional religious denominational leaders are having to take another look at the phenomenon of non-denominationalism. Recent social polls and surveys have indicated traditional religious denominations are declining drastically in membership and attendance numbers, while those Christians identifying themselves as "non-denominational" are increasing in much larger numbers. Some have said that those who identify as non-denominationalists have an identity crisis. They no longer identify as Lutheran Christians, Methodist Christians, or Baptist Christians, and just being a Christian has no meaning apart from a collective identity. That is ridiculous, for "the disciples in Antioch were first called 'Christians'" (Acts 11:26) without denominational affiliation.

Non-denominational groups of Christians are charged with being modern day personality cults. Some are, but most are not. One author stated, "Most non-denominational Christians are shallow and inconsistent in doctrine and practice." An unsubstantiated false charge! Other criticisms include absence of meaningful community, eclectic doctrinal standards, lack of behavioral consistency, and an individualized Christianity wherein everyone becomes their own denomination.

I think it is time for the denominational enthusiasts to examine their antiquated hierarchical structures, their perfunctory practices of worship, their lack of biblical support, and the extent to which their dogma has lost touch with the gospel of Jesus Christ. Christians are Christ-ones who understand that the living Lord Jesus lives within them. "The last Adam (Jesus) has become the life-giving Spirit" (I Cor. 15:45), and the Spirit of Christ is the dynamic leader and director of Christian individuals as well as collective groups of Christians. As for me, I want only to be denominated by my identity with and in Jesus Christ.

JUNE 6

KAIROS

Kairos is one of the Greek words for time. Another, more commonly known Greek word is *chronos*, from which we get "chronological" time, the kind of time that can be measured by clocks (seconds, minutes, hours) and even calendars (days, months, years). *Kairos* time cannot be measured by such instruments. It has been referred to as "God's time" or "those times when God breaks into human lives with the revelation of Himself" – a *kairos* God-moment within *chronos* time. If *kairos*-time is God's time or eternal-time, then *chronos*-time might be regarded as the temporal time wherein humans attempt to calculate human progress to become more than they really are?

In 1962, Madeleine L'Engle published a science-fiction young adult novel entitled *A Wrinkle in Time* wherein the characters engage in time-travel. Behind the storyline, she employs the interplay between *chronos* and *kairos* time. Her novel won the John Newberry Medal from the Association for Library Service to Children in 1963. The movie adaptation of the story, *A Wrinkle in Time*, was released by Disney Productions in 2018 with the common artistic license that excised the Christian elements of the story. The movie was not a box-office success. The story is about the battle between good and evil, and the triumph of love.

Whereas *chronos* is quantitative, *kairos* is qualitative. Paul Tillich referred to *kairos* as "the eternal breaking into the temporal." *Kairos* might be viewed as the existential moment when in God's perfect timing, He deems it the "right time" to speak to a person's heart in a meaningful manner – the appointed time in God's time when God does what He wants to do in a person's life, or even in history at large. When Jesus began His ministry, He said, "The *kairos* is fulfilled, the kingdom of God is at hand" (Mk. 1:15). Paul wrote, "Now is the acceptable *kairos*, behold, now is the day of salvation" (II Cor. 6:2).

INSIDE AND OUT

A Christ-one should be a person that others might observe and refer to as "beautiful inside and out" or "kind inside and out" or "gentle inside and out." The idiom "inside and out" first became common in English in the nineteenth century. The extreme opposite would be reference to a person as "having a depraved heart that is manifested in toxic influence of others." The idiom "inside and out" is particularly pertinent to describing a Christ-one who has the internal reality of the Triune God living in their spirit and allows the divine character to permeate into the mind, emotions, and decision-making of their soul, thus manifesting in their bodily behavior the character of Christ.

Everyone lives from the inside out, from a spirit-source that manifests character in ones' thought, emotions, and determinations. But it should be particularly obvious that a Christ-one has a distinctively different character and behavior than those of the world around them and stands out like a light in the world of darkness. We do not want a Christian faith that only affirms the inner spiritual reality of our spiritual identity and fails to allow the character of the Christ-live to be lived out in everyday behavior. Christian religion has become renowned for the kind of hypocrisy that wears a pasted-on "evangelical smile" and knows how to "put on the charm."

We want to have the character of Christ, the "fruit of the Spirit, which is love, joy, peace, patience, kindness, goodness, faithfulness, gentleness, and the Godly control of ourselves" (Gal. 5:22,23), exhibited in our behavioral actions. Like an unending artesian well that just keeps flowing from within the earth, we can "keep being filled with the Spirit" (Eph. 5:18) and thereby manifest the character of the living Lord Jesus from "the inside out." This is not a matter of "trying to be like Jesus," or "trying to be Christ-like;" it is the opportunity of allowing Jesus to be who He is "inside and out" of our lives.

JUNE 8

BE THE UNIQUE YOU THAT YOU ARE

David declares, "I will give thanks to You (God), for I am fearfully and wonderfully made; wonderful are Your works" (Ps.139:14). Another version reads, "I am Your *unique* creation, filled with wonder and awe" (*Voice*). Every person is unique, one of a kind. God doesn't create with a "cookie cutter" or a Xerox machine. The question is: Are we willing to be the unique ones that we are made to be? Are we willing to avoid all comparison with others, and attempts to be like the others? Are we willing to eschew the world's attempts to force us into egalitarian molds of conformity and sameness – to cause everyone to engage in "group-think" and "herd-mentality" so the world can control us? As Rhett says to Scarlett in *Gone with the Wind*, "The one unforgivable sin in any society – be different and be damned!"

Do you want to say with David, "It's so amazing to be the me that You, God, made me to be, and I want to express that singularity in the authenticity of being uniquely available to Your grace, even if that makes me idiosyncratic, unusual, and eccentric? Are you willing to stand out as unique in a way that drives our neurotic society, and its religious subset, crazy?

I have people say to me, "No one else seems to think or believe like you. No one else seems to teach what you are teaching." My response: "Well, everyone must think and teach what they know. I ponder and teach what I have come to know by the revelation of Jesus Christ as my life. If I am a lone voice in the wilderness of religion, the single anti-religionist who proclaims the living Jesus as life, then "so be it." I must be the unique me that I am. I must live life as I have chosen to let Jesus live life as me. Uniqueness is an attribute of those who determine to live life on God's terms, by His grace. I want to operate from the unique grace-giftedness by which Christ expresses Himself as me." Be the unique you that God created you to be!

"THE BEST LAID PLANS..."

Scottish poet, Robert (Robbie) Burns, wrote a poem, *To a Mouse*, after inadvertently plowing up the nest of a mother mouse and her young offspring. The most quoted words of the poem are, "The best laid plans of mice and men oft go awry." American author, John Steinbeck, picked up on Burns' words and wrote his novella, *Of Mice and Men*, about migrant farm workers in California in the 1930s. Both authors address the often-frustrated plans of mankind as various circumstances impinge upon our human plans and necessitate adjustments and acceptance of a plan greater than our own.

My wife had plans to retire from her position as a college professor so we could travel around the world together. She retired in 2020, right after the Covid-19 pandemic began. I soon began to have health problems. Three months after her retirement, we moved from CA to TX to be nearer to children and grandchildren. Less than two years later, I had both of my legs amputated due to diabetes. She saw her plans going down the drain. She claimed this verse as her verse of comfort. "For I know the plans I have for you, declares the Lord, plans for your good and not for evil, to give you a future and a hope" (Jere. 29:11).

There is often a disparity between the plans of men and the plans of God. James points this out, "Just a moment, now, you who say, 'We are going to such-and-such a city today or tomorrow. We shall stay there a year doing business and make a profit'! How do you know what will happen even tomorrow?" (James 4:13 JBP). Solomon, in his wisdom, made this clear: "The mind of man plans his way, But the Lord directs his steps. (Prov. 16:9). "Many plans are in a man's heart, but the counsel of the Lord will stand (Prov. 19:21). In submission to God, we must recognize that our "best laid plans" may have to be laid aside as God overrides them to arrange what is best for us.

JUNE 10

IN PROCESS

We do not want to forget that although we can affirm the wondrous spiritual realities that have transpired in our lives by means of the finished work of Christ, how by our spiritual regeneration we have become "new creatures in Christ" (II Cor. 5:17) with the nature of Christ in us (II Pet. 1:4) and a new identity as "Christ-ones," that does not mean that we have "arrived" at the completeness of what God wants to do in our lives. Paul wrote, "Not that I have already arrived, or obtained all that God has for me, but I press on to pursue and take hold of all that was taken hold of by Christ for me" (Phil. 3:12).

As Christians, we are continually "in process" because the Christ-life is dynamic, ever-moving, ever-growing, ever-pursuing the goal before us which is the fulness of Christ. (Yes, there is a paradox here: we have received His fulness, yet we pursue the fulness of Christ). We walk by faith (II Cor. 5:7; Col. 2:6) and the idea of "walk" implies forward movement and progress. We must not "go static," in our Christian life, thinking that the "rest" we have in Christ is like stopping at a "rest stop" on the highway, where we can "rest on our laurels" reiterating what Christ has done for us historically and experientially in the past.

We have not reached the end of the road in "the walk of obedience" (2 Jn. 1:6), walking in truth (3 Jn. 1:4) and love (Eph. 5:2). It's a paradox again: we have received all that God has for us in Jesus, but we continue to move forward toward all that God has for us in Jesus. We do not want to get "stuck," thinking that we have arrived, that we have everything figured out and have all the answers. Far too many are "stuck" in an undisciplined life, not moving forward on the journey, the trajectory of the unique purpose He has for each of our lives in expressing the Christ-life. We are all "in process" of "growing in the grace and knowledge of our Lord and Savior, Jesus Christ" (II Pet. 3:18).

THE "WORD OF GOD" IS JESUS

When the phrase "the word of God" is used in the New Testament it usually refers to the gospel. What else? ...Who else? ...is the gospel, but Jesus. The good news of the gospel is a Person, i.e., Jesus. When one proclaims or shares the gospel, they are necessarily sharing Jesus: not a message, not a philosophy, not principles, but the Person of the living Lord Jesus. It is obvious that "the Word" in the first chapter of John's gospel refers to Jesus. "In the beginning was the Word, and the Word was with God, and the Word was God" (Jn. 1:1). "The Word was made flesh and dwelt among us" (Jn. 1:14). Jesus is the Word of God.

Many contemporary Christians tend to use the phrase, "the word of God," in reference to the bible. The "word of God" is not a book, but the very Being of Jesus. How many times have we heard Christians read Hebrews 4:13, thinking that it refers to the bible. "The *word of God* is living and active and sharper than any two-edged sword, piercing as far as the division of soul and spirit, of both joints and marrow, and able to judge the thoughts and intentions of the heart." The very next verse goes on to say, "there is no creature hidden from *His* (God in Christ) sight, but all things are open and laid bare to the eyes of *Him* (God in Christ) with whom we have to do" (Heb. 4:14).

Paul wrote to the Thessalonian Christians, "We thank God that when you received the *word of God* (the gospel which is Jesus) which you heard from us, you accepted it (the gospel of Jesus) not as the word of men, but for what it (the gospel of Jesus) really is, the *word of God,* which also performs its work in you who believe" (I Thess. 2:13). We could read the final phrase as, "the *Word of God* (Jesus) who energizes in you who have faith (i.e., the receptivity of His activity)." We must beware of reverting back to a "religion of the book" like the Jewish religion which elevated the Torah text into an idolatrous position.

JUNE 12

CHRISTOCENTRIC CHRISTIANITY

Everything about Christianity is centered in the Person of Jesus Christ. Jesus was aware that everything He had to bring to the world was Himself. Jesus said, "I AM the way, the truth, and the life" (Jn. 14:6). "I AM the resurrection and the life" (Jn. 11:25). "Before Abraham was, I AM" (Jn. 8:58). The gospel is not a message about Jesus Christ to be passed on to others. Jesus is not the dispenser of an abstract salvation or eternal life package that is separate from Himself. The gospel is Jesus Christ and Him alone. Paul recognized the Christocentric reality of the gospel. "Christ Jesus became to us wisdom from God, and righteousness and sanctification, and redemption" (I Cor. 1:30).

What has been called "Christianity" for almost two millennia is but an empty shell apart from the living Lord Jesus. It is most unfortunate that the misrepresentation of Christianity called "Christian religion" has been just that, a misrepresentative shell of the reality of the Person and life of Jesus Christ – like a mollusk shell on the seashore wherein the organism within has died, yet people spend much time collecting their exoskeletons for their beauty and interesting shapes. Christian religion has always been concerned with the externals, the pomp and the circumstance, rather than the living reality of the Lord Jesus Christ.

Early Christianity was called "the Way" – the Way of Jesus Christ (Acts 9:2; 19:9), who is the Way. It is most unfortunate that the identification and union with Jesus was disconnected in a form best called "Christianism." (Any word ending in the affixed suffix "ism" is likely to be a man-made system of thought.) Everything that can rightly be called "Christian" is only found in the Person and life of Jesus Christ. Christianity is the Christocentric re-presentation of the Christ-life. We are Christ-ones who are partakers of the Christ-life, the "divine nature" (II Pet. 1:4).

IT'S ALL IN THE PERSON OF JESUS

Everything in the Christian gospel is comprised of, constituted of, and operative by the Person of Jesus. We're not referring just to the historical Person of Jesus in the first century, though that is the advent of His personal incarnational presence in the temporal realm, but we're talking about the risen and living Lord Jesus that is alive in every age and available to those who will receive Him by faith to become their indwelling life. The historical Jesus is the experiential Jesus, and the living Lord Jesus is the personal presence that constitutes everything Christian.

The "good news" of the gospel is the Person of Jesus.
Salvation is the saving activity of the Person of Jesus.
Grace is the dynamic energizing of the Person of Jesus.
The kingdom of God is the reign of the Person of Jesus.
The new covenant is God's arrangement in the Person of Jesus.
All of God's promises are fulfilled in the Person of Jesus.
All righteousness is in the Person of the Righteous One, Jesus.
All holiness is in the Person of the Holy One, Jesus.
All perfection is in the perfect Person of Jesus.
All goodness is in the Person of the divine Jesus.
All Love is in the Person of the divine Jesus.
The fullness of joy is in the Person of Jesus.
All peace is in the Prince of Peace, Jesus.
All hope is in the Person of Jesus.
The Spirit of Christ is the Person of Jesus.
The "fruit of the Spirit" is the character of Jesus.
Our spirit is meant to be occupied by the Person of Jesus.
The identity of a Christ-one is in the Person of Christ Jesus.
The church is comprised of the Person of Jesus.
All ministry is by the giftedness of the Person of Jesus.
All eschatological expectation is for the Person of Jesus.
All we have in heaven is the eternal life of the Person of Jesus.
Everything Christian is by means of the Person of Christ Jesus.

JUNE 14

JESUS PEOPLE

"The disciples were first called 'Christians' in Antioch" (Acts 11:26). Whether the designation "Christian" was first used as a term of denigration or derogation, we cannot be certain, but it was no doubt a term that referred to persons who were identified with the historical person of Jesus Christ. Considering the generalized use of the word "Christian" in our day, the designation seems to have been drained of any real meaning. The use of the label "Christian" has evolved to refer to a particular variety of religious person, perhaps a "Baptist Christian," a "Methodist Christian," a "Catholic Christian," a "charismatic Christian," etc., but it is a designation without meaning apart from an adjectival additive to clarify the type of religious person being referenced.

This is the reason why I have of late (last couple of years) been using the designation "Christ-ones" rather that the designation "Christians." By this term, I intend to refer to individuals who have received the risen and living Lord Jesus into their spirit and in whom the living Christ now resides. "Christ in you, the hope of glory" (Col. 1:27). Such designation of "Christ-ones" narrows and refines the somewhat ambiguous meaning of "Christians" as first used in reference to the believers in Antioch.

The designation "Christ-one" might rightfully be used synonymously with the designation "Jesus-person" because by such we want to indicate that it is the Person of the living Lord Jesus Christ that defines who we are. There was a movement referred to as "The Jesus People" in the 1970's among the avant-garde youth, sometimes referred to as "hippies," but it was eventually absorbed into charismatic Christianity. The designation of a Christ-one or a Jesus-person more specifically provides a meaningful name to Christ-indwelt believers indicating that the living Person of Jesus Christ forms their spiritual identity and character.

STANDING IN CHRIST

I am posting this just a few days after I was able to stand upright with my new prosthetic limbs and feet since the amputation of my lower legs – an almost five-month interval. I am like a one-year-old child learning to stand and walk, but it is farther down to the ground when I lose my balance and fall, and my seventy-five-year-old bones and skin do not fare as well as my latest grandson falling 12" on his diapered butt. My initial attempts have been most unsteady and wobbly, for learning to stand and walk with prosthetics requires finding a new center of gravity in the core of one's torso. It may take some time before I can walk across the room without parallel bars or a walker.

It takes time as we learn to stand and walk "in Christ" also. When we are spiritually newborn Christ-ones, we must learn to stand in Christ. This is more than what some call a "positional standing," as if we were standing on the parade grounds before God at attention, hands at our side, rigidly upright, static without twitching. Yes, Paul refers to "standing firm" (I Cor. 16:13; Eph. 6:11; Phil. 1:27; 4:1), but that does not mean a static standing without movement. Our standing in Christ is a dynamic standing that necessitates maintaining balance and is meant to lead to the dynamic peripatetic movement of walking in Christ.

We stand so we can walk. I am in that dynamic transition physically. The same is true in our spiritual life. We are to "walk in the light, as He is in the light" (I Jn. 1:7) for Jesus said, "whoever follows Me will never walk in darkness" (Jn. 8:12). We "walk in the way of love" (Eph. 5:2; II Jn. 1:6), "walking in the truth" (II Jn. 1:4; III Jn. 1:4), and we can only do so by "walking by the Spirit, so we will not gratify the desires of the flesh" (Gal. 5:16). Standing in Christ and walking in Christ are the dynamic outworking of His life within our human vessels. Jesus in on the move in us and manifesting His character wherever we go.

JUNE 16

FROM CROSSWAYS TO THE CROSS-WAY

Is there anyone who you are at odds with? Anyone with whom your relationship has gone crossways, and you are now at cross-purposes with that person? It seems to be the natural selfish way of mankind to demand one's own way and agenda, leading to conflicting ideas, opinions, and directions and thereby to relational clashes and engagement in disagreement with others. Are you crossways with your spouse? ...or your children? ...or your neighbors? ...or a friend? ...or a workplace colleague? ...or a brother or sister in Christ in the *ecclesia*? Such was the case in the *ecclesia* at Philippi between Euodia and Syntyche (4:2).

The well-known passage regarding the incarnation of Jesus as the God-man (2:5-11) has long been dissected as a theological discourse, but it is contextually located in Paul's epistle about practical personal relationships. Paul is using an analogy of the attitude of Jesus in becoming a human being to the attitude we need to have to reconcile and be of the same mind with our brothers and sisters in Christ. Jesus, knowing that He had the "same mind" as the Father, was willing to humble Himself and not grasp at His rights and privileges of equality, but deferred and become human, even accepting the mortality of humanity, humbling Himself "unto death, even death on the cross" (2:8).

Humanity had become crossways with God, alienated (Col. 1;21) from God. The Son of God was willing to become the God-man, the "one mediator between God and man" (I Tim. 2:5) who could reconcile man with God. By Jesus' willingness to become incarnate, to be the atoning death-sacrifice, and thus be exalted as Lord, He took the crossways relationship of God and man and via the CROSS-way reconciled God and man. Following the model of Jesus and by His living work in us, we too can take the CROSS-way of the Christ-life, putting aside selfishness, not looking out for our personal interests, but reconciling with others in love.

IS THERE A FEUD WITHIN THE TRINITY?

Western theology (at least for the last four hundred years) has given the impression that God the Father and God the Son are at odds with one another. God the Father is thought to be piqued and angry because of man's rebellion into sin. God the Son is thought to have lovingly agreed to take the consequence of man's sin in death to "pay the price" and reconcile God with mankind. This had led many Christians to think that the God of the Old Testament is a God of wrath and vengeance, whereas the God of the New Testament is a God of love who seeks reconciliation between God and man via the substitutional sacrifice of Jesus, the Son, "being obedience unto death" (Phil. 2:8).

The perceived feud between the divine Father and Son seems to be the popular outcome of the "Penal Substitution Model of the Atonement," that has been most prominent in Western theology since its explanation in the theology of John Calvin. Even if this is an unintended result of the legal and forensic interpretation that implies that a substitutional sacrifice was necessary to satisfy God the Father's justice or wrath, whereupon God could and would forgive the sin of mankind, it is nonetheless a popular perception among Christian people, and leads to the idea that there was a division and feud between Father and Son.

Such thought fails to maintain the oneness of the Trinity, for Father, Son, and Holy Spirit are always of one mind and purpose. When Jesus declared, "I and the Father are One" (Jn. 10:30; 17:11,21), He meant essentially one as well as of one mind and purpose. Proper understanding of the Trinity does not allow for severance or feud or differing mind and purposes in the Persons of the Trinity. The singularity and unity of the Persons of the Triune God acted as the One God that they are to draw humanity into participation in the loving and accepting fellowship with the loving interpersonal relations of the Trinity.

JUNE 18

WHAT ARE YOU LOOKING FOR?

Gabriel Marcel (1889-1973) was a French philosopher who distinguished between problem and mystery, noting that the approach is different in the disciplines that approach what they're looking for as a problem and those that approach what they're looking for as a mystery. In what are sometimes called the objective categories of science and mathematics, they address problems and seek determinative answers to those problems. In the more subjective categories of philosophy and theology, they address mysteries and seek personal awareness (even though logically indeterminate) of those mysteries.

Science demands external empirical observations and evidence to seek answers that they then establish as scientific theories equally as valid for every seeker. Mathematical problems seek quantitative answers that are objectively determined to be correct or not correct. Philosophy considers mysteries such as ontological being, the awareness of which will be subjectively differentiated by each personal being. Theology concerns itself with God and His creation of human beings, the mysteries of which can only be satisfied in the personal awareness of a qualitative I-Thou relationship between man and God.

Spirit-matters are obviously not hard science. The subject matter is not tangible or empirical. The "mystery of Christ" (Eph. 3:4; 5:32; Col. 2:2; 4:3) and the mystery of "Christ in you, the hope of glory" (Col. 1:27) can only be satisfied in personal awareness and relationship with the Spirit of Christ dwelling within our human spirit. Moral categories such as "good" and "evil" cannot find definitive answers in science or mathematics, and even philosophy and theology struggle to come to awareness of these abstract realities. The mysteries of good and evil only find experiential awareness in the character of the spirit-sources of the God who is good or in the Satanic Evil One.

"MIND THE GAP!"

Anyone who has ridden the subway, the "Underground," "The Tube" in London will recall the constant reminders at every station stop to "mind the gap," i.e., to be cautious of the gap between the train and the station platform as you enter or exit from the train. The gap differs at different stations – it may be minimal or up to 12 inches wide. They do not want passengers to inadvertently fall into the gap between the train and the platform. Life seems to be comprised of many treacherous gaps that we must navigate across and avoid falling into. Some of these are not small gaps; they appear more like a large crevasse or chasm that seems impossible to cross.

In my recent personal experience, such gaps came after the amputation of both of my feet. Very aware of the "gap" between the wheelchair and the places where I wanted to transfer my body, the most difficult transfer was from the wheelchair into and out of an automobile. Rehab therapists instructed us how to use an oak "slider board" to traverse over the imposing gap, but on more than one occasion, I have slipped into the gap when gravity pulled my torso down between the wheelchair and the seat of the automobile. How does one get up with no feet to assist? It requires upper-body strength and help from others.

The world around us seems to be filled with land mines and gravity-feed gaps. Some have fallen into the gap of drug addiction. Others have been pulled into the gap of sexual addiction. Others into the gap of acquisition and commercial shopping (even at "The Gap, Inc."). It is even possible to fall into the gap of isolated impersonalism. Satan seems to use every situation in life to create a self-oriented, self-destructive gap into which we might fall and thus fail to engage in the relationality of love with other Christ-ones. God's grace provides the means by which to cross over all the gaps that exist at every station in life.

JUNE 20

LEARNING TO LIVE LOVED

It is unimaginable for some to believe or comprehend what it means to be encompassed in the peaceful security of God's arms of love. This is especially true for those who did not experience a loving environment in the family of their youth. Some lived in abusive homes where parents were always at each other's throats, and they took it out on the children. Some children were abandoned (perhaps by death, divorce, or drugs), and had to develop "independent" survival skills of self-sufficiency which are hard to overcome as one learns to live loved in a personal relationship with God and in the family of God, the *ecclesia*.

Only when we know who we are as a Christ-one, a child of God, can we learn to live loved. Some may need to put aside all perceptions of an earthly father and his abuse to experience the loving Fatherhood of a kind and loving God. Those who lived in fear of a parent's response to what they were doing, or not doing, tend to transfer that kind of quivering fear to an angry God figure who is continuing to demand performance. "Perfect Love" (the Triune God) "casts out fear" (I Jn. 4:18). God loves us unconditionally – no performance required. There is nothing – nothing – nothing – we can do that will separate us from God's love and grace (Rom. 8:35-39).

Overcoming patterned "trust issues" takes time but learning to live loved in a loving relationship with God in Christ is worth all the time it takes. Jesus wants to lovingly free us from all our "issues." He wants us to be secure and at peace in His love. What a sense of freedom and security in learning to live loved. God loves me "just as I am" apart from anything I might do or not do. In fact, there is nothing I can do (not any sin) that will cause God to love me less. So, I can rest from all my performance concerns (whether I am doing it right or wrong), relaxed and contented and trusting in His love. I am His "beloved" one!

SEEING JESUS IN OUR SUFFERINGS

Suffering is part of human life in this fallen world. Such suffering takes many forms: physical suffering is not necessarily the most difficult sense of suffering, for there is psychological suffering in the mind, emotional suffering that can be so devastating as it lingers in our subconsciousness, and the suffering that results from our selfish decision-making. But the Christ-one must recognize that we are never alone in our suffering, though we are tempted to wallow in such a "separated concept." When we suffer, the living Lord Jesus is "one spirit" (I Cor. 6:17) with us, and He vicariously suffers in us and as us.

The inquiring minds of humans always ask the question, "Who caused this suffering?" We want to "pin it" on someone, some source-being on whom we can blame our sufferings. Though the Creator God is the ultimate cause of all things, He is never the cause of actions that are not consistent with His character; He is never the blameworthy or culpable cause of evil. Though they are unpleasant and uncomfortable, pain and suffering are not in every case to be identified with evil. God's good purposes (Rom. 8:28) can be realized in and through human suffering. Paul explained, "affliction is producing for us an eternal weight of glory far beyond all comparison" (II Cor. 4:17). "The sufferings of this present time are not worthy to be compared with the glory that is to be revealed to us" (Rom. 8:18).

Many people have said, "That hardship was the most difficult time of my life, yet at the same time, I can say, that was the most beneficial thing that ever happened in my life." In our trials and sufferings, we often learn the deeper realities of God and His ways. Suffering is the opportunity to allow Jesus to endure our pain and hardship with us. When we suffer, we should patiently wait until we see Jesus in our subjective experience of suffering, knowing that His eternality will see us through to His objective.

JUNE 22

"THE LIGHT OF THE WORLD"

The world (Greek *cosmos*) is a dark place. Physically, there is the darkness of outer space with its dark matter and dark energy. On the spiritual plane, we have the fallen world-system where Satan's power of darkness (Acts 26:18) prevails. Spiritual darkness is not merely the absence of light but is ontologically generated by Satan. In his gospel, John writes about the incarnated Son of God, "in him was life, and that life was the light of all mankind. The light shines in the darkness, but the darkness has not overcome it" (Jn. 1:4,5). Light overcomes darkness, rather than vice-versa. The positive overcomes the negative.

Jesus said, "I am the light of the world" (Jn. 8:12; 9:5). He also said to His followers, "You are the light of the world" (Matt. 5:14). We are only the light as He is the light in and through us. We do not self-generate our own light; it is His light that shines through us. "You were formerly darkness, but now you are Light in the Lord; walk as children of Light" (Eph. 5:8). "For God, who said, 'Let light shine out of darkness,' made his light to shine in our hearts to give us the light of the knowledge of God's glory displayed in the face of Christ" (II Cor. 4:6). "We proclaim the excellencies of Him who has called us out of darkness into His marvelous light" (I Pet. 2:9).

The Light who is Christ in us is more than a luminary in the abstraction of darkness. The practical character of divine light is evidenced in Jesus' admonition that we are to "let our light shine before men in such a way that they may see your good works and glorify the Father who is in heaven" (Matt. 5:16). Paul explained, "The fruit of the Light consists in all goodness and righteousness and truth" (Eph. 5:9). John adds, "The one who says he is in the Light and yet hates his brother is in the darkness until now. The one who loves his brother abides in the Light" (I Jn. 2:9-10). The luminance of God is the expressed character of God, His glory.

A FREEDOM MOVEMENT

There have been many "freedom movements" throughout history, as people have sought freedom from enslavement, persecution, and oppression, or freedom of speech, opportunity, and religion (religious freedom is an oxymoron). Many of these freedom movements were inspired by the rhetoric of such men as Mahatma Gandhi, Martin Luther King, and... could we, should we include Jesus?

Jesus began His public ministry by explaining His objective via a quotation from Isaiah 61: "The Spirit of the Lord is upon Me, because He anointed Me to preach the gospel to the poor; He has sent Me to proclaim release to the captives, to set free those who are oppressed..." (Lk. 4:18). The original Jesus movement might be viewed as a revolutionary freedom movement: freedom from the sin-slavery of Satan; freedom from the rigid conformity-strictures of the Law; freedom from the performance regulations of all religion. But such a Christian freedom movement must move beyond the "aginner mentality" of freedom *from* something to the positive mind-set of freedom *for* or freedom *to* a greater good, freedom *to* participate in the very life of the Lord Jesus both now and for eternity.

The message of the gospel is an advocacy of the freedom *to* use our God-given freedom of choice, freedom *to* discover that everything God has given to mankind is in the person of Jesus Christ, freedom *to* discover rest (Heb. 4:1-11) and "the peace that passes understanding" (Phil. 4:7), freedom *to* be the unique you that you are in Him, freedom *to* participate in the intimate spiritual realities and loving relations of the Trinity. "If the Son sets you free, you will be free indeed" (Jn. 8:36). "It was for freedom that Christ set us free; therefore, keep standing firm and do not be subject again to a yoke of slavery" (Gal. 5:1). "You were called to freedom, brethren..." (Gal. 5:13).

JUNE 24

WHO ARE YOU LISTENING TO?

Just as Herod "used to enjoy listening to John the Baptist" (Mk. 6:20) but ceased to do so, I used to enjoy listening to various preachers and teachers but can no longer stomach what they say. I will not do as Herod did and cut off their heads, but I can certainly turn off their incessant podcasts, videos, and social media and look elsewhere for meaningful input.

There was a time when I listened to conservative fundamentalist preachers, but I have ceased to do so because all they talk about is performance-works of what we should do to be right with God and go to heaven in the future. They have no understanding of all they have received "in Christ" or of the present dynamic reality of God's grace in Jesus Christ in Christ-ones. They are trying to get what they already have "in Christ."

In like manner, I have ceased to listen to the "exchanged life" teachers who want to participate in an exchange beyond the spiritual exchange (cf. Acts 26:18) that has already been realized "in Christ." They live in the historical and experiential past, focused on the "finished work" of Christ and how they have identified with such to have a new identity in Christ. They are camped out at the "rest stop," and have little to say about the practicalities of Jesus presently living in us today. They seem to be satisfied with where they are and who they have become and are content with their new identity and with their being "one with Jesus" in "spiritual union," even to the point of thinking they are Christ in their unique form.

I am looking for honest and authentic sharing about the dynamic of God's grace in Jesus Christ for everyday life ...with its problems ...with its sufferings ...with its problematic relationships ...with our stumbling and fumbling missteps in allowing the Christ-life to be lived out in our daily lives to the glory of God.

THOUGHTFUL UNCERTAINTY OF MYSTERY

Mark Twain is credited with the statement: "Education is the process of turning cocksure ignorance into thoughtful uncertainty." I would change the statement to: "Spiritual maturity is moving past cocksure ignorance to thoughtful uncertainty." The objective is not to get everything "figured out" so we can "know it all." Such fundamentalism ends up in a gross cerebral logjam and a perspective of God that is no larger than one's cranial brain-bucket. God is so much bigger than we can wrap our minds around. What we really desire is the infinite and eternal God who by revelation lets us in on what He's up to.

Christian theology has long recognized the necessary dialectic of apophatic and kataphatic theology. Apophatic is derived from two Greek words: *apo* = away from; *phaino* = to shed light. Away from and despite whatever light of understanding has been shed, God remains a mystery, an unknown God, an infinite God not capable of full understanding by our finite minds. Kataphatic is derived from two Greek words: *kata* = according to; *phaino* = to shed light. In accord with how God has revealed Himself in His creation and in His personal Self-revelation by His Son, God makes Himself known and receivable by our receiving Jesus.

To be able to hold the dialectic tension of the unknown God of mystery with the known God of Self-revelation is a sign of Christian maturity. We do not have to try to get God figured out in neat theological categories. We want our God to be personally and relationally approachable, but not manageable by human thought processes. It is because God is infinite and beyond human knowledge categories that we approach Him with the awe and reverence and worship that Divine mystery inspires. It is because God has made Himself known as a loving relational God in Jesus Christ that we can enter the holy place of relational intimacy with the Triune God.

JUNE 26

LORDING IT OVER OTHERS

Jesus referred to the rulers of the Gentiles who "lord it over others" and "exercise authority over the people" (Matt. 20:25; Mk.10:42; Lk. 22:25) to the extent that the people think that the authorities are their benefactors providing protection and monetary welfare. The people accept the oppressive authority because they think they are subject to and dependent on what the rulers can do for them. Jesus was contrasting such dominance and dependence with how it should be in the kingdom of God where Lordship is invested in Jesus Christ alone "having "all authority given to Him in heaven and on earth" (Matt. 28:18).

Writing to the Corinthians, Paul explained that "we do not lord it over your faith, but we are coworkers with you for your joy, that you may stand firm in your faith" (I Cor. 1:24). Even the apostles are not to be regarded as more important and elevated to positions of prestige over any other Christian in any age. "All are one in Christ Jesus" (Gal. 3:28). We are in the community of faith, the Body of Christ together and no one should have an advantage over or dominate another. Only the Lord Jesus Christ has the authority over our lives. If any other Christian claims to have authority over another and tries to subject another to their way of belief or practice, they should be avoided.

Writing to persecuted Christians living in Asia Minor, Peter cautioned the elders of the churches to "shepherd the flock of God among you, exercising oversight not under compulsion, but voluntarily ... not lording it over those allotted to your charge, but proving to be examples to the flock (I Pet. 5:1-3). Elders of local churches, and this includes those designated as pastors of local churches, should not claim an authority to dominate or compel or subject other Christians to think, believe, or act in the manner they deem acceptable. Be cautious of and avoid those who claim "pastoral authority" over you.

STATIC OR DYNAMIC?

Fallen humanity seems to want to get things figured out and to conceive of them in a static state. The purpose of both tendencies is that man might "get a handle" on the subject or object at hand and thereby to be in control of it, able to manipulate it for their own purposes. We begin with the subject of "salvation." Theologs have for centuries tried to develop an *ordo salutis* (order of salvation) to explain the steps that a man must take to possess salvation. In the process they have thought of salvation as a static object, debating whether the object is secure or can be lost. Ridiculous! Salvation is not something that can be put in a "safety box" for security. We are not "made safe" (Greek *sozo*) so we can put it (an object?) in a safe! Salvation is the dynamic function of the risen and living Lord and Savior, Jesus Christ, in our lives.

Those who seek to address more advanced spirituality refer to the Christ-one's spiritual identity in Christ, how the "finished work of Christ" (Jn. 19:30) allows us to partake of Christ's nature (II Pet. 1:4) and character, being made righteous, holy, and perfect. But even those realities can be regarded in a static sense indicating that the possession of the indwelling Christ and all that He provides in us makes us "heaven-ready," so for the present we need only rest and enjoy what we have in Him.

Everything in the Christian life is dynamic. We "serve a living Savior; He lives within our heart." I find it impossible to conceive of the "saving life of Christ" (Rom. 5:10) being static. Neither can I think that the resurrection-life of Jesus is static. He rose from the dead (static) to live (dynamic) in us. Can you imagine static "love, joy, peace, patience, kindness, goodness, faithfulness, gentleness" (Gal. 5:22,23)? Can righteousness, holiness, and perfection be static states of settled being? The Christ-life is living and dynamic as He manifests Himself in the behavior of our soul and body.

JUNE 28

SPIRIT, SOUL, AND BODY – ANOTHER LOOK

Man is a human being – not a divine being (like God) and not a spirit-being (as are the angels and the devil). A human being functions on three levels: spiritual function in the spirit; psychological function in the soul; physical function in the body (cf. I Thess. 5:23; Heb. 4:12). Man is a derivative being deriving spiritual nature, identity, life, and character from the Spirit of God or the spirit of Satan (I Cor. 2:12; Eph. 2:2; I Jn. 4:6). The human spirit has no capacity to function independently on its own, only the capacity to be a receptacle of one spirit or the other; otherwise, man would be a god-like "independent self."

Every human being comes into being with "the spirit that works in the sons of disobedience" (Eph. 2:2), i.e., Satan, indwelling in and functioning through the human spirit. The "whole world of fallen mankind lies in the Evil One" (I Jn. 5:19). That is why God told Saul (Acts 26:18) that men needed to be turned "from (ek = out of) the dominion (deriving out of the being of) Satan to the dominion of (deriving out of the Being of) God. This spiritual exchange is the essence of spiritual regeneration wherein the Spirit of the living Jesus is received into the human spirit, without which a person cannot be considered a Christ-one (Rom. 8:9

That is but the commencement of the gospel work of Jesus in His Christ-ones. The Spirit of Christ in the Christian brings His nature (II Pet. 1:4), His life (Jn. 14:6), His righteousness (Rom. 5:19), His mind (I Cor. 2:16), His character (Gal. 5:22,23) into our human spirit. The process must then ensue in the human soul of renewing the mind (Rom. 12:2; Eph. 4:23) to accommodate God's thought and wisdom; in our emotions to accommodate the divine love of God (I Jn. 3:10,14; 4:8,16), and in our human will to be receptive to the Will of God (Rom. 12:2; Col. 4:12). Christians thereby allow for the re-presentation and manifestation (II Cor. 4:10,11) of the Christ-life in their human behavior.

JUNE 29

OTHER PEOPLE'S PROBLEMS

You have no doubt noticed that some people, often emotionally
needy people, will try to drag you into their problems. Miserable
people want others to share their misery. Religious people often
attempt to do so by asking you to pray for them, then going into a
litany of their problems for which they want you to intercede
before God. How do you respond to such tactics? I am told that
the Polish have a proverb by which they explain that "it's not my
problem – not my issues. The proverb can be translated as, "Not
my circus – not my monkeys!" Humorous, but it can be construed
as a rather calloused unconcern for others.

We do not want to brush people off as if we are not concerned
about them or their problems. Neither is it wrong that they
should ask for prayer concerning their problems. The Lord Jesus
Christ in His earthly ministry always seemed to be sensitive to
people and their problems. Christ in us will be invested in other
people's problems, willing to come alongside as a *paraclete*
(comforter) and intercessor for others. But we are unable to deal
with all the problems of mankind. Each Christ-one must listen
under the promptings of God in obedience to ascertain when and
how Christ wants to be available to others in them.

God has allowed (or purposed) the specific set of circumstances,
problems, trials, and tribulations that each of us encounters in
our lives. It is not necessarily another person's responsibility to
deal with our problems. We are individually response-able to
make the necessary choices by which we confront and overcome
our "light and transient troubles" (II Cor. 4:17). As Christ-ones
we can exercise the faith-choices that allow for the "receptivity of
Christ's activity" whereby we cast our care on Him and trust Him
to exercise His love in seeking our highest good, amid which we
seek to be content even if the solutions to our problems are less
than pleasant or desirable.

JUNE 30

REWARD INCENTIVIZATION

Recognizing the self-orientation of natural man, the world's strategists encourage reward incentivization to provide tangible rewards to make the stated goals more attractive and entice people to work harder to increase the bottom-line. Companies offer bonuses and promotions to maximize productivity. Teachers offer shiny stars on homework and blue ribbons for those who excel. Such incentive-coerced performance achieves temporary results, but theorists in the fields of economics and education realized that such tangible rewards back-fired in the long-term, no longer producing the desired results.

Religion, which always follows along behind other world disciplines, began to employ reward incentivization to increase attendance and giving. Children and adults wore attendance pins with additional bars hanging to their belly button. Attractive (even expensive) Vacation Bible School prizes are awarded for those who bring the most friends to participate in V.B.S. Reward incentives for adults include year-end postings and bronze plaques for generous contributions, as well as leadership positions in the church for those who "go above and beyond" in their performance endeavors for the church.

Many religious church people are still incentivized by the enticing carrots of rewards such as more stars in their crown and a bigger mansion in heaven. Do these incentives educe or evoke any sense of godliness? No, only greedy and mercenary aspirations for tangible merit-rewards, which in the long-term instill hard-heartedness. Contrary to the world's ways, Jesus is the eternal fulfillment reward (II Cor. 1:21). All other rewards (cf. Matt. 5:12; 6:6,18; I Cor. 3:8,14; Col. 3:24; Heb. 11:6,26) are "in Him" and "of Him." God's grace prompts us to derive all from the Lord Jesus and allow Him to work all outcome results through us toward *Theosis* participation in the Triune deity.

BUT WHAT ABOUT ....?

Some people listen to the speaker, or the preacher, as he/she shares concerning all that has become ours in Jesus Christ. They affirm what has been shared, but then their comment is "but what about...."? They may want to go on and consider the very things that contradict what they have consented to; or proceed to consider the possible negations of what they have just affirmed. This is usually a quest to focus on their known experience of sin rather than on the Savior who has once and for all cancelled their sin in His death on the cross. Their attempt to "turn the table" of the discussion may reveal that they do not fully understand all that Jesus accomplished on their behalf – but maybe not!

We do not want to give the impression that it is not proper to seek to consider "the other side of the coin," the other options and possible variations of explaining the topic at hand.
It is also true that a truth can be presented in such a triumphalist manner that disallows any differing opinions, thereby appearing "too good to be true." When that occurs an honest seeker after truth will want to explore whether some points have been left unsaid in the speaker's gleeful recitation of the glories that are ours in Christ Jesus. There is a time to pose the difficult questions of seemingly contradictory avenues of thought.

When we refer to the objective triumph of Jesus Christ over all the powers of evil (cf. Col. 2:14) and the resultant spiritual condition wherein the living Lord Jesus reigns (Rom. 5:21) in our spirit and "leads us in triumph" (II Cor. 2:14), the "but what about...?" questions may not be an attempt to be objectionable, but an attempt to turn the discussion from the objective affirmation to the subjective consideration of the experiential conflict in the Christian life. Yes, the "flesh patterns" of selfish and sinful tendencies are present in the desires of our soul to counter the working of the Spirit of Christ (Gal. 5:16-21).

JULY 2

INCONSISTENCIES AND MISREPRESENTATIONS

All Christ-ones have inconsistencies and misrepresentations in their behavior. No, you are not the only one! Though we are perfect in our spiritual condition because of the Spirit-presence of the Perfect One, Jesus Christ (cf. Phil. 3:15; Heb. 10:14; 12:23), Paul explains that we are "not yet perfect" (Phil. 3:12) in the behavioral expression of His life but are in the process of "standing perfect and fully assured in the will of God" (Col. 4:12). Peter goes on to explain that "the God of all grace "will perfect, confirm, strengthen, and establish us" (I Pet. 5:10) as we continue to allow the Christ-life to be manifested in our behavior.

It is so easy to be self-deceived about the extent to which we are allowing the Christ-life to be expressed in our behavior. Some might think they are failing miserably at being available to the expression of the Christ-life, when really, they are being far too hard on themselves and need to lighten up and continue to be receptive in faith to what He wants to do in their lives. Others might think they are doing quite well in Christ's behavioral expression, when really their pride is deceiving them as to how well they are doing. Satan is so sneaky in his attempts to camouflage his selfish and sinful character in our behavior.

Self-evaluation of our progression in the process of manifesting the Christ-life behaviorally is susceptible to the falsification of Satan's misleading encouragement or discouragement. Satan's religious evaluators will also send false signals concerning whether we are adequately conforming to their legalistic criteria of growth and advancement. Each Christ-one must listen in obedience to the Spirit of Christ within to spiritually discern (I Cor. 2:14) how it is that the indwelling Lord Jesus desires that we avail ourselves to all that He wants to be and do in us, as He manifests His character to a watching world that is disenchanted with the charades of pseudo-Christianity.

PROGRESSSIVE REVELATION

Not one of us knows all there is to know about Jesus, the kingdom, or the new covenant. We are learners (disciples) who must always remain teachable, allowing the Spirit-teacher, to teach us all things (Jn. 14:26). The book of *Acts* provides an historical sketch of the progressive revelation of Jesus and His kingdom in the early church. When the Holy Spirit was poured out on Pentecost (Acts 2), He continued to reveal the implications of the risen and living Lord Jesus to the new believers. The early Christ-ones lived with a constant sense of awe as they learned from the Spirit how broad, expansive, and inclusive the Jesus-kingdom was intended to be.

In the early stages of this fledgling *ecclesia* of Christ-ones, they had to learn that the Holy Spirit was indeed the Person of the living Jesus (cf. Rom. 8:9; I Cor. 15:45; II Cor. 3:18), that the Holy Spirit, Jesus, and God the Father are inseparably One. They had to learn that discrimination against Gentile believers was not to be condoned in the Kingdom-Way (Acts 6:2-6). God loves all people with the same love (Gal. 3:28).

Even Peter, the Rock, had to learn by way of progressive revelation. The exclusivist superiority of his Jewish background had to be overcome by the inclusivism of the Kingdom wherein all peoples of all nations, Gentiles as well as Jews, could form a loving community (Acts 10). Perhaps the most difficult part of progressive revelation for the early Christ-ones was recognizing that Law was replaced by Grace as the operative and functional basis of Kingdom living. The Judaizers from the "mother-church" in Jerusalem fought this revelation everywhere Paul planted a church. All of Paul's letters promote the progressive revelation of freedom and liberty in Jesus Christ (cf. Gal. 5:1,13). On a personal level, we must continue to see that God is employing progressive revelation as He grows up other believers into Himself.

JULY 4

BREAKING OUT OF THE RELIGION BOX

Some people are born into the religion box because their parents were confined in the box at the time of their birth. They were soon thoroughly propagandized by all the believe-right, do-right religious dictums, having been told that only those in the box were "going to heaven." The religion-culture had a tight grip on the thought processes of everyone in the box, warning everyone that those outside of the box were "worldly," and worse yet "liberal." By such labelling of everyone other than the tight-knit group of fellow-ideologues, those in the box were granted the liberty to engage in the judgmentalism of castigating everyone who did not believe and behave as they were taught.

Occasionally, someone in the religion box looked through a knothole in the box to observe what people are doing outside of the box. At first, they are aghast that these persons seemed to be breaking all the carefully crafted rules of religious thought and practice. But further observation showed that those on the outside enjoyed a sense of light-heartedness, joy, and incomprehensible freedom. For varying reasons, some slipped through a crack in the box and made their exit from the controlled oppressiveness of living in the box.

Breaking out of the religion box has its own trials. Many of one's friends and acquaintances are still wrapped up in "box-think," the closed-minded introverted perspective that everything occurring in the world is to be evaluated by how it affects those in the religion box. One must be cautious of not offending these prior box-mates, while still desiring to share with them the freedom that can be enjoyed in simply living the Christ-life in whatever context one might find oneself (even to some extent while visiting the religion-box). It is agonizingly painful to be patient until God reveals to others that real life and freedom of thought are found in Jesus, usually outside of the box.

MIGRANTS, FOREIGNERS, AND REFUGEES

Living, as we do, in south-central Texas, we are as close to the southern border of the United States as we were when we lived in southern California, San Diego County. This forces us to consider God's perspective concerning people who cross the border into another country seeking safety from persecution and violence, seeking to find a place beyond the poverty and starvation they have been subjected to, seeking employment to care and raise their families. Much of the time they do not have the legal paperwork necessary to cross the U.S. border but are simply needy people desperate for a sustainable life.

We must see God's perspective for such hurting people. There is no doubt that God loves these down-and-out people because God loves all people. Many of Jesus' parables were about people who were lowly, lost, "losers" in social standing, those with the least skills and assets, and Jesus was addressing the religious people concerning their attitudes toward such people. Do we see Jesus in these people who are crying for mercy and grace, desiring a way out of their morass, begging for an opportunity to better themselves? Jesus said, "Inasmuch as you have done it to the least of these, you have done it unto Me" (Matt. 25:35-45).

Fully cognizant of the right and responsibility of any sovereign nation to control the ingress and egress across their borders, our national leadership must take care of such. My concern as a Christ-one is to express loving care for people and their needs, regardless of race, gender, social status, nationality, etc. The scripture has much to say about concern and care for the foreigner, the stranger, the alien, and refugees: we must not oppress them or do them wrong; we are to love them and provide sustenance for them, even show hospitality to such peoples (Heb. 13:2). When Jesus lives within us as our life, He will always approach the uprooted migrants, foreigners, and refugees with compassion.

JULY 6

MEASURING ONE'S PROGRESS

In a world where technique reigns supreme and there are ever-increasing technological apps to measure one's progress and performance in every activity of life, it becomes quite counterintuitive and even blasphemous in the world's understanding that we should be unconcerned about our progress. Religion, being the world's handmaiden, has likewise used techniques, formulas, and how-to procedures to attempt measurement evaluation of one's progress in the Christian life. The world's ways of progress-measurement know nothing of how God views our spiritual growth effected by His grace.

When we are concerned about measurement of our spiritual progress our focus is inevitably on ourselves – us – rather than on God in Christ moving by His Spirit. Spiritual realities and the movement of the Spirit in our lives is God's business – certainly not the business of any religious evaluators – and should be none of our business for it fosters self-concern about how well we think we are doing in what only God can manage. There are no measurement standards for progress in spiritual growth – we can only trust that God knows what He is doing in bringing His children along for His own unique purposes.

It is but a tragicomedy to observe how the disciplines of psychology, sociology, religion, and spirituality run around in circles trying to establish an objective empirical base to measure what only God can orchestrate. As one academic stated, "Spirituality lacks a ground in empirical evidence and is therefore incapable of objective measurement. That is why those demanding scientific evidence for such often conclude that spiritual growth is just an airy-fairy exercise for those inclined to be involved in such." That is an accurate assessment from the view of scientific objectivity! Christ-ones must live with such ambiguity as they "walk by the Spirit" (Rom. 8:4; Gal. 5:16,25) unconcerned with measuring their progress.

LEARNING OBEDIENCE THROUGH SUFFERING

In his epistle to the Hebrews, Paul explained that Jesus was "like us" in all ways (Heb. 2:17) except that He did not succumb to the temptation of the tempter (Heb. 4:15) and misrepresent His divine nature and character. Because of His being tempted in all that He suffered (Heb. 2:18) and not surrendering to the tempter, the living Lord Jesus is able to come to the aid of those who are still being tempted. In submitting to the acceptance of humanity, though never less than God, He accepted the human derivative function that required His deriving all from the Father by faith – human receptivity of divine activity – nothing of His own initiative (cf. Jn. 5:30, 8:28; 12:49; 14:10).

Paul proceeds to explain that "although He was a Son, He learned obedience from the things which He suffered" (Heb. 5:8). Here, we must recognize that obedience in the new covenant era is not the same as legalistic obedience to the Law in the old covenant era. In the new covenant wherein God dwells in mankind once again, obedience is the Greek word *hupakouo* (*hupo* = under; *akouo* = to listen or hear), "to listen under" God's voice and direction to ascertain what it is that He wants to be and do in us. Jesus listened and learned from the Father in order to be obedient as a human being in the midst of human suffering.

How, then, did Jesus "learn obedience from the things which He suffered?" In the midst of His human suffering, He was "listening under" the Father's direction, learning to derive all His responses to the pain and suffering that was occurring against Him by faithful receptivity of the Father's grace provision. Do we also learn obedience through what we suffer? No doubt! We, too, listen under the direction of the indwelling Lord Jesus amid the inevitable pain and suffering of living in this world, aware that "affliction is producing for us an eternal weight of glory far beyond all comparison" (II Cor. 4:17; cf. Rom. 8:18).

JULY 8

OUTLANDISH GRACE

The one-of-a-kind Episcopalian priest, Robert Farrar Capon (1925-2013), provided many outlandish, yet astute and accurate statements, about the radical grace of God in Jesus Christ. I share a few of them with you:

"Grace doesn't sell; you can hardly even give it away, because it works only for losers and no one wants to stand in their line. The world of winners will buy case lots of moral advice, grosses of guilt-edged prohibitions, skids of self-improvement techniques, and whole truckloads of transcendental hot air. But it will not accept free forgiveness because that threatens to let the riffraff into the Supper of the Lamb."

"Even to this day, grace remains hard to swallow. Religiosity and moralism go down easier than free forgiveness."

"Grace cannot prevail until our lifelong certainty that someone is keeping score has run out of steam and collapsed." (May I add: Until we realize that God is not a scorekeeper in the game of life, and only wants to be the energizer of all we do by His grace, then and only then can we sigh a great sign of relief and get on with Jesus' desire to live life as us.)

"Anything authentically Christian is going to have to keep off the kick of human merit and demerit and stick resolutely to a universal grace that overrides the subject of human works."

"The life of grace is not an effort on our part to achieve a goal we set ourselves. It is a continually renewed attempt simply to believe that someone else has done all the achieving that is needed and to live in relationship with that person."

"Grace is the celebration of life, relentlessly hounding all the non-celebrants in the world. It is a floating, cosmic bash shouting its way through the streets of the universe, flinging the sweetness of its cassations to every window, pounding at every door in a hilarity beyond all liking and happening, until the prodigals come out at last and dance, and the elder brothers finally take their fingers out of their ears."

ANTI-RELIGION

I have been accused of being an anti-religionist. I plead guilty!
I am in good company, as these witnesses attest:

"The revelation of God (*Jesus*) – The Abolition of Religion" (Karl Barth)

"Christianity is not a religion. Christianity is the proclamation of the end of religion, not of a new religion, or even of the best of all religions. If the cross is the sign of anything, it's the sign that God has gone out of the religion business and solved all of the world's problems without requiring a single human being to do a single religious thing. What the cross is actually a sign of is the fact that religion can't do a thing about the world's problems - that it never did work and it never will." (Robert Farrar Capon)

"When Christianity first appeared in the world, nobody called it a religion. It wasn't seen as another religion. It was called the "anti-religion." The Romans called the Christians for two hundred years "atheists.' And the reason was that the Romans understood that what Christianity was saying about God was so different than what any other religion, that it really shouldn't be given the same name. It's in a whole other category all together – and they were right." (an historian quoted by Tim Keller)

"Christianity is not a religion. Religion is humans trying to work their way to God through good works. Christianity is God coming to men and women through Jesus Christ." (Josh McDowell)

"Made up religions always rely, one way or another, on works. There is something which must be done in order to achieve the goal. But the idea that salvation is a gift from God (Ephesians 2:8-9) is the heart of the Christian message and not the sort of thing anyone would have made up." (C.S. Lewis)

I rest my case: Christianity is NOT religion! (Acts 17:22; Col. 2:23)

JULY 10

GOD'S SMUGGLER

A book by this title was published in 1964, written by John and Elizabeth Sherrill recounting thrilling events in the life of "Brother Andrew" (Andrew van der Bijl), a Dutch Christian who was led to smuggle Bibles into Communist countries after World War II. Andrew founded Open Doors Ministries to encourage others to share the message of Christ in countries whose borders were closed to mission activity. Later, as Communism began to wane, the thrust of the ministry was expanded to the closed doors of the Muslim countries and peoples. A film was made of "Brother Andrew" and his life in 2014.

Soren Kierkegaard, the Danish Christian thinker, regarded himself as a spy whose mission was "to smuggle Christianity back into Christendom." He commented on how difficult it was to explain what it really meant to be a Christian with those who thought they were Christians already because they were born into the state church. I can identify with Kierkegaard, as I want to share the message of the indwelling spiritual life in Christ Jesus to those who think they have life already because they walked down the aisle and joined the church. I am seeking to infiltrate the "closed doors" of institutional Christian religion with the message of a living Lord Jesus and His abundant life.

Soren Kierkegaard wrote, "The human race in the course of time has taken the liberty of softening and softening Christianity until at last we have contrived to make it exactly the opposite of what it is in the New Testament." Sad to say, but that is certainly what has happened, and it began to happen in the first centuries of the church's history and has only progressed in worse and worse forms through the years and the centuries. Whereas "Brother Andrew" was known as the "God Smuggler," I would prefer to be known as the Jesus Smuggler, seeking to smuggle the message of Jesus behind the lines of churchianity.

TRIFUNCTIONALITY

God created human beings to function on three levels. The most externally observable is the physiological function of human bodies. Beneath the surface of the body and its function is the psychological mental function of the human mind, the feelings and affections of the human emotions, and the volitional freedom of choice in the human will. At the core of one's being as a human being is the spiritual function of necessary receptivity to and residency of a spirit-being that serves as the source of character within the psychological behavioral function and the physiological function and expression of that behavior externally.

These three levels of human function are exercised in every activity that a human being might be involved. The apostle Paul prays that the God of peace might set us apart to function properly and entirely, and that our spirit function, soul function, and body function might remain intact without faulty dysfunction unto the coming of our Lord Jesus Christ (cf. I Thess. 5:23). Such complete trifunctionality of human activity is preserved as the *logos* of God personified in the Son of God, Jesus Christ, serves to properly sort and divide the psychological thoughts of our soul and His spiritual intents in our spirit (cf. Heb. 4:12) to facilitate expression of His character in our body.

The anthropocentric humanism that has prevailed since mankind succumbed to the lie of the alternative spirit (Satan) in the garden keeps advocating that a human being is an independent self-operative being (like God) serving as his own source of determination and implemented action (free-will). The mistaken teaching of Christian religion has correspondingly failed to recognize the necessary spirit-source of derived human functionality, by perpetuating the muddled and undistinguished merging of psychological and spiritual functionality, thus failing to appreciate the trifunctionality of human beings.

JULY 12

THE CHARACTER OF GOD

Consideration of the Triune God (Christian theology) must begin and end with the character of God. Our thoughts of God must begin with the essential character of God (Who He is in Himself, *a se, en autos*) and end with the expressed character of God in His people whom He indwells and manifests Himself through their behavior. The essential character of God is distinct and unique to God – there is none like Him (I Chron. 17:20). What God is, only God is! The Triune God desired to make Himself known to the personal human beings He created, and by the revelation of Himself in creation and especially in the incarnated Son, He manifested and expressed His nature and character.

The essential character of God has often been discussed in terms of the attributes of God, and then subdivided into non-transferrable and transferrable attributes. Since God uniquely does what He does, because He is Who He is, it is best to say that God's essential character is completely non-transferrable, but that does not mean that He does not invite us to be participants in His character. His essential character (*homoousion* - same being) was exhibited in the incarnate Son who is the "exact character and nature" and evidences the glory of God's character (Heb. 1:3) ."If you have seen Me, you have seen the Father" (Jn. 14:9). We can be partakers of the divine nature (II Pet. 1:4).

The expressed character of God was made visible when Jesus, the Son, served as "the image of God" (II Cor. 4:4; Col. 1:15). "We all, are being transformed into the same image from glory to glory, just as from the Lord, the Spirit" (II Cor. 3:18). The visible manifestation of the character of God in Christ-ones is not something we can produce by our performance. It is always God expressing Himself in us, through us, as us – the "life of Jesus manifested in our mortal bodies" (II Cor. 4:10,11). The obviation of the expression of divine character is made evident is the expression of love and righteousness in our behavior (I Jn. 3:10).

THE GOSPEL IS NOT A SYSTEM OF MORALS

Those who conceive of the gospel of Jesus Christ as but another system of morality are gravely mistaken. The gospel is not a moral prescription; it is the Person of the risen and living Lord Jesus desirous of being received by faith into the spiritual core of our being to be our Life. Morality is external conformity to the social mores of a distinct social grouping, to the laws of social governance in the tribe or in the grouping wherein one might participate. Yes, morality can be legislated; morality standards are often made a matter of governmental law. Murder, rape, theft, abortion – there are laws governing these actions.

But the purpose of the Christ-community is not to engage in the morals business. That is the world's business, and they spend much time and energy categorizing actions into right and wrong, good from bad, acceptable or non-acceptable, trying to sort out "the tree of the knowledge of good and evil" (Gen. 2:17). It's a dead-end task energized by "the one having the power of death, that is the devil" (Heb. 2:14). Religion, the moralistic handmaid of the world-system, is particularly adept at formulizing behavior in moral standards of "the good and evil game," and they have convinced people that such constitutes Christianity.

Just because religion and the world make moral codes, and endeavor to compel people to conform obediently to the social-moral laws does not, and will not, result in a righteous social order. They can banter about ethics and morality until they are blue in the face, but it is "much ado about nothing" (Wm. Shakespeare) when contrasted with God's intent in Jesus Christ to image His character from the inside out (spirit, soul, body), manifesting the indwelling life of Jesus in our mortal bodies (II Cor. 4:10,11). The Spirit of Christ within the spirit of the Christ-one is necessary for the manifestation of the "fruit of the Spirit" ((Gal. 5:22,23), the character of Christ in Christian behavior.

JULY 14

PARENTING ADULT CHILDREN

Just because your children grow up and become adults does not mean that they are not still your children, and you are not still their parents. But there is a big difference between their being your legal and biological children and maintaining a long-term relationship between parent and child as adults. There are some children who are so desirous to "fly the coop" that they leave and never look back. They don't even attempt to maintain an ongoing relationship with their parents – so much for "Honor your father and mother." On the other hand, there are children who make no attempt to leave the nest to develop an independent life apart from their parents. Some children must be asked to leave the home to learn what it means to be a responsible adult.

The ideal is that a child has been prepared by the parents to face the challenges of life as an adult, nurtured and instructed how to navigate the difficulties of relationships, finances, job responsibilities, and social interactions; prepared to become an adult who can live independent of their parents. Otherwise, we observe the sad situations where adult children remain dependent on their parents, or *vice versa*. There are parents who are codependent on the neediness of a grown child, and there are grown children who are codependent, to the point of being held emotionally hostage to the neediness of a parent.

A healthy relationship between parents and adult children will necessarily involve respect for the adulthood of the child, allowing them to be independent to the extent that they can fail and learn how to resolve the problems of their own making. Parents should be available and responsive but should not "butt in" or meddle in the lives of their adult children. Be a good listener and encourager but avoid any unsolicited advice. If the adult child is married, respect the privacy of their home, and avoid expressing opinions about their spouse or children.

TO KNOW JESUS IS TO KNOW GOD

The greatest and highest desire among mankind is to know God. No greater quest and no deeper desire can be found among mankind. We are not referring to the knowing of informational knowledge, but to the relational knowing of intimate oneness. Paul explained, "the world through its wisdom did not know God" (I Cor. 1:21). He goes on to explain, "when you did not know God, you were slaves to those which by nature are no gods" (Gal. 4:8), i.e., idolatrous false gods. But we do not come to know God by our human seeking. Those who "come to know God, or rather to be known by God (Gal. 4:9) are only responding to God's knowing of us through His Son, Jesus.

To know God in intimate personal relationship is unlike any other personal relationship among mankind. "No one knows the Father except the Son and those to whom the Son chooses to reveal him" (Matthew 11:27). "Anyone who has seen me," Jesus said, "has seen the Father" (John 14:9). To see God with spiritual eyes is to know Him. To know God, one must know Jesus, receiving Him by faith to dwell in the spirit-core of our being. "If anyone does not have the Spirit of Christ, he does not belong to Him" (Rom. 8:9) and does not know God. To know God is to participate in the Triune Godhead, Father, Son, and Holy Spirit.

To know God is to receive Jesus, His life and character, and to allow His character to be manifested through us. "The one who does not love does not know God, for God is love" (I Jn. 4:8). "Everyone who loves is born of God and knows God" (I Jn. 4:7). A dying soldier asked the chaplain, "Is God like Jesus?" The chaplain assured him that to see Jesus was to see God. To know Jesus is to know God. To know God is to be spiritually united with the Triune Godhead and to be an available vessel to share the divine life and character with others. Jesus told His disciples, "No one comes to the Father but through Me" (Jn. 14:6).

JULY 16

ATTRACTED BY A LURE OR ALLURE?

The words "lure" and "allure" are sometimes used synonymously, but there is a definite difference, and often it is whether the attraction has negative (destructive) or positive (constructive) purposes. The word "lure" is likely derived from the Germanic word *luder* meaning "bait," used in training hawks and eventually in fishing. The word "allure" on the other hand is derived from the Old French *alure* or *aleure* meaning "walk" or "gait," and means to be drawn towards and to move towards that which is appealing. We need to consider how the attraction is used by the contrasting spirit-beings of Satan and God.

Satan, the tempter, lures people into his character and action by enticing them by guile and deception, seeking to seduce and entrap them with his baited solicitations. This can be seen in James 1:14, "each person is tempted (by the tempter) being lured and enticed under their own desires." Using a fishing metaphor, James explains how the tempter lures and entices us to evil. The same Greek word *deleazo* is used in II Pet. 2:14 of the false teachers "who having eyes full of adultery that never cease from sin, enticing (*deleazo*) unstable souls," and in II Pet. 2:18 of how "they entice (*deleazo*) by fleshly desires, by sensuality." Satan lures people by the enticement to self-satisfying evil.

God in Christ and by the Holy Spirit, on the other hand, uses the alluring attraction of the quality of His own character to draw men to Himself. The allure of God's love in Jesus Christ is the attractive quality by which He invites us into a love relationship with Himself. The Greek word *helkuo* meaning "to draw or attract by an inward power" is used by Jesus in John 6:44, "No one can come to Me unless the Father who sent Me draws (*helkuso*) him," and in Jn. 12:32, ""When I am lifted up from the earth, I will draw (*helkuso*) all people to myself." The attraction and allure of God's character of love invites us into His Triune love.

ACCEPTING THE CIRCUMSTANCES

How does one keep standing firm with all that is happening around us? How do we react when it seems like we are encircled by sharks? The English word "circumstance" is derived from Latin: *circum* = around; *stance* = to stand. When confronted with all the situations that encompass us, or stand around us, how do we keep standing with our head above water?

We all have unexpected circumstances that break into our lives. Situations that pierce our status-quo of the way we planned and expected life to go. The New Testament Greek word is *peirasmoi*, meaning "to pierce in order to test." It is translated as "trials, tests, temptations, even troubles." Modern Greek translates this word as "experiences." Paul explained, "No (*peirasmos*) trial/temptation/experience/test has overtaken you but such as is common to man; and God is faithful, who will not allow you to be *peirazoed* tested/tempted beyond what you are able, but with the *peirasmos* trial/temptation/test/experience will provide the way to move beyond and the power to endure it" (I Cor. 10:13). These trials or circumstances may include accidents, diseases like cancer and diabetes, the idiosyncrasies of our spouse, the rejection by our children, even destructive addictive tendencies.

It certainly does not help to claim that we are a "victim" of our circumstances. "Poor me, I am buried under the circumstances." What are you doing under there? "Well, everything is piled up against me. Life is not going my way. Life's not fair. I'm not happy. This is all bad! Why do bad things happen to good people?" Our self-orientation tries to make it into a moral dilemma, but it is just a choice of faith. Will we be receptive to the activity of God's all sufficient grace and strength to be the necessary empowerment to move forward? It was so for the Israelites in the wilderness: "The way out of this desert is through the desert" by God's provision.

JULY 18

ADAPTING TO CHANGING CIRCUMSTANCES

Most will be familiar with the "Serenity Prayer" written by American theologian, Reinhold Niebuhr, and made popular by its use in the twelve-step anonymity groups such as Alcoholics Anonymous:

> God, grant me the serenity to accept the things I cannot change,
> courage to change the things I can,
> and wisdom to know the difference.

After acceptance of the changing circumstances there comes the necessary process of adapting to the changes. This adaptation often involves adjusting to a "new normal" wherein things will never be the same as before. After the amputation of both of my feet, I will never walk in the same manner that I did before, but I can accept the "new normal" of learning to walk with prosthetics.

We are meant to be overcomers, not letting the circumstances overwhelm us, rising above the occasion to recognize the sovereign God is in control and "all things work together for good for those who love the Lord" (Rom. 8:28). That does not mean that we will consider everything to "be good," but we know that "God is good" (Lk. 18:19) and we can thank Him for His "good grace" in all circumstances (Eph 5:20; I Thess. 5:18).

We must always remember that life is not in the circumstances, but life is in Christ Jesus (cf. Jn. 14:6). The life that we receive in Jesus is the life that functions, prevails, and overcomes whatever the circumstances might be. It is the life that has been tested and proven in the incarnated life of our Lord and is now made available to receptive individuals. This life of Jesus has been tested in the crucible (a word derived from crucifixion on a cross) and rose victorious in the resurrection – life out of death. His life can adapt to all changing circumstances.

GOD IS FAITHFUL

God is faithful, does no wrong, and is always upright and just. He is as faithful as an unmovable Rock, and always works in perfection." (Deut. 32:4)

God is faithful to fulfill His every promise. Not one of His good promises to Israel in the old covenant ever failed, every one of them was fulfilled." (Josh. 21:45).

God is faithful and will not withhold His mercy from His people. His loving faithfulness is always present to protect His children." (Ps. 40:11)

God is faithful, and because of His perfect love we are not consumed or destroyed. His compassions never fail; they are new every morning." (Lam. 3:23,24)

God is faithful to not allow us to experience any situation but what His provision of grace is sufficient to see us through the situation to His glory. (I Cor. 10:13)

God is faithful to have called us to Himself in His Son, Jesus Christ, and thereupon He will bring to pass all that He wants to do in our lives. (I Thess. 5:24)

God is faithful, and by the work of His Son, Jesus, He protects us from the Evil One, and provides us with the strength to persevere." (II Thess. 3:3)

God is faithful. Even though we are oftentimes faithless, He cannot disown Himself or violate His character of faithfulness." (II Tim. 2:13).

God is faithful to forgive our sins and cleanse from all unrighteousness when we agree with Him that sin is sin, a transgressing of His character. (I Jn. 1:9)

JULY 20

TRYING OR TRUSTING

There are two ways of dealing with the inevitable problems of life. They can be boiled down into man's way of trying to solve his own problems, often via the abundant self-help manuals and the pop-psychological suggestions. Or alternatively, man can admit his own inability to change himself or solve his problems and recognize that there is a power greater than himself, entrusting his predicaments to that divine power and trusting the power of God to act on his behalf. This is the great divide between man's way and God's way, which Watchman Nee indicated was "the difference between hell and heaven."

The same divide exists in the life of the Christ-one as well. Are we trying to live the Christian life, trying to be good, trying to be righteous, trying to be holy, trying to be perfect, or are we trusting that God has made us good, righteous, holy, and perfect by the indwelling presence of the Good, Righteous, Holy, and Perfect One, Jesus Christ? Are we trusting that the Christian life, the Christ-life, can only be lived by the living Christ Himself as we are available by faith to let Him manifest Himself in our behavior? This great divide in understanding our source is the difference between religion and the Christ-life.

The choice between the two must be made. Will we rely on what we perceive to be our own self-effort, when it is really Satan's humanistic lie that we can self-generate our own character and action? Or will we exercise the faith-receptivity to God's activity, allowing God in Christ to do what He wants to do to His own glory. "He will bring it to pass" (I Thess. 5:24). Our religious performance of trying our best to live for God will always leave us exhausted, ready to throw up our hands and give up. The faithful acceptance of accepting and trusting the grace-dynamic of God will allow us to "rest" in His sufficiency as God in Christ does what only He can do in our lives.

SPIRITUAL SELF-STIMULATED EROTICA

I came across this title phrase in a place I would least expect to find such. I was reading a book of philosophical theology, a place where few would find anything stimulating, for they are often tomes of lofty logical machinations. What could a philosopher have meant by the phrase "spiritual self-stimulated erotica?"

Let's begin with the last word in the phrase, "erotica." It is derived from the Greek word *eros* which indicates a form of love that is pursued for self-interest, a selfish form of love that is vastly different than the highest form of unselfish love found only in the perfect, unconditional love of divine *agape*. God's *agape* love can only be expressed by human beings when it is derived from God. So, the imperative inculcations to "love (*agape*) one another' (Jn. 13:34,35; 15:12,17; Rom. 13:8; I Jn. 3:11,23; 4:11,12) require the indicative presence and function of God in a man to be obeyed. *Eros* love, on the other hand, is derived from the self-serving character of the spiritual antithesis of God, Satan.

The derivative source of what is being referred to in the phrase should have been evident in the word "self-stimulated." Satan is the spirit-being (Eph. 2:2; I Cor. 2:12; I Jn. 4:6) who is intent on self-pleasuring via the *eros* of self-love. Self-pleasuring does not have to be physical; it can be self-pleasuring thoughts and opinions wherein we are self-stimulated to pride in our minds where as "lovers of self" we find our real self-gratification.

I must confess with heartfelt humility that I have been guilty of "spiritual self-stimulated erotica." I have enjoyed the heady pride of being able to stroke vocabulary words in the self-pleasuring of articulating thoughts that I have taken great delight in even though in the end they produce nothing but the emptiness of dissatisfaction. Our delight and satisfaction should be found in the relational *agape* love of Jesus Christ alone!

JULY 22

PLAYING MUSIC ON THE ORGAN

My brother-in-law, James S. Rogers, was an excellent organist. He earned master's degrees in church music and organ performance from Yale University in New Haven, Connecticut. When I observed him playing the organ pedals with his feet while at the same time playing on several manuals of keyboards with stops, I was in awe. I can recall the occasion when he and his sister, Gracie, were playing Johann Sebastian Bach's *"Jesu, Joy of Man's Desiring"* as a duet with organ and oboe. It was performed masterfully and sounded heavenly. Gracie and her brother had both developed the talent and the art of playing the best classical music on their respectively chosen instruments.

If I might draw an analogous thought-picture necessitating another meaning of the word "organ," I would suggest that God's intent is that we might all allow heavenly music to be played on the organ-instrument of the human heart. This also requires a serious mindset and much practice. The human heart was not designed to engage in the cacophony of discordant dissonance that has no patterns or purpose. In fact, to play God's music on the heart-organ must begin with the very opposite of cacophony – with silence and stillness that waits for the Master to create the music. "Be still and know that I am God" (Ps. 46:10).

May I proceed to suggest that the heavenly music intended to be played on the human heart-organ is the glorious heavenly music of the character of the Triune God. This music with its intricate variations within a composite unity is the divine music for the soul of humanity. It is the music made known to humanity by the God-man, Jesus Christ. Jesus is indeed "the joy of man's desiring" whereby the heart is delighted and made glad by His presence. The "fruit of the Spirit" (Gal. 5:22,23) expresses the melodious harmony of "love, joy, peace, patience, kindness, goodness, gentleness, faithful, and the Godly control of oneself."

PERSONAL UNION

The closest bond of personal union between persons on earth is the marital union of a man and a woman. That is why Paul compares the personal union of Christ and the Christian to the personal union of husband and wife in Ephesians 5:22-33.

As I used to tell couples in premarital counselling, the physical union is not the epitome of what marriage union is meant to be. When those with a sadistic bent take two cats and tie their tails together, it can rightfully be said that those cats are married, i.e., joined, but they are not happy with the situation and will claw each other's guts out until they are loosed or disjoined. This perverse illustration evidences the need to consider the deeper senses of the personal union of marriage. Even though sexual union of a man and a woman can be quite enjoyable, it loses its luster if there is not personal union that goes much deeper.

It is quite common in today's vernacular to refer to one's marriage partner as their "soulmate." But just as marriage is more than just physical union of bodies, compatibility of mind, emotion, and will in the souls of those who regard themselves as soulmates can become frazzled and disconnected over time. Whereas there was once a commonality of thought, feelings, and volitional determinations in the will, these are often insufficient to maintain the marital union for the duration of a lifetime. There must be a deeper sense of union and unity.

The relationship of Christ and the Christ-one is a spiritual union. "The one who joins himself to the Lord is one spirit with Him" (I Cor. 6:17). If two persons, in this case a man and a woman, have the "one spirit" personal union with the living Lord Jesus, they can then come together in a "one spirit" personal union with each other wherein they will experience the deepest sense of the personal and spiritual union of marriage.

JULY 24

SUBVERSIVE DOUBLE AGENCY

The title will cause some people to think of "double agents" in the subversive world of surveillance and spying. Double agents are those working for two opposing sides at the same time, usually without conviction but only for mercenary purposes. The French author, Jacques Ellul, wrote a book which when translated into English was *The Subversion of Christianity* (French title, *La subversion du christianisme*). Within this book there is the double entendre of the double agency of how the Christian gospel is subversive to the world's agenda and the world's agenda attempts to subvert the Christian gospel.

The gospel of the living Lord Jesus and the world-system of which Satan is the "ruler of this world" (Jn. 12:31; 16:11) stand as antithetical and incompatible spiritual antagonists – contradictory and counteractive. That does not disallow that the dynamics of each can subversively permeate into and serve as contrary subversions designed for the detrimental disintegration of the other. There can be no doubt that the gospel of the risen Christ is meant to overcome the world. "For whatever is born of God overcomes the world; and this is the victory that has overcome the world—our faith" (I Jn. 5:4,5).

Amid the subversive double agency of conflict between Christ and the world, the "elementary principles of the world" (Col. 2:8) have also subverted Christian thought to the extent that Christianity is largely conceived of as "Christian religion," which in French is "*Christianism*," and has in many cases become but the religious subset of the world. Paul clearly stated, "We have received, not the spirit of the world, but the Spirit who is from God" (I Cor. 2:12); "our struggle is against the world forces of darkness, the spiritual forces of wickedness" (Eph. 6:12). We are "not to be conformed to this world" (Rom. 12:2). The spiritual war between Jesus Christ and the world is intense.

LOYALTY

When I think of loyalty, my mind goes to our 12-year-old Maltipoo named "Peaches." The dog has bonded with me over the years. She sits on the recliner with me every day as I write. She sleeps in my bed every night. Every morning as I shave and brush my teeth, she sits under the counter looking up at me. On one occasion when my blood pressure dropped too low, I passed out on the floor. My wife tells me that Peaches sat on my chest growling and snarling at anyone who sought to help me, even the E.M.T.'s who arrived with the ambulance. She was faithfully protecting me, somehow aware that I could not protect myself. She has been a loyal pet for many years.

Loyalty, however, goes much deeper than canine loyalty. Personal relations of human beings with God and with one another find their deepest bond based on loyalty, on faithfulness. Consider, for example, a person in the military who has loyalty to their country as well as to the fellow soldiers in their military unit. The marital love of husbands and wives is based on loyalty and faithfulness to one another. Some families develop a sense of family loyalty wherein all the members of the family share a sense of loyalty to one another and the need to keep in contact with one another on a regular basis. Other families lack such. Loyalty is a choice, just as unfaithfulness is a choice to pursue one's own selfishness interests.

The faithfulness of God is firmly established. "The Lord your God, He is the faithful God" (Deut. 7:9); a "firm foundation" (II Tim. 2:19) indeed." Our continuing relationship with God in Christ will necessitate our faithfulness and loyalty to Him, but this is not something that we must work to accomplish and achieve. Our faithfulness is a result of the Spirit working in us. "The fruit of the Spirit is love, joy, peace, patience, kindness, goodness, gentleness, faithfulness, and the Godly control of oneself" (Gal. 5:22,23).

JULY 26

A TRIBUTE TO SOCRATES

Socrates (c. 470-399 B.C.) is credited with being the founder of Western philosophy. He authored no texts of his thinking but is known for his Socratic method of dialogic teaching by question and answer. He was an itinerant gadfly in Athens who attracted "groupies" who were his pupils, including Plato and Xenophon. When the Oracle of Delphi indicated that Socrates was the wisest man in Athens, he self-effacingly indicated that such was only the case because "I know that I know nothing." Those who think themselves knowledgeable think themselves wise, but they are only wise in their own eyes – inflated ideologues.

Socrates was averse to teaching doctrines or belief-tenets. He sought to convey his ideas by asking leading questions and by the practicum of lived-out character. His highest aspiration was to be humble, rather than to teach philosophical truths. Humbly proclaiming his own ignorance, he taught indirectly by what has been called "Socratic questioning," posing leading questions and then facilitating the discussion among those who seek to answer the questions. Since humility is a component of respect, he did not attempt to coerce others to think or believe like he did but allow them to come to their own conclusions.

As an "outside of the box" thinker, Socrates became a polarizing and problematic figure in Athens. In a one-day public trial, Socrates was charged with corrupting the youth of Athens by his individualistic ideas, and the political charge of failure to regard and worship the imperial state officials as gods (a form of atheism). In his defense he declared, "the unexamined life is not worth living" and chose to accept their death penalty by drinking poisoned hemlock. Plato and Xenophon both wrote of what they learned from Socrates (though from different perspectives of remembrance). Plato's pupil, Aristotle, became the third philosopher in the foremost triad of Greek philosophers.

THE ART OF CHRISTIAN LIVING

In the process of pondering how the Christ-life is lived out in us in a practical manner, three words came to mind. Those three words form the acrostic "art" – acceptance, rest, and trust. We know that the Christ-life is not what we do, but what He does. There is a complementary side to His action, and that is encompassed in our receptivity of His activity by faith. As we confront the inevitable circumstances of life, we must accept what is happening, learn to rest amid what is occurring, and trust that God sufficiently seeks our highest good by grace as we move through those circumstances.

The Christian response to what is happening in our lives as Christ-ones, is certainly more than merely enduring the circumstances hoping against hope that they will soon go away. To accept what God has allowed to come into our lives is to consent that this was God's intent, to approve without protest, acquiescing to the will of God. C.S. Lewis said that "there are in the end only two kinds of people in the world: those who say to God, 'Thy will be done!', and those to whom God says, 'thy will be done." The first of those two options represents the attitude of acceptance: "Thy will be done!"

Accepting what God has in store for us allows us, then, to rest amid what He is continuing to do. Instead of getting "all worked up" about what we should and can do for God, we can refrain from our human exertion and be free from any anxiety about what will come our way. "Anyone who enters God's rest also rests from their works, just as God did from his. Let us, therefore, make every effort to enter that rest" (Heb. 4:10,11). The only effort we make in resting is the choice of faith to trust that God has everything under control. "God is able to make all grace abound to you, so you may have all sufficiency in everything" (II Cor. 9:8).

JULY 28

TWO SIGNIFICANT FRENCH THINKERS

In seventeenth-century Europe there were two thinkers who are of significance for sparking human thought in the ensuing centuries. Both were French creative scientists, mathematicians, and philosophers, contemporaries of one another, and aware of the other's thought and writing. But they were vastly separated by the presuppositions of their thought.

René Descartes (1596–1650) was a foremost figure in igniting the Enlightenment Age of Reason wherein human reason was touted as the primary criteria for determining truth and knowledge, in contrast to what were regarded as the superstitions of Christian thought and faith. His famous dictum, "I think, therefore I am," was developed into the "Cartesian doubt" that accepted only rational deduction for positing truth in any category. Anthropology was elevated above theology, for a rational human being was regarded as an autonomous "independent self" and such anthropocentrism led to the deification of humanity and human reason over God. His thought is central to the humanistic thought of the modern age.

Blaise Pascal (1623–1662) rejected Descartes' rationalistic arguments that elevated man's reason over God's revelation of Himself in Jesus Christ. Pascal is regarded as the foremost philosopher that challenges what developed into the worship of the scientific method and human reasoning as the supreme arbiter of truth. In his later years Pascal turned his attention to philosophical theology. Being in ill-health most of his life, he died at only 39 years of age. At his death, he was writing what he called "Defense of the Christian Religion," but it was collected as thought fragments that were published as The *Pensees*, i.e. *The Thoughts of Pascal on Religion*, seven years after his death. Pascal is remembered for his Christian convictions, writing, "the heart has its own reason which reason does not know."

JULY 29

A MARRIAGE PROPOSAL

A young man is infatuated with love for the young lady who has captured his heart. He has decided that he wants to spend the rest of his life with this delicate dear one whom he has decided he cannot live without. So, he advises his sweetheart that they need to study together a course of Christian doctrine to make sure she assents to every point in the same manner as he does. Doesn't sound very romantic, does it? But that seems to be the approach that Christian religion has often taken to presenting the gospel to people in the world today. Christianity is not a course in Christian doctrine; it is a heartfelt and romantic proposal of marriage by Jesus the prospective groom.

The gospel of Jesus Christ is not primarily informational, but relational – intimately relational. God is love (I Jn. 4:8,16). Jesus Christ is God (Jn. 10:30). Therefore, Jesus is the expressor of God's love – the Lover who proposes to draw us into Himself. God in Christ has proposed that we might be joined in the oneness of intimacy (cf. I Cor. 6:17), in a marriage relationship wherein Jesus is our bridegroom, and we are His bride. Paul explained that physical marriage between husband and wife is patterned after the eternal marital relationship of Christ and the Christian (cf. Eph. 5:25-33).

"Blessed are those who are invited to the marriage supper of the Lamb" (Rev. 19:9). The blessing of God, wherein "God has blessed us with every spiritual blessing in the heavenly places in Christ Jesus "(Eph. 1:3) has been made available to all who accept the proposal of Jesus Christ to be united in oneness with Himself and wish to enjoy the celebration of the marriage supper with Him. The Triune God, Father, Son, and Holy Spirit, has invited us into participation in His eternal love relationship and marital union. All who will respond with a "Yes," will enjoy the marriage supper and enjoy the honeymoon with Jesus.

JULY 30

PERSONAL CORRESPONDENCE

You have no doubt received mail that was addressed "Dear occupant," or "Dear resident." Most impersonal! When we receive such mail, we recognize it is likely "junk mail" for the sender apparently did not even know who we are else they would have addressed us by name. It is just a mass-mailing, phishing for the gullible soul who might take the bait of their con-game to get your money. The best place for such unsolicited correspondence is in the round file in the corner – the waste basket.

Rest assured that you will never receive correspondence from God addressed to "Dear occupant," for God is a personal God, and we have a personal relationship with God through His Son, Jesus Christ. God knows our name, knows where we live and how to contact us, and beyond that He knows every detail of our thought life, and what our deepest desires really are. God's children are not nameless residents in His kingdom. Jesus who reigns as King in His kingdom doesn't address us as "Hey, you!" or "Do I know you?" or "Mrs. so-and-so!" No one in the kingdom wears a nameless name tag inscribed, "Whoever." The functional basis of the kingdom of God's community is relational connectedness.

God in Christ knows us by name because He is personally invested within us; He is the occupant residing in our spirit. Yes, we have an identity as a "Christ-one," but God knows us in a more intimate personal relationship. He knows us inside and out! "Nothing is hidden from God's sight. Everything is uncovered and laid bare before the eyes of him to whom we must give account" (Heb. 4:13). We can be sure that in all personal correspondence and communication between God and us He will be knowingly aware of our name and everything about us. That kind of transparency should not bring discomfort, but the realization that genuine love knows everything about us – our every flaw – and despite such and in full awareness, loves us anyway.

PARDOXICAL CHRISTIAN FAITH

If "knowing good and evil" was the forbidden choice (Gen. 2:17 of the original couple and making that choice led to the original sin of mankind (Gen. 3:22), why does Paul write that those who are mature in their Christian faith should have their senses trained to discern good and evil? (Heb. 5:14).

Who would aspire to become a teacher of spiritual things when James writes, "Let not many become teachers, my brethren, knowing that as such we will incur a stricter judgment" (James 3:1)? Yet, Paul explained that "God has appointed in the church, first apostles, second prophets, third teachers (I Cor. 12:28). Does God appoint some people for greater judgment?

We have received all that God has to give in Christ, every spiritual blessing in heavenly places in Christ Jesus (Eph. 1:3), yet we are encouraged to "press on to press on lay hold of that for which we have been laid hold of by Christ Jesus (Phil. 3:12).

"We are to grow in the grace and knowledge of our Lord and Savior Jesus Christ (II Pet. 3:18) and seek maturity (Eph. 4:13; Col. 1:28; Heb. 5:14), but there are no "adult Christians," because as we grow in Christ, we are humbled to recognize that we proceed with a child-like faith like a little child (rather than an adult). (Matt. 18:3,4; Mk. 10:14,15; Lk.18:16,17; Jn.1:12; I Jn. 3:2).

"We are useless slaves" (Luke 17:9,10), only doing what is expected of a slave, but are encouraged to be "useful to the Master" (II Tim. 2:21). The usefulness of uselessness?

Paul wrote, "A person is justified by faith apart from works of the law." (Romans 3:28), yet James explained that "a person is justified by works and not by faith alone (James 2:24), for faith without works is useless and dead" (James 2:17,26).

AUGUST 1

LIFE IS A STRUGGLE

Life in this world is a struggle. If anyone tries to tell you that life is not a struggle, they are likely living in an insulated and isolated bubble of unreality. Religion provides just such a bubble, encouraging the denial of the inevitable human struggles, pain, problems, trials, and tribulations to project the idea that religious faith provides a problem-free panacea that fixes all human ailments, and allows one to live a "life of victory." In diminishing the severity of pain and struggle, religion is often attempting to protect God's reputation against any thought that He has failed to meet the felt needs of those who worship Him.

God knows that we struggle and suffer pain from physical ailments, addictive propensities of the flesh, the wounds of broken relationships, being taken advantage of, and the death of loved ones. These do not take Him by surprise as we live "in the world, but not of the world" (Jn. 17:10,14). Religion does no one a favor in attempting to cover-up, diminish, or gloss over the harsh realities of life on earth. The anonymity groups are more honest in admitting their problems, and more transparent about their struggles than are many who flash their pious smiles and the contented attitude: "Ain't it nice to be nice to nice people."

Those who would intimate that the Christian life is a problem-free panacea from suffering are lying to you. Try telling that to Jesus as He suffered while hanging on the cross. Paul wouldn't buy that lie, for he wrote, "we are afflicted in every way, but not crushed; perplexed, but not despairing; persecuted, but not forsaken; struck down, but not destroyed; always carrying about in the body the dying of Jesus, so that the life of Jesus also may be manifested in our body" (II Cor. 4:8-10). "I am well content with weaknesses, with insults, with distresses, with persecutions, with difficulties, for Christ's sake; for when I am weak, then I am strong" (II Cor. 12:10).

AUGUST 2

SELFISM

Any word (noun, verb, adjective, or adverb) that one might place behind the prefix "self–" creates a compound word that usually describes the fallacy of the inherent potential and ability of a human being to generate and activate their own behavior. Selfism is the pivotal premise of the philosophy of humanism that prevails in the thought of the modern world. It is not a new thought, for it is as old as the serpent's false declaration in the Garden of Eden. "You too will be like God" (Gen. 3:5). Selfism posits the self-deification of mankind, falsely suggesting that human beings can be and do what only God can be and do.

Oh the subtlety of the many words prefixed with the word "self–": self-righteous, self-justifying, self-elevating, self-initiating, self-starter, self-activating, self-absorbed, self-magnifying, self-evaluating, self-concern, self-love, self-belonging, self-sovereign, self-affective, self-interested, self-determinative, self-assurance, self-confidence, self-esteem, self-image, self-worth, self-value, self-identity, self-control, self-reliance, self-conscious, self-governing, self-motivated, self-assured, self-made, self-opinionated, self-taught, self-devoted, self-knowledge, self-effacing, self-obsessed, self-protective, self-aggrandizing....

The accurate essence of selfism would be to substitute Satanic or diabolic as the prefix of all the words before which the self-prefix has been attached. Selfism is the character of Satan, who from his beginning as Lucifer declared, "I will be like the Most High God" (Isa. 14:14). Such egocentricity is the primary trait of Satan's character. The only true alternative to the fallacy of humanistic selfism is to "turn from the dominion of Satan to the dominion of God" (Acts 26:18), to submit to the spiritual exchange whereby the Spirit of Christ (Rom. 8:9) enters in and occupies the human spirit (Rom. 8:16) and becomes the basis of our true derived spiritual identity and spiritual energizing.

AUGUST 3

RELIGION: THE GREAT COVER-UP

As difficult as it might be for some people to agree and admit, religion (as distinguished from Christianity – "Christ-in-you-ity") is a systemic system of selfish dishonesty, hypocrisy, and cover-up. Religion is the codependent enabler of sin, collectively engaging in the deceitfulness of behavior that does not represent the character of God. Religion does not produce or facilitate holiness of character, and never brings about godliness. Religion always seems to hide behind a smokescreen of respectability, while covering up the most egregious sins of mankind (ex. child abuse, adultery, murder, rape, theft, drunkenness, lies, etc.).

Moses was engaged as a minister of death and condemnation when he delivered the Law to the Israelite people 430 years after they received the promises of God through Abraham (cf. Gal. 3:17). It was the beginning of an onerous religion that heaped legalistic performance standards upon the Jewish people. Moses had seen God on the mountain and his face glowed but then he engaged in the cover-up, covering his face with a veil (II Cor. 3:12-18) to hide the Ichabod effect (I Sam. 4:21), "the glory of the Lord has departed." Religious pride and arrogance attempt again and again to cover-up their lack of glorious reality.

One of the poignant features of the religious cover-up game is to tout how glorious the religious life is while covering-up the disappointment, the failure, the less than satisfactory elements of their hypocritical role-playing façade. Religion often tries to hype how they are living in victory, peace, and a state of bountiful blessings. "This is the good life." "I know my perfect identify as an overcomer." "I am living in heavenly glory." But they cover-up and are less than candid or forthright about the problems, weaknesses, sins, addictions, pain and suffering they are enduring day by day. Like Moses, religion arrogantly assumes they can hide the lack of glory behind the thin veil of cover-up.

"JUST AS I AM"

Charlotte Elliott (1789-1871) wrote this poem in 1834. Twelve years earlier, she had contracted a disease that left her an invalid in a wheelchair. Out of the pain of feeling useless and unneeded, she wrote these words. Although often used today as an invitation hymn inviting people to come forward and accept Jesus, it was not originally written with that objective in mind.

> Just as I am, without one plea
> But that Thy blood was shed for me
> And that Thou bid'st me come to Thee
> Oh, Lamb of God, I come, I come
>
> Just as I am, though tossed about
> With many a conflict, many a doubt
> Fighting and fears within without
> Oh, Lamb of God, I come, I come
>
> Just as I am, Thou wilt receive
> Wilt welcome, pardon, cleanse, relieve
> Because Thy promise I believe
> Oh, Lamb of God, I come, I come.

When people walk down the aisle during the singing of this invitation hymn, they should be advised that this will likely be the last time they will be accepted by the church "just as they are." After responding to the gospel of Jesus Christ and becoming a participant in a local evangelical fellowship there will inevitably be pressure to conform to the acceptable thought and action parameters of that particular religious group. Implied in the very word "religion" are the performance expectations required to conform to the rules and regulations of acceptable moral behavior in that group. "Just as I am" will get you in but conforming to "who we are" will be required henceforth.

AUGUST 5

GLIMPSES OF GLORY

Have you ever had a time when you felt you experienced a transcendent, heavenly experience – an "out of this world" experience, as if "heaven was opened" and you were seeing the "glory of God"? "Wow; this is unreal; this is surreal." Perhaps it was an occasion of grandeur, beauty or excellence in God's creation that inspired admiration, awe, and reverence; so out of the ordinary that it took your breath away. Perhaps it was during an intimate time of prayer, or while reading the bible or another book, or during a time of worship. It may have been while listening to music; it may have been while hiking in the mountains. It was as if you had been transported into the presence of God. You sensed the love of God, and it was as if the God of loving acceptance was giving you an embrace, and it was reassuring that you were in right relation with God, right where He wanted you.

Such an occasion can occur as a spiritual experience within any context in our ordinary lives as Christians. In fact, it should be a purposed objective in our Christian lives to long for and appreciate those "glimpses of glory" wherein God reveals Himself – His love and beauty and power – wherein we are sure that we have just had the privilege of being in the presence of God, of having observed his divine magnificence.

Religion often attempts to orchestrate or create what only God can do in our lives. The magnificent cathedrals were intended to draw people's focus upward. The exquisite sounds of the pipe organs produce awe. We want to explain, however, that these experiential "glimpses of glory" *can … should …* and *do* happen while engaged in a normal Christian life. Many Christians have been missing out on the sublimity of a personal revelation of God that can experientially confirm His love and concern for them. Stay receptive to God's presence everywhere.

TEMPTATIONS OF THE HIGHLY REGARDED

Many persons have gained prominence in their field and are highly regarded by others because of their knowledge and expertise. There are, however, specific temptations that accompany being held in high regard – of being the expert, the celebrity, or the star. Foremost, of course, is the pride that can go as far as haughty arrogance looking down with condescension from an elevated position on those who haven't achieved recognition, on those in a lesser position. Far better to have been kept in a lesser place, allowing God to work in us the character of humility, than to allow pride to trip us up in a fall of abasement.

The highly regarded often have people clamoring for their attention and advice. The temptation is to respond with expedience that simply tells people what they want to hear. There is also the temptation to make promises to people that are not kept. One must remember that integrity is the integral oneness between what one says and what one does. The follow-through is of utmost importance. The deceitful "father of lies" (Jn. 8:44) is often operative in unkept promises, in exaggeration and embellishment of the facts, in the half-truths that constitute full falsehood. Those held in high regard are greatly tempted to such.

Those who might aspire to a position of being in the limelight, of being at the top of the ladder of success in their field, should carefully consider the possible pitfalls which include becoming insular and isolated. The loneliest place can often be when one is "king of the mountain," when others are jealous of your position and are attempting to knock you off the pedestal. The mother of James and John wanted her sons to be in preferred places next to Jesus in the kingdom (Matt. 20:20-23). "You know not what you seek," Jesus responded, for such places of significance will likely require them to drink the cup of humiliation and suffering, even death, that I will have to endure.

AUGUST 7

MOSAIC LAW WAS ONLY FOR JEWS

Why is it that Christians have attempted to hijack, or otherwise self-appropriate, the Mosaic Law and place the burden of law-keeping on themselves and others? When the Jewish scriptures, the old covenant, identified as the Old Testament, was bound together in the same book as the Christian scriptures, the new covenant writings, identified as the New Testament, Christians failed to understand that the Jewish scriptures were included only for the purpose of historical background leading up to the introduction and incarnation of the expected Jewish Messiah, as well as showing the ever-consistent character of God.

Our intent is not to denigrate any portion of the divinely "inspired scripture" (cf. II Tim. 3:16), but to emphasize that the Christian new covenant writings about Jesus Christ and the development of His collective Body in the Church are meant to have primary emphasis within Christian thought. The two major portions of scripture must be kept in the context of the People of God for whom they were intended. The collection of both Jewish and Christian scriptures in a single Bible was not meant to create an amalgam of variant and contrasting thought whereby Christian thinkers have confusingly attempted to merge the works of Law and the freedom of grace in one gospel.

When Moses was on the mountain, God said, "Write down these words, for I made a covenant with you and with Israel" (Exod. 34:27). *The Jewish Encyclopedia* explains, "Moses presented the Jewish religious laws to the Jewish people, and those laws do not apply to Gentiles." Paul referred to "Gentiles who do not have the law" (Rom. 2:14) and referred to Gentiles as "those without the Law" (I Cor. 9:21). These statements serve to demonstrate the Mosaic Law was only intended for the Jewish people. An entirely different divine *modus operandi* was implemented in the Christian new covenant of God's grace in Jesus Christ.

THE ULTIMATE HEALING

There have been some, predominantly in the Pentecostal and Charismatic portions of the Church of Jesus Christ, who have taught that all human healing is guaranteed by the atonement of Jesus Christ on the cross. They have proceeded to explain that all Christians have a right and responsibility to claim God's physical healing for themselves and for others based on the atoning death of Jesus. Their primary biblical text used for justifying this teaching is found in Isaiah 53:5, where the death of Jesus is prophesied, "He was pierced through for our transgressions, He was crushed for our iniquities...and by His scourging (stripes, welts) we are healed."

In the New Testament, Peter alludes to this Isaiah prophecy, and he does so in the context of the spiritual healing from sin that is available by means of the death of Jesus Christ. "He Himself bore our sins in His body on the cross, so that we might die to sin and live to righteousness; for by His wounds you were healed" (I Pet. 2:24). Since the scripture best serves as the commentary on other scripture, it seems likely that the healing referred to in Isaiah is meant to refer primarily to the spiritual healing of mankind from the death consequences of sin by the vicarious substitutionary death of Jesus on the cross for our sins.

Rather than presuming that every Christian who has enough faith has a guaranteed right to physical healing, Paul explains, "we groan within ourselves, waiting eagerly for our adoption as sons, the redemption of our body" (Rom. 8:23), seeming to indicate that full physical healing of our bodies is expected in the future. That would certainly accord with the revelation of Jesus Christ given to the apostle John explaining that in the heavenly perpetuity of the Christ-life, "there will no longer be any death; there will no longer be any mourning, or crying, or pain; the first things have passed away" (Rev. 21:4).

AUGUST 9

WHAT DOES GOD EXPECT OF US?

God is quite realistic. He is quite aware that there are many things that we are incapable of doing. He created us that way! Contrary to the humanistic premises of human potential and ability, constantly touting that we can be and do whatever we set our minds and energies to be and do, God did not create little human-gods who could "do their own thing." God created human beings who must derive from a spirit-source to be and do all that they might be and do. The alternatives are simple – there is only the antithesis of deriving character from God or Satan, good or evil, sinfulness or righteousness, selfishness or love for others. We have a simple binary choice of one or the other.

Jesus explained that in and of ourselves, we human beings are not able to enter the narrow door of access to God (Lk. 13:24). For that reason, God took the initiative of grace to open that door of access to participation in the Triune community of love through His Son, Jesus Christ. Jesus also explained to His disciples, "Apart from Me, you can do nothing" (Jn. 15:5) – nothing that is invested with divine character that brings glory to God. The mind set on the flesh (Rom. 8:7) is not able to submit itself to what God expects of us. It is always desiring to go its own way, thinking it can be its own god, and does not want to submit to God.

God only desires that we should be and do what we were created to be and do – receptive, derivative, dependent creatures – receivers and not doers. God Himself intends to be the Doer – it's called "grace." Our being receptive and dependent – it's called "faith." "For by grace you have been saved through faith; and that not of yourselves, it (being saved) is the gift of God; not a result of works, so that no one may boast. For we are His workmanship, created in Christ Jesus for good works, which God prepared beforehand so that we would walk in them" (Eph. 2:8-10). God desires that we trust Him for everything.

AUGUST 10

RELIGION IS A KILLER

In religion, human beings think they are living the "good life," but they will die trying to keep all the rules, attempting to perform all the duties that religion requires. Humans will work themselves to death trying their best to be the best they think God wants them to be. Religion creates burnout among the most ardent adherents of performance righteousness because in giving it their all they try to please God with "the mind set on the flesh" (Rom. 8:5-7), and inevitably come to realize the futility of their efforts. They give up! Of course, God rejoices when we come to the end of ourselves and become available to the unlimited spiritual resources of His grace in Jesus Christ.

The apostle Paul explained that the old covenant of law performance, which is the operative premise of all religion, was a "ministry of condemnation" (II Cor. 3:9) and a "ministry of death" (II Cor. 3:7). Religion can never provide righteousness (Rom. 3:20; 10:4; Gal. 2:16,21). Religion can never provide life (Gal. 3:21). Religion can never provide salvation (Heb. 10:4,11). Religion can never provide holiness (Heb. 12:14). Religion can never provide freedom (Acts 13:39). Religion is a bankrupt enterprise, the legal regulations of which have nothing to do with living the Christ-life. It is the death-knell of the grace-life.

Religion views God's grace as a pathway to license, rather than viewing grace as the liberty of joyful living in Christ. Religion kills humanity's God-given desire for loving relationship with the Triune God in the context of genuine personal freedom. Religion would have us to believe that grace is a form of tyranny whereby God seeks to control our every thought and action. The opposite is true. Religion should be held culpable for its crimes against humanity. It is a slave master that has abused humanity through the ages in its various oppressive forms of enslavement. and has been the cause of death to many people – a killer!

AUGUST 11

A LOVER OR A PROSTITUTE?

In an article entitled, "The Question that Changed My Life," David Ryser posed the question used in the title. He used a quotation attributed to Richard Halverson that seems to give a brief history of Western Christianity. "Christianity started in Palestine as a fellowship; it moved to Greece and became a philosophy; it moved to Rome and became an institution; it moved to Europe and became a culture; it came to America and became an enterprise." A young lady raised her hand and asked, "How can the church be a business? Isn't it a Body? When a body becomes a business, isn't that a prostitute?" The question forces us to ask ourselves, "Are we Christ-lovers, or religious prostitutes?

Let us first admit that human bodies involved in business do not necessarily comprise the body-business of prostitution. But we still must ask: Are we lovers of the Lord Jesus Christ or are we going through the motions of religious prostitution? Perhaps we should ask, "What is the difference between a lover and a prostitute?" On one level, they may engage in some of the same activities, but a lover is motivated to do so based on a deep relational sense of loving intimacy, whereas a prostitute goes through the motions and pretends to love someone physically provided she/he is getting paid for the services rendered.

The Church in America today must consider whether we are engaged in the business enterprise of merchandising the blessings and benefits of God or whether we are engaged in introducing people to the love relationship with Jesus that is available to all who will receive Him by faith. Are we functioning as the Bride of Christ intimately involved with the Bridegroom, Jesus Christ, or are we prostitutes, engaged in going through the motions of religion? Individually, we might have to examine our motivations: Do we love Jesus for the blessings we get out of such, or do we love Jesus in an intimate relationship of love?

AUGUST 12

THE IDOLATRY OF MINISTRY

There is no doubt a legitimate sense of ministry in which each Christ-one is to be involved. This reading is not an attempt to denigrate those involved in ministry, whether professional or otherwise. But there is a need to rethink some common contemporary misconceptions of ministry in the Body of Christ, the *ecclesia* of God's people. There are some Christian leaders who so emphasize involvement in ministry they incentivize Christians to think that the epitome of spirituality is to be elevated to a position of ministry in the local congregation or in the broader Body of Christ, the Church at large.

If ministry becomes a personal goal that we strive to achieve or obtain, then it is likely that we have taken our eyes off Jesus (Heb. 12:2) and perhaps inadvertently replaced our first love (Rev. 2:4), making our aspiration to be involved in ministry into an object of idolatry. The idolatry of seeking ministry soon overtakes the proper desire to know Jesus (Phil. 3:10) and to listen under His voice (Jn. 10:27) in obedience. Rather than a role we seek, ministry is the spontaneous overflow of Jesus from within us into the lives of others. The means by which that takes place is the spiritual giftedness of Jesus manifesting His ministry through us, and that in the manifestation of the fruit of His character (Matt. 7:20; Gal. 5:22,23).

It is interesting to note that the original Greek word *diakonia* is translated into English as both "ministry" and "service" (cf. Eph. 4:12). One who ministers is a servant both of Jesus Christ and to others. It is not a higher or more elevated position of ministry that we should seek, but a more lowly and humble heart whereby we "regard another as more important than ourselves" (Phil. 2:3). The Greek word was transliterated into the English word "deacon," meaning "one who serves" those in the Body – not just a leadership position in the church.

AUGUST 13

THE LOGOS OF GOD

The gospel of John begins, "in the beginning was the Word (*logos*), and the Word (*logos*) was with God, and the Word (*logos*) was God" (Jn. 1:1). Thirteen verses later John explains, "The Word (*logos*) was made flesh and tabernacled (as the divine dwelling place) among us…" In the context of the ancient Greek world the *logos* was the revelation and rationale of the gods that provided meaning from a divine perspective. People came from all over the world to visit the oracle of Delphi (four others also) to hear the spoken *logos* revelation, the word from the gods regarding the meaning of all that was occurring in their lives and in the world. John's connection of the *Logos* with the divine revelation would have made sense to the Greek mind, but the incarnated personification of the *Logos* would have been a totally novel and dubious concept to the Greek mind.

In Christian thought, God has revealed Himself in His Son, and the theological and logical (*logos*) revelation of the divine rationale of reality has been substantiated personally in the Person of the Son, Jesus Christ. The pre-existent Son of God, existing within the Trinity since the beginning, i.e. the commencement of God's presence and activity among men, has voluntarily (cf. Phil. 2:6-8) made His advent on earth as the incarnated God-man (cf. I Tim. 2:5), the expressive agency of God whereby He makes Himself known, the Revealed Word of God, the Christic revelation that is the full and final revelation of the *logos* of God to man.

The gospel ("good news") of God is the Gospel of the *Logos*, personified and incarnated in the Person of Jesus Christ, the Son of God having become the God-man (*Theanthropos*). Jesus Christ, the historical revelation of God now perpetually alive and active as the Spirit (cf. I Cor. 15:45), continues to reveal the Triune God as the ultimate reality (*logos*) of the universe.

AUGUST 14

"HERE I STAND"

Martin Luther was an Augustinian monk in the Roman Catholic Church. As he studied the scriptures, he came to understand that salvation was acquired by faith alone, with good works being the outworking fruit of that faith as opposed to a meritorious means to reaching heaven. He stood up for his newfound beliefs and made the bold move in A.D. 1517of attaching a list of ninety-five theses on the door of the Castle Church in Wittenburg, expressing his repudiation of the sale of indulgences as a mercenary ecclesiastical gimmick whereby people could allegedly pay for penance and buy their way out of purgatory and into heaven.

Taking his stand against Roman Church thought and practice was not greeted graciously by Church authorities. Martin Luther was regarded as a rebellious heretic and slated for excommunication. In 1521, he was granted safe passage to the Imperial Diet of Worms where he was interrogated about his nonconformist statements, but he would not recant what he believed. Luther is alleged to have declared, "Here I stand; I can do no other, so help me God. Amen!" His resolute stand was a history-making stance that changed the church as well as history. Are we willing to take a stand for what we believe, despite the consequences?

The consideration of what we know and believe is often termed epistemology (*epi* = upon; *histemi* = to stand) – to take a stand on what one believes to be true. Standing in the steps of Martin Luther, I am willing to take my stand in stating that I do not believe in combining Christian faith with any ideology, be it nationalism, socialism, ecclesiasticism, isolationism, creedalism, biblicism, sacramentalism, religionism, or any other man-made -ism of human thought. I take my stand in Jesus Christ alone (*solus Christus*) as the living Lord who has come to live in me (Col. 1:27) as my Life and sole sufficiency for living; and my expectancy of expressing His glory both now and forever.

AUGUST 15

"IT'S JUST RELIGION!"

Perhaps you have heard, as I have, the dismissive and often disparaging comment made by some in the world today, "It's just religion!" They might be saying that you should disregard what that person or group of people might say or do, because "It's just religion." The comment might be made with an attitude of disdain and derision, even contemptuous scorn, about the thinking and actions of a particular group of people; "It's just religion." Rejecting the strict morality of their upbringing and discarding what they consider to be but "the trappings of provincial respectability," some might declare, "It's just religion."

When one's faith is merely a recapitulation of a belief-system of yesteryear, it may be "just religion." If one's faith is just an extracurricular sideline hobby that does not affect how they live, doesn't have any depth of character, and is nothing more than a gathering wherein "nice people are being nice to nice people," such socialization might be "just religion." Some enjoy engaging in superficial probes of the philosophical and so-called deeper intellectual thought and are not interested in involving themselves in the spiritual realities of understanding the connections that all men have with either Satan or God. For such brainiacs and elitists "It's just religion."

It doesn't take a learned person to see through the thin guise and folderol of religious activities. Those who are dismissive of the repetitive activities of the adherents and devotees of the innumerable varieties of Christian religion are correct in their analysis that "It's just religion." What they see is not the Christian gospel – not the dynamic of God's grace in Jesus Christ manifesting the divine character of God in human behavior – it's just religion! But as such, it continues to deceive so many innocent people who fail to realize that religion is the playground of the Deceiver, the Devil, the "father of lies" (Jn. 8:44).

AUGUST 16

MORTIFICATION

"Mortification" is not a word that is used much in the English language anymore. It means "to put to death," and was commonly used in older religious language because the *King James Bible* used the verb form "to mortify" in two New Testament verses (Rom. 8:13; Col. 3:5). The Roman Catholic Church continues to encourage self-mortification through such disciplines as fasting, abstinence, confession, using rosary beads, and self-deprivation. The Lenten season is a particular occasion for such activities. Lent begins on Ash Wednesday and commemorates the 40 days Jesus spent fasting in the wilderness. Catholicism encourages abstaining from various activities in replication of Christ's sacrifice and abstinence "to be more spiritually prepared for Easter season. Lent was not practiced until the 4th century.

The Catholic Encyclopedia states: "The purpose of mortification is to train the soul to virtuous and holy living." Such a definition is certainly devoid of any understanding of God's grace – advocating instead legalistic works of mortification to die to the "old man" or the "old nature," and to put to death "the flesh" and the "deeds of the flesh." Such a process of allegedly developing holiness or sanctification by human performance is "works".

Yes, all Christ-ones have residual flesh patterns. We need only be honest in saying, "Lord, I can't; only You can overcome these inclinations; I want You to do so by Your grace." The Christ-one has already "put to death the old man" identity (cf. Eph. 4:22-24; Col. 3:9,10), and the Lord, the Spirit, dwelling within each Christ-one will continue to function by grace to "put to death" the residual misrepresentative expressions of sin and death in our soul. The Divine Positive swallows up the negative. The Spirit manifesting the fruit of the Spirit overcomes the deeds of the flesh (Gal. 5:16-23). We simply get out of the way and let God "put to death" whatever needs mortifying.

AUGUST 17

CHRISTMAS AND EASTER

Perhaps you have heard persons speak disparagingly of "C. E. Christians," i.e., believers who only attend the services of the church on Christmas and Easter and are otherwise not involved in the church program. Those who have this attitude of judging others are often assuming the attitude of the older brother in the parable of the lost son (Lk. 15:11-32), proud of their own loyalty, and viewing condescendingly those less involved. Even those who are faithfully and religiously involved in the church often do not adequately understand the full import of Christmas and Easter, and the experiential impact of these historical events.

In the Christmas celebration, we recall when God deliberately broke into space and time in the incarnation of the Son as the God-man. He did so in the humble and lowly form of a baby laid in a manger, and this child, given the name of Jesus, partook of the full experience of humanity with all the vulnerability of our temptations and the susceptibility of mortality. The import of the incarnated birth of Jesus in Bethlehem is that the Spirit of the living Lord Jesus can now, by means of the resurrection, be born in the spirits of receptive individuals, born of the Spirit (Jn. 3:6,8), with the expectancy of living by the Life of Jesus.

In the Easter celebration, we focus on the death and resurrection of Jesus, seeing the perpetuity of life out of death, even eternal life beyond space and time. God deliberately allowed Jesus to vicariously "taste death for everyone" (Heb. 2:9), and raised up Jesus out of death, "rendering powerless him who had the power of death, that is the devil" (Heb. 2:14). "It was impossible for Jesus to be held in Satan's power of death" (Acts. 2:24). The resurrection of Jesus is the birth (Acts 13:33) of the life out of death paradigm, allowing receptive individuals to be "born again to a living hope through the resurrection of Jesus from the dead" (I Pet. 1;3). Spiritual life out of spiritual death!

AUGUST 18

CONSISTENCY OF THOUGHT

I was pondering the trajectory of my thinking from the time I first began to understand spiritual things (*pneumatikoi*) in 1973 until my continuing growth in the grace and knowledge of the Lord and Savior, Jesus Christ (II Pet. 3:18) presently. Has it been consistent from its commencement to the present? There were a few rabbit trails of questionable thinking, but for the most part the trajectory has been a Spirit-led consistency focused on the living Lord Jesus and His indwelling in Christ-ones (cf. Gal. 2:20; Col. 1:27; II Cor. 13:5). "Christ in you, the hope of glory."

The basic thoughts and formatting of "Man as God Intended" were formed in the mid 70s, in large part influenced by the thought of W. Ian Thomas. The theme of "Christ in you" was enhanced later in the 70s by the awareness of "union with Christ," through the ministry of Norman Grubb (who also had some aberrant thinking). Through additional studies in the scriptures by the instruction of the Spirit, I developed the themes that have been the structure of God's ministry through me.

Humanity's creation as a derivative creature, deriving all things from either Satan or God has been foundational. Contrary to all the humanistic thought of the world, man is not an "independent self" functioning as his own center of reference, having the ability to do whatever he sets out to do. Human beings were created with freedom of choice, but not free-will (defined as determinative choice with the self-generative ability to implement that choice). Our essential humanity was not corrupted by "original sin," but Satan's working in the sons of disobedience (Eph. 2;2) explains the selfishness and sinfulness of the natural man. Human beings were designed to derive God's character of love, holiness, and righteousness, and to manifest that character by His grace dynamic in the living Lord Jesus. Thank you, Lord, for Your constancy and consistency!

231

AUGUST 19

A RELATIONSHIP EXERCISE

Personal relationships are important and are worth taking the time to evaluate. All relationships are to be love relationships wherein we love one another. Marital and intimate relationships are particularly important and vulnerable – often in need of evaluating the loving interactions between the partners. The following exercise has been helpful to many in facilitating communication and understanding.

Each person should take a piece of paper.
On side-one write these two questions:
- How do I express love to ___*(the other)*__?
- How have I failed to express love to ___*(the other)*__?

On side-two write these two questions:
- How do I want __*(the other)*__ to express love to me?
- How has _*(the other)*__ failed to express love to me?

Take adequate time to seriously reflect and answer all four questions. Then, make a time to sit down with your relationship partner. Compare the answers on side-one of your paper with the answers of side-two of your relationship partner's paper. How do they correspond and align with one another? Then switch and do the same thing with the other sides of the pages.

The first purpose of this exercise is to consider how well you have communicated your love with one another. The second purpose is to consider the extent to which selfishness has sabotaged your love for one another.

On the spiritual side, we must understand that pure, unselfish, and unconditional love requires the God who "is love" (I Jn. 4:8,16) dwelling in all parties of the relationship, being allowed to express His love through each one to the other. This presence and function of the love of God is essential to the relationship.

AUGUST 20

COMPARING YOURSELF WITH OTHERS

We all seem to have this tendency to want to self-evaluate how we are doing in the Christ-life, and to compare how we are doing with how others are allowing the expression of the life of Jesus. In the first place, it is none of our business what Jesus Christ is doing in the lives of others. Paul wrote to the Corinthians, "We are not like those who compare themselves with themselves; they are without understanding." Perhaps Paul meant that they are lacking understanding of how God's grace works uniquely in every individual Christ-one. Each Christ-one is to keep their eyes on Jesus (Heb. 12:2), rather than on what He is doing in the lives of another.

Each Christ-one must understand and accept that it is the prerogative of the Lord Jesus Christ to work individually and uniquely in the life of each child of God. He will do what He has determined to do in each person's life, for "we are His workmanship, created in Christ Jesus for good works, which God prepared beforehand so that we would walk in them" (Eph. 2:10). Any attempt to preempt or modify God's work in us or others is ultimately an exercise in futility. We must continue to BE who we are in Christ, and allow Him to manifest Himself in us, through us, and as us in the unique way He has determined.

Self-concern with how God is working in our life often plays into the hands of Satan's character of pride or self-denigration. We must know who we are (our identity) "in Christ," and be willing to allow Christ to be lived out in us, through us, and as us. Each Christ-one is special, unique, novel, incomparable, and beyond comparison. Can we stand up and say, "I don't care how I compare, or what anyone else thinks of me, because I know I am "accepted in the Beloved" (Eph. 1:6 *KJV*), and I am willing to stand alone as one-of-a-kind, a solitary voice crying in the wilderness of the world (including the rejective religious world).

AUGUST 21

THE THREE IN ONE GOD

The distinctive understanding of God in the Christian faith is that God is Trinity – historically explained as three Persons in one Divine Being. The triunity of God is difficult, yea impossible, to explain to anyone who has not experienced Christian regeneration and received "the mind of Christ" (I Cor. 2:16) in order to "understand spiritual things" (I Cor. 2:14). There have been innumerable theoretical speculations attempting to explain the Trinity of God in logical sentential propositions of human thought, but they are all inadequate because a derived Theo-logic is required for such human understanding.

Since God can only be understood to the extent and in the manner that He reveals Himself to mankind, we can only understand His triunity in His Self-revelation. Hebrew words and phrases give intimation of His plurality. *Elohim* is a plural noun used as God's name. In the creation narrative, God uses plural pronouns, "Let *us* make man in *our* image" (Gen. 1:26). In the new covenant, Jesus says, "I and the Father are one" (Jn. 10:30; 17:11,21). Paul explains that "the Lord is the Spirit" (2 Cor. 3:17; I Cor. 15:45). Other references to the three personages of the Trinity include Matt. 28:19; Jn. 15:26; Gal. 4:6; 2 Cor. 13:14).

From the ontological Trinity, we proceed to the operational Trinity. The perfect loving relationality of the Father, Son, and Holy Spirit in the Trinity provides the foundation for understanding and experiencing the unity in diversity of our relationship with God, as well as the unity in plurality of our relationships in the *ecclesia* of the Body of Christ. Those who would suggest a relational Christian unity and fellowship based on anything other than the Trinity are simply offering a humanistic socialism that lacks the dynamic of divine grace enacted only by the Triune God. The divine Trinity is the spiritual source and substance of our conjunctive Christian fellowship.

THERE IS NO MORE THAN JESUS

God has provided everything mankind needs to remedy the human rejection of God in the garden. He provided His only Son in the incarnation (Jn. 3:16)), who in turn gave His own life for the sins of mankind (Gal. 2:20), and henceforth became the life-giving Spirit (I Cor. 15:45) to provide the living presence of Jesus to all who receive Him (Jn. 1:12,13). Those who do so and become Christ-ones are "blessed with every spiritual blessing in heavenly places in Christ Jesus (Eph. 1:3) and "filled with the fullness of God in Christ" (Eph. 3:19). We must realize we have all God has to give – "all things belong to you" (I Cor. 3:21,22).

There is no more than Jesus. He is "the sum of all spiritual things" (Eph. 1:10). "Of His fullness we have all received, and grace upon grace" (Jn. 1:16). If we should seek anything more than Jesus, then we imply that Jesus in Himself was not adequate or sufficient to restore humanity. If Jesus is not enough to restore humanity to God's intent for mankind, then we are doomed and damned forever. If Jesus is not enough to save mankind, "our faith is worthless, we are still in our sins" (I Cor. 15:17). Jesus is the one and only Savior of mankind, who gave His life on the cross once and for all that we might have His eternal life.

All history is consummated and brought to its intended goal in the Person and work of Jesus Christ. The Gregorian calendar, the most widely used calendar for international representation of dates, divides history into B.C. and A.D. (BCE and CE) based on the advent of Jesus. Paul wrote of "and an administration suitable to the fullness of the times, *that is*, the summing up of all things in Christ, things in the heavens and things on the earth" (Eph. 1:10). God has no more to give than Jesus. He has given us Himself in His Son, and by His Spirit. Jesus is the all-sufficient provision of God's grace, who keeps on dynamically giving and providing everything we need. *Solus Christus* – Christ alone.

AUGUST 23

TOO MUCH YOU, NOT ENOUGH JESUS

There are stacks and stacks of books written about *The New You*, allegedly achieved through nutrition, diet, exercise, mindfulness, makeup, meditation, and many other techniques. It seems that many Christian teachers are just adding to the stacks by referring to and writing about the realization and affirmation of one's new spiritual condition as a "new you." The emphasis is on the change in *you*, with inadequate emphasis on the reality of the One who comprises and IS the reality of the radical change of identity in you. There is too much "you," and not enough Jesus.

Many of these teachers claim Galatians 2:20 as their core verse, but it seems that it has ever-so-slightly been twisted into, "It is no longer I who lives, but the *new I* that lives in me." Most would claim that the "new I" is the living Christ, but their emphasis is on *my* new identity, *my* new understanding, *my* new provision, *my* new empowering, and there is inadequate emphasis on the presence and activity of JESUS CHRIST. It seems this teaching has fallen victim to the narcissistic preoccupation of the humanistic philosophy of our day: "It's all about ME!

What this leads to is a glorified or spiritualized form of humanism – pressed even to a humanistic gloss on grace, wherein we begin to think grace is a means to a "new ME." The one to be glorified in genuine divine grace is always JESUS. He is the dynamic of divine grace. He is the focus of divine grace. He is the re-presentation of Himself by His grace. We could call this disoriented teaching a form of "humanistic grace," were not such an incongruous oxymoron an impossible and inconceivable formulation. Divine grace comes into form only in the Person of Jesus (cf. Jn. 1:17). Grace is a Person – and that person is not me (or you), but the risen and living Lord Jesus by the Spirit (II Cor. 3:18). It is time that we should be more like the Greeks who came to Philip pleading, "We would see Jesus' (Jn. 12:21).

THE JESUS YOU

Many books have been published with such titles as "The New You," "The Righteous You," "The Holy You," "The Perfect You," etc. Perhaps someone should write a book entitled, "The Jesus You." That seems to better express what Paul wrote, "It is no longer I who live, but Christ lives in me" (Gal. 2:20), and it certainly identifies that the basis of my new identity is Jesus. I am a new creature because JESUS has come to live in me. It's not about me; it is about HIM. We must speak of JESUS instead of ourselves. I am only perfect because Jesus is the Perfect One in me; I am only holy because Jesus is the Holy One in me; I am only righteous because Jesus is the Righteous One in me.

A Christ-one can only be a Christ-one because the risen and living Christ Jesus has been invited into one's spirit to be the basis of one's new identity as a Christ-one. The one to be emphasized is Jesus, not ourselves; not our "newness," not our "righteousness," not our perfection. There is a sense of spiritual union and oneness, but such is not an essential oneness, but a relational oneness that retains the distinction between He and me. "The one who is joined with the Lord, is one spirit with Him" (I Cor. 6:17). We become a new creature, a new person in Christ – the Jesus you, the Christocentric you, the Christ-one.

We must be careful with our words and phrases. Reference to "the Jesus you," can and has been pushed to such an identification of Jesus and me that some would exclaim, "Jesus is me, and I am Jesus." That becomes a blasphemous identification of equivalence. The truth of our spiritual oneness must not be pushed to the extent that we exclaim, "I am Jesus" To push the distinctive divine "I AM" designation too far in identifying ourselves impinges on divine equivalence with Jesus. Jesus could say, "I AM" in that sense of essential oneness, but we cannot. But we can say, "There is no explanation for me apart from Jesus."

AUGUST 25

LOYAL FOLLOWERS OF JESUS

Our objective in ministry should be to facilitate the development of loyal followers of Jesus. We cannot make that happen, and then look back and say, "See what I've done!" It must be the work of the Holy Spirit in each person's life to direct and mold the thinking, emotions, and volitional actions of an individual in the process of "growing in the grace and knowledge of the Lord and Savior, Jesus Christ" (II Pet. 3:18). Every Christian is a disciple (Acts 11:26), and the Greek word for "disciple" is *mathētés*, meaning follower, learner, or apprentice. A learner-follower is "listening under" (*hupakouo – hupo* = under; *akouo* = to listen, to hear) the Spirit of Christ in obedience.

Typical religious forms of discipleship advocated in many religious contexts today are often framed in performance disciplines of prescribed prayer times and procedures of Bible memory, meditation, reading, or study, with the objective of learning the acceptable doctrines of the organization being represented. Such a format is quite inadequate to produce the outcome of true disciples who are loyal followers of the living Lord Jesus. It might produce loyal church members engaged in the performance criteria of their organization, but seldom do they learn how to live in the dynamic of God's grace.

We want to avoid any connotation of performance works comprising one's loyalty to Jesus Christ. We want also to avoid any sense of being faithful to or loyal followers of the those who have been involved in teaching and training of a disciple. I would be most chagrined, distressed, and upset, should it be revealed that anyone was a follower of Jim Fowler, instead of being a loyal follower of Jesus. I do not want to develop any Fowlerites, Fowlerians, or Fowlerists who would parrot what I have taught. I want people to be faithful and loyal followers of Jesus Christ, listening under the Spirit of Christ for leading and direction.

MY PERSONAL IMAGE OF HEAVEN

Most of the images of heaven that I have viewed have ascending steps, a stairway into heaven. Just go to Google images and type in "heaven." This is not the way I visualize heaven. Why steps of a stairway or ladder? Is this a leftover religious perspective that still clings to the concept of our having to climb our way up and into heaven? In my present physical body, having had my feet amputated, to think of having to climb steps is not a heavenly ideal for me; even walking on prosthetics is problematic. But heaven is a most desirable place that, if need be, I would crawl on hands and knees into the painless presence of Jesus.

My personal imagery of heaven is simply a transitional threshold. There is not even a door or gate to pass through. Just a flat threshold that enters a marvelously lighted place of peaceful serenity. It is so simple that one simply walks (floats) across the threshold into the place of glorious light – the glorious light of God's presence – into the loving arms of the Father, Son, and Holy Spirit, the Triune welcoming party. Physical death is but the transition into the eternality of God's presence and character. What a grace-full place it will be – everything functioning by the dynamic of God's grace in the Lord Jesus Christ.

In the moment that we are allowed to cross that threshold there will be an immediate change of form. Our body-form will be changed (I Cor. 15:52) from corporeal to incorporeal, from perishable to imperishable (I Cor. 15:42; 50, 53,54), from physical to spiritual (I Cor. 15:44). Paul refers to our body-form as a "house" (cf. II Cor. 5:1-10) and the physical will be transformed into a spiritual body (I Cor. 15:44), an ethereal body, a heavenly body (I Cor. 15:40,48,49), a glorified body. We will have a body-form that is suited to the heavenly context where we will be residing in eternal life, in Jesus. I can imagine myself exclaiming, "Glory, Glory to God in the Highest."

AUGUST 27

CONTROL AND FREEDOM

I was watching a documentary on the television show "60 Minutes," featuring the Chinese dissident artist, Badiucao. He was inspired by "tank man," the man who stood in front of the military tanks in Tiananmen Square in 1989 as the communist authorities were attempting to squelch the uprising of people demanding more freedom. Thousands died in their attempt to stand up against the repressive authorities. When Badiucao saw the videos of the stand-off occurring 30 years earlier, he took up the banner of dissent by drawing images that exposed and mocked the government. He was imprisoned for his actions, and eventually had to flee to Australia to avoid persecution.

Badiucao noted that the communist leaders sought to be in complete control of people's thought and action, and this always results in taking away personal freedoms by oppressing and repressing the people. The spark arced in my mind to the realization that religious control of people's thought and action also represses freedom. Religious authorities are in great fear of allowing the freedom that is found in grace. The very definition of religion, derived as it is from the Latin *religio* and *religare*, meaning to bind up or tie down, points to the control of people in a way that disallows personal freedom.

I identified with the dissident artist, Badiucao. I, too, am a dissident voice in a religious world, exposing religion and its control of people's thought and action in a manner that limits the freedom of God's grace. Selfish human control of others necessarily limits the freedom of others, but only the Lordship control of the living Lord Jesus in people's lives allows for freedom in the context of God's loving grace that seeks the fullness of human function. When we are controlled by God's grace (which always allows for freedom of choice), we have the freedom and liberty to be all that God intends us to be.

"THAT'S JUST THE WAY I AM"

Some people attempt to explain away their personality flaws, their fleshly selfishness traits, by retorting, "that's just the way I am!" It may be true that "it's the way a person is," given their fallen spiritual condition and the natural patterns of the "flesh," their variations of selfishness and sinfulness in the desires of their soul that comprise their natural personality traits. But is that a valid excuse for justifying their subsequent attitudes and behavior if that person claims to be a Christian?

A Christ-one who has received the presence and character of the living Lord Jesus into their spirit in regeneration (cf. Rom. 8:9), has become a "new creature" (II Cor. 5:17) in Christ, a "new person" (Eph. 4:24; Col. 3:10), with a new identity in their spirit based on the presence of the Spirit of Christ. Such a Christ-one does retain most of the "flesh" patterns of selfishness and sinfulness in their soul, but now has the provision of the Spirit of Christ in their spirit (cf. Rom. 8:16) to overcome the natural patterns. "The flesh sets its desire against the Spirit, and the Spirit against the flesh; for these are in opposition to one another, so that you may not do the things that you please" (Gal. 5:17). We have a choice to make about our identity and actions.

The Christ-one can no longer legitimately use the excuse, "That's just the way I am," and continue to do what they please in accord with their natural personality traits. The Christ-one is obliged to make moment-by-moment choices of faith to be receptive to the provision of the character of Christ within their spirit and thereby to be an overcomer of their natural propensities. "As you have received Christ Jesus the Lord (*by faith*), so walk in Him (*by faith*)" (Col. 2:6). "Walk by the Spirit (by faith), and you will not carry out the desires of the flesh" (Gal. 5:16). The Christ-one has a new "I am" identity in their spirit and can no longer fall back on the old natural default of "that's just the way I am" in their soul.

AUGUST 29

MOODINESS

Do you remember Eeyore? Winnie-the-Pooh fans will remember the old grey stuffed donkey that was a friend of Winnie-the-Pooh in the fictional books by A.A. Milne. He was a pessimistic, gloomy, depressed, unhappy, moody, and always looking-on-the down-side-of-life character. My favorite scene is where Eeyore is wandering around looking for his lost tail, lamenting in a slow drawl to everyone he encounters, "I think I've lost my tail." It's a great set-up for "pin the tail on the donkey." We have all known people who tend to be like Eeyore. We often categorize such persons as moody, gloomy, or depressive.

Some personalities are more prone to moodiness than others. It is often the particular manner these people express their selfishness. It is often indicative of the melancholy personality that allows their emotions to predominate in wide swings of happiness or unhappiness. Some would-be-psychologists might even call it "bipolar disorder," which in the past was termed "manic-depressive" disorder. Whatever we might entitle this personality disorder and natural behavioral characteristic, it always comes across as a negative "downer" that repels other people who don't want to be pulled down.

When the person exhibiting moodiness claims to be a Christ-one who knows "the joy of the Lord" (Neh. 8:10; I Thess. 1:6), observers are left bewildered by the discrepancy and incompatibility of the divergent character expressions. Rightly so! The attitude of dejected despondency is likely expressing the selfish patterns of fleshliness in the soul, whereas the "joy of the Lord" is derived from the presence of Jesus in one's spirit. It is the contrast of the flesh and the Spirit (Gal. 5:16,17). A moody Christian has a choice to make – the faith-choice of whether to continue to exhibit glumness, or whether to be receptive to the joy of Jesus that is included in "the fruit of the Spirit" (Gal. 5:22).

THE PAST, THE PRESENT, THE FUTURE

When we were in grammar school, we learned that the English language has three tenses of verbs: the past, the present, and the future. Yes, these can be broken down into the subdivisions of continuous, perfect, and continuous perfect, but the three major tenses of English verbs are past, present, and future. When it comes to how Christians perceive the three tenses, it has been noted that many Christians seem to realize that their past is forgiven, and their future is assured, but the present is the pits! Many Christians are at a loss to know how to live in the present. They often seek to bring the past into the present with regrets, or to bring the future into the present by speculation.

There are many people who seem to be stuck in the past, dragging old memories, regrets, and slights that remain as open wounds. We must regard the past as water under the bridge. Paul explained, "Forgetting what lies behind, I press on what lies ahead" (Phil. 3:13). This often requires forgiveness – forgiving ourself and forgiving others. The Forgiver, Jesus Christ, in us can heal our minds, memories and emotions. Forgiveness means to "let go" or "move away from;" coming from the Greek *aphiemi* (*apo* = from; *hiemi* = to move, to distance). Experiential forgiveness allows us to move on, letting bygones be bygones.

On the other hand, some become preoccupied with the future, the prophetic speculation of the "signs of the times" and "end times." The present becomes filled with projections of longed-for and expected future hope, often failing to realize that "Christ Jesus is our hope" (I Tim. 1:1) right now in the present. Christ-ones must learn to live in the NOW, the present reality and opportunity to manifest our true nature and identity "in Christ", to manifest Christ (II Cor. 4:10,11) as us. The present can be the unique re-presentation of the living Lord Jesus through our behavior as we derive life and character from Him day-by-day.

AUGUST 31

PRAISE GOD FOR TRIALS AND TEMPTATIONS

James, the Lord's brother, begins his epistle, "Consider it all joy, my brethren, when you encounter various trials, knowing that the testing of your faith produces endurance, and let endurance have its perfect result, so that you may be perfect and complete, lacking in nothing" (James 1:2-4). The Greek word for "trials" is *peirazmois* derived from *peiro* which means "to pierce in order to examine." The Greek word *peirazmos* referred to a trial or temptation, as well as a testing. The active source of a *peirazmoi* must be determined by its spiritual intent. If there is evil intent to the trial, testing, or temptation, then we can be assured that it is not from God. James explains, "Let no one say when he is tempted, 'I am being tempted by God'; for God cannot be tempted by evil, and He Himself does not tempt anyone (to evil)" (James 1:13). God never tempts us with evil intent.

The very same verb, *peirazo,* is used to explain why Jesus was asking Philip where they could get food to feed the multitude of people on the far side of the Sea of Galilee. He asked the question "to test him, for He knew what He was going to do" (Jn. 6:5,6). There was no evil intent in Jesus' question, just a test to see whether Philip would recognize the divine source of sufficiency to meet the need. We are likewise tried and tested.

Writing to the church at Corinth, Paul explained, "No temptation has overtaken you but such as is common to man; and God is faithful, who will not allow you to be tempted beyond what you are able, but with the temptation will provide the way of escape also, so that you will be able to endure it (I Cor. 10:13). The "temptation" referred to is the word *peirazmos*, which as noted can be translated "trial," "temptation," or "testing." Different English translations use each of the various words. If there is evil intent, then "temptation" is the word to use; if there is positive intent, then "trial" or "testing" might be the best translation.

SEPTEMBER 1

FREE TO BE THE REAL YOU

The" real you" is the "new creature" (II Cor. 5:17) that you have become" in Christ." We have become a new person (Eph. 4:24; Col. 3:10), but sometimes we try to hide behind the old persona we previously developed in our unregenerate and religious existence. That's the way people have known us. "That's how they relate to me, and me to them." "It's the way I am." "It's who I am!" some would reason. NO, the "real you" is now determined by your derived spiritual nature and identity in your spirit (cf. Rom. 8:16). We have become a Christ-one, spiritually united with the living Lord Jesus (I Cor. 6:17) to be the vessels through which Jesus re-presents (cf. II Cor. 4:10,11) Himself as us in the context of the world in which we live.

You are no longer the "old person" (Eph. 4:22; Col. 3:9) that you were when you were trapped and enslaved by the Evil One (II Tim. 2:26). Jesus took that old identity to the cross and it was crucified (Gal. 2:20; Col. 2:20; 3:3). So, stop trying to hide behind that old natural and religious persona. Quit living the lie (Jn. 8:44). Take off the mask and remove the fake evangelical smile. You are no longer the party girl who would do anything to get attention. You are no longer the "know it all," or the stuffed shirt nerd sitting at the computer trying to avoid people. Leave the baggage of the "old you" and its false identity behind you.

By God's grace in Jesus Christ, we are free to be the "real person" that we now are "in union with Christ" as a Christ-one. What freedom! We must not take ourselves too seriously. Self-consciousness just means that we are focusing on ourselves, rather than on Jesus. We must be willing to be vulnerable and genuine. We can be spontaneous in our expression of the character of Christ. There should be no fear of rejection, for we 'accepted in the Beloved" (Eph. 1:6). I am who I am in Christ Jesus, and those I interact with will have to take it or leave it!

SEPTEMBER 2

HUMANOLOGY

Frederic Buechner was a most interesting Christian writer. He studied to be a Presbyterian minister, but he never pastored a local congregation. His ministry was through Christian writing (some 30 books: novels, essays, theology, sermons, autobiography, etc.). He was a finalist for the Pulitzer Prize in literature in 1981.

Consider this quote from Buechner: "Theology is the study of God and His ways. For all we know, dung beetles may study us and our ways and call it humanology. If so, we would probably be more touched and amused than irritated. One hopes that God feels likewise" (*Wishful Thinking*). What is Buechner saying? Theology is humanity's attempt to explain God, but he whimsically labels the attempt of lesser creatures to explain humanity as "humanology."

The academic study of humanity is called "anthropology" (Greek *anthropos* = man; -ology from *logos*, word, logic, the study of). Christian thought has historically been weak in explaining how God created humanity: human constitution, function, what happened to mankind in the fall into sin, and how this is remedied by the Person and work of Jesus Christ. Early councils sought to clarify the theology of the Triune God, and the Christology of Jesus as *Theoanthropos*, the God-man, fully divine and human, but theological anthropology has been neglected. For this reason, much of my ministry and writing has sought to explain the derivativeness of humanity. In contradistinction to the world's philosophy of humanism which posits humans as gods who can determine and implement their own actions, it is important to understand that God is the dynamic of His action of grace in Jesus Christ (Jn. 1:17), whereas humans are receivers of God's grace by faith. Humans derive all that they are and do from one spirit-source of the other, God or Satan.

WHY ARE RELIGIOUS PEOPLE HYPOCRITICAL?

This question has been asked by many a thoughtful person over the years trying to figure out the blatant inconsistencies in the lives of those who are religiously active. How would you answer the question? I think the best place to start is to help the questioner to understand that religion, by definition, is not the reality of genuine participation in God. The word "religion," coming as it does from the Latin words *religare* and *religio*, pertains to "binding up" or "tying down," usually to rules and regulations of behavior or to rituals of devotion. Religion is a treadmill of performance standards dictated by human leaders.

Again, religion is not reality; there is no divine spiritual reality in religious exercises. Religion is a counterfeit charade inspired and energized by the "father of lies" (Jn. 8:44). Religion is the devil's showcase. Religious people may think they are working to please God but fail to recognize they are unable to perform as they might perceive God requires of them. So, they engage in the role-playing of religion like second-rate actors on a stage. That is the basis of religion – play-acting and pretending to be what one is not. And that is also the definition of hypocrisy – play-acting and pretending to be what one is not.

This is not a new game. It is the same-old never-ending charade. The Judaic religious Pharisees in the first century were indicted by Jesus for their hypocrisy. He called them "hypocrites" (Matt. 6:2,5,16; 23:13,14,15,23,25,27,29) and characterized them as "white-washed tombs" of corpses without life (Matt. 23:27). Paul indicted Peter for allowing his Judaic religion to carry-over into the Christian fellowship in Antioch (Gal. 2:13). Christianity is not religion! Christians are set free from the hypocritical bondage to the religious charade. Christians are free to allow the indwelling Lord Jesus to manifest His consistent life and character in their behavior to the glory of God.

SEPTEMBER 4

GHOST HUNTERS

I must confess that I have little (like none) interest in any of the television programs that speculate about aliens, extraterrestrial beings, ghost-hunting, paranormal phenomena, etc. I consider it unfortunate that the King James Bible refers to "the Holy Ghost" instead of the Holy Spirit. Perhaps I am predisposed to want to only consider data that can be conclusively verified historically or scientifically. Yet, at the same time, I am quite willing to accept the Theo-logic that is beyond human reasoning (I Cor. 2:14), the spiritual realities of the *pneumatikoi*, of spiritual things, (I Cor. 2:13). Though "unseen" (II Cor. 4:18), I do not question the reality of the Spirit of the living Lord Jesus dwelling and functioning within my spirit (Rom. 5:5; 8:9,11,16).

Such a personal disclosure probably explains (at least in part) why I have little interest in hunting or chasing the ghosts of speculation about demonic and sinister forces threatening to manipulate the government, the economy, or the ideological values that many people want to conserve (and have deified as non-negotiable). I have no interest in chasing rabbits or bopping gophers – things that are always popping up like a "new world order," the "illuminati," the "critical race theory," "wokeness," or "QAnon," or a plethora of other perceived threats.

The interest of Christ-ones should be focused on the Person and work of Jesus Christ (Heb.12:2; Col. 3:2). Yes, "the last Adam became the life-giving Spirit" (I Cor. 15:45), the Spirit of Christ (Rom. 8:9; I Pet. 1:11), so the spiritual is not outside of the realm of reasonable faith. Christ-ones are to be "renewed in the spirit of their minds" (Eph. 4:23), "the mind set on the Spirit is life and peace" (Rom. 8:6). I Jn. 4:4 – "Greater is He (Jesus) who is in you, than he (Satan) who is in the world (the ruler of this world). The world is going to do what the world is going to do, and it will always express the character of evil, but God overcomes all evil.

"AS HE IS SO ARE WE IN THIS WORLD"

A Christian cannot rightfully declare, "That's just the way I am," and continue in their old natural fleshly ways, exhibiting the selfish and sinful patterns of action and reaction that they have uniquely developed in the desires of their soul during their unregenerate life as the Satanic "spirit worked in the sons of disobedience" (Eph. 2:2), forming their personality and identity, i.e., their "flesh" expression. There has been a radical exchange of spiritual presence and identity (cf. Acts 26:18; Col. 1:13) within every Christ-one who has received the living Lord Jesus by faith, providing a new basis for the manifestation of godly character in their behavior.

John, the apostle of love, specifically mentions that God's character of love (I Jn. 4:8,16) is brought to maturity and perfection in the Christ-one: "By this, love is perfected with us, so that we may have confidence in the day of judgment; because as He is, so also are we in this world" (I Jn. 4:17). John is not saying that we are as God is in terms of essential being, but he is saying that in our union with Christ (I Cor. 6:17), we are Christ-ones intended to manifest godly character by deriving such from the divine presence of Jesus Christ who lives and functions within us. "Christ in us, the hope of glory" (Col. 1:27).

Our behavior as Christ-ones is intended to be derived from the character of the spiritual presence of the Triune God in our spirit. Because Christ in us is righteous, holy, perfect, and loving, we have the provision to evidence His righteousness, holiness, perfection and love, His character, the "fruit of His Spirit" (Gal. 5:22,23; Eph. 5:9; Phil. 1:11) in our human behavior. This is our ultimate teleological purpose and objective as human beings, our *raison d'etre*; we are "created for His glory" (Isa. 43:7). God is glorified when His character is manifested in His creatures, and in this manner His glorious character is made known.

SEPTEMBER 6

DERIVED CHARACTER IN HUMAN BEINGS

The Creator God alone is independent, autonomous, and is Who He is in Himself (*a se*). He created human creatures who are **not** little gods functioning independent, autonomous, and acting out of themselves (*ek autos*) as is the thesis of humanism, but humans are instead dependent, derivative creatures who must derive from a spirit-source (God or Satan) to manifest character (good or evil). This is an important foundation for understanding the relationship between God and mankind which is the objective of the gospel of Jesus Christ. The function of God's grace dynamic is the provision for all human beings are to be and to do as they receive God's character and action by the receptivity of faith.

Human beings are not independent selves or beings. There is no inherent or intrinsic character within the spirit or soul of human beings. There is no righteousness (Isa. 45:21; Rom. 3:10) or goodness (Mk. 10:18; Rom. 3:12). On the other hand, there is no inherent or intrinsic sinfulness or evil in mankind. All such character will necessarily be derived from either the good and righteous God, or from the Evil One (2 Thess. 3:3; I Jn. 3:12; 5:19) who inspires all sin (I Jn. 3:8) and selfishness. Derivative man will inevitably derive from one or the other – godliness is derived from God, while sin and evil is derived from the Evil One.

Historical Christian theology went awry when they accepted Augustine's theory that Adam's original sin corrupted the entire humanness of humanity and left human beings with an intrinsic sinfulness which could never be remedied or resolved, even by the work of Jesus Christ. That's right, Augustine and Calvin taught that the condition of original sin leaves humanity in a permanent condition of defiled humanness. That is why a Christian is but a permanent "sinner saved be grace," never to be declared righteous or good through Jesus Christ.

HUMANITY IS NOT AUTOGENERATIVE

First, we must explain what we mean by "autogenerative." The word simply means that we do not create or generate actions out of ourselves (*ek autos*). Human beings are not the source or origin of what they think or do. Yes, I know that this is totally counter to all the world tells us in their philosophy of humanism which begins with the premise that there is no God, so man is his own god. But rejecting the premises of humanism, we must begin with the Self-existent and Self-generative Creator God who created humans as derivative creatures intended to freely derive character and action receptively from God.

Only God is independent, autonomous and noncontingent, able to act with free-will, i.e., to freely determine to act, constrained only by consistency with His own character, with the coincident power to implement His Self-determined actions with His Self-generative (autogenerative) omnipotence. Human beings are not such independent beings (selves) with the inherent ability to self-determine from intrinsic character and self-generate action in accord with free-will. As derivative creatures, humans are choosing creatures with freedom of choice (not free-will) to self-determine to engage in this or than human action with the character of that action received from a spirit-source.

Human creatures cannot function like the Creator God. When we make a self-determined decision to act, we do not have the inherent power to implement and empower (autogenerate) that action with any positive or negative character, because we do not have any intrinsic character. We cannot self-determine to act righteously (with the character of God), nor can we simply choose to act sinfully (with the character of Satan). Instead, we choose to receive and derive from either God or Satan as the spirit-sources of character. Righteousness is generated by the Righteous One. Sinfulness is generated by the Evil One.

SEPTEMBER 8

WHY DO CHRISTIANS STILL SIN?

Christians are Christ-ones, spiritually united with the Spirit of Christ (I Cor. 6:17; Rom. 8:9). As such we are made righteous (Rom. 5:16,18,21; II Cor. 5:21) by the presence of the Righteous One (Acts 3:14; 7:52; 22:14), Jesus in us. Christ-ones are made holy, and called "holy ones", i.e., "saints" (Rom. 1:7; I Cor. 1:2) because of the presence of the Holy One (Acts 3:14; 13:35), Jesus Christ in our spirit. We are even referred to as "perfect" in spiritual condition (Phil. 3:15) by the presence of Jesus, the Perfect One (Heb. 5:9) in us. These are not essential attributions of identity in the Christ-one, but the character of God that we derive from His presence in our spirit.

Why, then, do Christians still manifest sinful behavior? It is certainly not the indwelling Jesus within their spirit that prompts them to express sinful behavior. The apostle John explained, "We know that everyone born out of God (*ek Theos*) does not keep on sinning" (I Jn. 5:18). Christ-ones are "born out of God" (Jn. 1:13), and the life of God in Christ is that of perfection that cannot and does not manifest the misrepresentative character of sinfulness and evil. So, the question remains: Why do Christ-ones make the choice to manifest character that is contrary to the character of Christ within which forms their new identity?

It can only be explained by the behavioral contrast and conflict that Paul identifies as "the mind set on the Spirit" versus "the mind set on the flesh" (Rom. 8:6,7,13; Gal. 3:3; 5:16,17;6:8; Phil. 3:3). Christ-ones continue to make choices of behavioral expression. Will they live out of the Spirit dynamic of God's grace and behave like who they have become, expressing the character of Christ, the fruit of the Spirit (Gal. 5:22,23), or will they revert to the fleshly patterns of selfishness and sinfulness in the Satan-contorted desires in their soul and express misrepresentative sinful behavior derived from the Evil One?

SEPTEMBER 9

THE SNARE OF RELIGION

In his attempt to warn the Galatian Christians about reverting to the bondage of religion, Paul provides an interesting word picture that is not evident in many English translations. The *King James Bible* translates Galatian 5:1, "Stand fast therefore in the liberty wherewith Christ hath made us free and be not entangled again with the yoke of bondage." *The New American Standard Bible* translates, "It was for freedom that Christ set us free; therefore, keep standing firm and do not be subject again to a yoke of slavery." The original Greek word for "be entangled" or "be subject" is *enecho* (*en* = in; *echo* = to hold).

The word picture is that of a snare trap that is often used by hunters and trappers. It is a simple piece of wire or strong string looped through a smaller loop which closes around the neck of an animal that runs through it. It does not appear to be threatening to an animal, but when an animal runs through the loop it serves as a noose or a ligature that tightens down on the neck. The more an animal struggles to free itself, the more the snare tightens and cuts into the neck until the animal is strangled and choked to death. It's not a pleasant way to die, but that is the intent of the hunter or trapper to kill the animal for food or for its fur pelt or other parts.

Paul is warning the Galatian Christians to avoid being ensnared, entrapped, and entangled by what may appear to be insignificant additions to the simplicity of the gospel, for by such they will be choked and strangled and held fast in a yoke of bondage that leads to death. This has been the sad fate of so many believers who have been receptive to God's grace in faith but are subsequently captured in the snare of religion. The more they struggle to get out of the snare trap, the tighter the restriction of their freedom becomes until they can no longer breathe in the grace of God, and they succumb to the death of quenched life.

SEPTEMBER 10

"I STAND AMAZED IN THE PRESENCE"

Charles H. Gabriel (1856-1932) wrote the words of a popular Christian song, known as "I Stand Amazed in the Presence." The lyrics of the first verse are:

> I stand amazed in the presence
> Of Jesus the Nazarene,
> And wonder how He could love me,
> A sinner, condemned, unclean.
> Oh, how marvelous! Oh, how wonderful!
> And my song shall ever be;
> Oh, how marvelous! Oh, how wonderful!
> Is my Savior's love for me.

I really like the melody, harmony, and rhythm of the song, but would prefer that the words be adjusted beyond the initial redemptive action of Jesus, to account for the ongoing amazement of all that He is to us in the restoration of our humanity. Perhaps something like this:

> I stand amazed in the presence
> Of Jesus, my Savior and Lord,
> And ponder how He does love me,
> Causing all of me to be restored.
> Oh, how marvelous! Oh, how wonderful!
> And my song shall ever be;
> Oh, how marvelous! Oh, how wonderful!
> Is my Savior's love for me.

The experiential awareness and awe of being united with the Lord of the universe is amazing beyond words. To ponder His presence functioning as me is mind-boggling. This constitutes genuine worship as I stand amazed in the presence of Jesus, my Savior and Lord."

SEPTEMBER 11

OVERWHELMED BY JESUS

The grace of God in Jesus Christ overwhelms us and overcomes us, pervading every aspect of our being. Our very identity, our very understanding of who we are and our *raison d'etre* is conjoined with Jesus. One cannot understand and know me apart from knowing Him (otherwise, I am a total enigma). There is an old truism that states, "What you take takes you." Well, I have taken/received Jesus by faith into the spiritual core of my being and am now known as a Christ-one. Jesus is completely absorbed into the core of my being, His Spirit united with my Spirit (I Cor. 6:17), testifying that I am indeed a child of God (Rom. 8:16).

I am not saying that such absorption of my being in Christ implies that my humanity is so totally absorbed in Jesus to the extent that I am no longer human. I remain fully human, with my spirit overwhelmed and personally engulfed in Jesus. I do not become Jesus in any essential way, but He has so complexly overtaken me, and taken over as presiding Lord of my life by means of the willingness of my freedom of choice, that He is allowed to live out His life and character as me. He re-presents His life in the totality of my human being, and those observing such may think it is me producing such behavior, but it is really He as me manifesting Himself, His character in my behavior.

In such union with Jesus (I Cor. 6:17), I do not want to sin and misrepresent the character of who He and we are. The real me, the deepest sense of the me who is spiritually united with Jesus, wants only to allow His character to be manifested in all I think, feel, and do to His glory. Hebrews 4:12 differentiates "the thoughts and intents of the heart," and the "intent of my heart (spirit) is to be a consistent Christ-one, allowing Him to override the "thoughts" suggested by the deceiving tempter to express behavior via the sinful and selfish patterns of the "flesh" that do not manifest the "fruit (character) of the Spirit" (Gal. 5:22,23).

SEPTEMBER 12

ATHEISTS AND AGNOSTICS

When I left seminary, I was not sure that I believed in the kind of God that was proffered and explained by the Augustinian-Calvinist theological paradigm. In fact, I was quite sure that I did not believe in a God who imposed Himself on mankind in a mechanical way and therefore disallowed a meaningful and relational response and interaction between God and man. So, I was essentially agnostic (Greek, *a* = no; *gnosis* = knowledge). I did not know what God was like or how to understand such a God. The problem with such a position of unknowing is that the Latin equivalent to the Greek "agnostic" is "ignoramus."

It is important to note that I was not an atheist. An atheist (Greek, *a* = no; *theos* = god) makes an assertion that "there is no God." The problem with making such an atheistic assertion is that you will likely be called upon to "prove your point," to provide evidence that there is no God. That is quite impossible – to attempt to prove the non-existence of an intangible entity. For just such a reason, many atheists do not claim to be atheists, but fall back on claiming to be agnostics who "do not know" if there is a god, or what such a god may be like, and thereby throw the onus of verification on the one who says "there is a God" to prove and explain what their God is like.

I can appreciate a genuine agnostic who is searching to find an adequate understanding of the invisible God of the universe. Paul explained, "the natural man does not understand spiritual things" (I Cor. 2:14). Such a person, an agnostic natural man, must be open to a revelation beyond empirical evidence and beyond natural reasoning whereby God can reveal Himself in a personal and spiritual way that is beyond mere human explanation. Such a personal revelation and personal invitation to join in personal participation with the Triune God via the Savior and Lord Jesus Christ will forever meet and fill the agnostic's quest.

SEPTEMBER 13

"GOTTA DO THIS; GOTTA DO THAT"

One individual who had just sat through another church service with the typical sermonic admonitions of performance, summed up the experience as having to endure the usual message of "You gotta do this; you gotta do that" and explained that it was "boring as hell." That person went on to say that they were tired of being accosted by the repetitive barrage of religious admonitions, surmising that those who subjected themselves to such tyranny week after week were apparently religious masochists who enjoyed the pain of being abused by charges of indolence, backsliding, lack of commitment, being shames with false guilt.

Many can identify with the sentiments of this discontented churchgoer. Christian religion and its practices have often degenerated into meaningless repetitive motions and monotonous maneuvers and machinations. The performance-based religion that is so entrenched in the churches seems to be lacking two vital ingredients: 1.) An understanding and experience of God's divine grace in Jesus Christ, whereby God serves as the dynamic for everything He desires to do in us. 2.) An awareness of how God created mankind as derivative creatures to be receptive to God's grace action, and to receive such by faith – the receptivity of God's activity.

Paul's way of expressing the interaction of these two important elements was, "For by grace you are being saved through faith, and that saving action is not of your own doing or making, for such salvation is given only by means of a gift from God, so no one can boast about what they have done or accomplished. For we Christ-ones are God's workmanship, created in Christ Jesus for good works expressed by means of the grace-dynamic of God's character of goodness – specific actions of Christ's character expression in us that were prepared from eternity that we should walk in them" (Eph. 2:8-10 paraphrased).

SEPTEMBER 14

TWO MOST IMPORTANT DAYS

Samuel Langhorne Clemens, best known by his pseudonym, Mark Twain, is quoted as saying, "The two most important days in your life are the day you are born and the day you find out why." Those are, without a doubt, important days in every person's life. From the moment of our birth, when we come into physical existence, we come complete with our distinctive sequence of DNA which will affect much of our physical actions throughout life. We are also born with natural temperament propensities that will structure our psychological personality and behavioral perspectives throughout our entire lives.

Mark Twain went on to explain that the second most important day of our lives is when we discover why we were born, why we exist. To understand our *raison d'etre*, our "reason for being," is more important than knowing our DNA and our psychological temperament type. The insular self-absorbed natural man may set out to "make a mark" for himself that will at least create a blip on the historical radar screen. Others will have a larger perspective that perceives a purpose, plan, or objective beyond themselves that will lead them to choices that will format the entire direction and activity of their lives.

The purpose of my existence is not simply to "serve my time" on earth as another insignificant historical personage. I am convinced that there is a greater divine plan ordained for me. Isaiah explained that "we were created for His glory" (Isa. 43:7). Jesus explained that the greatest commandment of our purpose was to "love the Lord your God with all your heart, and with all your soul, and with all your mind" (Matt 22:37). How do we love God and glorify God? God is glorified by our allowing His all-glorious character to be manifested in His creation, and more specifically through His human creatures indwelt by the Spirit of Christ (Rom. 8:9) to exhibit "the fruit of the Spirit" (Gal. 5:22,23).

JUST LIVE LIFE

These thoughts developed as a take-off from a quote attributed to C.S. Lewis: "Life is too deep for words, so don't try to describe it, just live it." In the same vein of thought, Soren Kierkegaard wrote, "Life is not a problem to be solved, but a reality to be experienced." Some people get distracted with all the petty details, and their life becomes a helter-skelter pinball with a meaningless trajectory. Kierkegaard also wrote, "Life can only be understood backwards; but it must be lived forwards." It is with 20/20 hindsight that we can analyze and perhaps develop some understanding of what has transpired, but we move forward in life trusting in divine foresight, as we are often groping and seemingly punching holes in the darkness.

As we move forward just living life, we do not need to understand all the "whys" and "wherefores" along the way. Our only preoccupation should be to live life, day-by-day, moment-by-moment to the glory of God (Isa. 43:7; Rom. 4:20; I Cor. 10:31). When one is preoccupied with trying to figure-out the hindrances, the nuances of their "fleshliness," or their patterns of sinfulness, they have lost their focus, and may soon lose their way. There is One who is the Way (Jn. 14:6), and we are to "fix our eyes on Jesus, the author and finisher or faith" (Heb. 12:2), allowing Him to serve as the orienting North Star.

To be able to "just live life" one must know Who is their life (Jn. 14:6; I Jn. 5:12,13; Col. 3:4). In conjunction with C.S. Lewis and Soren Kierkegaard, the Christ-one has received the life of Jesus into his or her spirit, into the core of one's being (Rom. 8:9;16). When we do encounter problems (they are inevitable), we are to allow Him to be the problem-solver, the icebreaker, the overcomer in every circumstance. Our only responsibility is to let Him live His live through us and as us. So, just live life by His life, receptive to all that He wants to be and do in you.

SEPTEMBER 16

PONDERING OUR EXISTENCE

Everyone is probably aware of Rene Descartes' (1596-1650) dictum: In Latin, *cogito, ergo sum*; first published in French, *je pense, donc je suis*; but in English, "I think, therefore I am." Lesser known is the statement of Albert Camus (1913-1960), who wrote, "I rebel, therefore I exist." Ponder with me. Can the syllogisms proposed by these philosophers be reversed to state, "If I fail to think and rebel, therefore I cease to exist – I am not? Can it be said, "I think not, therefore I cease to exist?" Both philosophers and their dictums are based on humanistic understanding of human beings being independent selves.

I propose another perspective. I exist as a derivative creature, and only as I make the moment-by-moment choices to derive from God or Satan does my existence have meaning or is it wasted without constructive purpose. My existence is not desultory, random, or the product of cursory chance, and the objective of my life, my *raison d'etre*, is not to make me "happy" (Old English *hap* = chance). As the happenstances happen haphazardly, perhaps one might be happy, provided there are no mishaps. Happiness is the chance that my self-desires might perchance be fulfilled to my selfish satisfaction.

Failure to understand the created derivativeness of mankind, that human beings are derivative creatures who will of necessity derive from one spirit-source or the other, God or Satan, will always lead to the humanistic premise first proposed in the Garden of Eden by the serpent, "You, too, can be like God" (Gen. 3:5). What a fallacious statement! God and man, deity and humanity are of two distinct categories of being. God is God; man is man, "wholly other from one another" (Barth), and it will always be so. That is why the introduction of a God-man is such an "absolute paradox" (Kierkegaard).

SEPTEMBER 17

NONCONFORMIST MISFITS

My wife bought me a t-shirt. On the front it reads, "Blessed are the weird people, the writers, the artists, the dreamers, and the outsiders for they force us to see the world differently." She knows me, and she has inquired on more than one occasion, "Why do you attract all the weirdos who want to glom on to you and your teaching? Why do you give them so much of your attention?" My only response is, "Because I think Jesus in me loves everybody, and everybody deserves my attention if they should want such." The truth is: I am one of those nonconformist misfits who "thinks outside of the box" and is unafraid to challenge the status-quo. A Christian college professor recently referred to me as "the controversial theologian."

Consider this statement: "Here's to the crazy ones, the misfits, the rebels, the troublemakers, the round pegs in the square holes, the ones who see things differently. They're not fond of conforming to rules. You can quote them, disagree with them, glorify or vilify them, but the only thing you can't do is ignore them because they change things. They push the human race forward, and while some may see them as the crazy ones, we see genius." This quote is attributed to Steve Jobs, cofounder of Apple Inc.

For those familiar with the King James Bible, it reads, "Christ "gave himself for us, that he might redeem us from all iniquity, and purify unto himself a *peculiar* people, zealous of good works" (Titus 2:14). And also, "You are a chosen generation, a royal priesthood, an holy nation, a *peculiar* people; that ye should shew forth the praises of him who hath called you out of darkness into his marvelous light" (I Pet. 2:9). Peculiar people often have a great desire to be and do what God wants to be and do in them, and unconcern for what those around them think of their individualized trajectory. I see in them "Pilgrim" in John Bunyan's *Pilgrims Progress*, trudging toward the goal (cf. Phil. 3:14).

SEPTEMBER 18

WE ARE BLESSED

The Greek word most often translated "blessing" is *eulogia* (*eu* = good; *logos* = word). God's "good word blessing" for us is, of course, the only-begotten Word, His Son (Jn. 1:1,14). That is why Paul explains in Ephesians 1:3 that "God has blessed (*eulogia*) us with every spiritual blessing (*eulogia*) in heavenly places **in Christ Jesus**." God has blessed us by means of the presence of His Son, Jesus Christ. Those who are "in (union with) Christ" have and experience God's blessing. Jesus in His Christ-ones continually serves as the blessing of our lives. There is no need to seek multiplied blessings that we attempt to pile up on top of Jesus. Jesus is all the blessing that we need.

In what we call the "beatitudes" of Matthew 5:3-12, we have another Greek word for "blessed." The word used by Jesus is *makarioi*, and this word is a congratulatory word meaning "fortunate," genuinely "prospered" by God. We call them "beatitudes" because Jerome's Latin *Vulgate* used the Latin word *beatus* for "blessed." We could read the beatitudes as "Blessed of God with many (plural) good fortunes and the genuine prosperity of God are the poor in spirit, those who mourn, etc. Jesus could have added, "Far greater than the *makarioi* will be your realization of the *eulogia* that I bring to you in Myself.

The blessing of Abraham (Gen. 12:3) "has come to the Gentiles in Christ Jesus" (Gal. 3:14) that we might receive the promise of the Spirit through faith." The blessing promised to Abraham was the "good Word" (*eulogia*) of Jesus Christ, and the fulness of Who He is in us. Many conceive of God's blessings as receiving good things or good circumstances. That can be part of God's blessing (cf. Matt. 5:45), but it is of utmost importance that every person be receptive to the spiritual and eternal blessings in Jesus Christ. Some will have noticed that the Greek word *eulogia* is the basis of the English word "eulogy," used to refer to the "good words."

SEPTEMBER 19

GOD IS NOT PLEASED

In Isaiah's heartfelt prayer, he confesses to God: cf. Isa. 64:6 – "all our righteous deeds are as a filthy rag (meaning in Hebrew, a dirty menstrual cloth)". God is not pleased with all our alleged righteous performance-efforts to do things for Him. Picture it like this: you come before God, and your sacrificial offering to Him is a dirty Kotex. God is not pleased! You have brought Him a symbol of death. But that is all we can do, in and of ourselves. In like manner, all the righteous deeds of religious performance are likewise an expression of death (II Cor. 3:7). God is not pleased with our human-engineered religion (cf. Isa. 1:14; Amos 5:21).

Performance-driven piety is a slam "in your face" rejection of what God has done. Yet, those who claim to have accepted the new covenant grace-dynamic in Jesus Christ, keep beating people down with inculcations of "what they must DO to please God." God is not pleased with the best we can do! This is a reintroduction of the Law-paradigm of human DOing, which puts people under God's curse (Gal. 3:10-14). Law-based human performance is an abomination in the sight of God. It is a rejection of God's grace in Jesus Christ. Considering all that God has done in the life and work of His Son Jesus Christ to provide His grace-dynamic to Christ-ones, to subsequently revert to LAW is to "spit in God's face," to participate in what God has cursed.

The apostle Paul saw this so clearly after his radical conversion (cf. Acts 9:1-22; 26:18). He had ardently attempted to keep every detail of the Law, but then he exclaims, "what I thought was my gain before God by my Law-keeping, I now count but rubbish (King James Bible "dung;" contemporary vernacular, "not worth a pile of shit), but it was all that I might know and gain Christ" (cf. Phil. 3:8). God is not pleased with any our attempts at obedience through performance-law. God is pleased with those who will function as receivers of His grace activity in Jesus Christ.

SEPTEMBER 20

"LET'S GET ALL EXCITED..."

Many Christ-ones today seem to be rather disappointed, unenthused, even verging on depressed that Christianity (Christ-in-you-ity) doesn't seem to be growing and making a big impact on people today. Well, if you are just looking at the surface statistics of ecclesiastical growth, the progress may appear rather dismal. I want to look at the deeper reality of what God by His Spirit is doing in the hearts of so many people across our nation and throughout the world as the Gospel of grace in Jesus Christ is taking root, spiritual regeneration and growth is occurring, and the awareness of "Christ in you, the hope of glory" (Col. 1:26,27) is burgeoning.

In fact, I am going to be bold in asserting that I believe there are more people in the world today who understand and have accepted the indwelling Lord Jesus, who understand that "works" performance to please God has been terminated at the cross, and realize that the Christian life is the manifestation of the Christ-life by the grace-dynamic of divine action, than there has ever been in world history. That is a bold proclamation, but I believe it! There are an ever-increasing number of grace-ministries operative today. Yes, they may have varying emphases, but they are introducing many people to abundant Life in Christ.

I am not discouraged but encouraged; even giddy about what God is doing by the grace-dynamic of His Spirit to expand the wonderful awareness of the living Lord Jesus who wants to live out His life in His Christ-ones, to re-present His supernatural Life in the Body of Christ today. I want to exclaim along with Bill and Gloria Gaither (©1972 – with a few revisions of their words), "Let's get all excited, go tell everybody, that Jesus Christ is Life; Let's get all excited, go tell everybody, that Jesus Christ wants to be their life, and they can be united in spirit with Him and live by His life." Be bold! Let's get all excited and tell everybody.

SEPTEMBER 21

EXPERIENCING AN EPISODE

Those of us with lingering health problems might speak of having an episode of light-headedness or ill-health. What is an episode? In Greek dramas there was often an *episodios* between the various segments of the dramatic story. The Greek root words: *epi* = upon; *eis* = into; *hodos* = way. An episode was an incidental insertion into the dramatic story. In like manner, we experience incidental insertions that God, the Divine Playwright, writes into the story of our lives, and allows Him "to enter into the story upon the stage of our lives" in various experiences. These episodes may feel like intrusions, but oftentimes they provide amplification of what God is doing behind the scenes.

The timing of these divine episodes in our lives is not ours to call. They often come unexpectedly. They may come in periodic installments. They come as "breaks" in the status-quo of our life-experience. We never know what God is going to do next and cannot schedule or stereotype the activities of God. God in Christ by His Spirit orchestrates and directs these episodes – these inserted incidents. They may be trials (*peirasmoi*); they may be glimpses of glory (*analampés dóxas*). Whatever form they might take, we can be sure that these diversions are not random, and they do serve God's purpose in our life-drama.

Without such episodes, our life-story might become so monotonous that it would lull us to sleep as we proceed in the rut of ordinary routine. An episode can serve as a "wake up" call interjected into the storyline of our lives, or it can serve as a spotlight to bring into focus a particular perspective that enlightens God's storyline. God has His ways and means of creating episodes in our lives, of breaking into the ordinary with His extraordinary events. It must be noted that His timing and His ways do not always coincide with our convenience. "His ways are not our ways" (Isa. 55:8,9); they are "past finding out."

SEPTEMBER 22

SHARING THE PROCESS

My first action of the day when I awake is to listen to what the Spirit of Christ has to say to me. He doesn't just bring to my mind biblical or theological ideas, for the thoughts are sometimes quite mundane and ordinary, but I know that they contain something I am to ponder and/or implement. Sometimes the idea comes to my mind while I am still in bed, and other times after I sit in my recliner. And sometimes I have to wait patiently, keep an open mind, and simply listen. Such listening is not seeking an audible word or statement from the living Lord Jesus Christ but is the openness whereby God puts an idea or a word in my mind. I think such divine communication and receptivity is **prayer**!

To listen is to be obedient. The new covenant Greek word for obedience is *hupakouo* (*hupo* = under; *akouo* = to hear or listen). Obedience is not trying to keep the rules and laws (that is old covenant obedience) but is to "listen under" God in personal relationship. But it must not stop there. We "listen under" in order to engage in "the obedience of faith" (Rom. 1:15; 16:26). In our "listening under," we ascertain what it is that God wants to be and do in us today, and then choose to allow for the receptivity of His activity whereby we become the open conduit in and through whom God acts – and that is the essence of **faith**!

My objective in listening is not to figure out how I can serve God or be engaged in ministry for God. Having a "one spirit" union with Jesus Christ (I Cor. 6:17), my concern is to ascertain God's direction in a relational impetus from God. It is not a matter of seeking what God wants me to do for Him, but what God wants to be and do in me today. All my doing will be ineffectual if it is not energized by His divine empowering (cf. Phil. 2:13). I often admit to God, "God, I can't; only You can; and I want you to do so." Only God can do God's work in a manner that produces godliness. God in action – God being God as only God can be – that is **grace**!

SEPTEMBER 23

IMPULSIVE ACTIONS

I knew a young couple who were driving down the highway together, when they saw an advertising sign that read, "Just do it!" They surmised this was a sign from God that they should get married. They did so, that very day, driving straight to the courthouse and getting married by a "justice of the peace." Let's just say that it was not "a marriage made in heaven." They had a couple of children, but the marriage ended in divorce a few years later. Their impulsive action lacked planning and forethought. They did not seek counsel from those who might have been willing to assist them in the major life-choice they were making.

Most of us can probably look back and recall impulsive actions and reactions in our own lives. We have all made impulsive determinations in shopping, both in-store and on-line. Some have made an impulsive decision to join a particular group or church. Can anyone say they have not acted or reacted impulsively, making an unadvised decision without sufficient planning and without seeking the advice or counsel of others? The Jewish scriptures had much to say about the counsel or two or three witnesses (cf. Deut. 19:15; Josh. 9:14; II Chron. 10:8; Job. 12:13; Ps. 106:13; Prov. 1:5; 12:15; 13:10; 24:6; Isa. 9:6). We must live with the consequences of our choices.

As Christ-ones, we do not want to merely react to the stimuli of the present moment, but to listen to God's direction via the Spirit-Counsellor. This does not imply a paranoid uncertainty about what God wants to do next. Is this of God, or is this of my own desires? Rather, we can participate in a spontaneous Spirit-led response of faith, acting out of receptivity to the available activity of God's grace. Instead of an impulsive reaction to the events around us, we want to make a thoughtful response of faith with an inner assurance that what we have chosen is what God wants to be and do in us.

SEPTEMBER 24

ABIDING IN CHRIST

In the context of Jesus' teaching the analogy of "the vine and the branches" (Jn. 15:1-11), He tells His disciples, ""Abide in Me, and I in you." (Jn. 15:4). The concept of "abiding" has been ambiguous in the minds of many Christians over the years. What does it mean to "abide"? Let's begin by noting that we abide in an abode, we live in a house or a home. The Greek word *méno* translated "abide," means "to stay, remain, live, dwell, make yourself at home." When combined with *oikos* ("house") we get the word *oikoumenē*, transliterated as "ecumenical," which refers to groups of people with differing opinions willing to abide in the same house, i.e., the Church of Jesus Christ.

Experientially, in our lives as individual Christ-ones, "abiding" is a choice of faith to "stay put" in the placement where God has "put us" and where He wants us to stay and make ourselves at home. By the regenerative action of the Spirit of Christ, we have been "put" or placed "in Christ," or "in the Vine" as Jesus was illustrating. So, to "stay put" where we have been "put" is an internal spiritual, as well as psychological (mental, emotional, volitional), willingness to make ourselves at home in union with (I Cor. 6:17) Christ, to settle into the deep personal relationship that we as Christ-ones have with our Lord Jesus Christ.

It is important to note that our "abiding in Christ" is not a performance that is required of the Christ-one; it is not something we have to DO to continue to be a Christ-one. In His next statement to His disciples, Jesus explained, "Apart from Me, you can DO nothing" (Jn. 15:5). Our "abiding in Christ" is a faith-abiding, and faith is not a meritorious "work." When we abide in Christ, we settle in and make ourselves at home in the realization that God's grace in Jesus Christ is sufficient for all that God wants to be and do in us. We choose to moment-by-moment derive from Him, allowing for the receptivity of His activity.

SEPTEMBER 25

"MY GOD, HE KNOWETH NONE"

Many Christians have struggled with the recollection of past sins. They know their sins are forgiven by God (or do they?) based on Jesus' taking them to the cross, but they struggle with forgiving themselves. One might ask, "Who are you to think that you can be more judgmental than God is alleged to be?" God's forgiveness in Christ is extensive and inclusive. The prophets foretold that He would "forgive our iniquity and remember our sins no more" (Jere. 31:34); that He would "cast our sins into the depths of the sea" (Micah 7:19). "As far as the east is from the west, He has removed our transgressions from us. (Ps. 103:12).

God's forgiveness, pardon, and absolution are beyond measure. "The blood of Jesus cleanses from all sin... from all unrighteousness (I Jn. 1:7,9). "The blood of Christ will cleanse your conscience from dead works to serve the living God" (Heb. 9:14), and "having been cleansed there will be no more consciousness of sins" (Heb. 10:2). Paul reiterated, "Blessed is the man whose sin the Lord will not take into account" (Rom. 4:8), and he lived it out with Philemon, writing, "Put that on my account" (Philemon. 1:18). Peter had to learn this lesson tangibly and viscerally on the rooftop in Joppa, "What God has cleansed, no longer consider unholy" (Acts 11:19).

Consider the words of this old hymn, written almost 300 years ago by Anglican vicar, Samuel Whitelock Gandy (1780-1851):

My sin is cast into the sea Of God's forgotten memory,
No more to haunt accusingly, For Christ has lived and died
for me.

What though the vile accuser roar of sins that I have done;
I know them well, and thousands more:
My God, He knoweth none.

SEPTEMBER 26

THE CRUX OF THE NEW COVENANT

If I might function as a systems analyst (broadly speaking), and boil-down the new covenant message to its core content, its central theme, the heart or crux of the *kerygma* proclamation of the gospel, I think the statement of the Swiss theologian Karl Barth best expresses the outcome: "The Revelation of God – the Abolition of Religion." The revelation of God is His Self-revelation in the Person, life and work of the Son, Jesus Christ. Jesus said, "No one knows the Father except those to whom the Son wills to reveal Him" (Matt. 11:27). His words to His disciples, "If you have seen Me, you have seen the Father" (Jn. 14:7,9).

Every assertion has its corollary, a flipside, a converse, obverse, or reverse. The necessary consequential contrary action to the Revelation of God in Jesus Christ is that it creates the negation and abolition of man-made religion (cf. Col. 2:20-23). Since Jesus is the Self-revelation of the Triune God, and "no one comes to the Father except through the Son" (Jn. 14:6) by the work of the Spirit, then the revelation of God's grace in Jesus Christ is necessarily the abolition of all the performance-religion of mankind trying to reach God. Religion is unnecessary, pointless, ineffectual, and to be rejected as but man's unbelieving quest.

Question: Can this double-sided theme be used to understand every portion of the new covenant literature? I think it can.

Gospels – narratives of Jesus confronting religion
Acts – religion counters progressive revelation of risen Christ
Paul's epistles – to the *ecclesia* – polemic of Judaizing religion
John's epistles - to the *ecclesia* – polemic of mystery religions
Revelation – cryptic illustration of Jesus' victory over religion

No portion of the new covenant literature should be isolated from this central organizing theme of the contextual whole.

CONTROL FREAKS

In the psychobabble of contemporary communication, there is a lot of talk about "control freaks." It is a colloquial indictment that describes a person with an obsession with getting things done "their way," with little or no tolerance for those who deviate from their way. If that sounds like a narcissist, you have correctly noted that a "control freak" selfishly wants to do everything "their way." Deep down, psychologically, control freaks are anxious, insecure, and angry – terrified of being vulnerable, always trying to protect their elevated self-opinion by constantly criticizing others and never accepting any blame themselves.

If that sounds like attitudes and techniques you have observed in religious interactions, you have sniffed out the rats in the religious woodpile. Religion thrives on the development of "control freaks" – self-obsessed individuals who want to control others and be the center of attention by asserting that they are "right" and know better than others seem to be candidates for religious leadership. Inflexible and unwilling to compromise, they are notorious for criticizing and "putting down" others in a legalistic and judgmental manner to elevate opinion of themselves, and to exercise leadership control over others.

Religious communities are replete with narcissistic "control freaks" manifesting Satan's character of selfishness instead of God's character of love. Observe the abundance of "the deeds of the flesh" (cf. Gal. 5:19-21), i.e., enmities, strife, jealousy, anger, disputes, dissensions, factions, etc. There is always infighting because narcissistic "control freaks" cannot tolerate people like themselves. But if you try to "buck" them, they are notorious for blame-shifting and twisting the truth into lies that indict you for precisely what they are guilty of. This is so misrepresentative of what the *ecclesia* is supposed to be, wherein the living Jesus is to function as the Truth (Reality) of His Body.

SEPTEMBER 28

AN AGNOSTIC GNOSTIC

This may appear at first glance to be an oxymoron – two words that should not be combined because together they negate or deny each other. Before we adjudge it to be an impossible construction, we need to define our terms. Historically, the philosophical religious phenomenon of Gnosticism rose to prominence in Asia Minor (now western Turkey) in the late 1st and early 2nd centuries A.D. Reference to Gnosticism was based on the Greek word *gnosis* meaning "knowledge," referring to a mystical or esoteric knowledge that could be attained by elite initiates enabling the release of the human spirit from the prison-house of the human body, in accord with Platonic dualism.

Gnostic thought also produced the sub-concept of Docetism, the idea that Jesus only appeared (Greek *dokein*) to be human because the physical was too far removed from the higher *gnosis* of spiritual reality to be united in one person. The apostle John appears to be addressing some of the concerns of Gnosticism in his writings late in the 1st century. Christian theologians of the ensuing centuries, particularly Irenaeus of Lyons (c. A.D. 130-203) labelled Gnosticism as heretical (*Against Heresies*). Modern linguistic usage of the term "gnostic" is expanded to refer to an inordinate emphasis on cerebral knowledge of factual data.

The term "agnostic," (from Greek *a* = no; *gnosis* = knowledge) is used to refer to someone who claims to have inadequate knowledge of God to be persuaded to believe in God, particularly the Trinitarian monotheistic God of Christian faith. Such a claim of agnosticism is often an escapism to avoid having to take a position of belief or unbelief about God. So, an individual may be termed a "gnostic," regarded as having much cerebral knowledge of factual data, and at the same time claim to be an "agnostic" when it comes to having insufficient knowledge to believe in God, or desire to experience God.

CHRISTIAN APOLOGETICS

The word "apologetics" comes from the Greek word *apologia* (*apo* = from; *logia, logos* = word, logic, reason), and linguistically meant "to argue, to make a reasoned defense." Peter used the word when he wrote, "always being ready to make a defense to everyone who asks you to give an account for the hope that is in you" (I Pet. 3:15). What are we trying to defend? God doesn't need any defense. He is indefensible by human argument. He already has a good defense attorney, an Advocate, in the Spirit of Christ. What God has done does not need any logical defense. He did what He did. Just study your history – the incarnation, the resurrection, the ascension of Jesus – they, and their extended implications are indefensible by human logic.

There was a time in my youth when I was quite enamored by "apologetics," the logical and rational defense of Christian "truths". After my regeneration in 1973, and my experience of the *pneumatikoi,* "spiritual things" (I Cor. 2:13-16), my interest in rationalist apologetics waned and faded into oblivion. Christian faith isn't logical in that way. It is reality experienced. If I can "get my head around" a particular topic to argue for it, then you can be sure that my argument is probably paltry and quite specious and doesn't hold much water – just words in the wind – just head-games. The discipline of Christian apologetics is practiced in the playpen of childish concern – the Tinker-toys and Legos of religious playtime. "When I was a child, I concerned myself with such, but now such interest has faded away."

Peter referred to "making a defense" for "the hope that is in you." Should I ever need to make a defense for why I am so hopeful, why I have such confident expectation (hope) that "All is well" in Christ Jesus? I shall answer, "I have found Him quite sufficient for all I need." Will that satisfy a rationalistic skeptic? NO, but I need not, nor can I go any farther to make human sense of the matter.

SEPTEMBER 30

SCRIPTURE INTERPRETATION

Many people misuse the scriptures, reading into them the concepts and thought grids they have picked up in whatever religious training they have experienced. To read into scripture the bias of one's previous understanding is called "eisegesis" (Greek *eis* = into; Latin *egeisthai* = to explain). Proper scripture interpretation should involve "exegesis" (*ex* = out of; *egeisthai* = to explain), i.e., to allow the scriptures to explain themselves as the interpreter draws the meaning "out of" the text. This is the basic procedure for proper interpretation of scripture – the study of which is called "hermeneutics."

An initial premise underlying our interpretation of scripture should be to remember that "it can't mean now what it didn't mean then" in the context of which it was first written. Otherwise, a text can mean anything to anyone at any time, in which case it doesn't mean anything to anyone. The context of any written document is of prime importance. This includes historical context and cultural context as well as the textual context in which the passage is found (ex. old covenant or new covenant literature and their overall thematic structure). In addition, grammatical context of authorship and the flow of the author's thought in the text must be take into consideration.

Those attempting to write or speak about the meaning of scripture must avoid conjecture and prior perspectives. They should come at the text with "fresh eyes" every time they commence to study the text. Recognizing that the best commentary on the bible is the bible, they should allow it to explain itself by the use of the same words and concepts elsewhere in the text. Those who write or speak about the scripture should provide scriptural documentation for every assertion. Unsupported suppositions about the meaning of scripture often leads to aberrant interpretations and even heretical teaching.

OCTOBER 1

WHERE IS HOME?

We have all heard the dictum, "Home is where you lay your head." Jesus said, "The foxes have holes and the birds of the air have nests, but the Son of Man has nowhere to lay His head" (Matt. 8:20). So, we ask, "Where was home for Jesus? Was Jesus a homeless man wandering around aimlessly?

I have never been "homeless" in the physical sense of not having a house to go to, to sleep in, to "lay my head." But I have been so lost that I could not find my way out of the lostness. Even then, I didn't know I was lost, for in physical terms I had found my way and my "home." I was a pastor. I had found my home, my career, my way in the ecclesiastical system, doing the things that ecclesiastical pastors do (preach, teach, counsel, say prayers, etc.), but I was lost; I did not know where I was going; I did not know where "home" really was. Yes, I was an unregenerate pastor, but by God's grace and in His time, He led me to my spiritual home in the relational presence and spiritual union with the Triune God, Father, Son, and Holy Spirit.

On the physical plane, it might be true that "home is where you lay your head," but on the more important spiritual plane, it might be said "home is where you conjoin your heart in relational spiritual union with the Eternal. In that sense, Jesus knew where His "home" was, and it was not in any physical structure where He could "lay His head" – His home was in the conjoined Triunity of the Three Persons in the one Godhead.

In like manner, we Christ-ones know where our "home" is. No GPS (Global Positioning System) can orient us toward our home. Our computer may have a "home" button, but that will not get us home either. We are "home" wherever Jesus is present and operative in our lives, now and hereafter. When we are dwelling in relationship with the living Lord Jesus, we are at "home."

OCTOBER 2

YESTERDAY

Yesterday is not just the day before today – not just the day that ended at midnight last night and ushered in today. If all we know is what occurred yesterday, we have a severely limited perspective, and all our tomorrows will be shortsighted in the shadows (cf. Job. 8:9). Yesterday came and went and now is gone. Have no regrets! Regrets about yesterday just indicate that you haven't let go of it; that it still looms large in your thinking and emotions. Yesterday is "water under the bridge," and we must let all the flotsam go downstream in the flow of the river. It is most miserable to try to relive or duplicate yesterday today. We must not allow yesterday to rob us of today, and cloud over tomorrow.

This seems to have been Paul's perspective of his yesterday of the past. "Forgetting what lies behind, I reach forward to what lies ahead, ...pressing on toward the heavenward call of God in Christ Jesus" (Phil. 3:7-13), all the while living in the NOW of today. The Psalmist voiced his perspective to God: "For a thousand years in Your sight are like yesterday when it passes by (Ps. 90:4). The past extends back as far as one might want to consider, but everything in the past is merely a bygone occurrence, and not to be syndicated in reruns. Moving beyond yesterday, we look forward to the new season.

"Jesus Christ *is* the same yesterday and today and forever" (Heb. 13:8). Our Lord is unchangeable in His consistency of character, ever new in His newness of life, and forever faithful to His every promise. The Danish thinker, Soren Kierkegaard explained that we may look back at yesterday with 20/20 hindsight and have some understanding of what God was doing, but we must live life with eyes straight ahead, often not knowing where God is leading, but proceeding in faith. Yesterday is history, the future is mystery, today is the present, so enjoy it as just such a gift and opportunity to be who Christ wants to be in you.

OCTOBER 3

TODAY

Chronological time is often divided into past, present and future
– yesterday, today, and tomorrow. The attitude of many Christ-
ones toward these time divisions has sometimes been to surmise
that my past is forgiven (by the death of Jesus on the cross), my
future is assured (I am confident of going to heaven), but the
present is the pits (where do I find strength for today?). Such an
attitude can be remedied by understanding the dynamic of God's
grace in Jesus Christ, whereby the Triune God has provided
everything necessary for the Christ-one to manifest the Christ-
life in any circumstances we encounter.

What is your attitude when you wake up to a new day? Do you
dread facing another day that may be a monotonous repetition of
yesterday? "Here we go again – I am getting tired of this daily
grind that is wearing down my resolve to be all that I can be – all
that God wants me to be!" That doesn't sound like a triumphant
Christian life, does it? Or do you awake to another day excited
about the possibilities of what God might want to do in your life
in this new day? The psalmist exclaimed, "This is the day that the
Lord has made, I will rejoice" (Ps. 118:24). Paul advised, "now is
the time of God's favor, now is the day of salvation" (II Cor. 6:2);
another day to live by the saving life of Jesus Christ (Rom. 5:10).

I choose to live every day with the expectant anticipation of God's
opportunities. Yesterday is in the rear-view mirror; today is a
wide-open road which serves as a bridge to tomorrow. I am
excited for every new day, anticipating that I will hear God's
voice and His word for me today. Hearing God's gentle loving
voice and responding with faith-receptivity to His activity is the
pathway of obedience. I want to live in the reality of the Christ-
life "as long as it is still called 'Today'" (Heb. 3:13), and manifest
the character of Christ, the "fruit of the Spirit" (Gal. 5:22,23) in
every opportunity afforded to me today.

OCTOBER 4

TOMORROW

Hedonistic humanism declares, "Let us eat and drink, for tomorrow we die" (I Cor. 15:32). Materialistic humanism explains, "Tomorrow we will go and engage in business and make a profit" (James 4:13,14). But life is so tenuous, and we are not in control of the circumstances, not today or tomorrow. Jesus said, "Do not be overly concerned about tomorrow, for tomorrow will care for itself" (Matt. 6:34). Have you noticed that the world tends to be overly concerned about tomorrow? "Plan ahead for tomorrow," they declare, buy insurance to hedge your bets, cover your tracks. Your future depends on what you do today.

The philosophical minded might say, "Tomorrow never comes," but the more practical say, "Don't put off until tomorrow what you can do today; don't procrastinate. There is truth in the realization that tomorrow is unending and unknown. Tomorrow is everything that occurs after and beyond today, and the extended duration of such can be any length of time in the future. Life is progressive – tomorrow's situation depends to some extent on what you do today – tomorrow's pleasures, troubles, workload, direction, etc. Annie sang expectantly: "Tomorrow, tomorrow, tomorrow; it's only a day away."

Many Christ-ones spend much time speculating on the blessings that will be theirs in heaven in the future. Many who yearn for what they hope to have tomorrow, in heaven, fail to realize that what they yearn for is already theirs today. Jesus is eternal life, and to have His life dwelling and functioning in us is to participate in heavenly eternity. How much better can it get? Christ is my life tomorrow because, and to the extent that Christ is my life today! Bill and Gloria Gaither gave us the words, "Because He lives, I can face tomorrow; because He lives all fear is gone. Because I know He holds the future; Life is worth the living just because He lives." He lives in us, today and forever.

OCTOBER 5

TRINITARIAN GRACE

It seems that Christ-ones often have only a concept of redemptive grace, i.e., the grace afforded to us in the historic Person and work of Jesus Christ. Such is the only revelation (cf. Jn. 1:17) by which we can understand a broader Trinitarian grace, but it should be the bridge which the parameters of our understanding of God's grace should expand in ever broader circles of inclusion. The very concept of Trinity implies a relational community of love wherein personal concern radiates out to the other. Each Person of the Godhead functions "in character" with loving concern for the other, and then the "other" expands to the entire created human people group they (God) created (Gen. 1:26).

The grace that we experience as Christ-ones is always Trinitarian grace, the functional expression of the Triune God, Father, Son, and Holy Spirit acting on us, in us, through us, as us, in relational love that leads us to genuine community (common unity) in Christ (in union with Christ). The relational community of the *ecclesia* is intended to be the living expression of Trinitarian grace, tangible evidence of the Trinity in every action that Christ-ones make individually and collectively. The Trinity will still be an enigmatic mystery to those who view it from the outside, but the visible manifestation of God's character in His people should be an undeniable testimony of Trinitarian grace.

Grace as the flow of divine activity of the Triune Godhead, one to the other is a reality that will forever be unreasonable, and incapable of being understood, by those who deny the Trinitarian understanding of the Godhead. But it is a sad indictment upon the contemporary institutional Church that so few have any concept of Trinitarian grace as the dynamic basis of God's interactive expression of love within the Body of Christ. It is only because of the grace of the Trinity that we can properly "love one another" in the loving community of Christ-ones.

OCTOBER 6

UNIDIRECTIONAL UNQUALIFIED LOVE

"God is Love" (I Jn. 4;8,16). His divine love is *agape* love, a kind of love that humans know nothing about, much less exhibit, unless they are in spirit-union (I Cor. 6:17) with the living Lord Jesus, whereby the divine Spirit has come to dwell within their spirit (Rom. 8:9, 16), and they allow such divine love to flow through them by deriving such in faithful receptivity of the loving activity of God for others. Apart from the Triune God, we will never know such *agape* love. God's *agape* love is only expressed *ek Theos,* out of God, in expression of His character. Humans cannot express such love unless it is His love through them.

There are no contingencies in God's *agape* love. There is no "I will love you if...." Or "I will love you when..." Or "I will love you because..." Or "I will love you provided...." Or "I will love you in order to..." Or "I will love you as long as..." *Agape* love is a free-flow spigot of God's love to others. There is no cut-off valve. There is nothing that the recipients of God's love can do to deserve God's love or to disqualify themselves from God's love. His love is not contingent on our reciprocation. Then, when Christ-ones become the conduits of His love, His love cannot be manipulated with any expectation of personal return benefits. God's love toward us, and through us toward others, will always be "I will love you regardless...". "I will love you despite....". "I will love you no matter who you are and what you do ....".

Such unqualified and egalitarian love is expressed. "God so loved the world of mankind that He gave His only begotten Son..." (Jn. 3:16). God's *agape* love is not a two-way street, but always a one-way, unidirectional expression for the highest good of others, with no return or reciprocal element or component. *Agape* love flows outward to others, in contrast to the selfishness that is always directed inward toward me, me, me. Love is the diametric opposite of all selfishness, self-concern and self-satisfaction.

OCTOBER 7

RESTING IN HIS "FINISHED WORK"

The evidence that one has truly entered experientially into the "finished work" of Jesus Christ on the cross (cf. Jn. 19:30) is when a person gives up all their performance-doing with any expectations of pleasing God thereby and accepts the "rest" of grace that God provides. When we "rest," we cease from attempting to do what has already been done to the full extent in the "finished work" of Jesus Christ on the cross. There is nothing that we need to do to finish the "finished work" of Jesus, nothing we can add to or supplement what Jesus has done. Accepting God's grace by faith, we allow Him to continue to do His doing to manifest His character by His empowering.

This means that those who persist in "playing religion" do not likely understand or appreciate the "finished work" of Jesus Christ. The religious performance-game is totally contrary to the gospel of grace that was put into efficacious motion by the death of Jesus on the cross. The death of Jesus on the cross of Calvary was the terminating deathblow to all performance-law for pleasing God and for formulating righteousness by means of performance. The apostle Paul explicitly advises the Galatian Christians, "If a law (religious rule) had been given which was able to impart life, then righteousness would indeed have been based on law" (Gal. 3:21). Performance law-keeping could not impart life or righteousness, and most definitely did not do so for the old covenant peoples. Paul proceeds to emphasize, "if righteousness could come through the Law (religious rules), then Christ died needlessly" (Gal. 2:21). Do you see what he is saying? If any religious performance could please God, appease God, or bring about righteousness before God, then the death of Jesus on the cross was an impertinence, a charade, a redundancy. Obviously not! Jesus' dying on the cross was the "finished work" of Jesus, by which henceforth connection and union with God could only be accomplished by God's grace-action.

OCTOBER 8

GRACE: THE ENERGY OF CHRIST

The Eastern Orthodox (Greek speaking) Church refers to "the energies of Christ" (*energeies tou Christou*). They point out that we do not partake of the essence of God or His Son, Jesus Christ, i.e., we do not become God or Jesus essentially, but the Christian does partake of the function of Jesus, which they call "the energies of God in Christ." By such energies, they explain that we are led to achieve *Theosis*, i.e., salvation and participation in God. This seems not unlike what Western Christianity identifies as the functional provision of the grace of God. Grace is the biblical word that seems to best describe the divine activity and empowering of God in Christ in our lives.

Grace is God in Christ at work in our lives, energizing His character and by the Spirit empowering our ministry activities. By the "sanctifying work of the Spirit" (I Pet. 1:2), the Triune God is manifesting His character in Christ-ones. "The fruit of the Spirit is love, joy, peace, patience, kindness, goodness, faithfulness, gentleness, and the godly control of oneself" (Gal. 5:22,23). The Triune God (Father, Son, and Holy Spirit) "is at work (*energon*) in us, both to will and to work (*energein*) for His good pleasure" (Phil. 2:13). God is *energizing* in us, both to will and to *energize* for His good pleasure.

The energies of God in Christ and by the Spirit are the divine actuation of His grace. Not only is divine character, the "fruit of the Spirit," energized by His grace, but the divine actuation of all Christian ministry is energized via the "gifts of the Spirit" whereby Jesus manifests His ministry in His Christ-ones. Jesus came to dwell in our spirit complete with His character and the continuation of His ministry – all energized by divine grace. We can never take credit for our character nor our ministry activities, for they are Jesus' energizing in us by divine grace. "God works (*energon*) all things in all His people" (I Cor. 12:6).

OCTOBER 9

THE HUMBLING OF THE PROUD

We have all observed the selfish actions of proud, arrogant, and self-sufficient individuals. Tragically, many of them are pastors and church leaders within the charade of religion, but there are even greater numbers among those who have sold out to their self-concerns in the world. The proverbial dictum, "Pride goes before a fall" is well-known. "Pride goeth before destruction, and a haughty spirit before a fall" (Pro. 16:18-KJV). We can be sure that the proud will be humbled (Isa. 2:12). God has His ways to "burst their bubble," to bring them down from their lofty perches, and to undermine their shaky empires. God's humbling process is not a vengeful or punitive process. The natural process is quite evident that if you give a proud person enough rope, he/she will hang themselves without any awareness that they have marched off of the edge of the gallows platform.

But, Oh the surprise of the proud when the façade of their lives crumbles and falls around them. When their carefully constructed "house of cards" crumbles, they will stand in the midst of the debris-field and ask, "What happened?" They never see it coming. They are blinded by their aspirations of successful advance to the top of the rubble pile. They are blinded by "the god of this world" (II Cor. 4:4), the "ruler of this world" (Jn. 12:31; 16:11) who has fueled them with his satanic character of selfish pride. It is an intoxicating elixir indeed.

The proud are convinced they cannot fail, that by the invincible means of the world's self-help incentives they have climbed the ladder of success. They have overcome the lesser foes in the process of the survival of the fittest. They have cast off the snares of social and family commitments and trampled their own people. They envision that they will stand triumphant as victors in the awards ceremonies of life. Pride goeth before a fall! "A man's pride will bring him low" (Prov. 29:23).

OCTOBER 10

LETTING DINOSAURS DIE

There was a time when dinosaurs roamed much of the planet earth. The word "dinosaur" comes from the Greek, meaning "terrible lizard." According to paleontologists, dinosaurs lived in the Triassic, Jurassic, and Cretaceous periods, which are collectively known as the Mesozoic era. This was a period when most of the planet was hot and humid, allowing for lush vegetation to sustain the abundant population of the herbivore, carnivore, and omnivore types of dinosaurs. A sudden climactic change seems to have led to the loss of the abundant vegetation and the mass extinction of dinosaurs around the globe.

What we observe is that dinosaurs lived in a particular period when they were sustainable by the global availability of vegetation. When climate change disallowed the sustainability of the food-source, dinosaurs died. This principle has been transferred to many other categories of thought. When the viability of objects or living things is no longer sustainable, then we should allow such to die or be terminated. People have even suggested that "dinosaur laws" should be enacted that would mandate the termination of unsustainable resources or agencies. Why perpetuate or put on life-support that which is not going to serve a viable purpose?

All of this reminds me of a sign I saw in Cambridge, England years ago. A church building was boarded up to avoid vandalism, and the sign read: "This building is maintained by the Trust for Redundant Churches." There comes a time when even church fellowships and church buildings reach the limit of their viable sustainability, and we must let dinosaurs die. I pastored a church fellowship called "The Neighborhood Church, in Fallbrook, CA, and there came a time when the glorious fellowship we enjoyed in that *ecclesia* congregation had served its purpose and needed to be terminated, whereupon the assembly was dissolved.

THE BIBLE AS A WINDOW

No doubt you have windows in your home. Do you look *at* your windows, or do you look *through* your windows? There may be occasions when we look *at* windows, like the stained-glass windows in cathedrals (ex. the circular Rose Windows at Rheims, Strasbourg, Sainte Chapelle, etc.). But we usually look *through* the clear, transparent glass windows in our homes to see what is on the other side. We would likely not want to look too closely *at* the windows in our homes, for we would see dirt smudges, cobwebs, insect remains, and imperfections in the glass.

The Bible is like a window that we look *through* to see Jesus. Religion has approached the Bible as something we look *at* to gain knowledge, and to develop our theology. Religion, like the Pharisees, has approached the Bible as an end-in-itself. Jesus told the Pharisees, "You search the Scriptures because you think that in them you have eternal life; it is these that testify about Me; and you are unwilling to come to Me so that you may have life" (Jn. 5:39,40). The Bible is not an end-in-itself, but a window that we look *through* to see Jesus Christ and enjoy personal relationship.

What did Paul mean when he wrote, "For now we see through a glass, darkly; but then face to face" (I Cor. 13:12 KJV)? Paul was likely referring to a mirror that reflects everything back at you in reverse. Mirrors didn't have the quality in Paul's day that they have today. What one saw in "the looking glass" was often a dim, blurred, distorted reflection of oneself. The window-glass of the Bible is not for the purpose of seeing a reflection of ourselves, but a window whereby we might have a vision of Jesus. The biblical writers (Luke, John, Paul) provided us with various lenses to see *through* to Jesus from various perspectives. Most biblical commentaries are the result of "scholars" looking *at* the Bible window with microscopes, looking *at* and seeing the imperfections and the bugs.

OCTOBER 12

NOT WORTH DOING

Religion is all about the human performance of doing things for God. This process has a snowball effect, for as the religious ball gets rolling it adds and collects an abundance of additional rules and regulations. The Judaic religion was constantly adding *chumrot*, i.e., "fence laws" (cf. Deut. 22:8) around the *mitzvot* (commandments) of the *Torah* (the first five books of the Pentateuch). Rabbinic tradition numbered the commandments of the *Torah* to be 613, but there was an unending number of additional *chumrot* to clarify the laws of the *Torah* text, and these *Halacha* were recorded in the *Talmud* and *Mishnah*.

The reality is that much/most/all of this religious doing is not worth doing. This is also true of the abundance of ecclesiastical rules that have developed in the Christian religion through the ages, with the various denominations each having their own collections thereof. The rules and regulations of religion that have bound up, tied up, wrapped up, snared and enslaved people through the ages are just extraneous religious activities that serve no benefit for those duped by such in the sight of God. The religious performance-rules are just not worth doing – it's just spinning one's wheels on the slippery slopes of worldliness.

Christ-ones must understand that if their activity is not the result of His (Jesus') ministry expressed through "the gifts of the Spirit" (Rom. 12; I Cor. 12; Eph. 4) in the Christ-one, and if His (Jesus') character is not expressed in their activities consonant with and by means of "the fruit of the Spirit (Gal. 5:22,23), then no matter how religious and numerous their activities might be, they are just "not worthy doing." Paul's explanation of the result of such impertinent activity is that it amounts to nothing but "wood, hay and stubble" (I Cor. 3:12-15) that will be burned up and revealed to be of no value – smoke up the chimney. He counted all his religious activity as but rubbish (Phil. 3:8).

GRACE AND HUMILITY

Many Christ-ones rightfully consider humility to be a trait beyond their reach. If they are still dabbling in religion, then humility is a totally foreign value, for it is contrary to the performance recommendations and commendations that religion lifts up as the standard of success before God. Religion does not foster humility, for religion is a means of self-elevation by self-performance. The lowliness of humility can never be achieved by the path of religion. Religious people will never achieve humility because their sense of self-worth and self-value is derived from how people see and applaud them (yes, Pharisaism). They do not realize that this aspiration leads inevitably to pride and never leads to humility.

Religion wants you to focus on what you can do for God, but God wants you to focus on what He has done for you and wants to continue to do in and through you by His grace. Religious legalistic performance gives birth to pride; God's grace gives birth to humility. Both Peter and James tell us that ""God is opposed to the proud but gives grace unto the humble" (James 4:6; I Pet. 5:5). God gives His grace to instill in us His character of humility. No one can work up or produce humility; it must be derived from the character of Christ. It's not about me, It's about HIM. This was the attitude of John the Baptist, "I must decrease; He must increase" (Jn. 3:30).

Jesus said He could do nothing except what He sees His Father say and do (John 8:28). Humility is simply turning everything over to God, and saying, "I can't; only You can; I want You to do so." The attitude of humility is the recognition that it is the power of God, not of man, that activates all things in His creation. Humility hands over the reins of actuation and power to the Almighty and omnipotent God. Humility does not desire any credit or commendation for what is done.

OCTOBER 14

LIVING BY CHOICES, NOT BY FEELINGS

God created human beings as choosing creatures with freedom of choice (not free-will), and many of the choices we make have consequences that determine how we live our lives here on earth. If God had created us as choosing creatures making choices without consequences, we would be living in a vacuum with no meaning to our choices. It is also true that choices without a source to implement those choices would also be but a vacuum. God did not create humans to live in a vacuum, but in the dynamic of His grace whereby He would provide the implementation and consequences of our choices. The necessary alternative is that humans might choose to derive from Satan, falsely thinking that they are engaging in self-implementation of action leading to self-fulfillment of consequences. That is not a vacuum, but a negatively charged spirit-source.

God also created us with emotions, affections, and feelings. The resultant expression of such is meant to correspond with our thoughts, feelings, and decisions. We are not little gods, and cannot will things into existence *ek autos* (out of ourselves). But we do make determinative choices. Ours is a willed life, not just an emotive life. If we do not feel like having fellowship with others, the consequence may be that we feel alone and left out. If we do not feel like going to bed, and therefore get only a few hours of sleep, the consequences may be that we wake up grumpy and weary.

Human choices are of necessity invested with character, and such comes from the spirit-source from whom we derive. Human choices are, for the most part, choices to derive from a spirit-source, either God or Satan, with the character of one or the other implicit in our actions. Faith is a choice. Are we going to live by faith or by feelings? We are intended to live by our choices of faith, and not by our feelings.

OCTOBER 15

THE COMING DEMISE OF RELIGION

I do not claim to be a prophet, but if the living Christ in me wants to speak in advance (Greek *pro* = before; *phanai* = to speak) through me, He certainly has every right, as my Lord, to do so. Who am I to say, "Not so...Lord" (Acts 10:14)? One doesn't have to be much of a prophet or social analyst to see the coming demise of religion. Even as crafty and resilient as the Evil One is in creating new variations of religion every hour of every day around the world, there is abundant evidence that the major religions are diminishing, and their ability to keep their followers and adherents in line and filling the coffers is declining.

The social signs are obvious as less and less people have any interest in religion. In fact, the word "religion" is rapidly developing such a negative connotation that it is often spoken with a snarl of contempt. Social analysts indicate that religion, particularly the Christian religion, has suffered a steep decline in the last twenty years, except for Pentecostalism in some areas of the world that are receptive to such sensate religion. When Christianity becomes something less than "Christ-in-you-ity" operative by God's grace as the living Lord Jesus lives His life in the Christ-one, then the bankruptcy of mere Christian religion will be evident.

The *Apocalypse* of the Apostle John, the last book of the Christian bible that we identify as "The Revelation," seems to explain that Jesus is and will be the victor over religion, and religion will eventually meet its demise when the Evil One and all of his religious performance regulations, and the entire world-system that he rules over will be cast into the "lake of fire" (Rev. 19:20–20:11). Satan and his world-kingdom which includes religion of every kind will meet their final fate. All the deception, all forms of death, all the religious counterfeits of what the Triune God wants to do will disappear and only those "in Christ" will remain.

OCTOBER 16

THE CHARACTER OF GRACE

Grace is the divine dynamic of God in Jesus Christ – God at work by means of the Son and by the power of the Holy Spirit. Grace is the impetus and empowering of all that God does to express who He is in His Triunity for His own divine purposes. We must be cautious, however, of simply thinking of grace as the divine energizing dynamic of God. Grace is God's activity, but God's activity always has a quality, i.e., consistency with His Being and character. The empowering of God in action is always expressive of His character of love, joy, peace, patience, kindness, goodness, gentleness, faithfulness, and the Godly control of oneself –the "fruit of the Spirit" (Gal. 5:22,23).

The holy (Isa. 6:3; 57:15; Ps. 22:3) and righteous (Ps. 119:137, 142; Isa. 45:21) God will always express Himself as who He IS. God does what He does because He IS who He IS. His grace-action is an expression of His Being. His character of compassionate love (Lam. 3:22,23; Ps. 86:15) is always, without fail, expressed in compassionate grace (Ps. 103:13; Isa. 49:13). God's character of sacrificial love will always be the grace-impetus whereby He acts in sacrifice for others in the Person of His Son (Eph. 5:1,2; Heb. 10:12), and continues to act in sacrificial love through Christ-ones (Jn. 15:13; Heb. 13:15; I Pet. 2:5) to others.

God's grace always has a purpose, a teleology. God acts to express His grace for others, and in so doing unto His own glory. The grace-action of God is for others' benefit, and unto His own glory. God is glorified when His own all-glorious character is exhibited in His creation unto His own glory. We were "created for His glory" (Isa. 43:7), and Christ-ones have "Christ in you, the hope of glory" (Col. 1:27), and are "to do all for the glory of God (I Cor. 10:31). We are "filled with the fruit of righteousness...to the glory and praise of God" (Phil. 1:11). God calls us to express His character of godliness to His own glory (II Pet. 1:3).

OCTOBER 17

CORRUPTION OF GRACE

When a person takes the liberty that is found in God's grace beyond its intended God-designed parameters prescribed by God's character and allows the pendulum to swing to the opposite extreme in license and libertinism, i.e., the misrepresentation of God's character in the selfish expression of Satanic character, it evidences human beings are attempting to use God's grace for their own purposes. Such serves as an example of the misused and corrupted grace of God. That is exactly what Satan always attempts to do – to twist that which is of God and "make crooked the straight ways of God" (Acts 13:10).

It must be noted that in the most basic sense God and His character are absolute and eternal, and essentially incapable of corruption, but His functional actions of grace can be misconstrued, misused, and misrepresented, even by those who claim to be operating in His grace – even by those who indicate that they are involved in a "grace ministry." The question that must always be asked, "Do the activities alleged to be expressive of God's grace manifest the character of Christ for others via "the fruit of the Spirit" (Gal. 5:22,23), or do they misrepresent God's divine character in selfish pursuits of personal pleasure, financial gain, or advancement of prestige?"

The corrupted misappropriation of God's grace-action can be so subtle, so cloaked in what seems to be legitimate reactions to the legalistic restrictions of religion while seeking the liberty and freedom of God's grace-action. But in that process such reactive pursuits are easily masked in self-justification that allows the pendulum to swing to counterfeit expressions of God's grace, flaunting freedoms that step over the bounds of the manifestations of "the fruit of the Spirit," and causing God's grace to be formularized in categories of freedom and liberty that do not account for the character of God.

OCTOBER 18

JUST A HUMBLE SERVANT

Humility is a character trait that is so completely "upside down" and outside of the world's wheelhouse of humanistic encouragement to "climb the ladder" and "be all you can be" as you become "king of the mountain." The world seems to think that to be humble is to be a "push-over," a form of passivity that "rolls over" and plays dead, and never accomplishes anything for the betterment of mankind. Humility is considered a form of weakness, evidence of powerlessness, a failure of the assertiveness necessary to achieve the great things that men are expected to achieve for the continual advancement of humanity.

There is a little-known parable that Jesus told, sometimes referred to as "The parable of the useless/worthless servant" (Lk. 17:7-10). He refers to a servant/slave who recognizes that he is just doing the job he is intended to do for the Master, simply a servant without worth or power in and of himself, or of any particular significance because of what he does. Just a humble servant, functioning as the available servant he is meant to be, receptive to the master's bidding without any expectation of praise, commendation, or adulation. Merely a servant who has simply done what was expected of him, and that without any expectation of getting a bonus or a raise for what he has done.

As far as the performance and productivity concerns of the world are evaluated, such a humble servant is useless in his slavish efforts to serve as a human tool for the benefit of another without commensurate compensation. The Christian perspective that understands humans created as derivative beings, views humility as knowing our rightful place of availability and receptivity in reference to the Triune God. It is totally backwards to the humanistic ways of the world, but Christ-ones can understand what it means to be "just a humble servant," accepting the usefulness of uselessness, and the uselessness of usefulness.

OCTOBER 19

THE PERFORMANCE PARADIGM

The world and its humanistic ways are increasingly emphasizing human performance in every sphere of functionality. A journal entitled *Performance Paradigm: a journal of performance and contemporary culture* is published annually, focusing on performance in art, productivity in the workplace, and the functionality of technological systems. Jon McKenzie has authored a book entitled, *Perform or Else* examining the relationship between cultural, organizational, and technological performance. Another journal, *Performance, Religion and Spirituality* explores performance in religious realms.

Performance has been the premier principle in religious thought and practice since its inception soon after the creation of mankind. The must-dos, the should-dos, and the how-to-dos are the incentivization of religious performance, regardless of what type of religion one is tied or bound to. Based, as it always is, on humanistic premises of human performance, religion is always proclaiming "God wants you to do it; please do it; we need you to do it," and this has been reinforced by the *Nike* motto of "Just do it!" *Nike* was the Greek goddess of victory, alleged to provide the performance enhancement for triumph.

The entire performance paradigm, whether in religion, business, or artistic and theatric endeavors stands in contrast to the dynamic of God's grace. God created human beings with the functional intent that humanity should be derivative creatures, receptively deriving from God's grace-performance in each individual. Religious performance with its Satan-inspired self-incentives of performance is the antithesis of God's grace. We are confronted with the either/or alternative of deriving from one spirit-source of the other – either from the Satan-prompted self-performance paradigm of thought or from the dynamic of God's grace provision whereby He energizes His character in us.

OCTOBER 20

OFF THE HOOK AND OFF THE BOOKS

For those inclined and disposed to consider the relationship of God and human individuals from a legalistic perspective wherein the primary concern is how human sin is the major criteria whereby humans became estranged from God, and then proceed to explain how this was remedied and rectified by God's Son, Jesus, who became a human being (cf. Jn. 1:1,14; Phil. 2:5-8), took the penalty of human sin upon Himself in crucifixion, and thereby served as our vicarious substitute to get us "off the hook" for our trespasses and off the books" of juridical accounting wherein we were considered as a liability to God – perhaps it is time to go beyond the images of a "hook" and a "book."

Our sins are not the means whereby we are identified as "sinners" (Rom. 5:8,19). Our sins are not like a meat-hook on which we hang before God prior to our being quartered and fileted. Our sins are not marked in red in the liability column of God's accounting ledger-books. By Jesus' identification with us and our identification with Him, every Christ-one can view themselves as God's asset. Since Jesus is God's asset, and we are "in Christ," then we are God's asset. The alleged sin-liability column has been cancelled out, erased, blotted out, and sins removed as far as the east is from the west

Jesus took all the sins of mankind unto and into Himself, and by His death took the consequences of all human sin (He Himself was "without sin" – II Cor. 5:21), so that sin-consequences are no longer a Damocles sword hanging over human beings with impending doom. In His Son, He arranged for relational restoration of God with man by means of His love drawing us into His Trinitarian community. When we keep bringing up sins in our prayer conversations with God, He simply says, "What sins?" God remembers them no more. We are off the hook, and off the books. Henceforth, we just look unto Him!

JESUS – MAN AS GOD INTENDED

At the heart of Christian thought is the understanding that Jesus was and is the God-man, the *Theanthropos* (*Theos* = God; *anthropos* = man) as the early Christians identified Him. The Word, the Son of God, "was made flesh" (Jn. 1:14). He was "made in the likeness of man" (Phil. 2:7), the "one mediator between God and men" (I Tim. 2:5), "the man Christ Jesus." As difficult as it is to grasp, He could be fully God and fully man simultaneously, but He could not function independently and autonomously as God while functioning dependently, derivatively, and receptively as man at the same time for such functions are incompatible.

After the Enlightenment of the 17th and 18th centuries when human reason was thought to triumph over all religious tradition and the supernatural, Christian thinkers thought it necessary to emphasize the deity of Jesus, emphasizing that He was God. Such thought prevailed in the apologetics of the 19th and 20th centuries into the 21st century, but now Christians need to understand that He was man and functioned as a man. We now find Christians saying that Jesus lived as He lived because He was God, and that we as Christians cannot live and function in the manner that Jesus did because we are just men.

As a man, Jesus functioned in spirit, soul, and body (I Thess. 5:23), and as a human choosing creature he had to live by the consequences of his choices. He was tempted "in all ways as we are" (Heb. 4:15) and was mortally "obedient unto death" (Phil. 2:8). Whereas God does everything autonomously of His own initiative (*ek autos*), Jesus said, "I do nothing of My own initiative; the Father abiding in Me does His works" (Jn. 14:10). Jesus lived out His life as a derivative man, by human receptivity of the Father's activity (faith). Although inherently divine, He lived His functional life as a human being by deriving from the Father by the power of the Spirit for every moment He lived.

OCTOBER 22

GOD IS SELF-GENERATIVE; MAN IS DERIVATIVE

"God is God" and "man is man," and to confuse this basic dialectic of being and function always produces confusion. The Triune God is the Creator-God and everything else is created being. Human beings, being the highest of created beings, are necessarily designed and limited to derivative creaturely function. To say that "derivativeness is tyranny," as humanists have claimed is but creatureliness clamoring for unachievable creative divinity. Man can conceptualize such but cannot create or effect such an operative paradigm. The parameters of being and function between deity and humanity are divinely established.

God is independent; man is dependent. Humanity cannot be an independent self-being. God did not create lesser gods and call them "humans." The greater (Creator God) can create the lesser (human creatures) who do not possess any of the essential Being, character or function of the Creator, and He has done so. Such human creatures are designed and intended by the Creator to derive from and receive from the Creator God to be and function as the human creatures they were created to be. It takes God in a man, for man to be man as God intended, but the ontological being and operational function of each remains distinct as God determined from the beginning.

God does what He does because He IS who he IS. He acts *ek autos* (out of Himself). He is self-generative of His own activity, and His character pervades His every activity. God never acts "out of character." God is the giver of all good things; man is the receiver. God's activity of givingness is called "Grace." Man's receiving of God's grace-givingness is called "faith." Faith is the response-ability of human beings to partake of all that God IS and Does. Faith is the ability of the human creature to make a receptive response to the character-invested activity of the Creator God. Faith allows God to be and to do as He wills in His creatures.

RESPONSE-ABILITY

In the minds of some English speakers, the word "responsibility" carries with it the connotation that "I must do this." For that reason, I have chosen to think and speak of personal "responsibility" as personal response-ability – the ability to freely respond with freedom of choice to what God has made available (and continues to make available) by His grace-dynamic in Jesus Christ. God is the dynamic for all that He demands and desires in our lives. We cannot, and are not, to attempt to "crank out" or self-produce the actuation of God's intents by self-effort. Instead, we are response-able to respond with faith-receptivity to God's grace-activity.

The denial of human response-ability has been prominent in Christian thought since the fourth century when Augustine formulated his novel concept of "original sin." This hypothesis suggests that Adam's sin of rebellion in the garden left every human being depraved and corrupted to the extent that the created abilities of humanity, such as response-ability to God's action, were destroyed and incapable of functioning. On this foundation of "total depravity," they proceed to suggest there are no conditions (such as faith) to respond to what God has made available in the redemptive work of Jesus.

Because man is not response-able, it is suggested that faith is "the gift of God," that God performs the act of response in us and for us, but that only for the predetermined "elect" who are limited by God's pre-selection. In such case His redemptive grace in Jesus is irresistible, i.e., pre-emptively imposed upon those previously chosen, who will then be preserved in their imposed placement without any need and with no ability to respond to the grace of God in the Christian life. Such a closed system of predetermination and divine imposition is man-made theorizing and indoctrination without scriptural base.

OCTOBER 24

CONCOMITANCE

Concomitance pertains to one being or substance being conjoined together with another being or substance. The term has been used in reference to the concomitant conjoining of the bread and the wine of the Eucharist to the presence of the physical blood and body of Christ, in the process of transubstantiation. Jesus' concomitant Being as the *Theanthropos* God-man dwells and functions in all Christ-ones by the "one spirit" (cf. I Cor. 6:17) union with the living Lord Jesus. Our spiritual concomitancy, coexistence and correlation so conjoins us, not in essential Being, but in unity of functionality to the extent that it can be said that Christ is at work in us (Heb. 13:21).

In like manner as the living Lord Jesus interjects Himself into concomitant Being with humanity in the incarnation, He subsequently, by means of the resurrection, stands ready to interject Himself into faithfully receptive Christ-ones to be their derived Being, life, identity, and character. This is not a co-essential or integral intermingling of natures, but HIS nature becomes our derived "divine nature" (II Pet. 1;4), for the spiritual nature of an individual is identified as the nature of the spiritual personage who indwells his spirit, meaning the Christ-one is spiritually united with the Spirit of the living Jesus (Rom. 8:9).

There is definitely a concomitant conjoining of function between Christ and the Christian as there was between the Father and the Son in the function of the Jesus as the God-man (cf. Jn. 14:10). The Father abiding in the Son always did what was consistent with the divine character, and thus was pleasing to the Father, and the divine Son without exception yielded Himself by faith to the Father's will, in human reception to the Father's activity. The Christian, in like manner, with the Spirit of Christ dwelling within his spirit (Rom. 8:9,16), is to be receptive to what the Lord Jesus desires to be and do in us.

OCTOBER 25

I APPROACH THE DOORS OF ETERNAL GLORY

It appears that I am on the final departure and evaporation of the "vapor" (cf. James 4:4) that has been my physical life on earth. Now, this final approach to the "departure doors of physical death" is simultaneous to the approach to the entrance doors into the already existent and realized eternal life that is the presence of the living Lord Jesus. "United with Jesus, we continue to live even if we die physically" (Jn. 11:25). "Believing in and living in Jesus, we never die on all life planes" (Jn. 11:26), specifically, the spiritual life-plane wherein Jesus is our life (Col. 3:4), and we are imbued with all that He is eternally and forever.

Those who do NOT know Jesus in the union of spiritual life remain subject to the slavery of the fear of dying physically (Heb. 2:15), enslaved to the "one who has the power of death, that is the devil" (Heb. 2:14). But we who know and are spiritually united with the living Jesus have confident expectation (i.e., hope) that being united with Jesus' life "in Christ" takes us on through eternity. "Christ Jesus is our hope" (I Tim. 1:1) of eternal life, and continual union with all that is identified with (as) Him (righteousness, holiness, goodness, etc.

O Lord, grant me the most expedient departure from this physical earth-suit that we call physical life and my simultaneous expected transfer into the eternal house of a spiritual body (I Cor. 15:44), a heavenly body (I Cor. 15:40; II Cor. 5:2), an imperishable body (I Cor. 15:42; 52-54) without pain (Rev. 21:4), an immortal body (I Cor. 15:53,54) without death (Rev. 21:4), a glorified body (I Cor. 15:40) that will forever glorify the name of Jesus by exhibiting His character and praising His name. I would hope that my friends would not mourn at my body transfer, for it will be I who grieves that they must remain behind in this diabolic world of physical hindrances until "their time has come" to make their contextual body transfer.

OCTOBER 26

PAIN ALWAYS HAS A PERSPECTIVE

My wife is a trained classical musician and finds great joy in listening to and playing classical music on her double-reed instruments. But she expresses a certain 'pain' at having to listen to rock music, and even some of the "happy-clappy religious music." Despite the psychological pain of having to listen to music in genres outside of her musical preferences, she recognizes that the musical preferences of others must be tolerated, and accommodated, and respected.

The act of sexual union via physical intercourse can be a painful experience for some, but it can at the same time be an enjoyable experience of personal sexual union. Physical pain can be superseded in the tolerance and endurance of the perspective in which it occurs. Even the practice of sexual BDSM (bondage, domination, sadism, and masochism) and the physical pain experienced therein may have its place in viable sexual relationships. The popular trilogy of books and movies, *Fifty Shades of Grey*, written by British author, E.L. James, featuring actors Jamie Dorman and Dakota Johnson, revealed the reality and social acceptability of pain in this perspective.

The intense physical pain I am presently experiencing in the degeneration of my lower extremities as I suffer the consequences of several years of decay from the disease of diabetes is most debilitating. I cry out in pain, both in the day and in the night, sometimes audibly and other times silently. I have, in particularly painful moments, asked God to "take me to my heavenly home," to avoid the pain. But such a request is qualified by the fact that He knows better than me, and if He has a purpose for my pain, such as my continuing to write about my trials leading up to physical death, I want to remain cooperative in the trajectory of His grace through the pain. The Lord knows better than I do the perspectives of how my pain serves His purpose.

GRATITUDE IS THE GRACE ATTITUDE

Some have suggested that we need to teach people the character-trait of gratitude. The problem with that suggestion is that one cannot teach or develop a how-to instruction manual for the development of an attitude of gratitude. Gratitude is the spiritually derived awareness that God is at work in our lives and/or the situation we are confronting. Gratitude must come from the spontaneous reception of grace and the recognition that the dynamic of grace is God's action. Gratitude is recognizing the "good grace," the Eucharist (*eu* = good; *charis* = grace) attitude of realizing, remembering, and giving thanks for God's grace-provision in the Person of the living Lord Jesus Christ.

When we who are "in Christ" ponder all that God has graciously provided in the historic redemptive reality of His Son, Jesus Christ; all that God so graciously provides presently in the grace-dynamic of Christ's life, and all that we confidently expect in hope that God will provide for our eternity in the contentment of His presence, how can we help but experience the eucharistic grace-attitude wherein we are thankful beyond measure – the grace-attitude of gratitude that is aware of the "good grace" of God in every circumstance and experience of our lives as He graciously directs our every step.

Despite the centuries of instructional writings on gratitude by the foremost philosophers of the world who have called gratitude "the mother of all virtues," and extolled the necessity of engaging in the performance of developing and cultivating the gratitude-attitude as a virtuous character-trait, we are suggesting that only those who have experienced the grace of God in Jesus Christ have the necessary internal provision of divine grace to recognize the eucharistic "good grace" of God, as well as the linguistic meaning of the thanksgiving of gratitude in order to participate in the gratitude grace-attitude of Christians.

OCTOBER 28

PERSPECTIVE ON WHAT GOD IS DOING

In the midst of severe pain from the diabetic decay of the tissue of my feet, I found myself crying out, "No, No, No!" whereby I was articulating that I did not want to tolerate the pain, that I considered the pain to be unbearable and I wanted God to stop the pain in one way or another. In other words, I was trying to selfishly "call the shots" in the present circumstance of my life. Recognizing such, I changed the word of my cries to "Yes, Yes, Yes!" What difference did that make in my pain? None! But it caused me to change my mental focus to recognize that "Yes, Jesus was with me right in the pain of the circumstance; Yes, Jesus knew what was going on and was empathetic; Yes, Jesus knew how much it hurts, for He endured the ultimate pain of vicariously suffering in our stead, even unto death (Phil. 2:8).

This reminds me of the incident where Simon Peter was on the rooftop of the home of Simon the Tanner on the seacoast of Joppa (Acts 10:1-16). God was preparing Peter to go to the home of Cornelius, a Gentile, to share the gospel of inclusion for all men in Jesus Christ regardless of race, religion, or circumstance. While sleeping on the rooftop, he became hungry and a king-sized sheet was lowered full of many animals, many of them not "kosher" in the Jewish religion. A voice said to Peter, "Kill and eat!" Peter answered, "Not so, Lord, for I have never eaten anything not kosher." The voice from God said, "What God has cleansed, you should no longer consider unholy." When Peter went to the home of Cornelius with the three escorts sent for him, he seems to have learned the lesson of the sheet, and did not say, "Not so, Lord; it is forbidden that I go into the home of an unclean Gentile."

Our reactions of "No" and "Not so Lord," can be converted to "Yes," and "Yes, Lord," with a changed perspective of what God is doing in the situation. This is an ongoing lesson I am still in the process of learning.

OCTOBER 29

THE NATIVITY SET-UP

During the Christmas season, many Christians around the world set up nativity scenes in their homes, depicting in various ways the manger where Jesus was born and the many personages and animals surrounding that historical event. In the United States where citizens make a big issue out of their personal rights, there have even been legal battles over whether nativity scenes should be allowed to be constructed in public places, like the courthouse lawn or in shopping malls. This issue of the right to construct nativity scenes can become a smokescreen that diverts people from seeing the spiritual reality of the new birth in those who receive the Lord Jesus by faith.

The birth of Jesus as a baby in Bethlehem was never intended to be an end-all of reverence and adoration, verging on idolatry, among Christians. Celebration of the incarnational advent of Jesus was not even practiced among the Christian community until the 4th century after Constantine's mother, Helena, made a pilgrimage to Palestine to find the place of Jesus' birth. It is inconceivable that Paul could ever have imagined making an issue out of constructing the physical peripherals of nativity scenes in public places. The birth of Jesus as a baby was but the historical set-up, the physical precursor of Christ's birth in human hearts in the subsequent history of Christianity.

The poet, Angelus Silesius, whose real name was John Scheffler (1624-1677), wrote these words in the 17th century:

> Though Christ a thousand times in Bethlehem be born,
> If He's not born in you, your soul is still forlorn.

The physical birth of Jesus was God's planned arrangement to prepare, to set up for the commencement of the spiritual birth of Jesus in receptive individuals. We must not allow a disconnect between these historical and eternal realities.

OCTOBER 30

"IN THE BEGINNING WAS THE WORD"

Most readers will recognize this phrase as the initial words of the Gospel of John. "In the beginning was the Word, and the Word was with God, and the Word was God" (John 1:1). In all three cases, "Word" is capitalized in most English translations, indicating, as the text indicates, that "Word" refers to One who is divine, i.e., God. The word "word" is translated from the Greek word *logos*. There was a long history of the usage of the word *logos* in ancient Greece. It went back at least as far as the 6th century B.C. philosopher, Heraclitus, who understood *logos* as the inner logic or soul of the universe ("logic" is from *logos*) which was often interpreted as communication from the gods (cf. the oracle of Delphi).

Early Christian thought agreed that *logos* was the "inner logic" of the universe, but personified the inner reality, purpose, and intent of the triune God in the Person of Jesus Christ. "The Word (*logos*) was made flesh" (Jn. 1:14.) The incarnation of the Son of God in the Person of Jesus Christ brought the divine Son of God down to man "made in the likeness of man" (Phil. 2:7) to identify with mankind in the experience of temptation and mortality. "He was tempted in all ways as we are, yet without sin" (Heb. 4:15), and all men are subject to death because of the sin of Adam in the Garden (Rom. 5:12,17,19). Jesus can thus serve as a High Priest who can sympathize with our weakness (Heb. 4:15).

Jesus is indeed the *logos*, the "inner logic" of God, of all that God intended from the beginning to do to redeem and restore humanity from their fall into sin by His Son, made man in Jesus Christ. Jesus is the way (the modality), the truth (the reality), and the life (the vitality) of God for mankind (Jn. 14:6). The Greeks did not understand the full import of the *logos*, but that was yet to be made known in the historical incarnational revelation of God in Jesus Christ.

OCTOBER 31

OVERSTATING THE TRUTH

There are some groups of Christians who have learned that Jesus Christ has totally transformed them and is willing to be their ALL in ALL. They have recognized that Jesus within them makes them righteous, holy, and perfect. But there seems to be some "zeal without knowledge" (Rom. 10:2) as they then begin to zealously proclaim, "I am righteous, I am holy, I am perfect!" Some have even gone so far as to proclaim, "I am Jesus Christ in my own distinct personal form!" Those who hear such acclamations are often "put off" by those claiming to be what they consider only Christ to be, considering the claims as blasphemy.

These Christians need to exercise caution about giving extravagant account of the truth they are so exuberant about, taking care to give full explanation of what they are declaring (even though the natural man cannot understand spiritual things – I Cor. 2:14), and not leaving out the contrasting dampeners (like the "flesh" and the reality of continued temptation) that will inevitably be experienced by one who is enjoying the reality of their new-found identification with Jesus Christ. It is possible to engage in a form of triumphalism that makes it appear that we are partaking of a Fantasyland in a spiritual Disneyland.

The Christ-one is indeed a "new creature" (II Cor. 5:17), a "new man" (Eph. 4:24; Col. 3:10) made righteous and holy. The "finished work" (Jn. 19:30) of Jesus Christ has made us "perfect" (Phil. 3:15; Heb. 12:23) and "complete in Christ" (Col. 1:28; 2:10). But in sharing these spiritual realities with others (even other Christ-ones), we must not sugar-coat or exaggerate the effect that the risen and living Lord Jesus has made in our lives. The Christian life is not a "bed of roses," and we must be honest about the experiential practicum of the "momentary, light affliction that is producing for us an eternal weight of glory far beyond all comparison" (II Cor. 4:17).

NOVEMBER 1

DERIVATION FROM THE DEVIL

Many in Christian religion doubt and reject that human-beings can derive from the spirit-source of Satan. We need to consider biblical references that appear to refer to derivation from Satan. John states in I John 5:19, "The whole world lies in the Evil One." The whole world of fallen mankind is in the Evil One, in similarity to how a Christian is in Christ – in spiritual union with Christ.

Paul states in Ephesians 2:2 that "the prince of the power of the air" (the devil) is "the spirit that works in the sons of disobedience." Satan is a spirit-being (not a divine being, and not a human-being) and he works (the Greek word is *energeo* – "energizes") in the sons of disobedience, identified as such because they are included in and identified with Adam's disobedience [cf. Rom. 5:19). Satan works spiritually in the unregenerate, in like manner as "God is at work" (Phil. 2:13) in regenerate Christians.

John wrote, "The one who sins if of the devil" (I Jn. 3:8). Sin-character must have a source. The source of sin-character is Satan. The Greek preposition that John used was the preposition *ek*, implying origin, source, or derivation. John is saying that the one who expresses the character of sin in sinful behavior is deriving what he/she does out of the devil.

When knocked down on the road to Damascus, Paul heard a heavenly voice telling him he was being sent to the Gentiles "to open their eyes so they may turn from darkness (reference to the devil) to light and from the dominion of Satan to God" (Acts 26:18). This is one of the clearest statements of spiritual conversion in the New Testament. Paul was being sent to advise Gentiles they must turn (be converted) from darkness to light (from the devil's darkness to the God of Light), turned from the dominion (*exousia*; *ex* = out of; *ousia* = being – deriving from the being of) Satan to God. This is the need of fallen mankind.

NOVEMBER 2

IDENTIFYING AND DEFINING SIN

There has been a tendency among Christians for centuries to identify and define sin as particular external actions – whether it be telling a lie, committing adultery, stealing items, or killing someone. Such externalization turns sin into a moralistic category of social wrongdoing contrary to the social mores of a particular social unit. Sin thus becomes relative to the particular group you associate with. It might be acceptable to one group of peoples, but unacceptable and abhorred in another group of peoples. The problem with such a definition is that there is no absolute standard by which to define sin.

From a biblical perspective, sin can be defined as any attitude or act contrary to the character of God. But furthermore it should be noted that such attitudes or acts contrary to the character of God are prompted by the Adversary, the Evil One, as he attempts to entice mankind to express his negative and evil character in place of the positive and righteous character of God. Any thought to engage in sinfulness does not just pop-up in our minds "out of the blue"; it is planted there by the spirit whose very objective is to "make crooked the straight ways of God" (Acts 13:10), to pervert God's ways.

Sin is not merely external improper behavioral actions that we might identify as "sinful," but sin is Satan manifesting his character of selfishness, sinfulness and evil in our attitudes and actions! The biblical justification for this view is made plain by the apostle John in his first epistle. "The one who practices sin is of the devil" (I Jn. 3:8), i.e., anyone continuing to do or commit sin is of (Greek *ek* = out of, meaning that person derives what they do from the spiritual source of the devil). When we thus identify and define sin, we can better understand why sin is so abhorrent to God, and why He hates it (Prov. 6:16-19) so – it is the perversion of His good and righteous character.

NOVEMBER 3

THEODICY AND THE ORIGIN OF EVIL

The term "theodicy" was introduced by the philosopher, Leibniz, in 1710, in his *Essays of Theodicy on the Goodness of God, the Freedom of Man and the Origin of Evil*. Long prior, Epicurus (341-270 B.C), questioned, "Is he [God] willing to prevent evil, but not able? Or "Is he able, but not willing?" A theodicy is designed to vindicate God and provide explanations for evil to enable people to continue to believe in God during pain and suffering.

Two primary explanations have been given in the history of Christian thought. Irenaeus (A.D. 130-202) believed that evil and suffering were part of the fallen world-system, creating a contrast so mankind would appreciate God's good. Augustine (A.D. 354-430) defined evil as the absence or deprivation of God's good. Evil is nothing in itself, merely the loss of the good. Neither of these explanations have biblical merit. The *Encyclopedia Britannica*, in an entry on "The Origin of Evil," begins, "In the Bible, especially in the New Testament, Satan (the Devil) appears as the representative of evil." After the Enlightenment, the idea of a personal devil was mocked and derided as being a product of the fantasy of the Middle Ages. C.S. Lewis noted that Enlightenment deprecation of the devil might be the camouflage of the devil himself, to give the impression that he just a fictional character.

Though the origin of evil creates a conundrum that is beyond what God has revealed, the traditional Christian explanation of Lucifer, the "shining one," the angelic light-bearer (Isa. 14:12), making a choice to defy being a derivative angelic creature, and to attempt to be "like the Most-High God" (Isa. 14:14), remains the best biblically revealed explanation. The question still is, "Did Lucifer's choice create the adversarial Evil One?" or "Did God determine to make Lucifer turned Satan, the Evil One? These options still leave us with inadequate incongruities.

CHRISTIANITY IS NOT A BOOK-RELIGION

Protestant Christians, particularly, have tended to make Christianity a "religion of the book" in their reverence and adoration for the biblical text of both the old covenant and new covenant scriptures. It is understandable that Protestants came to elevate the scriptures. Leading up to the sixteenth century Reformation, the bible was only available in the Latin language used by the Roman Church, and only in large cumbersome volumes. The availability of bibles in the common languages of the people was made possible by the printing press and proliferated with Luther's German translation and William Tyndale's translation of the New Testament into English (1526).

The Protestant Reformation coincided historically with the availability of printed scriptures; thanks to Gutenberg and the development of the printing press (c. 1455). Protestants, however, so identified with the printed scriptures, they began to conceive of Christianity as "a religion of the book," sometimes elevating the scriptures to a place of authority and adoration equivalent to Jesus Christ Himself, which is bibliolatry (idolatrous worship of the book). One Protestant author wrote, "Scripture imparts salvation," and added, "Believing God's Word (the Bible) results in eternal life." No, only Jesus can do so!

I appreciated the statement made in the *Catechism of the Catholic Church*, (#108). It reads, "The Christian faith ... is not a 'religion of the Book.' Christianity is the religion of the 'Word of God,' a word which is not written, but the Word which is incarnate and living. If the Scriptures are not to remain a dead letter, Christ, the eternal Word of the living God, must through the Holy Spirit open our mind to understand the Scriptures." The Bible is important, but unlike Judaism with the *Talmud* and Islam and its veneration of the *Koran*, Christianity is not a "religion of the book."

NOVEMBER 5

THE TRINITARIAN MONOTHEISTIC GOD

This is the unique and distinctive perspective of God in Christian thought. Early Christians had a Jewish background, and the *Shema* statement of Deut. 6:4, "The Lord is our God, the Lord is one!" was an important affirmation. Yet, Jesus said, "I and the Father are one!" (Jn. 10:30) and "If you have seen Me, you have seen the Father" (Jn. 14:7-11), which the Jewish listeners thought was blasphemous. How could these statements be reconciled? The Nicene Council (325) explained that Father and Son were *homoousion*, of the same Being, later at Constantinople (381) revised to include the Holy Spirit. This is a different understanding of God than the monadic monotheism of Judaism and Islam, both of which regard Christian teaching of the Trinity to be tritheism (three gods). The Council of Chalcedon (451) explained the Trinity by indicating there were three Persons in one Being, called the "hypostatic union."

The practical importance of the Christian view of Trinity is that Father, Son, and Holy Spirit form a perfect personal, relational, and loving community that is the derivative basis for all loving interpersonal relationships and community among Christian peoples. A singular monad cannot be love in the sense that "God is love" (I Jn. 4:8,16), for there has to be an "other" unto which to relate in love. Love always flows outward to another. A unity of two would allow for reciprocal relation (like a husband and wife), but a plurality of at least three is the basis of community. The divine Trinity is not to be thought of as a mathematical unity, but as a relational unity.

Christians believe that all three Persons of the Trinity, Father, Son, and Holy Spirit, come to dwell in the spirit of the person who is receptive to Jesus by faith. The experiential awareness of this spiritual reality is the basis of Christians deriving love and relationality to participate in the corporate reality of the Body of Christ, the *ecclesia*.

THE CREATION OF HUMANITY AND THE FALL

God created what which was not Himself "out of Himself," *ek
Theos* (cf. I Cor. 8:6; Rom. 11:36) All three Persons of the
Godhead were involved in creation (Gen. 1:1,2; Jn. 1:2). God the
Creator created human creatures as the apex of His creation,
with the purpose that they might participate in the personal
relationality of His triune Being (*Theosis*) and with one another.
Humans were created to function with "spirit, soul, and body" (I
Thess. 5:23; Heb. 4:12). They were created as receptive and
derivative creatures, intended to receive God's action of Grace by
the response-ability of receptive Faith.

Satan, the Evil One, the antithesis of God, with the character of
egocentricity and sinfulness, was allowed to test the freedom of
choice (not free-will) of the original human couple in the garden.
As the "father of lies" (Jn. 8:44), he lied to them indicating that
they could "be like God" (Gen. 3:5) and could "go it alone"
without the tyranny of derivation from God. In choosing against
God, humanity fell under tyrannical derivation of the devil, of
"the spirit that works in the sons of disobedience" (Eph. 2:2,3),
and were made "sinners' (Rom. 5:19) in spiritual identity, whose
consequent sins were derived from the devil (I Jn. 3:8). All
human beings were now spiritually dead (cf. Gen. 2:17) because
"the one having the power of death, the devil" (Heb. 2:14) was
operative within them.

Christians have had divergent opinions concerning how Adam's
sin affected the whole of humanity (cf. Rom. 5:12-21). A popular
opinion, suggested by Augustine of Hippo (354-430) is that
Adam's sin corrupted the entirety of human functionality
(depravity), making humans incapable of their created response-
ability (ability to respond to God's grace). This opinion, referred
to as "original sin," posits an inherent sinfulness to humanness,
in contrast to selfishness, sinfulness and evil being the character
of the Evil One.

NOVEMBER 7

OLD COVENANT AND NEW COVENANT

One has only to open what Christians call *The Bible* to note that it is divided into Old Testament (39 books) and New Testament (26 books) – two covenants. Early Christians referred to these as "the Jewish Bible" and "the Christian Bible." The story of God's covenants with mankind begins with the Promises of God to Abraham (Gen. 12-22). They include the promise of descendants (as numerous as the sand on the seashore and the stars in the sky), the nation promise, the land promise, and the promises of blessing among the nations. All the promises were fulfilled physically for the Jewish people (Josh. 21:45; 23:14; I Kgs. 8:56). Four hundred thirty years after the promises to Abraham, the Law was given through Moses for the Jewish people (not Gentiles – Rom. 2:14: I Cor. 9:21), but the promises precede and supersede the Law (Gal. 3:17,18). The Law could not make anyone righteous (Rom. 3:20: Gal. 2:16,20; 3:21) or perfect (Heb. 7:11-19; 9:9: 10:1). The Law ended at the cross (Rom. 10:4).

The Hebrew prophets prophesied of a "new covenant" (Jere. 31:31; Heb.8:13). The new covenant, the Jesus covenant, would be an inclusive covenant for "all peoples of all nations" (Jere. 3:17; 31:26), an internal spiritual covenant (Jere. 31:36; II Cor. 3:6), a Christ-centered covenant (Lk. 22:20; I Cor. 11:25), not legalistic but relational (Ezek. 37:26,27), a dynamic living relationship, rather than the static and dead outcomes of the old covenant (II Cor. 3:7). The new covenant provides the provision to manifest the divine life and character by God's grace and is truly an eternal covenant bringing divine eternal life to receptive humanity, the reality of the heavenly presence of the Triune God.

How tragic that misguided Christian teaching has attempted to put Christian people under the duress of old covenant Law. They have failed to understand the complete dichotomy of the old covenant for Israel and the new covenant reality of the grace provision of the living Lord Jesus in Christ-ones.

312

THE INCARNATON OF THE SON OF GOD

Humanity was unable to solve their fallen problem of sin and death. But "God so loved the world of fallen mankind that He gave His only begotten Son" (Jn. 3:16) to be the Messiah promised in the old covenant and the fulfillment of the Abrahamic promises. The Triune God determined to save mankind by identifying with them in their situation, allowing the Son of God to become a human being. The Son volunteered for the task (Phil. 2:5-8) by emptying Himself of His prerogative to function as God (though never less than God) and agreeing to function as a derivative human being. This was not a "Plan B", but God's plan from eternity past.

"The Word became flesh" (Jn. 1:14). The *Logos* which the Greeks regarded as the "inner logic of the universe" and "the unknown explanation for all things" became incarnated and personified. John identified the *Logos* as the Son of God. The eternally pre-existent Son of God became a human being, "being made in the likeness of men" (Phil. 2:8). How did Jesus live the life that He lived? Not as God (though He was) but as a human being who derived all He did from God the Father and the Spirit. "The Father abiding in Me does His works" (Jn. 14:10). He lived by faith, the receptivity of divine activity. "He humbled Himself by becoming obedient to the point of death (human mortality), even death on a cross" (Phil. 2:8). Jesus shared in human temptation (Heb. 4:15) and human mortality. "Since the children (humanity) share in flesh and blood, He Himself (Jesus) likewise partook of the same, that through death He might render powerless him who had the power of death that is, the devil" (Heb. 2:14).

"The only begotten of the Father, full of grace and truth" (Jn. 1:14) inaugurated and allowed grace and truth to be realized by mankind (Jn. 1:17). By His subsequent life and action as the God-man (I Tim. 2:5), "grace would reign through righteousness to eternal life through Jesus Christ our Lord" (Rom. 5:21).

NOVEMBER 9

THE CRUCIFIED LORD AND CHRIST

Jesus Christ, though immortal God, partook of mortality as a human being (Heb. 2:14). He was executed by crucifixion on a Roman cross at the instigation of the Jewish leaders (Matt. 26:57-68; 27:25;) with the complicity of the Roman authorities (Matt. 27:22; Acts 4:27) who implemented the gruesome task. Jesus, had, however, come to give His life as a ransom for all men (Mk. 10:45; I Tim. 2:6). The death consequence of sin (cf. Gen. 2:17) which occurred in Adam were incurred by Jesus vicariously, in our place, as us. "He who knew no sin was made to be sin on our behalf" (II Cor. 5:21). Jesus paid the price (I Cor. 6:20; 7:23; II Pet. 2:1) for our sin to provide God's forgiveness for sin.

One of the Greek words for "redemption" is *exagorazo* (*ex* = out of; *agora* = marketplace), and it was often used of buying slaves out of the slave market, redeeming them from slavery. The Hebrew concepts of substitutionary sacrifice, atonement (Lev. 23:7,8), and redemption of the disenfranchised (Ruth 4:4) are also used to explain the death of Jesus. There have been numerous theories of the atonement through the centuries of Christian thought. The word "atonement" is used once (Rom. 5:11) in the KJV, but in all modern translations it is translated as "reconciliation." We are "reconciled to God through the death of His Son" (Rom. 5:10. We should avoid the economic transaction theories with their questions of who paid the ransom, and to whom. "We preach Christ crucified, to Jews a stumbling block and to Gentiles, (moronic) foolishness" (I Cor. 1:23).

Jesus took all humanity to the cross objectively. The "old man" of every person was crucified with Christ (Gal. 2:20; Rom. 6:8; Col. 2:20). From the cross, Jesus exclaimed *tetelestai*, "It is Finished" – He could see the trajectory of the efficacy of His death (through resurrection, Pentecost, etc.). Every individual must enter by the receptivity of faith into the subjective realization of what Christ has done for them in His death.

THE RESURRECTION OF JESUS

The resurrection of Jesus from the dead was not just an historical miracle symbolizing life out of death (Jn. 5:24). When Jesus was unjustly crucified, the one having the power of death, that is the devil (Heb. 2:14) could not hold Him in death (Acts 2:24) for Jesus had no sin (II Cor. 5:21; Heb. 4:15), allowing Him to be resurrected (not resuscitated) from death to life. He took our death that we might have His resurrection life. Having declared, "I am the resurrection and the life" (Jn. 11:25), He came that we might have life" (Jn. 10:10) – His life! Jesus is eternal life!

The objective of the resurrection of Jesus was that He might be the "first-born from the dead" by resurrection "among many brethren" (Rom. 8:29), "so that as Christ was raised from the dead through the glory of the Father, so Christ-ones might also walk in newness of life" (Rom. 6:14). The saving life (Rom. 5:10) of the risen Lord Jesus becomes operative in a receptive individual when that individual receives Jesus by faith and is re-lifed, regenerated (Titus 3:5), "born from above" (Jn. 3:3,7), "born again to a living hope through the resurrection of Jesus Christ from the dead" (I Pet. 1:3). We are "born again" when Christ's resurrection-life is "brought into being" in our spirit by the presence of the Spirit of Christ (Rom. 8:9). Christ-ones are "raised up with Him," and "made alive together with Him" (Eph. 2:4,5), "united with Christ in His resurrection" (Rom. 6:5).

Christ-ones have experienced resurrection spiritually by being raised from spiritual death to spiritual life in regeneration. "Consider yourselves to be dead to sin, but alive to God in Christ Jesus (Rom. 6:11). We are "raised up with Him through faith in the working of God, who raised Him from the dead" (Col. 2:12,13). "In Christ all (who receive Him) will be made alive" (I Cor. 15:22) and we can presently experience "the power of His resurrection" (Phil. 3:10), while looking forward to the resurrection of our bodies in heaven (I Cor. 15:42) in the future.

NOVEMBER 11

SPIRIT CHRISTOLOGY

Jesus was not just the historical God-man executed on a cross. By His resurrection, He lives today; the Spirit of His life having been poured out at Pentecost (Acts 2). Christology (the study of Christ) moves beyond historical Christology to a Spirit Christology. Jesus told His disciples, "I will send another Helper" (Jn. 14:6) – not another of a different kind (*heteros*), but another of the same kind (*allos*), i.e., Jesus in Spirit-form (Jn. 14:17; 15:26). The very resurrection-life of Jesus lives in Christ-ones by the Spirit. "If the Spirit of Him who raised Jesus from the dead dwells in you, He who raised Christ Jesus from the dead will also give life...through His Spirit who dwells in you" (Rom. 8:11). The Spirit of Christ is the essential reality of being a Christ-one (Rom. 8:9,16). Paul asks, "Do you not recognize that Jesus lives in you, unless you believed in vain" (II Cor. 13:5)

The "mystery of the gospel" is "Christ in you, the hope of glory" (Col. 1:26,27). That is why Paul could write, "It is no longer I who lives, but Christ lives in me" (Gal. 2:20). "The last Adam (Jesus) became the life-giving Spirit" (I Cor. 15:45). The "Lord (Jesus) is Spirit" (Rom. 1:4; II Cor. 3:17). When the Spirit of Christ comes to occupy our spirit as our life (cf. Col. 3:4), we are in spiritual union with Him – "the one who joins himself to the Lord is one spirit with Him" (I Cor. 6:17). Christianity is "Christ-in-you-ity."

When we become Christ-ones and the Spirit of the living Lord Jesus dwells in us, we become "partakers of the divine nature" (II Pet. 1:4) of the triune God. The objective of Christ's indwelling in us is that His divine character and life might be manifested in our bodily behavior (II Cor. 4:10,11) by the expression of "the fruit of the Spirit" (Gal. 5:22,23). We were "created for His glory" (Isa. 43:7), and God is only glorified when His all-glorious character is manifested to His own glory. "Do all to the glory of God" (I Cor. 10:31). Christ is in us individually and collectively as we comprise the Body of Christ, the *ecclesia*.

FLESH AND SPIRIT CONFLICT

Some who become Christ-ones by faith-receptivity of the Spirit of Christ into their spirit have been misled into thinking that the Christ-life would be without problems. Didn't Jesus say, "Come unto Me, and I will give you rest"? (Matt. 11:28). Yes, but "rest" doesn't mean absence of trials, but provision within the problems. A new Christ-one soon realizes that there is ongoing conflict in their Christian life. Paul wrote, "If anyone is in Christ, he is a new creature; old things have passed away, behold all things have become new" (II Cor. 5:17). These latter phrases pertain to spiritual condition: "our old spiritual condition as an "old self" (cf. Rom. 6:6; Eph. 4:22; Col. 2:9) has been laid aside and died with Jesus; we are now a "new self" (Eph. 4:24; Col. 3:10) in Christ. The Spirit of Christ dwells in our spirit as our new derived spiritual identity of "children of God," and Christ-ones.

Paul grew up in Tarsus familiar with Greek culture and authors. He was likely aware of the philosopher, Epicurus (341-270 B.C.) and his association of the Greek word for "flesh" (*sarx*) with human desires. Paul refers to "desires of the flesh" (Eph. 2:3; Gal. 5:16-24), and Peter uses the phrase "fleshly desires" (II Pet. 2:18). Every person has a full set of God-given desires in their soul. There is nothing wrong with these desires, but they can be "urged upon" (*epithumioi*) and "yearned upon" (*epipotheo*) by "the spirit that works in the sons of disobedience" (Eph. 2:2) and twisted with patterns of the character of the Evil One. Everyone has such patterns of selfishness and sinfulness, and they remain in the soul when the spirit is regenerated.

Paul refers to the Christian conflict of one's "flesh" and the intents of the Spirit (Gal. 5:16-24). "The flesh sets its desire against the Spirit, and the Spirit against the flesh; for these are in opposition to one another" (Gal. 5:17). The Christian is not to battle the "flesh" by self-effort" – the divine Spirit is the positive power that overcomes the negative patterns of the "flesh."

NOVEMBER 13

THE SECOND COMING AND ETERNAL HEAVEN

After His resurrection, Jesus ascended into the presence of His Father with the promise to return (Acts 1:11) in what is referred to as the Second Coming (Matt. 24:30; Mk. 13:26) or "second advent. Christ's second coming is referred to as the "coming" (*parousia*), the revealing (*apocalypsis*), the appearance (*epiphaneia*), and "the day" (*hemera*). Christian eschatological thought is unique in that its primary focus is not on the future. Jewish hope was futuristic looking for a coming Messiah. Christians focus on the historic incarnation and the provision that was made available in His crucifixion, resurrection, and the Pentecostal provision of the Spirit of Christ. Our hope is in the revealed Jesus (I Tim. 1:1), not in a future expectation. Heavenly life is the continuity and perpetuity of the life we now enjoy in Jesus. We do not look for anything more than we have in Jesus.

It is from Paul's words, "The Lord (Jesus) will descend from heaven, and the dead in Christ will rise first ...then the living who are left, will be caught up in the clouds together with them to meet the Lord in the air" (I Thess. 4:16,17), that Christians refer to "the rapture." John refers to "the great tribulation" (Rev.7:14), but the timing and scope of this is not clarified. The "thousand years" of the millennium (Rev. 20:1-7) has been much debated (pre-, a-, post-). There is much speculation concerning the timing and signs of Christ's coming, and whether that coming is imminent (expected soon) or impending (forthcoming)? Christ's coming again will be to "judge the living and the dead" (I Tim. 4:1; I Pet. 4:5).

Christians find hope in the promise that physical death is not the end (Jn.6:58; 11:25,26). There is life after physical death – the continuity and perpetuity of the life of Jesus Christ that we now enjoy. Christians also expect the resurrection of the bodies of God's people who have died (I Cor. 15:14-18, 35-56).

DERIVATIVE HUMANITY

God did not create humans as God-like beings, as "little gods," or as demigods (lesser divine beings). He created that which was not Himself out of Himself (*ek Theos*). The greater (God) could create the lesser (humans) to be dependent upon Himself, intended to derive everything from Himself (*ek Theos*). God created humans as derivative creatures, who would of necessity derive from a spirit-being, either God or Satan. God is independent, but humans are dependent and derivative. God is the giver of all good things (James 1:17) by His grace, but humans are created as receivers, meant to receive God's grace by faith.

The lie suggested by Satan, the serpent, was that man could "be like God" (still suggested by Christian teachers today); that man could be an "independent self," functioning independently, *ek autos*, out of himself. That is the thesis of humanism that has been prominent ever since Satan beguiled Adam and Eve into thinking that they did not need to derive everything from God but could "go it alone." "You can be like God" (Gen. 3:5). Be who you want to be. You can live out of your own being and mental acumen. That God should make you depend on Him and intend that you derive from Him is tyranny; God is lording it over you.

Failing to understand that God created mankind as derivative creatures, Christian teachers ever since Augustine have tended to teach a form of "evangelical humanism," suggesting that when mankind chose to rebel against God in sin, he became "independent," living out of his own resources as an inherent "sinner." They are particularly reticent to accept that man apart from God is deriving from the devil, as "the spirit working (Greek *energountos* - energizing) in the sons of disobedience" (Eph. 2:2). It is imperative that the basic biblical doctrine of "derivative humanity" be reinstated in the teaching and thinking of Christian peoples to understand the relationship between God and man.

NOVEMBER 15

THE DERIVED CHRIST-LIFE

Everything in the Christian life is to be derived from the risen and living Lord Jesus. There is nothing that we have been given, and nothing that we can do that is not to be derived from Jesus. The entirety of the expression of the Christ-life in, through and as us is to be energized by the Spirit of Christ. We live by the life of another! It is not our best imitation of Christ, but the Christ-life must always be Christ manifesting His life and character in our behavior. The living Lord Jesus in the form of the Spirit has come to live in our human spirit (cf. Rom. 8:9,16) and is willing to BE who He is and DO what He does in our behavior, as us.

The religious incentivization to engage yourself in church activities to "be like Jesus," is a fallacious and demoralizing endeavor. Religious people soon run into the wall of their own inability and jettison the misconception of the Christian life by saying, "It doesn't work!" The activity of the Christian life must be divine activity. If God in Christ by the Spirit is not the energizing impetus of our activity, then we are just spinning our wheels in the religious mud-puddle. Religion is always a "go nowhere" endeavor that ends in a dead-end. The life of Jesus in us is an eternal endeavor that takes us to the presence of God.

The entire Christian life, i.e. the Christ-life, must be derived out of Christ (*ek Christos*), be the actuation of living through Christ (*dia Christos*), and be directed unto Christ (*eis Christos*). This cyclical structure: out of Christ, through Christ, and unto Christ, reveals that the dynamic of the Christ-life is always the living Lord Jesus as we derive all from Him. In likeness to Paul's statement in Rom. 11:36, after quoting from Isa. 40 and Job 41, "For from (*ek* = out of) Him, and through (*dia* = through), and unto (*eis* = unto) Him are all things," we recognize that the Christian life is the Christ-life, and we derive such by faith.

OUR DERIVED SPIRITUAL CONDITION

The religious world might talk of one's spiritual condition or refer to one's spirituality, but they usually conceive of such as a state of satisfaction, serenity or sobriety. Such a state of contentment or happiness might simply be the selfish pleasure of believing and enjoying that everything is going my way at the present time. Humans function at three levels: spiritual, psychological and physical function (I Thess. 5:23; Heb. 4:12). Our spiritual condition is predicated on what spirit-being (God or Satan) is dwelling in our spirit, and from whom we are deriving our character and disposition evidenced in our behavior.

The unregenerate, "natural man," having fallen into sin and death by means of the sin of Adam in the garden, has a spiritual condition wherein he is identified as a "sinner" (Rom. 5:19) – that because the spirit of evil, the spirit-source of all sin, the Evil One, Satan, the devil is "the spirit that works in the sons of disobedience" (Eph. 2:2), and is the spirit-source of their dysfunctional behavior. Since all human beings are derivative creatures, if they are not deriving from God they will necessarily be deriving from the spirit of this world (I Cor. 2:21), the spirit of error (I Jn. 4:6), the spirit of bondage (Rom. 8:15), i.e., Satan.

The spiritual condition of the Christian, however, is that of a "child of God" (Jn. 1:12; Rom. 8:16; I Jn.3:1,2). The spirit of the Christ-one is indwelt by the Spirit of Christ (Rom. 8:9,16), and the indwelling Jesus is the spirit-source from which a Christian is intended to derive character, best summed up by "the fruit of the Spirit" (Gal. 5:22,23). By deriving such godly character, the Christ-one is sanctified (set apart unto holiness) by the Spirit (I Pet. 1:2). Everyone's spiritual condition is derived from the presence of one spirit or the other, either from Satan or God. There are those, however, who are deceived by the Deceiver (II Jn. 1:7) into thinking they have an independent spiritual condition.

NOVEMBER 17

THE DERIVED LIFE OF GOD IN MAN

Spiritual life does not spontaneously erupt, but it can be brought into being *ek Theos* (out of God). No one can buy their way into life. No one can work their way into life. Everyone must be born into life. This is the reason that John wrote, "as many as received Him, to them He gave the right to become children of God, even to those who believe in His name, who were born, not of blood nor of the will of the flesh nor of the will of man, but of God (*ek Theos*)" (Jn 1:12,13). The purposed physical actions of man cannot produce divine spiritual life. Jesus, likewise, uses the imagery of being birthed into life. "You must be born of (*ek* = out of) the Spirit" (Jn. 3:6,8) "from above" (3:7).

The divine spiritual life of God can only come into being within man by means of derivation from God (*ek Theos*). God did originally create man with His life in man (Gen. 2:7), but after man's rejection of God in the Fall into sin and death, God does not impose His life upon humans who He created with freedom of choice. In his book, *Mere Christianity*, C.S. Lewis writes, "...the whole offer which Christianity makes is this: that we can, if we let God have His way, come to share in the life of Christ. If we do, we shall then be sharing a life which was begotten, not made, which always has existed and always will exist." Eternal life!

Jesus, being "one with God" (Jn. 10:30) has divine life in Himself (Jn. 5:26). "I am the life" (Jn. 14:6), Jesus explained. "He who believes in (receives) the Son has eternal life" (Jn. 3:36: 6:40,47). Paul wrote, "the free gift of God is eternal life in Christ Jesus our Lord" (Rom. 6:23). The apostle John added, "God has given us eternal life, and this life is in His Son" (I Jn. 5:11). "He who has the Son has the life; he who does not have the Son of God does not have the life" (I Jn. 5:12). Every person has the opportunity to derive the life of God into the human spirit by receiving such by faith. We "believe in Him for eternal life" (I Tim. 1:16).

NOVEMBER 18

DERIVED NATURE

It is common to hear people refer to "human nature," but what people mean by that is "all over the map." If ever there were an ambiguous word in the English language, it is the word "nature." "Mother Nature" is acclaimed as the cause of all natural occurrences. Is "human nature" comprised of our natural attributes given to us by "Mother Nature"? Is it legitimate to refer to "human nature" as the God-given capabilities of humanity, such as the abilities to think, to have desires, to have affective emotions, or to make volitional choices with "freedom of choice"? Some think that "human nature" is the inherent, intrinsic, and innate condition of sinfulness brought about by the sin of Adam.

The more biblical explanation is that all human beings have a derived spiritual nature, determined by the nature of the spiritual personage who indwells their human spirit. Writing to the Ephesians of their natural spiritual condition, Paul wrote, "We were by nature (Greek word *phusis*) children of wrath (a word referencing Satan)" (Eph. 2:3). We derived our spiritual nature from "the spirit that works in the sons of disobedience" (Eph. 2:2). Having received Christ, Peter explains that we "become partakers of the divine nature (*phusis*)" (II Pet. 1:4), deriving our spiritual nature from the presence of Christ within.

The spiritual nature of humanity is always derived from the nature of the spiritual personage who indwells our human spirit. We either have "the nature of wrath" derived from Satan or we have "the divine nature" derived from the presence of the Triune God within our spirit. Since God and Satan are mutually incompatible, it is impossible to have "two natures" (an "old nature" and a "new nature") in our spirit simultaneously, as has been popular in Christian religious teaching. One teacher explained that every Christian has both "the old sin nature" and "the Jesus nature" in their human spirit. Impossible!

NOVEMBER 19

DERIVED IDENTITY

The humanistic world around us attempts to find and establish an identity by what they do (professional occupation or talents), who they know (associations and affiliations), or what they possess (portfolio, homes, automobiles). We are much more than our given name, or what we possess, know, or do. These external criteria are inadequate to explain a person's deepest identity and are a most fragile sense of identification that is susceptible to collapse and the ostracism of rejection. Every person needs to find a sense of identity that is constructed in the core of their being, in their spirit, in union with the spiritual personage (either Satan or God) that occupies their human spirit.

The identity of an unregenerate person, a person who is not a Christ-one, is derived from the character of "the spirit who works in the sons of disobedience' (Eph. 2:2). "Natural men" (I Cor. 2:14) are identified with the identify of "sinners" (Rom. 5:8,19) – that identity is not based on any sins they have committed, but on the Satanic spiritual presence of the spirit-source of all sinful expression (cf. I Jn. 3:8). Non-Christians are also identified as "sons of disobedience" (Eph. 5:6), the "ungodly" (Rom. 5:6), the "unrighteous" (I Cor. 6:9), and the "condemned" (Mk. 16:16).

The Christ-one, on the other hand, is identified by the presence of the living Lord Jesus in his/her human spirit (cf. Acts 11:26). This does not mean that we have become Jesus, but that we derive our Christian identity from the One who lives in us. Christians have the derived identity of "saints" (Rom. 1:7; Eph. 1:18; 4:12) instead of "sinners;" "children of God" (Jn. 1:12; Rom. 8:16; I Jn. 3:1) instead of "sons of disobedience" (Eph. 5:6); the "redeemed" (Rom. 3:24; I Cor. 1:30); the "chosen of God" (Col. 3:12; Titus 1:1); the "sanctified" (I Cor. 1:2,30; 6:11) and set apart unto God's holiness. All of these are monikers for our derived identity in union with Jesus Christ.

DERIVED SPIRITUAL CHARACTER

Humanistic psychology regards character to be rooted in the natural characteristics of human personality and/or behavior patterns. Some would indicate that human character is innately determined by our unique combination of genetics – character is in our genes! Others would advocate that character is learned behavior patterns, and character can be developed with "character education" – we just need to teach people to change their character. Christian teaching indicates character is derived from a spirit, either Satan or God, who dwells within the human spirit and energizes his character in their behavior.

Those inhabited by the "the spirit that works in the sons of disobedience" (Eph. 2:2), i.e., by Satan, the Evil One, derive his character of selfishness and sinfulness. Lucifer, who became Satan, was selfish from the beginning (cf. Isa. 14:14). The devil takes that which is of God and "makes crooked the straight ways of God" (Acts 13:10), twisting and distorting the character of God. The character of the Evil One is evidenced in "the deed of the flesh" (Gal. 5:19-21); "enmities, strife, jealousy, outbursts of anger, disputes, dissensions, factions, envying, drunkenness, carousing, and things like these." To these we might add negativism, rejection, and all sinfulness. The apostle John explained that "the one committing sin is of the devil (*ek diabolos*), i.e., derives what he does from the devil.

Christ-ones have become "new creatures" in Christ (II Cor. 5:17), by the presence of the risen and living Lord Jesus in our spirit. Jesus desires to live out His character in our behavior. What will that look like? "The fruit of the Spirit is love, joy, peace, patience, kindness, goodness, faithfulness, gentleness, and the Godly control of oneself" (Gal. 5:22,23). This spiritual component and reality of derived character is missing in all humanistic concepts of human character.

NOVEMBER 21

DERIVED RIGHTEOUSNESS

Perhaps the greatest bone of contention in the Protestant Reformation was the issue of justification or righteousness. The reformers reacted against the Roman church concept that Christians could achieve righteousness by engaging in certain "works," such as the purchase of indulgences. Instead, they proposed a juridical paradigm that explained that God the Judge would declare or proclaim a person "righteous" when they assented to Christ's work on their behalf. The righteousness of Christ was then legally "imputed" or ascribed to the Christian "as if" it was their righteousness, but the Christian was never actually made righteous.

The scripture explicitly indicates that a Christ-one is "made righteous" in Christ. "He (God the Father) made Him (Jesus) who knew no sin to be sin on our behalf, so that we (Christ-ones) might become the righteousness of God in Him" (II Cor. 5:21). "Through the obedience of the One (obedient unto death) the many (all who are "in Christ") will be made righteous" (Rom. 5:19). We are not inherently or essentially righteous, for we cannot be what only God is (Isa. 45:21). Ours is a derived righteousness predicated on the presence of "the Righteous One" (Acts 3:14; 7:52; 22:14), i.e., Jesus Christ, dwelling in our spirit.

We are "righteous" in union with Jesus Christ (Rom. 8:10) – made righteous by His abiding presence. Having been made righteous in conjunction with the indwelling Jesus, the objective is that we should exercise the faith, the receptivity of His activity, expressing His righteous character in our human behavior (Phil. 1:11; 2 Tim. 2:22). We cannot produce righteous behavior by any of our religious activities, but Jesus, the Righteous One, is desirous of living out His righteous life and character in us. "Let the one who is righteous, continue to practice righteousness" (Rev. 22:11). "Those who do not practice righteousness are not of God" (I Jn. 3:10).

DERIVED HOLINESS

God alone is essentially and inherently holy. 'I the Lord your God am holy" (Lev. 19:2). "I am God and not man, the Holy One in your midst" (Hosea 11:9). "There is no one holy like the Lord" (I Sam 2:2). God is glorified by His own holiness (as evidenced by the Shekinah glory in the Holy of Holies of the Jewish temple). Because God is singularly Holy, He declares, "I will not give My glory to another" (Isa. 42:8; 48:11). Yet, when something or someone is associated with God, it may be identified as "holy" (ex. the Holy Place in the temple, the holy utensils of the temple, holy prophets, and the holy nation of Israel).

Christians are referred to as "holy ones," translated "saints" in most English translations of the New Testament (cf. Acts 9:13,32; Rom. 1:7; 12:13; Eph. 1:15; 4:12). Christians are "holy ones," not just because they are associated with Jesus, but they are made "holy" (Eph. 1:4; Col. 1:22; 3:12) by the derived holiness of the presence of the Holy One (Mk. 1:24; Jn. 6:69; Acts 2:27; 3:14; 13:35), Jesus Christ. Corporately, in the collective of the *ecclesia*, we become a "holy priesthood" (I Pet. 2:5), a "holy nation" (I Pet. 2:9), also by the derived holiness of Jesus as He lives within all Christ-ones in the Body of Christ.

Having been made holy in terms of spiritual condition and spiritual identity, Christ-ones are intended to allow that holy character of God the Father, God the Son, and God the Holy Spirit to be manifested in holy behavior. "Like the Holy One who called you, be holy yourselves also in all your behavior; because it is written (Lev. 19:2), "You shall be holy, for I am holy." When holy behavior is purposefully and intentionally derived from the holy character of God by faith, He is glorified, and we fulfill the purpose for which we were created (Isa. 43:7). When the holy character of Jesus is manifested in our mortal bodies (II Cor. 4:10,11), we express "the holiness without which no one will see the Lord" (Heb. 12:14)

NOVEMBER 23

DERIVED IMAGE

"God said, "Let Us make man in Our image, according to Our
likeness…" and "God created man in His own image, in
the image of God He created him" (Gen. 1:26,27). This does not
mean that there is anything about humanity that is like unto God
or God-like. Rather, it means that the reality of the invisible
character of God is to be made visible in the creature man, by the
derivation of God's character. Image has to do with visage and
visibility. Such visible image requires the presence of God in the
human individual to allow God to be imaged or made visible.
When humanity chose to rebel against God in the fall into sin,
God chose to no longer dwell where He was not wanted, and
Satan moved in to inhabit "the sons of disobedience" (Eph. 2:2).

Those estranged from God by sin and unbelief will derive the
image of character out of the devil (*ek diabolos*) who dwells
within them. Unable to exhibit the "image of God" because they
are "without God," they can only bear the image of the Evil One's
iniquity. Instead of "the mystery of godliness" (I Tim. 3:16), they
show forth "the mystery of iniquity" (II Thess. 2:7 – KJV) and
remain misused humanity, a tragic misrepresentation of what
God intended mankind to be.

Jesus is referred to as "the image of God" (II Cor. 4:4; Col. 1:15).
As the Son of God, voluntarily functioning as a human being, He
derived the divine character by faith to exhibit a perfect visible
image of the invisible God. As the Perfect Man, He could offer
Himself as the perfect sacrifice for the sins of mankind, making
available His Being in receptive believers to allow Christ-ones to
manifest the image of God again. Christ-ones "have put on the
new self who is being renewed to a true knowledge according to
the image of the One who created us" (Eph. 4:24) and are to
submit to "being transformed into the same image from glory to
glory, just as from the Lord, the Spirit" (II Cor. 3:18).

DERIVED CHRISTIAN ACTIVITY

In Romans 11:36, Paul provides the structure of a cyclical pattern of Christian activity that derives out of God (*ek Theos*) by the impetus of the Spirit, is enacted by means of or through Christ (*dia Christos*) and is directed unto God the Father (*eis Theos*) to the glory of God (Isa. 43:7; I Cor. 10:31). Our first example will be prayer. Paul explains, "We do not know how to pray as we should" (Rom. 8:26), "but the Spirit intercedes with groanings too deep for words." Christ is the pray-er in us, and our prayers ascend unto (*eis*) the Father as both Christ and the Spirit function to God's glory. Everything begins and ends with God's action.

The same cyclical pattern can be seen in reference to Christian worship, a topic that has a multitude of differing opinions among Christians. Jesus explained to the woman at the well in Samaria, "God is Spirit, and those who worship Him must worship in spirit and truth" (Jn. 4:24). The Spirit of God prompts us (*ek Theos*) to worship God. "The Lord our God is a jealous God," desiring that we should worship Him alone (Exod. 20:5). Christ in us wants to be the One through whom (*dia*) we express the worth-ship of God's character and action, directed unto (*eis*) God the Father that He might be glorified for who He is and what He does.

The same pattern can be seen in Christian ministry. Derived out of (*ek Theos*) God by the impetus of the Spirit, we are compelled to serve and minister to others in love. God's loving concern is always directed toward others. Ministry, however, is not a self-chosen, altruistic endeavor to help or assist in what we perceive to be the well-being of others. We minister to others (particularly in the context of the *ecclesia*) by means of the spiritual giftedness (often called "spiritual gifts") given to us by the Spirit. When we received Christ, we received the totality of His ability to minister through (*dia*) us, and by such *charismata* (grace giftedness), we minister to others unto (*eis*) the glory of God.

NOVEMBER 25

DERIVED IMMORTALITY

Paul wrote that "the mortal shall put on immortality" (I Cor. 15:53,54). He was referring to our bodies which will be resurrected as immortal bodies, immune to any of the effects of death (cf. Rev. 21:4). In this article, we shall be considering the immortality of God, who as the living God has life in Himself. God cannot be touched by death or mortality. "God alone possesses immortality" Paul explained to Timothy (I Tim. 6:16), meaning that no one else, certainly no creature, can claim inherent immortality which belongs to God alone. God can, however, because of the Son assuming human mortality and being "obedient unto death" (Phil. 2:7), taking the death consequences of sin for all mankind, make His immortal life available to those for whom Christ died.

Immortality is equivalent to "eternal life" (cf. Rom. 2:7; II Tim. 1:10). Such immortal, eternal life" is made available to be given to humanity by the presence of the One, Jesus Christ, who claimed to be Life in Himself. "I am the resurrection and the life; everyone who lives and believes in Me will never die" (Jn. 11:25), He declared to Martha. To His disciples, Jesus explained, "I am the way, the truth, and the life" (Jn. 14:6). When we receive the life of Jesus by faith, we receive His eternal life. Christ-ones have derived eternal life and immortality by means of the presence of the living Lord Jesus living within us and as us.

Immortality is rightly perceived as a state of "no death," beyond the death of our physical bodies. The continuity and perpetuity of the immortality and eternal life that we presently have in Jesus Christ extends beyond our physical life in this earthly world. We have the derived immortality of God in Christ already, but it is still hoped for in the not yet of heavenly existence. "Christ Jesus is our hope" (I Tim. 1:1), and Christ-ones believe that our union (I Cor. 6:17) with the presence of God in Christ by the Holy Spirit will take us into eternity.

PERSONAL DERIVATION OUT OF GOD

Apart from God in Christ, I *am* nothing and can *do* nothing (Jn. 15:5). Anything of any consequence on earth or in heaven must be derived out of God (*ek Theos*). He provides the meaning for everything that exists – everything that occurs in my life. "We are not adequate in ourselves to consider anything as coming out of ourselves (*ek autos*), but our adequacy is out of God (*ek Theos*)" (II Cor. 3:5). I confess, I have always had an attitude of self-sufficiency, an attitude that "I can do it" in selected areas of activity (not in athletics, but in knowledge and thought categories). I am still, and will always be, in God's training school of learning that I must derive everything out of Him.

We are simply "vessels for the Master's use" – "a vessel for honor, sanctified, useful to the Master, prepared for every good work" (II Tim. 2:21), by deriving all from Him. A "vessel" does not produce any action; it simply receives what is put into it. I want to be a vessel that is available to receive and derive everything from God, and to enjoy being such a vessel. Many a vessel, and I speak in the first person of myself, aspires to be more than just a vessel, to do something for Jesus, to engage in so-called Christian ministry. Genuine Christian ministry is derived out God (*ek Theos*) by means of Spirit-giftedness.

To come to the point of enjoying being a vessel or a conduit of God's activity, means that I have come to appreciate that my "old man" was crucified on the cross with Jesus. It means that I have come to accept Paul's statement that "it is no longer I who lives, but Christ lives in me" (Gal. 2:20). I want it to be true that "the life I now live, I live by faith (the receptivity of His activity) in the Son of God, who loved me and gave Himself up for me" (Gal. 2:20). Oh, the joy and peace of knowing that it is not what I do, but what He does that makes my life significant from the perspective of eternity. May the living Jesus be my "all in all."

NOVEMBER 27

THE QUEST FOR SOMETHING GLORIOUS

There is within the heart of every pondering human person, a quest for something more wonderful, more glorious, more exciting than what they have yet experienced. Those who appreciate music (classical, contemporary, etc.), wait with anticipation for the next concert where the music might take them into the euphoria (Greek *eu* = good; *pherein* = to bear) of good feelings. Those enamored with the natural beauty of the physical world anticipate the next trip to see the northern lights in Iceland or Alaska, or the fjords of Norway, or Victoria Falls in southern Africa, or the southern Alps in New Zealand, etc. Those who have been introduced to alcohol and drugs often long for the next "high" whereby they can experience the stimulation of being "over the top," or the depressant of not having to deal with the present unbearable troubles of life.

Does this universal desire for "something more" indicate that there must be some such wonderful, majestic, glorious reality or experience as these people long for? C.S. Lewis thought so, when he wrote, "If we find ourselves with a desire that nothing in this world can satisfy, the most probable explanation is that we were made for another world." He was suggesting that human desire can only be satisfied in God and the heaven that God has prepared for mankind. He continues, "If we are made for heaven, the desire for our proper place will be already in us." Despite how the world attempts to quench such, "we remain conscious of a desire which no natural happiness will satisfy."

Bruce Springsteen sang a song (released 1980), "Everybody's got a hungry heart." That has been interpreted to mean that everyone is greedy for love, affection, and relationships. But it might also be interpreted that in the core of our being, God made us hungry for Himself, and we will never be totally satisfied or fulfilled until we experience such glorious relationship with God.

HAVE YOU EXPERIENCED GOD'S GLORY?

Is it possible for human beings to experience God's glory? You may have had some glorious experiences (in music, art, travel, worship, etc.), but have you experienced God's glory? To experience God's glory, one must have experienced the presence of God, for out of the perfection of His Being He expresses His all-glorious character, and always unto His own glory. Those who are receptive to God's revealing of Himself in His manifold manners of manifestation have sometimes reported an ineffable awareness of the presence of God in various experiences in their lives. It was a genuine OMG, "Oh, my God!" revelation.

Is seeing the glory of God something that Christians should expect or desire? I think the answer is "yes." Writing in what we call the "Second epistle to the Corinthians," Paul wrote, "It is God who said, 'Let light shine out of the darkness' (Gen. 1:14-19), who did shine in our hearts, for our enlightened knowing of the glory of God by means of the face-to-face, heart-to-heart, spirit-to-spirit presence of Jesus Christ" (II Cor. 4:6 – Fowler translation). Later, in that same fourth chapter, Paul writes, "For fleeting, light troubles are producing for us an eternal weight of glory far beyond all comparison (II Cor. 4:17). Our trials and troubles often make us more open to seeing the glory of God at work.

Divine glory is an important motif throughout the old and new covenant scriptures. There is a basic understanding that God is the most glorious Being in existence; and that where God is there is glory. When God created human beings (male and female), He created them "in the image of God" (Gen. 1:27) to participate in His divine glory by being image-bearers to manifest His glorious character. We were "created for His glory" (Isa. 43:7). All Christians should be able to say, "Mine eyes have seen the glory of the coming of the Lord," not just as a future expectation, but having seen God in the magnificence of His workings.

NOVEMBER 29

NATURAL GOD-MOMENTS

I will never forget visiting the Yellow Mountains (aka Huangshan Mts.) in Eastern China in 2003. I had a "beyond my wildest imaginations," experience of appreciating the natural beauty of God's creation. The splendor of it was breathtaking. To get there required a several mile gondola ride over very deep canyons, and after arriving at the top one could walk for miles on narrow walking paths around the peaks which were treacherous (often with no handrail or cable). It was a jaw-dropping, awe-inspiring experience. If you have seen Chinese artwork with jagged mountain peaks shrouded in fog, those were probably depicting the Yellow Mountains. That was a natural God-moment that will forever be etched in my memory.

On another occasion, I had such an "eye-opening" epiphany of awe that took my breath away when I first entered into the *Academia Galleria* in Florence, Italy, and viewed Michelangelo's fourteen-foot-tall white marble statue of "David" – a masterpiece of Renaissance art. I was stopped in my tracks, transfixed at the sublime beauty of that sculpture. It was a surreal, "wow!" moment, wherein there was an epiphany of realization of how the creativity of God could be expressed through a human artist to create a sculpture of such exquisite beauty. It was another memorable God-moment.

It does not require a viewing of natural beauty or of human artwork to bring us to such an overwhelming experience of awe and appreciation. Such an occasion can occur as a spiritual experience within any context in our ordinary lives as Christians. In fact, it should be a purposed objective in our Christian lives to long for and appreciate those "glimpses of glory" wherein God reveals Himself – His love and beauty and power – wherein, we are sure that we have just had the privilege of being in the presence of God and seeing the handiwork of God.

EUCHARISTIC THANKSGIVING

Giving thanks for all that God is doing in our lives by His grace should be a spontaneous expression in the life of a Christ-one. We are living each moment by His grace, and gratitude should be an inner impulse or inclination of appreciation for all that He is to us – everything – and all that He is doing in our lives. The word "thanksgiving" or "to give thanks" in the original Greek language of the New Testament is *eucharistia* (*eu* = good; *charis* = grace). To give thanks is to recognize the "good grace" of God for everything that He is to us and is doing in our lives. That is why we can "give thanks" for everything and in everything (Phil. 4:6; I Thess. 5:18).

Christ-ones will recognize the Greek word *eucharistia* as the root word of what Christians have for centuries called the Eucharist or the Lord's Supper or Communion. The reason why we have referred to that celebratory remembrance of Jesus' death on our behalf as "Eucharist" is that Jesus "gave thanks" (*eucharisteo*) before partaking of the cup and the bread with His disciples at the Last Supper in the Upper Room (Matt. 26:27; Mk. 14:23; Lk. 22:17,19; I Cor. 11:24). Over the centuries Christian peoples have developed varying perspectives of the meaning of the Eucharist observance in their public worship. For some it is merely a time of remembrance, while for others it is the most important focal point of their weekly collective worship. Eucharist is regarded by some as "a means of grace," a human action wherein God's grace is suffused and infused into the participant.

In 1863 President Abraham Lincoln set a national day of Thanksgiving on the final Thursday in the month of November each year. The secular holiday is not invested with any religious meaning, as should be the case for a nation that espouses the separation of church and state. That does not mean that we cannot recognize the eucharistic meaning of thanksgiving.

DECEMBER 1

INTENDED TO BE RECEIVERS

As usual, organized institutional religion has turned everything around backwards. God created humanity to be dependent, derivative, and receptive creatures. When God sent His only begotten Son, Jesus, to be Savior and Lord of all men, the basic function of mankind did not change. We are still intended to be derivative receivers of what God provides. That is why we read in John 1:12,13, "As many as *received* Him (Jesus), to them He gave right to become the sons (deriving out of the Being) of God, even to those that believe on His name" (Jn. 1:12). Believing is not mere assent to the historicity of Jesus but receiving Him within.

Paul understood the receptivity of Jesus by faith. "Do you have anything that you did not *receive?*" (I Cor. 4:7). "Did you *receive* the Spirit by the works of the Law, or by hearing with faith?" (Gal. 3:2). "As you have *received* Christ Jesus the Lord (by faith), so walk in Him (by faith) (Col. 2:6). Faith is our receptivity of God's activity, whether it be the receiving of the initial redemptive and reconciling work of God in Christ or the continuing restorative and sanctifying work of God in Christ. To answer Paul's question in I Cor. 4:7, "NO, we do not have anything we did not receive by faith – not salvation, not righteousness, not anything!

Why, then, does religion seek to change the divine emphasis of our being receivers to an emphasis on our being givers? Religion encourages (sometimes demands) that Christian people give of their material resources (at least a ten percent tithe, they indicate). In addition, they want us to give of our time and talents. They want us to give ourselves in attempting to convince others that they should believe in Jesus (they call it "witnessing"). Religion wants us to give ourselves in "ministry," failing to understand that genuine ministry is received by means of the giftedness of the Spirit as the living Lord Jesus provides the grace of God through us to serve others.

DECEMBER 2

"LET MY PEOPLE GO!"

God told Moses from the burning bush that He was sending him back to Egypt, where he was a "wanted man," to tell Pharoah to "Let My people go!" Despite some reluctance, Moses and his brother, Aaron, approached the Pharoah with God's demand. God had promised Moses that He would stand behind His demand and apply the necessary divine leverage to convince the Pharoah of Egypt to allow the departure of the large population of Hebrew slaves, which would surely have had an economic impact. After nine devastating plagues Pharoah still refused, until the tenth plague which involved the death of the firstborn son of all Egyptians, including the son of the Pharoah himself. That convinced him to order the expulsion of the Hebrew peoples from the land of Egypt.

There comes a time when people need to be "let go" or expelled. For example, when Hagar's son, Ishmael, was bullying Sarah's son, Isaac, the son of promise, she had to convince Abraham that Hagar and Ishmael needed to be "cast out" from their community (cf. Gen. 21:9-19; Gal. 4:21-31). Paul likens this expulsion to the necessity of "casting out" the Judaizers, and religion in general, to preserve the community of promise.

Perhaps God is saying to the religious community today, to those who keep people in bondage and slavery (the Latin root of "religion," *religio*, means to "bind up"), "Let My people go!"; set them free to live in the freedom of My grace (Gal. 5:1). To those who are having to battle the legalism of religion, like the Galatians Christians battling the Judaizers, God may be saying, "Cast out those who continue to advocate religious performance, so you can enjoy the freedom of living in grace." "It was for freedom that Christ set us free, ...do not be subject again to a yoke of slavery" (Gal. 5:1), to the oppressive bondage of religious dos and don'ts. God wants us to live in the freedom of GRACE.

DECEMBER 3

DIFFICULT SPOUSES

There are many people who are living with difficult spouses – might be a husband and might be a wife. When we marry, we have no way of knowing the latent personality tendencies that may develop in a partner. We are often not aware that mental health issues and family dynamics can be passed on to children from generation to generation. The old covenant literature indicates that the consequences of iniquity can be passed on to the third and fourth generations (Exod. 20:5; 34:7; Numb. 14:18; Deut. 5:9). Neither are we always aware of the selfish and sinful patterns of fleshly desires in our prospective partner.

The psychological community refers to "personality disorders" which seem to have some overlap with the Pauline and Petrine references to "desires of the flesh" (Eph. 2:3: II Pet. 2:10,18). Individuals can develop selfish and sinful ways of thinking, feeling, and behaving that might be ascribed to mental illness or even demonic involvement. When we are attracted to a potential partner, we are quite unaware of how their personalities and behavior might develop into problematic interpersonal relations. One's spouse may be prone to paranoid, bipolar, borderline, schizoid, or narcissistic behavioral tendencies.

A spouse may develop tendencies to obsessive, compulsive fixations that can lead to demanding expectations. Some spouses develop addictive tendencies that may appear in alcoholism, abuse of drugs (whether illicit or prescriptive), or variant sexual expectations. Paul explained, "God is faithful, who will not allow you to be tested beyond what you are able, but with the testing will provide the way of escape also, so that you will be able to endure it" (I Cor. 10:13). Many marriages with difficult spouses have been preserved by one partner relying on God's sufficient grace (II Cor. 12:9), but that is not to say that dissolution by divorce is always out of the question.

DECEMBER 4

CHRIST OUR LIFE

Many Christians will explain that they have believed in Jesus Christ and received eternal life. Oftentimes, their belief in Jesus was merely mental assent to the historicity of the person of Jesus who lived on earth two millennium ago, on which basis they have been told they will receive the promise of future eternal life in heaven. They usually have a separated concept which does not recognize Jesus IS eternal life, the entirety of God's gift to redeem mankind, regenerate them, and restore them to the divine intent in creating them. Their need is to "grow in the grace and knowledge of the Lord Jesus Christ" (II Pet. 3:18).

Some Christians are more aware that in receiving Jesus in the new birth of regeneration, the very life of the risen and living Lord Jesus came to live within their spirit. The Spirit of Christ dwelling in their human spirit is evidence that they belong to God (Rom. 8:9). Their awareness of having "Christ in you, the hope of glory" (Col. 1:27) is the ever-present assurance of the indwelling provision whereby they can rely on the life of Jesus to be lived out in every facet of their daily lives. They live with the expectation of manifesting the glorious character of Jesus to the glory of God in all that they are engaged in.

The Christ-life, however, is not a life of concern about how we are doing in allowing Jesus to be lived out in us. When Christ is our life, there need be no concern about our doing, for we can simply BE who we are "in Christ," and live in constant receptivity of His activity. Paul explained, "For me to live is Christ" (Phil. 1:21). When we are "joined to the Lord, we are in one spirit (union) with Him" (I Cor. 6:17), and we can trust that the living Lord Jesus is living out His life as us. "Christ is our life" (Col. 3:4), and there is no explanation for who we are and what we do except that the Christ-life is being lived out in us, the Christ-ones, in a contemporary re-presentation of the life of Jesus.

DECEMBER 5

PROCLAMATION OR PROPAGANDA?

There are several words that might seem to be synonymous, and the procedures of which may overlap each other. Let's consider the words, proclamation, propagation, and propaganda. They might all be used to persuade and influence people's opinions, to shape personal perceptions, and to draw people into engaging in a particular action. Propaganda, however, attempts to manipulate others by misrepresentation. Propagation is an attempt to stimulate growth and increase expansion by various means. Proclamation seeks to make known the good news of something that fulfills the needs for those who hear it.

There has been an intense emphasis on propagation in many Christian communities – emphasizing evangelism and witnessing to others as the foremost Christian responsibility, i.e., to reproduce and create more Christian believers to fill our churches (and heaven, of course). This can, and often has, degenerated into methods of propaganda whereby influencing one to "make a decision" is little different from a high-pressure salesman, employing psychological persuasion to "make a sale." When the purpose of our persuasive argument is to promote an agenda or cause others to join us, it is likely propaganda.

The Greek word for proclamation or preaching is *kerygma*, derived from *kerusso*, meaning "to cry or proclaim as a herald." Proclamatory preaching of the gospel of Jesus Christ must be alive with the grace dynamic of God's Spirit, pointing to the risen and living Lord Jesus as the living reality of one's life. Preaching becomes propaganda when it promotes exclusivism, when it stoops to name-calling of those who think differently, when it becomes tireless repetition of familiar information, when it encourages agendas of achievement, and when it appeals to the authority of the proclaimer. God forgive us of such propaganda procedures and reveal our need to preach with pure motives.

DECEMBER 6

THE IMPORTANCE OF A LETTER

Letters can be important, for the change of one alphabetical letter in a word can change the whole meaning as in "bitter" changed to "better," or conversely "letter" changed to "litter." Such word-morphing has become the basis of many word-games today (cf. Jeopardy, Wordle, etc.) The concept of a "letter" must be differentiated between an alphabetical letter and an epistolary letter. The receipt of a letter (epistle) from someone meaningful to us can be very important, i.e., a parent, a child, a boyfriend or girlfriend, or even an educational institution advising us of our acceptance into the academic program we applied for.

The scriptures also differentiate between different types of "letters." Paul refers to "the letters" of the Mosaic Law engraved on stone tablets (II Cor. 3:7; Lk. 16:17; Gal. 6:11). In the same "letter" to the Corinthians, he refers to "the letter of the Law," referring to the precise performance requirements of the Mosaic Torah that serve to indict us for failure to keep and conform to every detail of the legalistic behavioral standards. The "letter" of the Law kills (II Cor. 3:6) by exposing our inability to perform perfectly, and Paul differentiates between old covenant (Rom. 2:27,29; 7:6) legalistic accountability and the new covenant provision of life by the Spirit of Christ.

Epistolary "letters" are also an important part of our New Testament. The apostle Peter wrote that the "letters" of Paul contain "some things hard to understand" (II Pet. 3:16), with which many have concurred. Writing to the Corinthians, Paul indicates that the Corinthian believers were "living letters," "being manifested that you are a letter of Christ, written not with ink but with the Spirit of the living God, not on tablets of stone but on tablets of human hearts" (II Cor. 3:2,3). All Christ-ones are living epistles, intended to manifest the life of Christ (II Cor. 4:10,11) by allowing the Christ-life to be lived out as us.

DECEMBER 7

DOES IT MAKE ONE IOTA OF DIFFERENCE?

Even people who do not know a lick of Greek know the phrase "not one iota." The question, "does it make one iota of difference?" may originate in the fourth century when Athanasius countered the Arians at the Council of Nicea (A.D. 325). The issue was whether the Father and the Son were "of the same divine Being," Greek word *homoousion (homo* = same; *ousia* = being), or whether they were "of similar being," Greek word *homoiousion (homoi* = similar; *ousia* = being). Can you see the difference? It is only one little iota (the 9th letter of the Greek alphabet) that has been inserted in the second spelling of the debated words.

Jesus said, "I and the Father are one" (Jn. 10:30). Does that mean "of one mind or objective" as the Arians would have argued (and as the Jehovah Witnesses still argue), or does it mean the Father, the Son and the Holy Spirit (included by the Council of Constantinople, A.D. 381) are of "one essential divine being." This assertion becomes the basis of the distinctive Christian understanding of the Godhead, "three Persons in one Being." There are modern translations of the Nicene Creed that have retranslated "of one Being" with the Latin-based word "consubstantial" meaning "together of the same substance."

The inherent and essential divine Being of the Father, Son, and Holy Spirit is important to the entire Christian message of redemption. Did the death of Jesus on the cross simply "force the hand" of the Father to begrudgingly redeem and forgive humanity, or did Jesus as the divine Son of God serve as the divine Savior in Himself to "pay the price" of the consequence of human death for sin in total eternal consensus with the Father and the Spirit? It means far more to indicate that Jesus was willing to be "made sin" (II Cor. 5:21) in submitting to the death-power of the devil (Heb. 2:14) vicariously in our place as man, and in order to forgive us of our sins, as only God can do.

DECEMBER 8

DELAYS, SETBACKS, AND INTERRUPTIONS

Some people seem to think that "the cards are stacked against them," or perhaps God is against them, because whenever they set out to do something they run into delays, postponements, and interruptions. Welcome to the "advancements" (setbacks?) of the twenty-first century! Computers were supposed to simplify our lives and make interactions more efficient, but they seem to unnecessarily extend the misery factor of our lives. Just this morning, I made what I thought would be a simple call to the bank. First, I had to answer a barrage of questions posed by a computer. Then, I was put "on hold," transferred to another department, and put "on hold" again. After thirty minutes of having to put up with such ineptness, the phone connection was "dropped, and I had to start all over again.

There is no doubt that these kinds of unnecessary delays can get frustrating and irritating. The biblical word for these occasions that "pierce our status-quo" and throw roadblocks in what we planned to do is the word *peirasmoi*, translated "trials" (sometimes "troubles" or "tribulations"). The word *peirasmos*, derived from the root of *peiro*, means "to pierce in order to examine." Amid these common trials (I Cor. 10:13), God examines whether we react with impatience and inflexibility, or whether we "roll with the punches" of the repetitive change of plans and let things happen as God sees fit to orchestrate them.

Scottish poet, Robbie Burns, in a poem entitled, "*To a Mouse*," wrote, "the best laid plans of mice and men oft go awry." When it happens, inevitably, the occasion requires adjustment of both our attitudes and our schedules. "Come now, you who say, 'Today or tomorrow we will go to such and such a city and spend a year there and engage in business and make a profit.' You do not know what your life will be like tomorrow. You ought to say, 'If the Lord wills, we will live and do this or that'" (James 4:13-15).

DECEMBER 9

HOW TO MAKE GOD LAUGH

Do you want to make God laugh – tell Him that you have a plan!
Tell Him you have a plan on how to live the Christian life. Tell
Him you have a plan to make yourself more spiritual. Tell Him
you have a plan that will make the church grow. Tell Him you
have a plan to reconcile the polarized parties in your church or in
the nation. You see, the plans of man are based on the abilities of
man to do and perform something that man has determined
should be pleasing to God. But God is not pleased by human
performance or "works." God only takes delight in His divine
character being expressed by the dynamic of His grace.

The psalmist noted that God would laugh at the audacity of
human endeavors. In the second psalm the psalmist writes of
how "the nations are in an uproar, and the peoples devise useless
and vain things" (vs. 1), but "He who sits in the heavens *laughs*
and scoffs at them" (vs. 4). God's laughter is not funny-ha-ha, but
derision and scorn. Psalm 37 refers to evildoers with wicked
plots against the righteous, but "God *laughs* at them, for He sees
that the day of their defeat is coming" (vs. 13). In Psalm 59 the
psalmist writes of the enemies of God who engage in iniquity and
even mock God, but the Lord "*laughs* at them and scoffs at their
threats" (vs. 8), recognizing the silliness of their posturing.

God shakes His head in disbelief at the hard-headed pointless
pursuits of driven-to-succeed humanity. Whenever human
beings think they can solve the problems of the world or of their
own lives by functioning *ek autos* (out of themselves) they are
destined to failure and defeat. The futile efforts of men trying to
do what only God can do causes God to chuckle at their wasted
efforts. God knows the outcome of all such human endeavors and
gets an empty laugh at their feeble plans. Only when humanity
derives their activity *ek Theos* (out of God) will their efforts be
pleasing to God and serve as worship of God.

DECEMBER 10

CROSSING THE LINE

There are many different concepts of "crossing the line." In the U.S. Navy, it refers to crossing the equator. In many sports, it refers to crossing the boundary line of fair play according to the rules of the game (basketball, soccer, football, etc.). The line may be an imaginary line, as in drawing "a line in the sand" to determine the limits of acceptability. Most of these indicate a "line of violation" that can be overstepped. A more positive "line" is when a competitor crosses the "finish line" in a foot race, bicycle race, or automobile race. In this case, the "line" represents progression, advancement, or completion.

In this article, we will be considering an imaginary "line of procession" where a person chooses to cross the line into another perspective or mode of operation. It is the line that seems to be suggested by Paul in II Corinthians 4:17,18 – the line between the "seen" and the "unseen," the line between the "temporal" and the "eternal." It is a line that is only available to a Christ-one who can "understand spiritual things" (I Cor. 2:14). To do so requires an individual to be designated as "spiritual" (I Cor. 2:15; 3:1) by the freely received presence of the Spirit of Christ in the human spirit (Rom. 8:9).

When we encounter problems and trials which are "common to man" (I Cor. 10:13) which Paul referred to as "light and temporary troubles/afflictions" (II Cor. 4:17), our natural human response is to determine how we can deal with the problems by means of our own self-effort. We all know that such effort often exposes our inability. That brings us to "the line." To cross the line, we must admit our inability (aka repentance), believe that there is a "greater power" on the other side of the line. By faith we "cross the line" to accept the provision of God's grace in the "unseen" means of the Christ-life and avail ourselves of the "eternal weight of glory" (II Cor. 4:17).

DECEMBER 11

MAN'S WAY OR GOD'S WAY

There are two antithetical M.O.s (*modus operandi*) for dealing with the issues of life. "There is a way that seems right to a man, but the end thereof is death" (Prov. 14:12; 16:25). Man's way is to determine "a plan of action," and then to address the issue with the strength of self-resolve, tackling the problem with common-sense and self-effort. The human way will vary among individuals, as they approach the situation with their own patterns of action and reaction. But man's way of acting *ek autos* (out of oneself), i.e., *ek diabolos* (deriving out of the devil), will inevitably have diametrically opposite outcomes than our choosing to act *ek Theos* (deriving out of God).

In Matthew 7:13,14, Jesus explained that "the gate is wide, and the way is broad that leads to destruction, and there are many who enter through it. But the gate is small, and the way is narrow that leads to life, and there are few who find it." There are two paths available to the one who is a Christ-one. In that we are still human creatures with freedom of choice, we can choose the natural broad way with a wide gate that leads to death and destruction. But Christ-ones have another option of choosing the narrow way with a small gate that leads to allowing the Christ-life to be energized and lived out through us by the grace of God.

The choice we make of choosing man's way or God's way requires that we approach the cross-roads (or "the line") by first admitting that we are unable to deal with life by our own power (even with the self-help books). We are failures at pulling off the project of life. That is repentance – admitting we can't do it. To proceed, then, on the narrow path of God's provision and empowering requires that we make the choice of faith, the receptivity of God's activity in our situation. God's way of divine grace received by faith opens the pathway for God to act in His Self-chosen way by the dynamic of His grace-action.

DECEMBER 12

GOD'S TIMING

I heard a gentleman say something so presumptuous that it took me aback. I think he was frustrated that he didn't get what he wanted at the time when he wanted it. He said, "I think God needs a course in time-management!" Writing to the Roman Christians, Paul quotes Isaiah 40:13, "Who has known the mind of the Lord? Who has been able to give the Lord advice?" (Rom. 11:34). God's ways and God's timing are always perfect, and that is why it is so presumptuous to suggest that God might need a humanly constructed course in time-management. It is not our place to dictate how and when God should act in our lives. We cannot set the timetable or the deadlines for God's action.

We are such impatient people. We want God to act in the way we want, and we want it NOW! That is why we are advised to "wait on the Lord." Jacob was nearing the end of his life, and gathered his sons together, and declared, "For Your salvation I *wait*, O Lord" (Gen. 49:18). The psalmist wrote, "I *waited* patiently for the Lord; And He inclined to me and heard my cry" (Ps. 40:1). "My soul, *wait* in silence for God only, for my hope is from Him" (Ps. 62:5). Hear the prophets: ""God acts on behalf of the one who *waits* for Him" (Isa. 64:6). "I will *wait* for the God of my salvation. My God will hear me" (Micah 7:7).

Waiting on God's timing requires patience. Patience is more than a virtue, as some have indicated; patience is the very character of God made available to Christ-ones by "the fruit of the Spirit" (Gal. 5:22,23). We cannot go fruit-picking for patience, however, for the fruit (singular) of the Spirit comes in the character-cluster of Christ's character. We should listen again to the psalmist: "This is the Lord for whom we have *waited*; Let us rejoice and be glad in His salvation" (Isa. 25:9). "My prayer is to You, O Lord: At an acceptable time, O God, in the greatness of Your lovingkindness, answer me with Your saving truth" (Ps. 69:13).

347

DECEMBER 13

CHRISTIAN PRINCIPLES?

How many times have I heard speakers saying or read in religious books the assertion that the Christian life is to be lived in accord with Christian "principles" that can be found in the bible? The dictionary definition of "principles" is "a fundamental truth or proposition that serves as the foundation for a system of belief or behavior." Is Christian truth or Christian living based on a fundamental foundation of propositional principles? I do not think so! This would make Christianity merely a "belief-system" of epistemological propositions. Christianity is the PERSON of Jesus Christ, not a religion of principles.

Frederick Buechner explained, "Principles are what people have instead of God." I would further explain, principles are the humanistic criteria by which the world and its humanistic religion attempts to develop acceptable doctrine and morality. Buechner went on to say, "principle" is an even duller word than "religion." The world-system in which religion is grounded and contextualized is always insistent on basing their positions and operations on "principles." Principles are merely static precepts, that like the performance-based Law, can never lead to life, righteousness, or perfection, only to death.

French philosopher, Jacques Ellul, wrote, "There is no such things as 'Christian principles'. There is the Person of Christ, who is the principle of everything." I would say, "Jesus is the reality of everything Christian." Ellul went on to state, "If we wish to be faithful to Jesus, we cannot dream of reducing Christianity to a certain number of principles (though this is often done), the consequences of which can be logically deduced. That makes Christianity into an ethic, a new law, a religion of 'principles' which need only to be 'applied'." We should eschew all the religious rhetoric that refers to basing our thought and action on "principles. Christianity is the Person of Jesus Christ (period).

THE THEMATIC CONTEXT OF SCRIPTURE

It has long been recognized that proper interpretation of scripture must reckon with the context of the text being considered. A text considered outside of its context allows the text to become a pretext for any aberrant teaching. Contextual consideration has a wide spectrum: historical context, cultural context, linguistic-grammatical context, authorial context (Pauline, Johannine, Petrine, etc.), literary context (gospel, history, epistle, apocalyptic), logical and rhetorical context (following the argument), etc. The prime point of contextual consideration is "It can't mean now, what it didn't mean then."

Not enough attention has been given to the thematic context of scripture. The thematic context of the New Testament writings, of the new covenant literature *en masse*, might be summed up in the statement of Karl Barth, "The Revelation of God – the Abolition of Religion." The revelation of God is the Self-revealing of the Godhead in the person of the incarnated Son of God, Jesus Christ. The realization of the grace-dynamic of the risen and living Lord Jesus bringing life in Himself to all receptive persons creates the abolishment and termination of the legitimacy of all religion with its performance regulations.

The gospels are full of the offense of the religious leaders at the teaching of Jesus. They finally realized that many of the parables were pointed at them. The book of Acts exposes the progression of the gospel and the conflict with religion. The Pauline epistles evidence a constant resistance of the interloping Judaizing religionists to the gospel of grace in Jesus. Hebrews is a warning against reverting to religion. The Johannine writings counter the mystery religions and nascent Gnosticism. The Apocalypse illustrates the constant battle of Christ and religion. The overriding theme is the contrast of the vital dynamic of the life of Jesus Christ with the antichrist orientation of all religion.

DECEMBER 15

FAITH, HOPE, AND LOVE

In the thirteenth verse of the thirteenth chapter of First Corinthians, Paul wrote, "Now faith, hope, and love abide, but the greatest of these is love." Let us consider the interrelations of these three abiding spiritual realities that Paul mentioned.

Faith is the basic human function of the receptivity of spirit activity, particularly intended to be the receptivity of God's activity in the Son, Jesus Christ, by means of the Holy Spirit. To the Ephesians, Paul wrote, "For by grace we are saved through faith, and that salvation is not *ek humon* (out of ourselves – for we cannot save themselves), but that salvation is the gift of God, not of human works lest anyone might boast that they did something to save themselves" (Eph. 2:8,9). Salvation is entirely derived from God, received by faith.

Hope is the expectation that the divine activity that we are receptive to in faith will continue to be perpetuated unto eternity. "We have obtained our introduction (to salvation in the Savior, Jesus Christ) by faith into this grace in which we stand; and we exult in hope of the glory of God" (Rom. 5:2)..."hope does not disappoint, because the love of God has been poured out within our hearts through the Holy Spirit who was given to us" (Rom. 5:5). The living "Christ Jesus is our hope" (I Tim. 1:1).

Love is the character of God (I Jn. 4:8,16; Gal. 5:22) expressed in His divine activity of grace received by faith, and we have expectant hope such divine love will be manifested into eternity. Love is necessarily a denial of our self-action, as we allow God to manifest His love in "loving one another" (Jn. 13:34,35). This "love of God has been poured out within our hearts through the Holy Spirit who was given to us" (Rom. 5:5) and will necessarily be poured out to others through us (I Jn. 4:20).

Faith receives, **Hope** expects, and **Love** flows outward to others.

CHRISTIAN FREEDOM TO BE AND TO DO

God's freedom is the freedom to BE Himself in His Self-manifestation, as only God can DO because He IS who He IS. What we are saying is that God's freedom is contextualized by His own BEING, and is not just an absolute, open-ended freedom to DO anything He pleases. All freedom, including God's freedom, is contextualized by some parameter. God's freedom is contextualized by His character. Human freedom is contextualized by the divinely established laws of governmental institution. Christian freedom is contextualized by the freely chosen constraint of Christ's character of loving action.

Christian freedom should not entail an emphasis on our freedom to BE who we are in Christ, but on the freedom to derive from the BEING of the living Christ within us by faith, and His freedom to BE who He IS in the Self-manifestation of His divine character in our human behavior. Freedom to BE (perfect, righteous, holy) without the corresponding chosen derivation from the risen and living Christ, and the choosing of the freedom to allow for the out-lived character of the Christ-life is but a penchant for the freedom of an "independent self."

Too often freedom is conceived only as a freedom **FROM** (sin, law, flesh), rather than a freedom **TO** (pray, serve, witness). To over-emphasize "freedom **FROM**" is to emphasize independence from something, and thus a clamoring for an "independent self" that eschews any regulation or submission. When we understand that we have been granted "freedom **TO**," this should indicate our submission **TO** the Lordship of Jesus Christ, and the willingness to allow Him to freely express His character in the practicality of His DOING in our behavior. Freedom is not freedom if it does not follow-through in lived-out freedom. Objective freedom is just a theoretical abstraction without the subjective freedom of allowing the Christ-life to be lived out in Christian behavior.

DECEMBER 17

THERE IS NO REST IN RELIGION

A passion for the Lord and commitment to do great things for the Lord does not a Christian make! Churches are filled with people with such religious sentiment and commitment, with such self-resolve and self-ambition. In fact, religion is constituted and characterized by such self-inspired self-effort to do "good works" for God, despite Paul's inculcation that "God has prepared good works that we should walk in them" (Eph. 2:10) by His empowering. Religion specializes in attempting to do good things for God, while simultaneously encouraging adherents to not do what is against the rules.

Paul refers to "the appearance of wisdom in *self-made religion* and self-abasement and severe treatment of the body, things that are of no value against fleshly indulgence, (*actions that are*) mere self-striving in accordance with the commandments and *religious* teachings of men" (Col. 2:22,23). Forget all that you have heard about what God is for and what God is against; what God wants you to do or wants you to avoid doing. Just be available and receptive to what God by the Spirit of Christ within prompts you to be and do, knowing that such will likely be criticized by the religious "peeping Toms" who have self-designated themselves as God's watchdogs.

The Christian life is a life of "rest" (Heb. 4:1-11). It is a life of restful relaxation from all the "to dos" and "not to dos," all the "thou shalts" and "thou shalt nots," all the religious guidelines and imposed boundaries that self-made religion attempts to bind people with. When we receive the risen and living Lord Jesus and become a Christ-one, we become a free-man – not free to do anything we want, but free to be responsible in allowing the Christ-life to be lived out through us, free to pray, free to love, free to be vessels of mercy as Jesus so chooses to act through us, free to live hilariously in the dynamic of His grace.

DECEMBER 18

MIND, EMOTION, WILL

Some of the brethren have expressed some confusion about the mental, emotional, and volitional function of those who are "in Christ," i.e., "in union with Christ." When the persons of the Triune Godhead come to dwell within the spirit of a Christ-one who is receptive to the gospel, the Father, Son, and Holy Spirit come complete with the divine mind, the divine affections, and the divine will of God. For this reason, Paul could write to the Corinthians, stating, "You have the mind of Christ" (I Cor. 2:16) – that in contrast to the "natural man" who "cannot understand spiritual things" (I Cor. 2:14). The divine mind, the love of God, and the will of God are in our spirit because God is there.

At the same time, we still have the human function of reasoning (mind), affection (emotions), and decision-making (will) in the human soul. The objective for the Christ-one is to allow the divine mind, affections, and determinations, to be worked into our human thinking, human emotions, and human decision-making. This is what Paul seems to be referring to when he wrote of being "renewed in the spirit of your mind" (Eph. 4:23) and "being transformed by the renewing of your (*human*) mind" so "you may prove what the will of God is, that which is good and acceptable and perfect" (Rom. 12:2).

We want the thoughts of the divine mind (naturally quite different from those of the human mind – cf. Isa. 55:8,9) to be developed into "established attitudes" in our human thinking. We want the affection of divine love to be developed into "established affections" of love in our human emotions. We want the determinations of the divine Will of God to be the basis of our human willing and volitional decision-making. That is the process of sanctification, allowing for the transfer of God's function to be imprinted on our human psychological function, to implement the character of God imaged in our behavior.

DECEMBER 19

FREEDOM AND INDEPENDENCE

The American citizens of the United States of America seem to equate freedom with independence. That is to be expected in their July 4th celebrations of a freedom which were initially tied to their independence from the control and taxation of Britain. The Declaration of Independence (July 4, 1776) declared the freedoms of life, liberty, and the pursuit of happiness, and the resulting constitution (1787) protected the five basic freedoms of speech, religion, press, assembly, and the right to petition the government. When speaking of spiritual realities, however, we must beware of equating the freedom we have in Jesus Christ with any sense of independence.

Derivative human creatures cannot function as God does, in autonomy and independence. Humans are always dependent on the spirit-presence and spirit-function of either God or Satan. Human freedom does not imply human independence. Adam and Eve were apparently duped to assume such. Strangely enough, evangelical theology still assumes such by declaring that natural man is independent, having human sovereignty, and able to "do his own thing." Such thought accepts the premise of secular humanism and thus fails to articulate the radical exchange of spiritual presence in spiritual regeneration.

Human freedom does not necessarily carry with it a sense of independence. Certainly not when we are referring to Christian freedom. Our freedom "in Christ" (in union with Christ) is not primarily a "freedom FROM," but rather a "freedom TO" manifest Jesus Christ in all we do. Christian freedom is not a hankering for independence, but a hunkering down in our identification with and faith in the Lord Jesus Christ to allow Him to function as Lord of our lives, in which case Christ-ones becomes "bond servants of Christ Jesus" (Phil. 1:1), "slaves of righteousness" (Rom. 6:18,19), and "servants of all" (Mk. 9:35).

DECEMBER 20

STRANGERS AND ALIENS

I suspect that God is going to give Christians a more poignant opportunity to function as "strangers and aliens" (Heb. 11:13-16; I Pet. 2:11) in the context of the world. As Satan, the "ruler of this world" (Jn. 12:31; 16:11) continues to express his hostility to Christianity in ever more hostile and malevolent forms, Christians will have opportunity to demonstrate the radical dichotomy between the character-works of the Evil One (Jn. 17:15) and the character-works of the living Lord Jesus. Christians are "in the world, but not of the world" (Jn. 17:11,14), dwelling as foreign sojourners and resident strangers.

In most countries, resident foreigners do not have the same rights as do the citizens of the country. Since the Christian's citizenship is in heaven (Phil. 3:20), yet we are living in the world from which we are disenfranchised, we cannot as foreign exiles expect to demand our rights and protection of personal freedoms. As we bank on God's promises of what is yet to transpire, we must eschew the ways of the world with its "fleshly lusts" (I Pet. 2:11), by manifesting character in our behavior that will stupefy and mystify the world around us. In fact, the world hates those who will not conform to its values (Jn. 15:18,19).

Living in the world context where we temporarily reside, we are called to allow Christ to live out His life and character despite possible ridicule, persecution, internment, imprisonment, etc. Uprooted from our former life, we are on pilgrimage to the country that God has promised, just as did Abraham and other persons of faith (Heb. 11:13-16). On the journey, we share the ultimate meaning of life inviting those in the world-system around us to disengage from the world, become resident-aliens together with us "in Christ", and in that process to realize that while living in the context of the world they can be citizens of heaven, living in hope for what is yet to come.

DECEMBER 21

COMPREHENSIVE SALVATION

There is a tendency among Christians today to confine or limit "salvation" to merely historical redemption, or to spiritual regeneration, or to a particular saving and/or sanctifying work of Jesus. Salvation is much more comprehensive that just a conversion experience or a subjective event in time when we "received Jesus." Salvation refers to everything God has done to "make us safe" from the misuse and dysfunction that we were subjected to in our natural state, when we were "slaves of sin" (Rom. 6:6,17) under the control of "the spirit that works in the sons of disobedience" (Eph. 2:2) i.e., of Satan.

"Salvation" seems to be used in Scripture as the comprehensive work of God in the Son, Jesus Christ. It includes the historical actions of Jesus, as well as the experiential actions of the living Lord Jesus in the lives of receptive people today. Modern Christians, in general, are unable to clearly define and differentiate between redemption, conversion, regeneration, reconciliation, sanctification, spiritual exchange, etc., often interchanging one or more of these terms with "salvation." In many evangelical environs, it is common to hear people refer to someone "getting saved," and by this phrase they seem to mean that someone has been converted, "born again" or regenerated.

The saving work of God in Jesus Christ encompasses all the divine work of God in redeeming and reconciling and restoring humanity to their divinely intended function. In the Eastern Orthodox churches, the comprehensive view of salvation is referred to as *Theosis*, meaning "participation with God." That seems to be much closer to the biblical meaning of salvation than what we find in the Western churches, where the theologians have argued for centuries about the *ordo salutis*, the order of salvation, rearranging the sequence of what a person must do to be saved, i.e. confess, believe, repent, be baptized, etc.

THE CONUNDRUM OF MARITAL DISSOLUTION

Not all relationships are sustainable. Some relationships can become so contentious as to necessitate dissolution. Yes, "God hates sending away one's spouse (*shalach*)" (Mal. 2:16) because it disintegrates the picture of relational union to which He intended to compare the relational union of Christ and the Christian (Eph. 5:25-22). But even in the old covenant context of strict legalism, God made allowance for divorce (Deut. 24:1) among the people of Israel. In fact, God's relationship with the people of Israel became so strained that God said, "I saw that for all the adulteries of faithless Israel, I had to send her away (*shalach*) and give her a writ of divorce (*kerithuth*)" (Jere. 3:8).

In the new covenant, Jesus addressed the subject of marital dissolution in the Sermon on the Mount, saying, "Whoever dismisses and sends his wife away (*apolouo*), let him give her a certificate of divorce (*apostasion*)" (Matt. 5:31). He quoted from Deuteronomy 24:1, but He adds that a wife should not be sent away except for the cause of marital infidelity (not just on a husband's whim of discontent). Later, the Jewish Pharisees questioned Jesus about marital dissolution (Matt. 19:3-9), and Jesus reiterates that a man should not send his wife away (*apolouo*) for petty reasons, but only based on sexual infidelity, and if a man then joins himself to another woman without providing a certificate of divorce, it is he that commits adultery.

Jesus was protecting women from being discarded (*apolouo*) without a divorce settlement (*apostasion*), and thus having to deal with the social stigma of being a castaway without recourse to legitimate employment and without adequate recompense (alimony). Marital dissolution should not be regarded as a blanket sin but can, if necessary, be enacted in righteousness that provides the spouse with provision for living and gives both parties the right of remarriage.

DECEMBER 23

ARE YOU A MEMBER?

When visiting various church fellowships, I have repetitively been queried, "Are you a member of our church? Do you want to become a member of our church? When are you going to become a member of our church?" To such questions, I might answer, "Yes, I am a member of the Body of Christ, the Church of God, the *ecclesia* that Jesus established based on faithful receptivity of Him into one's spirit (cf. Matt. 16:18; Rom. 8:9,16). Now, if I am a functional member (Rom. 12:4,5; I Cor. 12:14-27) of the Body of Christ, why is it important or imperative to have "membership" in a local church fellowship or congregation?

Being a functional member of the living worldwide Body of Christ is not equivalent to having legal or registered membership in an institutional denomination or congregational organization. In some church organizations, registered membership is required for the privilege of participation. If that means that I cannot worship with them if I do not have legal membership, then I consider them more restrictive and exclusive than the Church was ever intended to be. If registered membership in the legal entity is required to exercise "voting rights" in the local congregation, I can understand that necessity, but that should never be confused with being a member of the Body of Christ.

Registered legal membership has its rightful place in a legal organization, for if unregistered parties can exercise voting rights and thereby unduly control the direction and mission of the organization, then the organization is susceptible to being taken over by those with possible impure motives to sabotage and change the mission of the organization. At the same time, an *ecclesia* congregation of Christ's Body must always be open and inviting to all confessing Christ-ones to participate in the worship of the Triune God, to share in the study of the scriptures, and to commemorate the life and work of Jesus in the Eucharist.

DECEMBER 24

EVERYONE HAS A MESSAGE

Everyone seems to have "a message" these days, i.e., they have a distinctive bit of advice or information, a distinctive point or idea of thought, that they regard as important and wish to communicate and share either by verbal or written means. The pastor's sermon is often referred to as "The Message." A paraphrastic version of the Bible written by Eugene H. Peterson is entitled, *The Message: The Bible in Contemporary Language,* which many Christians have found beneficial. What concerns me is that many authors and religious ministries seem to think they have found a neglected "corner" on the truth and emphasize their newfound concept as the specific message all need to hear.

The New Testament does refer to "the message of life" (Acts 5:20), and "the message of salvation" (Acts 13:26), and "the message of truth, the gospel of your salvation" (Eph. 1:13). In each case reference is being made to "the message of JESUS." The Greek word for "message" is *angelia* from which we get the English word "angel." A blended extension of this word is *euangelion*, translated "good news" or "gospel." The good news of the gospel is JESUS. Whenever we use another word, other than JESUS, to explain our message, we risk the misinterpretation of our audience that we are refer to something other than JESUS.

It is so important to make clear that our message is JESUS and JESUS alone; *solus Christus* "Christ alone" was the Reformation motto. My concern is that many readers and listeners will be misled into thinking that a particular ministry "message "is something new, other than and different than, the message of JESUS that has been shared for two millennia by the *ecclesia* of Jesus Christ. When someone touts "the message of the finished work," or "the message of the new covenant," or "the message of freedom," or the "message of faith," or "the message of grace," be sure to discern if it is "the message of JESUS."

DECEMBER 25

THE COMPLETE CHRISTMAS STORY

For years, yea centuries, the Christmas story has been told and retold, and celebrated among those who appreciate the gospel. The beauty and pageantry of the retelling of the historical story of Christmas has elicited beautiful music and instrumentation presented in elaborate settings throughout the centuries. The uplifting and inspiring storytelling of Joseph and Mary and the baby Jesus in the manger has been emotionally moving for many people. But it is possible to enjoy the celebratory pageantry and miss the intended spiritual reality to which it all points – a tragic short-circuiting of the Christmas story.

The words of this poem always come to mind at the Christmas season. The Polish poet, Angelus Silesius, whose given name was Johann Scheffler, wrote these words in the 17th century:

> "Though Christ a thousand times in Bethlehem be born,
> If He's not born in you, your soul is still forlorn."

The birth of Jesus in Bethlehem was a prototype or a precursor to the spiritual birth (Jn. 3:1-6) of Jesus in the heart of every receptive believer who becomes a Christ-one.

The poem continues:

> "The Cross on Golgotha, is looked upon in vain,
> Unless within your heart, it is set up again."

The complete Christmas story must extend as far as the death of Jesus on the cross for our sins, and the consequential internal and purgatorial dying to selfish attitudes and actions as we allow the Christ-life to be manifested in our mortal bodies (II Cor. 4:10,11). The incarnation, crucifixion, and resurrection of Jesus must be subjectively experienced within every Christian.

DECEMBER 26

THE LIVING GRACE OF THE LIVING LORD

There are many "grace teachers" who adequately explain God's redemptive grace in the work of Jesus Christ on the cross and point to the resurrection of Jesus as the ratification of that redemptive grace. Most of these teachers proceed to mention that when Christ died, our old self was taken to the cross with Jesus and died with Him (cf. Gal. 2:20; Col. 2:20; 3:3; Rom. 6:8; II Tim. 2:11), and based on Christ's resurrection, we too are "raised to newness of life" (Rom. 6:4) to become "new creatures" (II Cor. 5:17) in Christ. These foundational truths are indeed critical to understanding the gospel of grace in Jesus Christ.

The part that seems to be missing from this emphasis on historical redemptive grace is the recognition that God's grace didn't end at the cross or the resurrection. Is God still the God of grace? Of course, He is! Then we must go on to explicate how the grace of God in Jesus Christ is not just an historical phenomenon but continues to be operative as the dynamic by which the Christ-life is re-presented and manifested in the contemporary Christian behavior of those in whom Christ lives. In other words, we need to focus on the living grace function of the living Lord Jesus as He is allowed to live out His life in Christians.

The weak link in the chain of the "grace message" has been the tendency to drive forward by constantly looking in the rearview mirror. While we must always preach "Christ crucified" (I Cor. 1:23; 2:2), and the "finished work" (Jn. 19:30) of Jesus Christ, and all the personal implications of our having "died with Christ" (Rom. 6:8; Gal. 2:20; Col. 2:20), it is imperative that we articulate the living grace of the living Lord Jesus. Christians need to understand "the word of His grace, which is able to build them up" (Acts 20:32), "the abundance of grace...by which we reign in life through Jesus Christ" (Rom. 5:17), and "the grace by which we conduct ourselves in the world" (II Cor. 1:12).

DECEMBER 27

THE MYSTERY OF THE KINGDOM OF GOD

Jesus was speaking in many parables and His disciples were confused by what He was saying. Jesus said, "To you has been given **the mystery of the kingdom of God**, but those who are outside get everything in parables" (Mk. 4:11). Mystery (Greek *musterion*) pertains to what was once concealed but has now been revealed. Jesus is the promised revelation of God (Jn. 14:7,9) and the promised King in the lineage of David (Mk. 11:10). Wherever the King is reigning the kingdom is present. Jesus is the kingdom of God in Himself (Greek *autobasileion*; *autos* = in himself; *basileion* = kingdom, from *basileuo* = to reign).

"Kingdom of God" (equivalent to "kingdom of heaven" in gospel of Matthew) is not a geographical area or realm. It is not a tangible or visible reality, referring rather to the intangible functional reign of King Jesus in Christ-ones. When the Pharisees questioned Jesus about when the kingdom of God would come, Jesus responded, "The kingdom of God is in your midst" (Lk. 17:21). The KJV reads "within you," but this does not refer to individual internalization, for Jesus was speaking to the Pharisees, and the plural prepositional phrase *entos humin* refers to Jesus' presence standing among those listening.

The Jewish people longed for a king who would restore their kingdom-nation. In the first century this would require a military king to rout the Romans. Using the same word but with a different meaning, Jesus indicated that His kingdom was "not of this world" (Jn. 18:36). Paul indicates that "God has rescued us (Christ-ones) from the dominion of darkness and brought us into the kingdom of the Son" (Col. 1:13). John explained that "Christ has made us (past tense) to be a kingdom" (Rev. 1:6). Jesus the King is reigning in the lives of individual Christ-ones and in the collective entity of the *ecclesia*, and we look forward to an eternity of kingdom-life in heaven.

DECEMBER 28

WHEN YOU CREST THE SUMMIT

When driving in mountainous areas the ascent is relatively easy compared to the descent after you have crested the summit. The downhill becomes more treacherous as gravity pulls the vehicle downward, and the driver must keep the vehicle from gaining too much speed while at the same time not overusing the brakes, so they do not overheat and become unusable. Shifting down to use lower gears to keep the vehicle slowed is usually the best course of action. But you have no doubt noticed the "runaway truck ramps" on many mountain descents where vehicles can exit into the sand and come to a stop.

Elijah had ascended to the top of Mount Carmel where he engaged in a contest with 450 prophets of Baal. The false gods of Baal were called upon to bring down fire to consume the sacrifice and nothing happened. Elijah mocked them, taunting them to cry louder for perhaps their gods could not hear. When Elijah called upon Jehovah, God sent down fire and consumed the sacrifice. After this stupendous success and victory of God, Queen Jezebel sent notice that she intended to kill Elijah. Seeming to forget what God had done on Mt. Carmel, Elijah feared for his life, descended the mountain, and went into the wilderness to sit under a juniper tree, and later in a cave (I Kgs. 19).

Have you noticed that when you engage in an endeavor where you know that God is working by His grace in what you have been doing, almost immediately thereafter the temptation comes to engage in an activity that you know is not of God? Satan seems to know that when we crest the summit of being receptive to God by faith, we are susceptible to letting down our guard and allowing him to tempt us into activities that exemplify the character of selfishness and sin. This downward pull of Satanic temptation bears a similarity to the downward pull of gravity when a vehicle begins to descend from the summit of a mountain.

DECEMBER 29

IT'S NOT ABOUT YOU

Our narcissistic culture has tainted so many with the egoistic orientation of me-ism and selfism to the extent that the attitude "it's all about me" seems to be the prevailing approach that many take to life. Such a self-absorbed attitude has not lent itself to meaningful interpersonal relationships wherein there must be a reciprocity of respect and concern for the other. Even in our vocations, we must go beyond self-preoccupation to consider the needs and desires of another, whether it be in leadership or in sales, whether it be in public speaking or on the stage in theatrics or performing in a musical concert.

Ghandi is quoted as saying, "The way to find yourself is to lose yourself in the service of others." Jesus said, "whoever wishes to save his life will lose it, but whoever loses his life for My sake and the gospel's will save it" (Mk. 8:35). As a preacher and a public speaker, I had to go beyond the self-conscious jitters to realize "it's not about me." I was only to be the mouthpiece through which the Spirit of God might share the content of the gospel of the living Lord Jesus. Any self-concern on my part needed to be put aside; I needed to get out of the way to allow God to do what He might want to do in the lives of those listening.

My wife is a musician having taught countless young students to play the piano, flute, and oboe. When they were preparing for a concert or audition, I heard her tell them, "It's not about you, so don't get nervous or freeze-up; you have a gift to contribute to your audience, so share it to the best of your ability." Some people are so quick to take the actions of others personally when they are snubbed or when another person makes an unflattering remark about them. My wife has a plague on the wall of her office that reads, "What others might say about you has less to say about you than it does about the attitude and values of the person who speaks it." "It's not about you!"

THE WORLD'S SELF-MOTIVATION

While listening to the broadcast of the Macy's Thanksgiving Day Parade in New York City, I jotted down some of the clichés that the broadcasters were spewing forth as motivational incentives to their television audience to be more like the stars who were appearing in the parade. These were the usual humanistic one-liners that the world ignorantly repeats to encourage one another in the self-motivation to "be all" and "do all" to achieve whatever their objectives might be. The minds of the unbelieving are blinded by the Evil One (II Cor. 4:4), failing to understand that human beings cannot create their own reality in this way.

"Do your best to be the best you can be" was one of the mottoes parroted by the hosts of the program. This variation of the humanistic self-betterment motif is based on the false assumption that a human being has within herself (or himself) the innate self-potential and self-ability to be a self-starter who can self-generate and self-actuate extraordinary behavioral performance that will be commended and applauded by those who observe such. The fallacy of such self-activation techniques is revealed when we understand that human beings were created to be derivative creatures, deriving from a spiritual source outside of themselves, either Satan or God.

"If you believe, you can do anything," was another humanistic motto expressed by the television hosts. This variation of the old motivational hype that "whatever you believe, you can achieve," is again founded on the fallacy that human belief self-generates the self-creation of a desired possibility. Not so! Human beings are not self-creators, little gods with the self-potential of bringing into being desired results. We derive character and the resultant quality of the outcomes of our behavioral activity from a spirit-source. Out motivation will either be selfish and sinful or the loving character of God in Jesus Christ.

DECEMBER 31

RELATIONSHIP MANAGEMENT

The pastor indicated in his sermon that most of Christian living is focused on "relationship management," and Christians need to commit themselves to restoring their conflicted personal relationships. This sounded to me like a call to Christians to engage in "fix-it" remedies to save and make right their broken relationships by overcoming their passive-aggressive attitudes. Get your stuff together and be reconciled with one another! Does this sound like another performance admonition, another "works" engagement to be what God wants you to be, and to get along with others in personal relationships?

There is no doubt that the indwelling Christ in Christ-ones, having effected the vertical reconciliation between God and man, will continue to function in the reconciliation of horizontal relationships between people, and especially between brothers and sisters in Christ. "God, who reconciled us to Himself through Christ gave us the ministry of reconciliation" (II Cor. 5:18). Paul earlier wrote, "I exhort you, brethren, by the name of our Lord Jesus Christ, that you all agree and that there be no divisions among you, but that you be made complete in the same mind and in the same purpose" (I Cor. 1:10).

The managing of all relationships is accomplished by the character of Christ manifested in those relationships. John wrote, "If someone says, 'I love God,' and hates his brother, he is a liar; for the one who does not love his brother whom he has seen, cannot love God whom he has not seen" (I John 4:20). Paul wrote, "make my joy complete by being of the same mind, maintaining the same love, united in spirit, intent on one purpose. Do nothing from selfishness or empty conceit, but with humility of mind regard one another as more important than yourselves" (Phil. 2:2,3). "If possible, so far as it depends on you, be at peace with all men" (Rom. 12:18).

Indices

TOPICAL INDEX

SCRIPTURAL INDEX

375

377

Made in United States
North Haven, CT
26 November 2022

27273907R00215